Movies on Home Ground

Movies on Home Ground: Explorations in Amateur Cinema

Edited by

Ian Craven

CAMBRIDGE SCHOLARS
PUBLISHING

Movies on Home Ground:
Explorations in Amateur Cinema,
Edited by Ian Craven

This book first published 2009. The present binding first published 2012.

Cambridge Scholars Publishing

12 Back Chapman Street, Newcastle upon Tyne, NE6 2XX, UK

British Library Cataloguing in Publication Data
A catalogue record for this book is available from the British Library

Copyright © 2012 by Ian Craven and contributors

All rights for this book reserved. No part of this book may be reproduced, stored in a retrieval system, or transmitted, in any form or by any means, electronic, mechanical, photocopying, recording or otherwise, without the prior permission of the copyright owner.

ISBN (10): 1-4438-4169-2, ISBN (13): 978-1-4438-4169-6

TABLE OF CONTENTS

List of Illustrations vii

Acknowledgements ix

Introduction
A Very Fishy Tale: The Curious Case of Amateur Subjectivity
Ian Craven 1

Part I: Activities

Chapter One.. 36
Innovation on a Shoestring: The Films and Filmmakers of the Scottish Amateur Film Festival
Ruth Washbrook

Chapter Two 65
Babies, Kids, Cartoons and Comedies: Children and Pathéscope's 9.5mm Home Cinema in Britain
Clare Watson

Chapter Three 93
Framing The View: Holiday Recording and Britain's Amateur Film Movement, 1925-1950
Heather Norris Nicholson

Part II: Controversies

Chapter Four.. 130
Putting Film on Nottingham's Cultural Map: Film Production and The Festival of Britain
Melanie Selfe

Chapter Five 156
Amateur Film Re-Located: Localism in Fact and Fiction
Ryan Shand

Chapter Six 182
Locating the Family Film: The Critics, the Competition and the Archive
Ian Goode

Chapter Seven 208
Screening Classics: Film Appreciation Canons and the Post-War
Film Societies
Richard MacDonald

Part III: Creativities

Chapter Eight 238
Animated Explorations: The Grasshopper Group 1953-1983
Sheila Chalke

Chapter Nine 270
Enrico Cocozza as Amateur Auteur—Ideas above his Station?
Mitchell Miller

Chapter Ten 301
"Ploughing a Lonely Furrow": Margaret Tait and Professional
Filmmaking Practices in 1950s Scotland
Sarah Neely

Appendix A
Chronology 327

Appendix B
Select Bibliography 336

Notes on Contributors 348

Index 351

LIST OF ILLUSTRATIONS

Intro-1 Frame enlargement from *A Very Fishy Tale* (1938) 3
Intro-2 Frame enlargement from *A Very Fishy Tale* (1938) 3
Intro-3 Frame enlargement from *A Very Fishy Tale* (1938) 4
Intro-4 Frame enlargement from *A Very Fishy Tale* (1938) 13
Intro-5 Frame enlargement from *A Very Fishy Tale* (1938) 17

1-1 Frame enlargement from *Hair* (1933) 39
1-2 Frame enlargement from *Robot Three* (1952) 52
1-3 Frame enlargement from *Nine O'Clock* (1952) 53

2-1 Pathéscope Company printed materials, 1920s-1930s 68
2-2 Aerial view of Pathéscope Cricklewood factory, 1930s 75
2-3 Pathéscope Baby and Kid projector advertisements, 1926 76
2-4 Pathéscope Ace projector advertisement, c. 1935 77

3-1 Frame enlargement from *Tour in the USSR* (1932) 104
3-2 Frame enlargement from *Gallipoli: A Pilgrimage Cruise* (1934) 105
3-3 Frame enlargement from *International Colonial Exhibition in Paris* (1931) 107
3-4 Frame enlargement from *Sykes family holiday in the Lake District* (1949) 113

4-1 Frame enlargement from *Old Market Square* (1951) 146
4-2 Frame enlargement from *Old Market Square* (1951) 146
4-3 Frame enlargement from *Old Market Square* (1951) 148
4-4 Frame enlargement from *Old Market Square* (1951) 149

5-1 Frame enlargement from *Seawards The Great Ships* (1960) 163
5-2 Frame enlargement from *Seawards The Great Ships* (1960) 164
5-3 Frame enlargement from *Fit O' The Toon* (1978) 167
5-4 Frame enlargement from *Fit O' The Toon* (1978) 168
5-5 Frame enlargement from *Seven Ages* (1957) 175
5-6 Frame enlargement from *Seven Ages* (1957) 175

6-1 Frame enlargement from *Tree for Two* (1957) 192
6-2 Frame enlargement from *A Hit and A Miss* (1956) 193
6-3 Frame enlargement from *Castlecary Events* (1932-1937) 197
6-4 Frame enlargement from *Agricultural and Highland Shows* (1928). 198

7-1 Poster for *Turksib* (1929) 218
7-2 Federation of Film Societies journal, *Film* (1957) 221
7-3 South London Film Society Yearbook, 1951-52 222
7-4 St Andrews Film Society Programme, 1951-52 229

8-1 Grasshopper Group production meeting for *The Battle of Wangapore* (1955) 247
8-2 Animation cell from *The Battle of Wangapore* (1955) 248
8-3 Frame enlargement from *Bride and Groom* (1955) 249
8-4 Frame enlargement from *Watch The Birdie* (1954) 250

9-1 Frame enlargement from *Fantasmagoria* (1948) 277
9-2 Frame enlargement from *Scherzo* (1955) 280
9-3 Frame enlargement from *Chick's Day* (1950) 282
9-4 Frame enlargement from *Corky* (1958) 285
9-5 Frame enlargement from *The Mirror* (1951) 294

10-1 Frame enlargement from *Colour Poems* (1974) 303
10-2 Frame enlargement from *The Drift Back* (1957) 308
10-3 Frame enlargement from *Orquil Burn* (1955) 313
10-4 Frame enlargement from *Happy Bees* (1954) 316

ACKNOWLEDGEMENTS

The present volume began life in two distinct but related settings; a new honours option in Amateur Cinema—offered within the M.A. degree in Film and Television Studies at the University of Glasgow, and within a symposium organised by the Centre for Screen Studies at the University, held in May 2006. Many individuals and organisations have subsequently contributed to the evolution of the present volume, and I am pleased to thank all those involved in its formulation and production.

Invaluable feedback on papers presented by the editor at Manchester Metropolitan University, the Institute of Education at the University of London, the University of Leeds, and the "Middlebrow Cultures" conference hosted by the University of Strathclyde, helped to clarify perspectives framing the Introduction. The arrangement of chapters and range of the chronology benefitted considerably from suggestions made in these various settings concerning links between key areas of practice, and the future directions of research in "substandard" cinema.

Scholarship within the emerging field of amateur cinema studies is especially dependent upon the support of colleagues within the archive sector: Janet McBain and the staff of the Scottish Screen Archive provided help and advice at every turn; the Media Archive of Central England furnished otherwise unviewable materials, whilst colleagues at the Northwest Film Archive offered ready access to their substantial collections of non-fiction amateur film. At a late stage in proceedings, Phillip Collins of the East Anglian Film Archive, supplied crucial information illuminating the development of two forgotten amateur cine organisations. The Pathé Archive in Paris provided Clare Watson with important paper records, and the editor with more general information concerning the development of Pathéscope apparatus.

I am especially pleased to acknowledge the assistance received from members of today's highly active amateur cine community: Linda Gough, currently President of the Institute of Amateur Cinematographers, and Grahame Newnham of the 9.5 Association, answered numerous questions with enthusiasm and precision, whilst members of the Edinburgh Cine and Video Society, recently celebrating its seventieth anniversary, offered limitless access to their collections, and long expertise in every aspect of amateur cine production. Ron Ashton located rare issues of journals and newsletters discussed in the volume, and furnished invaluable contact with fellow collectors and former practitioners.

Librarians in diverse locations provided substantial support: specific help was given by staff of the Glasgow Room at the city's Mitchell Library; Donald Tait, subject specialist in Film and Television Studies at Glasgow University Library, offered much appreciated assistance with the location of elusive cine materials; hard-pressed officers of the (now) IAC: Film and Video Institute, granted access to the organisation's collections and supplied copies of long-gone publications. Julia Hallam, currently pursuing her own research interests in amateur cinema at the University of Liverpool, found time to share her knowledge of the Liverpudlian amamteur cine scene in the post-war period, for which I am especially grateful.

Amanda Millar, Carol Koulikourdi and their colleagues at Cambridge Scholars Press guided the assembly of the anthology with patience and encouragement, whilst Michael McCann, at the University of Glasgow, provided invaluable technical support, and helped solve numerous problems of layout and design. Individual images are reproduced courtesy of the individuals, institutions and organisations listed as sources. I am especially indebted to the amateur enthusiasts who gave permission to reproduce items from their remarkable personal collections. Illustration 7-2 is copyright, British Federation of Film Societies: every effort has been made to trace other relevant copyright holders where appropriate.

The production of the anthology was made possible thanks to Study Leave in spring 2008, granted by the Research Committee of the Faculty of Arts at the University of Glasgow, and funding support from the Department of Theatre, Film and Television Studies.

Last, but by no means least, my thanks to Ryan Shand and Graeme Spurr, my research students in amateur cinema over the past few years, whose interests first re-kindled the editor's fascination with "small gauge", and to undergraduates on the Glasgow University Amateur Cinema option in 2005 and 2007—their critical response to arguments still very much in the course of formulation, and critical enthusiasm for the kinds of movies examined in the volume, provided early encouragement to embark upon this anthology, and the monograph which will follow it.

INTRODUCTION

A VERY FISHY TALE: THE CURIOUS CASE OF AMATEUR SUBJECTIVITY

IAN CRAVEN

A Very Fishy Tale is a 12-minute, silent "film play", put together by prize-winning amateur movie-maker Frank Marshall, during the summer of 1938. One of numerous drama shorts scattered through the amateur archive, the film marks a genre encouraged insistently and explored enthusiastically within the cine sector, throughout the interwar and post-1945 periods. Indicative of broader trends within a non-professional cinema increasingly organised as hobby movement, it also offers a typical example of Marshall's own steady output of such whimsical "kailyard" narratives: of the 120 or so projects completed before his death in 1979, around 50% fall comfortably into this popular category.[1] Most featured, as here, confined dramatic scenarios, involving the filmmaker's relatives or friends playing conspicuously typed roles, settings around the suburban home or various holiday locations visited by the Marshall family, and a mildly didactic attitude towards story-telling; like similar efforts such as *Payment Deferred* (1941), *Early Birds* (1956), or *Dream Holiday* (1970), *A Very Fishy Tale* is very much a parable or fable.

The combination of "kinship casting", lococentric emphasis, and vaguely "improving" narrative ambition involved, is suggestive of the mixed motivations of much amateur filmmaking—here stranding the

---

[1] Marshall (1896-1979) worked enthusiastically across a range of genres during his long amateur cine career: early "industrials" include *Filters and Filtration* (1934) and *From Byre to Buyer* (1949); domestic record movies such as *Our Fifth Anniversary* (1932) and *At Muriel's Wedding* (1955) are much in evidence; travelogues include *Pitlochry Welcomes You* (1958) and *Weekend in Skye* (1962), whilst "avant-garde" attitudes are well represented in work between *All On A Summer's Day* (1933) and *Joys of the Open Road* (1961).

finished text somewhere between the domestic record movie, holiday picture and one-reel "story film". A distinctive fusion of emulatory "fictional" realism, with the actuality emphases of more obviously "home mode" production, is particularly apparent,[2] indexing an aesthetic hybridisation designed to accommodate both the private-immediate and more public-distanced audiences, potentially addressed by such a work, within its envisaged exhibition environments. As the listing of family members in the credits implies, such films functioned as both memory texts (within the home) activating reminiscence for those involved, and as incentives to altogether less personal fiction-building and appreciation by the outsider (within the club, or even more public sphere such as the festival). A surviving leader-strip, inserted prior to the main title, reminds us also that *A Very Fishy Tale* was in part conceived as a competition film, entered in the Institute of Amateur Cinematographers' (IAC's) recently formalised "Ten Best" event, and recognised in the "Specially Commended" category, possibly proving something of a disappointment for its maker when it did so, following earlier successes.[3]

The narrative premise of *Fishy Tale* concerns "novice" ambitions realised and "experienced" orthodoxies over-turned, involving an endorsement of the underdog, echoed in a host of other such apparently idiosyncratic exercises. To summarise for the sake of clarity: captivated by his father's fly-tying expertise, a small boy begs to accompany his parent on a fishing trip, but is rebuffed: not to be outdone, the youngster improvises a rod, line, and hooks, from "borrowed" materials, and tackles up on the riverbank as his father does likewise, somewhere further downstream. Both settle into an afternoon's angling, as parallel editing establishes the motif of comparative enterprise that will persist throughout the remainder of the film. (see Figs. Intro-1 and -2) Despite the interruptions of nearby chickens (which steal his live-bait, and force the substitution of a feather lure), a troublesome cow (which makes off with

---

[2] "Home Mode" production is defined and explored in Chalfen, "Cinema Naiveté", 87.
[3] Collaboration on *All On A Summer's Day* (1933) had helped that film to gain an award in the "Interest" category at the first Scottish Amateur Film Festival, in October 1933. Marshall had, more recently, gained an "amateur oscar" for his earlier—and very similarly fashioned—work, *Christmas* (1937) in the IAC "Ten Best" competition of 1938. Many other prizes followed, including "Highly Commended" for *Coming of the Camerons* (1944) at the 1945 IAC National Contest, and "A" classification for *Mower Madness* (1938) at the 1947 UNICA festival.

A Very Fishy Tale: The Curious Case of Amateur Subjectivity 3

Fig. Intro-1 frame enlargement from *A Very Fishy Tale* (1938)
Source: Scottish Screen Archive

Fig. Intro-2 frame enlargement from *A Very Fishy Tale* (1938)
Source: Scottish Screen Archive

his gear), and other very literal entanglements (with surrounding undergrowth), the boy eventually succeeds in hooking and landing a sizeable fish, apparently under the nose of a patrolling game-keeper. His father meanwhile, equipped with full—one is tempted to suggest "professional"—tackle, catches nothing, and reluctantly abandons his pitch in disappointment. As the latter wanders homewards, he encounters his son, who displays his own catch proudly, makes his father a gift of his improvised lure, and offers advice on how to maximise chances of success in the future. (see Fig. Intro-3)

Fig. Intro-3 frame enlargement from *A Very Fishy Tale* (1938)
Source: Scottish Screen Archive

Father responds with appreciation and the film ends, as it began, with a neatly titled credit, introducing a formal symmetry beloved of amateur construction, which (quite literally) mirrors (via reversal dupe) the opening image of "tiddlers" swimming tirelessly upstream.

As with much of Marshall's early work, the fictional world of *Fishy Tale*, populated by apparently well-to-do nuclear families, surrounded by typed functionaries, tells us a great deal about the social milieu of such amateur filmmaking in the 1930s. Proudly displaying its coveted *Amateur Cine World* (ACW) leader-strip ahead of its titles, it speaks too of the "official" aesthetic preferences of the organised cine movement, within which Marshall himself would subsequently play such a prominent role.[4] In a conceptual vein however, perhaps appropriate to this introductory context, the movie might also be seen as generating certain theoretical perspectives, and as tracing latent meanings for the amateur itself, thereby suggesting a useful starting point for an exploration, more specifically, of the amateur "subjectivities" at stake in a number of the essays which follow. Such an appropriation of *A Very Fishy Tale* takes its lead from the film's own understated but unmistakeable instructionalism (offering a decidedly self-conscious advertisement for the superiority of amateur approaches) and from the discursive contexts of the sector from which it emerges, within which the status and capacity of amateurism figures as a question of persistent and unresolved concern. Its focus on angling too seems to register a curiously privileged recreational instance in the evolving theoretical literatures.[5]

Social Worlds and Diverse Ambitions

Valuable explorations of the origins and forms of cine amateurism have emerged in a range of disciplinary contexts, elaborated around concerns with technological innovation (the introduction of "sub-standard" equipments offer valuable case studies), the production and maintenance of the modern family (especially in the case of the home movie), and innovative media practices shaped by the application of industrial method in the cultural sphere, and varieties of critical and more "leisure-based" responses towards them.[6] On the evidence of the essays presented here, a

---

[4] Marshall remained a prominent figure on the Scottish, British and international film scene for almost forty years. An early member of the Meteor Film Producing Society formed in 1932, and supporter of the Scottish Educational Film Association formed in 1935, Marshall was elected first Chairman of the Scottish Association of Amateur Cinematographers on its creation in 1949, and subsequently served on the Board of the Scottish Film Council until 1972. An active member of UNICA, Marshall reported regularly on the organisation's activities for *Amateur Cine World* and other amateur cine publications.

[5] See for example, Hobson, "Leisure Value Systems and Recreational Specialization: the Case of Trout Fishermen", 174-187.

[6] Particularly valuable inroads are made by Kattelle, 2000, who tracks significant relationships between technical innovation and social practice; Zimmermann, 1995, whose "social history" of amateur film places an early emphasis on the role of ideology in forming amateur practices and institutions; Chalfen, 1987, whose ethnography of suburban home-movie-making illustrates a film practice and senses of creative virtue very much at odds with those of professional counterparts, and Hogenkamp and Lauwers, 1993, whose study of the motivations for "hobby

promising basis for the extension of such studies now derives from a return to emphases on the *voluntary* aspects of amateurism stressed by early commentators. Bliss Perry's reminder, in a 1904 essay appropriately entitled "Fishing With A Worm", that amateur participation is "not a necessary, but a freely assumed activity, born of surplusage of vitality", grounds approaches subsequently assuming firmer academic definition within the domains of Leisure Studies, and provides a connective thread through much of the material presented here on the more specific case of amateur cine.[7]

A particularly useful body of scholarship might be anchored around the work of Robert Stebbins, a key voice within the sociology of recreation over the past thirty years or so, and an active empirical researcher into those variants of leisure activity possessing a conspicuously amateur dimension (most obviously sport, science, entertainment and the arts) akin to amateur cine. Stebbins himself has worked suggestively on the cultures of amateur theatre and amateur music, spheres usefully located well towards the "expressive" end of discursive practice, and obviously both intimately related to the rise of hobby filmmaking—from the mid-1920s many cine clubs develop as off-shoots from drama groups, whilst local music societies often trigger film production alongside audio recording activity. A particular virtue of Stebbins' work in this context is its synthetic approach, and its stress on the formative contexts of amateurism's "occupational contact network". From this perspective, creative outcomes are understood as symptomatic of multiple-determinations and contradictory needs, played out across a "social world"—a phenomenon understood in David Unruh's succinct definition as simply: "a form of social organisation, which could, conceivably, create a common 'world view' and encompass the entire life-round of social actors."[8]

Attention to the formalised "scenes" of the amateur, via the participant-observation that Stebbins undertakes in *Amateurs on The Margin Between Work and Leisure* and elsewhere, typically reveals a diverse range of ambitions, investments, anxieties, and pleasures in play within such social worlds, of which "realised" outcomes are seen to speak in remarkably pertinent and often highly *self-conscious* ways.[9] Ongoing study outlines a

---

filmmaking" draw attention specifically to the importance of memory-making activity in the maintenance of "psychic security".
[7] Perry, "Fishing With A Worm", 162.
[8] Unruh, "The Nature of Social Worlds", 274.
[9] Stebbins, 1979; such formulations of "serious" leisure and "modern" amateurism" have stimulated a wide range of work in leisure studies. The "Serious Leisure

typical network of elements that help to map the social world of the recreational sportsperson, scientist, entertainer or artist, charting an imagined universe within which his or her amateur subjectivity will be projected and introjected, nurtured and sustained. Crucially, seven elements—all readily traceable in the case of amateur cine culture—emerge as axiomatic: *groups*, *events*, *routines*, *protocols*, *organisations*, *resources*, and *discourses* are all seen as playing key roles in maintaining self-definitions—which provide persistent points of reference for the non-professional "cine-participant", nurturing the "special beliefs, values, moral principles, norms and performance standards" seen as characterising the very ideology of amateurism.[10] Such networks are seen as framing the amateur as an essentially leisure pursuit, which expresses devotion to the activity involved, and generates forms of pleasurable gratification, rather than accountable remuneration—pointing towards oft-quoted definitions of the amateur as "lover" rather than worker—but never precluding levels of rational organisation and assessment akin to those of the more commercially-minded professional.[11]

What Stebbins recognises immediately, thanks to his familiarity with actual practitioners as well as definitional discourses, is that pleasurable gratification arises in *various* forms, and that the negotiation of these varieties helps to identify persistent fault-lines cutting across the generalised space of the amateur, enabling recognition of diverse configurations of its social world, and a range of attitudinal positions within it. Various essays contained here suggest clearly how such symptomatic differences find expression in the spectrum of discursive positions adopted by festival judging panels, editorial commentaries, and the promotional strategies of equipment manufacturers, as well in the preferred forms of more localised creative projects and outcomes. Stebbins' modelling therefore of the amateur's social world is scarcely monolithic, and indeed places a particular stress on the uneven-ness of its development, and tendency to fragment into cliques, factions and "subworlds".

One of Stebbins' enduring contributions in this context is his early establishment of a basic dynamic within leisure culture, between what he terms simply *serious* and *casual* activity.[12] Refining earlier taxonomies of

---

Perspective" website: *www.soci.ucalgary.ca/seriousleisure*, provides an invaluable point of entry into this ever-expanding field.
[10] Stebbins, "A Conceptual Statement", 257.
[11] Deren, "Amateur Versus Professional", 45.
[12] A basic formulation of the distinction is offered in Stebbins, "Two Sociological Definitions, 582-588.

involvement, the dynamic is elaborated across a substantial body of scholarship.[13] Synthesising a range of relevant formulations, the respective attributes which emerge might be tabulated thus:

SERIOUS LEISURE	CASUAL LEISURE
perseverance	intermittent interest
systematic pursuit	randomised distraction
special ethos	subsidiary element
careerist character	playful character
calculated	instinctive
outcome-oriented	process-oriented

Many other qualifications might be inserted of course, and as Stebbins reminds us, what's indicated here are "poles of a complicated dimension" rather than any set of fixed alternatives, but the general picture seems clear.[14] Although not without longer term benefits and costs, *casual* leisure is the domain of the "player, dabbler or novice" and remains typically "fleeting, mundane and commonplace";[15] *serious* leisure, by contrast, assumes many of the attributes of paid employment undertaken on professional terms, whilst remaining non-remunerative:

> serious leisure refers to the systematic pursuit of an amateur, hobbyist or volunteer activity that is sufficiently substantial and interesting for the participants to find a career there in the acquisition and expression of its special skills and knowledge.[16]

Stebbins' distinction is valuable here in allowing us to become more inclusive and "connective" about the instance of amateur cinema (necessarily seen as embracing a range of rather different investments in filmmaking), enabling linkage between apparently idiosyncratic participations, and encouraging sensitivity to the aggregated motives and structural relations,

---

[13] David Unruh, for example, distinguishes between "strangers, tourists, regulars and insiders", whose involvements are all readily traceable in the case of amateur cine's social world. See Unruh, "The Nature of Social Worlds", 280-282.

[14] Stebbins, "A Conceptual Statement", 255. The basic distinction may suggest further categorisations, such as "Project-based Leisure", defined as "a short-term, moderately complicated, either one-shot or occasional, though infrequent, creative undertaking", in Stebbins, "Project-Based Leisure", 2. Such a categorisation is especially pertinent to Ruth Washbrook's discussion of cine competition culture elsewhere in this volume.

[15] Stebbins, "Costs and Benefits of Hedonism", 308-309, and "A Conceptual Statement", 258.

[16] Stebbins, "Serious Leisure", 3.

evidenced in particular non-professional stances (from the would-be filmic auteur, to the serial experimentalist, to the pre-professional trainee dreaming of "cross-over", to the "point and shoot" tourist, and even the home cinema "technicist"—with less interest in the outcomes of pushing the exposure button than the performance of his or her equipment). Suggestive examples of possible configurations emerge throughout this volume, confirming the flexibility and utility of Stebbins' paradigm, and an underlying politics of amateur intervention.

A range of possible inclinations and a tangle of motivations and ambitions are clearly at stake here. Scrutiny of British amateur cine culture confirms quickly wider suspicions that "casual" hedonism and "serious" careerism are rarely mutually-exclusive tendencies, but more often regarded as welcome counter-balances. The co-dependency of the instincts—and the legitimisation of both—is quickly underlined, for example, on examining definitional discourses circulated within amateur cine's "social world" by service publications and specialist hobby literatures. Both a matter of standardising a definition of appropriate practices and goals, and of negotiating between diverse interests and priorities, such materials characterise the amateur sector as an endlessly contested sphere, an emphasis shared by a number of the essays which follow.

The address of journal publications such as *Home Movies and Home Talkies* (HMHT) (1932-1940), *Amateur Cine World* (ACW) (1934-1967), and *Amateur Movie Maker* (AMM) (1957-1964) for example, provides orientation for a spread of—more or less "serious"—cine constituencies. Like the specialist titles characterising any organised amateur culture, each represents a sometimes uncertain fusion of the trade journal and popular magazine, offering collations of the consequential and the trivial, interspersing "definitive" technical articles that should be "retained for reference" and ephemeral inclusions, aimed at distraction and temporary pleasure ("just to raise a smile"). Precisely "semi-formal" in Stebbins' suggestive characterisation, the rhetoric of particular articles often veers between an unapologetic high seriousness, and a kind of self-mockery: interestingly, all three titles include—alongside photographic exposure tables and electrical impedance charts—cartoon strips and light-hearted graphics, parodying the very activities which much of the rest of their content elaborates with such obvious conviction.[17]

---

[17] Stebbins places a recurrent emphasis on the importance of "semi-formal" communication in the maintenance of amateur social worlds. One of his most recent explorations of the terms occurs in "Erasing the Line Between Work and Leisure", 9.

From their opening editorials, HMHT and ACW strike a serious editorial tone, expressing tangible senses of mission. Both associate themselves with a "maturing" of amateur cinematography, and the organisation and centralisation of a "movement". HMHT unashamedly sets out to make itself "an institution" essential to the amateur cine "worker", defining its role around the provision of technical support and information, and reserving column space for formal concerns with the attributes of the "well-made" amateur movie. The initial editorial comments:

> Each month we shall endeavour to give you help and guidance in taking, editing, and showing your pictures—in selecting the right backgrounds and "props"—in finding good subjects for "family films", in choosing the right apparatus at the right price; in fact, in doing all the things you want to do—better.[18]

ACW perhaps styles itself in slightly less presumptuous terms, addresses a readership conceived with palpably more international reference, and defines its role as "opening up the limitless pleasures to be derived from the intelligent use of the camera and projector". With the editors dedicating themselves to coverage of their milieu as a whole "world", and the raising of standards via a practice of constructive criticism, manifesto ambitions are considerable indeed:

> We shall not hesitate to criticise where we think criticism is necessary. It is only thus, we think, that we can deserve and retain the confidence and goodwill of our readers. Beginner and advanced enthusiast alike will find their needs catered for in our pages, for we seek to make *Amateur Cine World* completely representative of the amateur cine movement. Our title implies it.[19]

Alongside the stentorian tones of serious amateurism, softer notes are again being struck however: even as the amateur "worker" is encouraged to adhere to stricter codes and more rational procedures, casual variants are acknowledged and legitimised within the spirit of inclusiveness animating amateur cine in this formative phase. Amateur cinema is thus recognised as a "hobby"—as well as something more serious, usually termed a "craft"—thus casualised practices sit side-by-side with more dedicated enterprise and investment. HMHT even sponsors and develops a "circles movement" which it recognises alongside the "club" sector as a

---

[18] Harris, "The Editor's News-Reel", 7.
[19] Malthouse, "The Editor to His Readers", 5.

less formal, more primarily social network of like-minded "funsters", linked by "round robin" packages of films and diaries, rather than by weekly meetings, collective projects or the galvanising deadlines of competition entry.[20] Suggesting its ideological necessity, ACW relaunches and helps to sustain this "circles" movement well into the 1950s and beyond,[21] before AMM acknowledges hedonism as a more key—and freshly legitimised—strand of amateurism as the 1960s approach, in terms which suggest a long-cultivated seriousness giving way to something more topical and casual:

> Over the years *Amateur Cine World* has come to be known as the amateur's Bible. We do our best to present a full compendium of fact and opinion every month, and take some pride in the authority which the magazine has attained throughout the world. Coming from the same stable, *Amateur Movie Maker* will be no less authoritative, but its main object will be to serve the comparative beginner who does not want to delve too deeply into cine.[22]

AMM then develops along these lines as a publication geared towards an altogether more casual readership: "we are dedicated editorially to the belief that film-making is fun!"[23]

Apocryphal Spheres and Invidious Contrasts

Stebbins expends much effort elaborating the dynamic between the serious and the casual illustrated here, in ever more sophisticated terms, but the main thrust of his work becomes increasingly historical, ever more concerned with the ways in which amateurism changes in relation to the shifting social contexts of modernity. Indeed the "splitting" of amateurism into the two variants recognised, is understood as a response in itself to a modernising cultural environment.

Both variants are seen as expressing senses of displacement. On the one hand, *serious* leisure represents a kind of compensation for the alienations of modernity: a space to express abilities, fulfil potentials and identify a subjectivity, in a manner no longer possible in the work-place or

---

[20] Harris, "Home Movie Cine Circles Leaders Wanted", 1933, 146; "The Good Companions: More about Home Movies Cine Circles", 1934, 302.
[21] Malthouse, "The ACW Cine Circles", 1951, 227-228; "Just Among Friends", 1951, 628; "Cine Circle Rally", 1957, 672.
[22] Rose, "First performance", 15.
[23] Ibid., 15.

domestic everyday, via a kind of median activity, akin to employment, but conducted in the name of play (Frank Marshall's amateur "career" seems to epitomise just such a model). *Casual* leisure, on the other hand, represents more of an evasion and a regression, a kind of longing for pre-social activity as sheer pastime, which regards success in incidental and fatalistic terms, rather than as a reward for calculated investment or scientific strategy (the serendipities of much "home mode" production perhaps?)—a strong sense of which is conspicuously at work in *Fishy Tale*, where expensive angling equipment proves ineffective, and the boy's catch is landed as much by luck as judgement. Interestingly, the operation of fate remains a remarkably persistent theme in suggestions for amateur "film play" production, as if speaking to such instincts, whilst seeking to negotiate and perhaps to transcend them.[24]

Following earlier observations of amateurism's evolution as response to the rise of professional cultures,[25] Stebbins sees *serious* leisure specifically as a kind of "modern amateurism" that infiltrates more ancient, and possibly more noble, amateur traditions—"the player of old in sport and music, was referred to as a gentleman", he reminds us.[26] At points, this feels like an account of the dilution of a "pure" amateur code, in favour of something compromising with, and increasingly *resembling*, the professional, with "modern amateurism" styling itself as a version, rather than a refusal of the professional ethos, and even seeking misrecognition *as* the professional. Although in the case of amateur cine, this tendency clearly comes to exist alongside, rather than to displace, the older tradition, with subsequent tension generated between resulting pulls towards an emulation of professional standards, and proponents of creative virtues imagined in altogether more "autonomous" and less outcome-oriented terms.[27] Stanley Godlovitch frames this elegantly as a distinction between a "strongly evaluative" *achievement-based* amateurism and an *attitude-based* amateurism "neutral as to results"—with the latter signalling an:

> aspect of amateurism deriving from its earlier tradition, but which is transfigured by modern preoccupations with institutional professionalism [and a] relative purity of spirit in a world in which career-building and the

---

[24] Rose, *Let's Make Movies*, 119-142.
[25] See Todd's essay "Amateur", 19.
[26] Stebbins, "Two Sociological Definitions", 583.
[27] See Godlovitch, "Amateurs, Professionals and the Ideal of the Creative Virtues", 354-367, for a useful discussion of traditional amateurism's more "autonomous" ambitions.

desire for money, rank and status compromise many virtues which remain vital to traditions of creativity and enquiry.[28]

Illustrating well the network of instincts involved, the boy's father in *Fishy Tale* seems both to caricature and celebrate this older tradition (see Fig. Intro-4), resuscitating the disciplines and styles of the "gentlemanly", which amusingly prove no match for the more opportunistic pragmatisms of the present, and the promise of the modern amateur future, here represented by the young boy.

Fig. Intro-4 frame enlargement from *A Very Fishy Tale* (1938)
Source: Scottish Screen Archive

One of the things that Stebbins make clear, is that what's at stake here is a matter of choice: the amateur can adopt a serious or casual approach, but that either way, his or her achievement will be measured against an absolute standard—in this case that defined by the mainstream professionalised cinema. The decision about how to proceed as an amateur is indeed triggered by *confrontation* with such definitional criteria on a day-to-day basis, especially in the sphere of cultural production. Encounter with the spectacular realisation of such standards here is routine-ised and intensified within modernity, by the increasingly insistent provision of

---

[28] Ibid., 355.

cultural goods (as services, performances or products), mass-produced to high tolerances, and delivered with an awesome regularity and efficiency inconceivable in earlier periods. It takes little effort to construe the commercial cinema of the 1930s, circulating somewhere in the background of *A Very Fishy Tale*, as epitomising this very modern—and intimidating—provision. Technically reinvigorated by the arrival of sound, and increasingly anchored by the formal protocols of the "classical", it is no coincidence that such a cinema quickly forms a very axiom of the "culture industry" within founding texts of Cultural Studies such as those generated by the Frankfurt School. In Adorno and Horkheimer's celebrated formulation, it quickly emerges as an ideological apparatus deemed socially coercive in its construction of the subject as consumer and *reproducer*, rather than genuine originator, of social meanings:

> Far more strongly than the theatre of illusion, film denies its audience any dimension in which they might roam freely in imagination—contained by the film's framework but unsupervised by its precise actualities—without losing the thread... The withering of imagination and spontaneity in the consumer of culture today need not be traced back to psychological mechanisms. The products themselves, especially the most characteristic, the sound film, cripple those faculties through their objective makeup.[29]

Stebbins' would-be amateur participant appreciates the proficiency—if not the political and social effectivity—of such "apparatuses" more intensely than most:

> With today's mass availability of professional performances (or products), whatever the field, new standards of excellence confront all participants, whether professional or not. The performances of the professionals are frequently impressive for anyone who beholds them, but no one is more impressed than the non-professional participant who, through direct experience, knows the activity intimately. Once he becomes aware of the professional standards, all that he has accomplished there seems mediocre by comparison.[30]

Social encounter with the professional is then imagined here in distinctly primal terms, with its modern spectacle figured as a dazzling image, which may well prove incapacitating. Elizabeth Todd concurs in 1930 that such confrontation with the provisions of the culture industry may block productive instincts:

---

[29] Adorno and Horkheimer, "Enlightenment as Mass Deception", 99-100.
[30] Stebbins, "Two Sociological Definitions", 583.

> The radio and moving pictures, social intercourse based on objective amusement, have made the individual of the present generation very largely a recipient rather than a communicant. He is more inclined to pay for his recreation than to supply it through his own efforts.[31]

Squaring such theoretical disincentives to participation with the steady expansion of organised leisure activity represented by the growth of amateur cine, represents a considerable critical challenge, and the inertias of "spectatoritis" will haunt even enthusiast discourse for decades.[32] For Adorno and Horkheimer, non-professional "transmissions" can only be acknowledged as a prelude to political dismissal:

> No mechanism of reply has been developed, and private transmissions are condemned to unfreedom. They confine themselves to the apocryphal sphere of "amateurs" who in any case, are organised from above.[33]

Subsequent social historians have tended to stress the more critical and creative dimensions of such voluntary "unfreedom". John Stevenson notes, for example, in *British Society 1914-1945*, that from the 1930s, a key reaction to the expansion of the culture industries was the growth, alongside mass commitment to particular activities, of more self-consciously specialised groups, furnished with managerial frameworks, dedicated literatures and retail outlets—described in terms which echo Stebbins closely, and anticipate emphases explored by essays included in the present volume:

> Dancing might have been a mass activity for millions on a *casual* basis, but a few thousand might take it *seriously* enough to develop ballroom dancing competitions, run dance schools and make it their principal leisure activity. Similarly, as jazz music became an increasingly commercialised and popular form, its *real devotees* formed themselves into jazz clubs and patronised more specialised outlets. The same thing happened in the cinema, where those impatient with an endless diet of Shirley Temple, George Formby or Clark Gable formed their own clubs or private cinemas to watch foreign-language films ... even individual leisure choices tended to operate within an increasingly *organised* and *centralised* framework.[34] [my emphasis]

---

[31] Todd, "Amateur", 19.
[32] Czurles, "Art Creativity Versus Spectatoritis", 104-107.
[33] Adorno and Horkheimer, "Enlightenment as Mass Deception", 96.
[34] Stevenson, *British Society 1914-1945*, 401-402.

For Stebbins, the aftermath of encounter with the professional is understood in more psychological terms, with the amateur struggling to resolve a complex—perhaps a "mediocrity" complex—that may develop along various lines, and stimulate conflicting drives.

Beyond incapacitating neurosis, or the distraction and carelessness often construed as the very essence of the "amateur*ish*", *Fishy Tale* reminds us that a memory may be formed in the encounter, that can easily institute a desire for participation—precisely the scenario played out at the start of the film in familial microcosm, as the small boy spies on his father through a closed window, and yearns to get involved. (see Fig. Intro-5) As well as retreats into the specialist "appreciation" of professional provision—a reading strategy understood as something more than mere consumption—outcomes may include a determination to succeed as producer "against the odds", a move characteristically expressed as the obsessiveness or over-ambitiousness, frequently reported in accounts of amateur enterprise. That such a "mediocrity complex" usually remains unresolved, is suggested perhaps by the *simultaneous* occurrence of such tendencies in differing strands of amateur activity, and in conspicuous attractions between them. In *Fishy Tale*—in one of a series of identificatory exchanges patterning the film—the boy seeks to emulate his father's (supposed) skill, whilst the father indulges a passion that allows him to regress (temporarily) to childhood. Through the work of the narration, serious and casual instincts are thus validated and re-charged, in an endless circuit of mutually reinforcing desires.

Stebbins' sense of amateurism as grounded in "lack" is certainly suggestive, sometimes palpably internalised within the cine sector, and surfacing within even the most encouraging of "how-to-do-it" discourses. Thus advice is often prefaced by an acknowledgement of disincentives and apparent obstacles. Tony Rose, editor of *Amateur Movie Maker* comments in his influential 1950s manual, for example:

> As he contemplates the vast complexities of the cinema industry and the many specialised skills which contribute to the production of a professional film, he [the novice amateur] may feel overwhelmed. How can he, with a minimum of equipment, little money, no studio and—possibly—a handful of helpers, hope to make a film that is worthy of the name?[35]

---

[35] Rose, *Let's Make Movies*, 9.

A Very Fishy Tale: The Curious Case of Amateur Subjectivity   17

Fig. Intro-5 frame enlargement from *A Very Fishy Tale* (1938)
Source: Scottish Screen Archive

Even if accepted however, the formulation clearly authors a range of symptomatic amateur behaviours. Feelings of intimidation may find expression in, precisely, a "high" seriousness, that bespeaks a determination to match professional standards, or alternatively develop into a full-blown "inferiorism" and a casualness indexing a kind of refusal of identification, anticipating withdrawal into highly privatised spheres of activity, and very personal senses of affective value. In Stebbins' own summary:

> The amateur is faced with a critical choice in his career as participant: restrict identification with the activity to a degree sufficient to remain largely unaffected by such invidious contrasts, or identify with it to a degree sufficient to spark an attempt to meet those standards.[36]

Whilst probably indexing the latter, rather more than the former option— the "story film" is often seen as the most challenging of amateur genres precisely *because* it invites comparison with its professional counterpart[37]—and ratified in this ambition through its commendation by

---

[36] Stebbins, "The Amateur: Two Sociological Definitions", 583.
[37] Malthouse, "In Defence of the Film Play", 225-226; Malthouse, "Amateur Story Film", 122-127.

the judges of ACW's competition, *A Very Fishy Tale* also points nervously perhaps towards a third responsive option. Involving relish of amateur difference as potential *transcendence* of professional standards, this finds expression in senses that amateur movie-making retains a creative integrity now lost to the merely "proficient" cinemas of the "culture industries". For Godlovitch, quite unambiguously, amateur traditions "enshrine and preserve in an unmortgaged fashion the best that the professions aim to achieve", and reminders of creative virtues beyond the reach of professional codes, often assail the amateur filmmaker.[38] Review sections of cine journals, for example, routinely scrutinise professional as well as amateur movies, finding instructional value in mainstream releases, whilst critiquing the former's failure to reach amateur standards. Entirely without irony, reviewers may be found "congratulating" professional films, for being *almost* as good as amateur ones, in a determined re-configuration of Stebbins' field-of-force, to the advantage of the amateur.[39] Something of this instinctive superiorism is perhaps tangible in even as polite as narrative as *Fishy Tale*, where "sub-standard" resources and improvisatory approaches win out over their supposedly better equipped, and more rationalised professional counterparts.

What emerges from this glance at Frank Marshall's fatalistic little parable on amateur accomplishment, and Leisure Studies accounts of the non-professional participant? Certainly, a sense of the amateur practitioner as an anxious and unresolved subject, whether "serious" devotee or "casual" dilettante, and that the amateur sphere might be most productively understood critically—very much as it sees itself—as a *relational* category, rather than the separate zone implied by the notions of "independent" or "alternative" cinema to which such filmmaking has sometimes been assimilated.[40] Whatever its particular configuration, designation as amateur probably implies a parallel cine world, elaborated less according to intrinsic norms or customised counter-strategies, than "similar" agendas and unapologetically emulatory reflexes, suggesting a kind of "echo cinema" simultaneously struggling for its own resonances. As Tony Rose puts it succinctly: "I think we must face the fact that audiences' mental reactions to amateur films are conditioned largely by what they see at the local cinema or on television."[41]

---

[38] Godlovitch, "Amateurs, Professionals and the Ideal of the Creative Virtues", 358, and "Lynx", "Why Not Try To Be Better?", 541-542.
[39] See for example, Hill, "Amateur Feature Beats Professional Picture", 560-562
[40] MacPherson, *Traditions of Independence*, 191-207.
[41] Rose, *Let's Make Movies*, 150.

Without pushing analogies too far, the value of *Fishy Tale* in this setting is that it helps us to see, within this peculiar field-of-force, just how deeply the professional functions as "alter ego" for a modern amateurism, involving a curiously self-conscious mix of resentments and infatuations. As the essays which follow suggest, the structures of feeling played out in this little film are reiterated in an endless inter-layering of identifications and refusals across much amateur cine activity. Contributors reveal interconnectedness with the professional at articulated levels, from the institutional (competitions, societies, governing bodies), to the behavioural (protocols surrounding shooting, assembly, exhibition), to the aesthetic (the qualified simulation of and allusion to professional modes of representation), and throughout the extended discursive field (of journals, newsletters, and incidental commentary) effectively marking the boundaries of amateur cine's social world. Such linkages are certainly evident it seems, in apparently "innocent" little films about angling, and the limited appeals to the trout of even the most professionally-tied fly.

Implications and Explorations

Understandings of amateurism as a structured subjectivity formed within concrete historical conjunctures and evolving social relations, ground the explorations which follow, as they present a range of overlapping, but distinct perspectives, on the amateur cine enterprise from conception to consumption. Together, the essays volunteer a unified introduction to the study of amateur cinema, exploring its constitutive relationship with notions of "professional" film practice, and offering specific case studies of amateur film production, circulation and critical reception. Starting from loosely Leisure Studies perspectives, amateur cinema is understood throughout as a "social world", as well as an assembly of texts, or critical-creative project, defined by a rich network of determinants, practices and locations. To clarify continuities and discrete levels of analysis, the essays are divided loosely into three sections: addressing activities, controversies and creativities, which aim to sketch the borders of this extensive field.

Activities

Part I, focussed on "activities", explores selected dimensions of amateur cine's social world, as expressed in particular behaviours, shaped by questions of creative evaluation, equipment supply, and the development of neighbouring leisure cultures. Ruth Washbrook's opening discussion of the Scottish Amateur Film Festival (SAFF) provides a suggestive starting point for the analysis, up-dating existing research on this key event in the amateur cine calendar for over fifty years, and offering a fascinating insight into the role of competition culture more generally within the amateur sector, variously endorsed as creative incentive, showcase for excellence, and stimulus to the overall improvement of technique.[42] Washbrook illuminates, in particular, ongoing tensions between SAFF's "serious" and "casual" participants, the work of evaluative discourse in disseminating aesthetic standards and cultural values, and the function of competitions in propagating a self-generated canon of amateur cinema, subsequently circulating alongside the authorised "Society" counterparts, discussed elsewhere in this volume. Such competitive activity is seen as playing a crucial role in integrating amateur cine culture, whilst simultaneously functioning as a prime site for direct contact with (and for some entrants, actual point of "cross-over" into…) the professional sector. In these contradictory respects, competitive activity is regarded as fundamental to "modern" amateur movie-making, helping to consolidate senses of an autonomous amateur cine world, whilst expressing and even realising dreams of cultural "equivalence" with the professional.

Technical specification plays a significant role within early definitions of amateur practice, initially seen as rooted, as Zimmermann notes in "nonconformity to more dominant professional standards."[43] Clare Watson's account of the Pathé company's 9.5mm "substandard" film gauge and its use as a medium for projecting films in Britain between 1924 and 1960, provides an opportunity to consider the significance of technical parameters in characterising amateur exhibition modes and their social uses, slowly emerging elsewhere as concerns in current scholarship.[44] Pathé launched their 9.5mm gauge in France in 1922, and from 1924 it was sold and distributed energetically in Britain by the Pathéscope Limited Company, as a compact standard which supposedly sacrificed nothing of the quality of broader formats, whilst offering users considerable cost-savings.[45] Although now primarily a collector's gauge, 9.5mm was widely used for over thirty years, both for the purposes of amateur filmmaking and for the domestic screening of professionally-

---

[42] Anon, "Our First Competition", 198-199; Malthouse, "Film Making and Film Judging", 990-1004; Watson, "How To Give Your Film A Better Chance", 106-117.
[43] Zimmermann, *Reel Families: A Social History of Amateur Film*, 12.
[44] Chalke, "Early Home Cinema", 223-230; Edmonds, "Amateur Widescreen", 401-413.
[45] Malthouse, "The Story of Pathéscope Apparatus." [Parts 1-3] 249-252; 367-369; 472-474.

produced material, made available in the format by a range of distributors. Developing slowly into a distinct sub-culture within the amateur sector, marked by its own "nine-five" competition classes, organisations and publications, the continuing history of the gauge following Pathé's withdrawal in 1960, offers a compelling case study of amateur attachment and perseverance. The chapter examines, in particular, the early relationship between 9.5mm projecting technology and the role of children as viewers, projectionists and consumers of the gauge, and establishes home exhibition as a key dimension of amateur cinema's social world, an element often existing in uneasy tension with more community-based counterparts such as the cine club, and the commercial matinée session aimed specifically at younger cinemagoers.

Discussion of Pathé's early development of home exhibition reminds us of wider trends in domestic leisure during the inter-war years, and of amateur cine's frequent articulation with a range of parallel recreational activities, well into the 1950s and beyond. Encouraged to cultivate "auxiliary pastimes" in order to ensure a supply of ideas for their films, or to secure the involvement of family or friends, practitioners respond with a startling range of "interest" pictures.[46] Heather Norris Nicholson examines the ways in which the production of such movies develops in relation to the specific expansion of holiday activity, and the encouragements of influential cine discourses—one commentator has "times of travel" offering "next to family life, the widest range of subjects to the amateur."[47] Scrutiny of the making and showing of amateur cine films about holidays, in and beyond Britain, she argues, serves not only to situate a distinctive genre of amateur film practice within patterns of middle- and upper-middle-class cultural consumption and social formation, but also to underline the *interdependent* characteristic of much amateur filmmaking. For affluent enthusiasts with sufficient time and money to indulge two costly hobbies, the availability of Kodak's lightweight cine cameras in Britain from the early 1920s, she suggests, offered a new travel accessory, and the possibility of creating moving records of travel experience. Thanks to the simultaneous diffusions of camera technology and such leisure activity, she shows how holiday experiences recorded in amateur footage now provide valuable insights into tourism history, and related recreational practices. The survival of such material, and the attendant development of amateur cinematic practice into a fully-fledged hobby industry which it indexes, is seen here as offering an incentive to scholarly revisionism at a

---

[46] See Goodlad, "The Case for Two Hobbies", 531, and Abbott, "Filming Hobbies—and Other Things", 278-303.
[47] Strasser, *Amateur Films: Planning, Directing and Cutting*, 44.

range of levels, above all raising the possibility of a more nuanced, and more inclusive, understanding of national cinematic history.

Controversies

Amateur cine culture is nurtured by critical, historical and theoretical debate conducted in a range of settings, with varying degrees of influence upon attendant filmmaking practices. "Controversialism" emerges as a key term early within the discursive field, and remains both a stimulus and frustration to the development of a coherent "movement" thereafter.[48] Part II extends this history of discussion into the academy, through attention to recurrent dilemmas of significance in both spheres, namely a stress on the challenge of the amateur circumstance to considerations of professional "national" cinema, the evaluative and ethical implications surrounding the acquisition and public circulation of "personal" filmic materials, and the status of "canonical" works as exemplars for amateur filmmakers.

Essays by Melanie Selfe and Ryan Shand offer suggestive microcosms of a national cinematic history, "re-nuanced" by attention to the amateur filmmaker. Both explorations shift focus away from master narratives of development and character supposedly shared across the nation, towards the "localisms" and regional differences often effaced by stresses on the strategic value of an imaginary national unity, and its prioritisation in the organisation of industry and representation. Scrutiny of amateur cine culture for both authors suggests an early awareness of what we may now be inclined to construct perhaps rather too swiftly as a "postmodern" turn towards the local. Cursory scanning of the amateur cine catalogue reveals a recurrent stress on "localist" initiatives from the outset, consistently characterised by both amateur enthusiasts and their professional patrons as peculiarly appropriate to the situation and resources of the non-professional participant. Amateur filmmakers are indeed typically invited to make sense of their lives, and to develop their skills, in decidedly local settings—sometimes as practical acceptance of narrowed horizons, sometimes as complicating qualification of broader understandings of social development. Peter Le Neve Foster comments in 1935, in typically "controversialist" terms, for example, that by:

> making films whose appeal is too localised or too specialised to attract commercial producers, amateurs are far more likely to make themselves of immediate practical assistance than they are by trying to become test tubes

---

[48] Watson, "Experimental... A Word That Covers a Multitude of Junk", 1036-1037.

for film theories, or by imagining themselves to be founders of a new school of film art.[49]

Civic filmmaking, involving attendance to the local as an *aspect* of the national, is subsequently defined as a key responsibility for the amateur filmmaker—although not always undertaken in practice at the remove from "test tube" theory or "film art" envisaged here.

Melanie Selfe explores the meaning of just such amateur production within the primarily exhibition-oriented film society context. Focusing on *Old Market Square* (1951), a film made by The Nottingham & District Film Society for the city's Festival of Britain celebrations, her chapter considers the ways in which the production of "local interest" film can be understood both as an attempt to attract attention to the wider aims of such a society, and as providing a sense of local relevance, with which to counter the metropolitan image of a national movement, often construed as élitist and remote. Analysis of both the finished film and its production context, suggests that such projects played an important role in securing a film society's involvement in official celebratory events, helping to promote the medium as the equal of more traditional arts, and generating work which dramatises formative relationships between the local amateur filmmaker, traditions securely coded as national (sponsored British documentary production) and continental film practice (particularly in this case, the inherited traditions of the European "city symphony film").

Such cultural transfer between region, nation and continent—mediated by the modern amateur filmmaker, ceaselessly scanning the horizon for templates, whilst simultaneously cultivating a sense of lococentric difference—also finds potent expression in the Scottish context. Ryan Shand considers the case of the amateur sector north of the border to sketch definitions of a more "de-centred" Scottish cinema, shaped by acutely parochial entailments of received tropes and base-reference figures. Representing as it does a smaller scale production and exhibition network, closer to *local* histories and artistic practices than the products of professional popular culture, and often claiming an affinity with explicitly *international* movements and their manifestoes, Shand argues that the amateur cinema offers an opportunity to trace a wide range of tributaries and counter-currents to established constructions of a "national" mainstream. With reference to a suggestive sample of films and filmmakers, his chapter explores the conjuncture between amateur initiatives sensitive to local priorities, and the professional priorities of filmmaking destined for projection to the Scottish nation and beyond.

---

[49] Le Neve Foster, "Amateur Film Maker", 9.

Attention to such "parochial-trans-national" amateur film cultures, it is argued, helps both to enrich reproductive constructions of Scottish cinema, typically hinged around the sponsored documentary and the feature film, and to assert the cultural resistance of a filmmaking sceptical of the value of national identifications and agendas to more transformative ends.

Accounts such as these clearly emphasise the strategic value of amateur material within polemics against established critical orthodoxies. The use-value of amateur material implicated in such initiatives also emerges as a central concern for Ian Goode, whose essay questions the ethical implications of amateur footage's characteristic journey from private collection, to supervised archive, to public screening space and "professionalised" scrutiny within the academy. Goode notes that anxieties now rightly attend the exposure of "family films" in particular to the public gaze, and their incorporation within both scholarly, and more commercial, production. As the most familiar and ubiquitous of amateur film genres, often sometimes regarded as synonymous with the mode itself, "home movies" now enjoy cultural mobility well beyond their original exhibition spaces, surfacing in a range of "remote" contexts, from the academic seminar room, to television "attic archive" programming, to the "self-post" internet site. The critical re-positioning of such material is examined here in relation to issues surrounding the incorporation of these often intimate records of family life into the critical and historical study of film, within the academy and elsewhere.

Amateur exhibition is equally central to Richard MacDonald's account of Britain's Film Society culture, exploring participations constructed early as essential preparations for filmmaking itself. An anonymous contributor (possibly Peter Le Neve Foster?) to *Close Up* in 1927 makes linkage explicit, in his account of the Manchester Film Society:

> Although we appreciate the obvious value of discussions and private shows of little seen films, our main object is practical experiment. Unless amateur film production on a large scale comes to stay, the cinema will never get an intelligently critical public.[50]

Connections are reiterated thereafter in the reminiscences of numerous celebrated "cross-over" amateurs, and indeed exhibition societies still often provide the organisational bases from which numerous would-be filmmakers still move into amateur production. The closely-linked development of non-professional exhibition and production sectors from the 1930s discussed by MacDonald, is again suggestive of unresolved

---

[50] Anon., "The Manchester Film Society", 69.

impulses towards emulation and distinction encountered by other essays in the volume. Under the overall guidance of the newly formed British Film Institute (BFI), Society screenings are seen as validating key films and filmmakers, and establishing a core history of film "art", subsequently assuming instructional as well as aesthetic pre-eminence.[51] The chapter examines the burgeoning film society movement's particular dependence on the National Film Library canon post-1945, a period when its influence is felt especially strongly within amateur film production.[52] MacDonald's account thus helps to contextualise the contributions of some of the filmmakers considered later in the volume, whose shifts into production betray suggestive exposure to some of the Society movement's perennial favourites. Focusing on their distinctive programming and exhibition practices, MacDonald argues that the voluntary societies negotiated the British Film Institute's growing authority in film pedagogy in complex ways, sustaining alternative conceptions of the educational and artistic potentials of film, which were sometimes taken up enthusiastically by amateur filmmakers, although rarely without controversy, or evidence of distinctly amateur transformations.

Creativities

Amateur circumstances seemingly enable a cinema of remarkable creative integrity, occupying a space beyond the restrictions of professional codes and inhibiting market determinations. The unique "freedom" of the amateur remains a persistent theme in the accompanying literatures: one standard manual from the 1930s locates the "real beauty" of the amateur film in the fact that "each worker must create as suits his immediate purpose" in contrast with his professional counterpart:

> When professional films are made, limits are set to this creative power by "censors" and "box-office" interests, so that the professional worker can never be entirely free to create as he wants. The amateur, though, has all fields open to him, and is unaffected by interests other than his own.[53]

---

[51] Reference to the canon is legion: Alex Strasser, for example, has "that old classic" *Battleship Potemkin*, and "our old friend" *The Cabinet of Dr Caligari* as standard references, *Amateur Films: Planning, Directing and Cutting*, 19.
[52] Tony Rose comments in 1963 that "early Russian films such as Eisenstein's *The Battleship Potemkin* (1925) and Pudovkin's *Mother* (1926) remain, with those of Griffith, classic models for the editor of silent films", whilst *Bicycle Thieves* (1948) is a film which "in terms of production is not far beyond the scope of the amateur unit.", *Let's Make Movies*, 60, 125.
[53] Strasser, *Amateur Films: Planning, Directing and Cutting*, 16.

By the 1960s, Maya Deren has the professional envying the amateur for such "freedom—both artistic and physical", whilst for Jonas Mekas substandard technologies and non-professional participations finally realise in cinema the possibilities of "a beautiful folk art, like songs and the lyric poetry... created by the people."[54] Amateur practitioners relishing very different creative potentials have routinely constructed the mode in such libertarian terms, although distinct ambivalence towards such "freedoms" is evidenced by a range of discourses bent on establishing disciplinary technique and the observance of recognised protocols, as an essential prelude to the exercise of "experimental" creative imagination. ACW's most celebrated "controversialist" in the 1960s, Ivan Watson, for example, cites Cocteau:

> "The camera", said Jean Cocteau, "should be like a fountain-pen which anyone may use to translate his soul onto paper". Fine! But think of the many would-be novelists with fountain-pens, bright ideas—and not the faintest glimmering of the technical requirements of the novel. They don't get published. And I've yet to hear of any painter, musician or actor of any consequence who did not first achieve technical mastery before he started to break the rules *deliberately*.[55]

Part III interrogates some particular instances of amateur creativity, with reference both to specialist "units" and more isolationist "lone workers", located within very different historical and geographical settings. The modes of production involved have long raised debate in themselves within the amateur cine movement, which often struggles to reconcile very deep-seated "collectivist" impulses, with an equally firm insistence on tolerance for the individual practitioner.

Certainly some of the amateur cinema's most remarkable creative initiatives emerge from collective, rather than more solitary, forms of production. For Sheila Chalke, formation of the London-based Grasshopper Group in the 1950s, under the leadership of John Daborn, represented a highly co-ordinated response to American dominance of the amateur animation film. The genre is a conspicuous one from early in the history of amateur cinema, often regarded as a particularly appropriate basis for the creation of truly original works, freed from difficulties surrounding performance—regarded as endemic with amateur cine—and

---

[54] Deren, "Amateur Versus Professional", 45, and Mekas, "8mm Cinema as Folk Art", 12.
[55] Watson, "Experimental... A Word That Covers a Multitude of Junk", 1036.

the scarcity of more concrete production resources. Daborn himself comments early that work in the medium:

> gives the creator a far greater sense of satisfaction than any live-action film he can make. He has complete control of his "actor", no set he desires is impossible. He is limited only by the extent of his imagination.[56]

Remarkable imagination is combined in the work examined here with astonishing determination and patience, illustrating well a perfectionism often seen as the hallmark of truly amateur enterprise. In a spirit of co-operation, pooling skills and resources, Chalke argues, Grasshopper activists developed highly original projects, pioneered fresh production techniques, and supported each other through the lengthy, and meticulous creative process typifying animation work, with remarkable results.

Of particular interest is Grasshopper's exploration of assembly methods involving remote collaboration, and a kind of sub-contracting of designated tasks to specialist "lone workers". Thanks to such innovative definitions of collectivity, the group could boast a membership of over 120 at the height of its activities, organising screenings and club competitions which provided a focus for amateurs committed to this very particular branch of hobby filmmaking. With awards won frequently in national and international festivals, and celebration of the work attracting offers of professional employment—significantly declined by members epitomising, for the amateur cine press and others, the true spirit of the amateur filmmaker—the Grasshoppers represent an undoubted amateur success story. Charting the development of this quickly mythologised group, and critiquing a body of work exposed widely within amateur circles through the post-war period, but now largely unviewable, Chalke assesses Grasshopper's likely positioning within a still largely unwritten history of the amateur animation film in Britain.

A stark contrast to the distinctly "rationalist-Fordist" operation of the Grasshopper Group is offered by Mitchell Miller's introduction to the work of Scots-Italian amateur auteur, Enrico Cocozza, whose films were produced as highly personal projects, with the support of fellow enthusiasts and family members. Comparable notoriety was achieved however: between 1947 and 1960, this part-time academic and café owner produced a string of low-budget psychodramas and comedies, recognised as achieving considerable artistic quality, and evidencing remarkable technical expertise. Exhibiting little in the way of Grasshopper puritanism, dreams of "cross-over" seem to have driven the filmmaker's early career,

---

[56] Daborn, "Making a Colour Cartoon", 782.

although Cocozza's idiosyncratic approaches diverged somewhat from professional norms, synthesising influences from European Art cinema, Hollywood B-movies and the most instrumental of documentary traditions. Exploring topics as diverse as juvenile delinquency in *Chick's Day* (1951)—a film which gained Cocozza a coveted ACW "Ten Best" plaque as "Film of The Year"—post-nuclear survivalism in *Twilight* (1955), and the nature of romantic love in *Before Time Came* (1958), Cocozza's output clearly resists easy categorisation. Miller offers here an early *critical* response to the work of this largely forgotten amateur filmmaker, described during his lifetime as both a Neorealist and Surrealist, within an always curious, but frequently scandalised amateur film movement, instinctively committed to more conservative modes and genres. Particular stress is placed upon the relation of his work to its professional counterparts, and Cocozza's abortive career as professional employee of Films of Scotland. Such an accounting of this far from untypical employment history is perhaps suggestive of the filmmaker's significance to future studies of amateur film more broadly.

Cocozza's yearning for recognition, and dreams of professional advancement, throw into relief the altogether more separatist instincts of Margaret Tait, an Orkney-based practitioner, epitomising for Sarah Neely, the rather more autonomous amateur of romantic imagination. With over thirty films—probably best described as "avant-garde"—to her credit, Tait's career emerges as a testament once again to amateur persistence and resourcefulness. Justifiably celebrated as a truly independent filmmaker, having started her own production company and self-financing the majority of her short experimental works, Tait's creative struggles emerge in highly symptomatic amateur terms in the course of Neely's analysis. While the filmmaker's freedom from industrial constraints undoubtedly enabled her to explore personal fascinations across a range of forms and media, lack of support from government and other agencies, Neely argues, offers little cause for celebration. Rather, Tait's case serves to demonstrate the challenges facing the amateur film artist, strongly rooted in a particular locale, but forced to seek endorsement and patronage from often distant sources. Ryan Shand's "parochial-trans-nationalism" is well illustrated here by the fate of Tait's films. Although her work was met with considerable interest overseas (particularly in the United States, India, and Germany), organisations closer to home, such as the Films of Scotland Committee and the Scottish Film Council remained uncertain as to the experimental film's validity. Typically, the films were chastised for a supposed failure to observe professional standards, and generally deemed unsuitable for the educational context, which they were assumed to be intended for. Tait's "independence" was retained therefore at some price, and "lone worker" status clearly represents something of a mixed blessing in this instance. Operating at a determined remove from the organised amateur movement, her case is nonetheless illustrative of a network of cherished self-sufficiencies and manifest dependencies, often characterising the situation of the "non-professional participant" trying to ensure the continuation of their work. Isolated from both the professionalised film sector, and any organised cine movement, Tait was indeed forced, as Hugh MacDiarmid put it: "to plough a lonely furrow." Neely's essay thus examines the very practical ways in which such filmmakers might secure their positions within film culture, and how Tait's particular body of work might be discussed within ongoing debates about the character of both amateur and Scottish cinema.

Conclusions

The diverse range of moments and approaches represented by the essays presented here, outline then a narrative of British amateur cinema as a decidedly "fishy tale", driven by a range of ambitions, identifications and contradictions, every bit as primal as those dramatised in Frank Marshall's endearing little "film play". For the pessimistic scrutineers of the "culture industries" referenced above, amateurism represents only an advanced state of acquiescence:

> One has only the choice of conforming or being consigned to the backwoods: the provincials who oppose cinema and radio by falling back on eternal beauty and amateur theatricals have already reached the political stance toward which the members of mass culture are still being driven.[57]

What emerges here however is a cinema of remarkable engagement scarcely confined to the "backwoods", always evolving both in relation to an acute awareness of its own origins and immediate circumstances, and in response to incentives from shifting professional counterparts which constantly re-define the terms of amateurism's still cherished sense of difference. Whether amateur conditions are regarded by filmmakers themselves as inhibiting aesthetic ambitions, or as underwriting unique opportunity, their still largely unexamined output of work represents a considerable encouragement to the revision of much received wisdom. The contributors to the present volume respond to such encouragement with suggestive indications of directions for future enquiry.

---

[57] Adorno and Horkheimer, "Enlightenment as Mass Deception", 118-119.

Works Cited

Abbott, Harold B. "Filming Hobbies—and Other Things." *Amateur Cine World* 4, no. 6 (1937): 278-303.

Adorno, Theodor and Max Horkheimer. "The Culture Industry: Enlightenment as Mass Deception." In their *Dialectic of Enlightenment: Philosophical Fragments*, 94-136. Stanford, California: Stanford University Press, 2002.

Anon. "The Manchester Film Society." *Close Up* 1, no. 4 (1927): 69-72.

—. "Our First Competition." *Amateur Cine World* 1, no. 5 (1934): 198-199.

Chalfen, Richard. "Cinema Naiveté: A Study of Home Movie-making as Visual Communication." *Studies in the Anthropology of Visual Communication* 2, no. 2 (1975): 87-103.

Chalke, Sheila. "Early Home Cinema: The Origins of Alternative Spectatorship." *Convergence* 13, no. 3 (2007): 223-230.

Czurles, Stanley. "Art Creativity Versus Spectatoritis." *Journal of Creative Behaviour* 10, No. 2 (1976): 104-107.

Daborn, John. "Making a Colour Cartoon." *Amateur Cine World* 16, no. 8 (1952): 782-784.

Deren, Maya. "Amateur Versus Professional." *Film Culture* 39, no. 2 (1965): 45-46.

Edmonds, Gary. "Amateur Widescreen: or Some Forgotten Skirmishes in the Battle of the Gauges." *Film History* 19, no. 4 (2007): 401-413.

Godlovitch, Stanley. "Amateurs, Professionals and the Ideal of the Creative Virtues." In *Time Out: Leisure, Recreation and Tourism in New Zealand and Australia*, edited by Harvey C. Perkins and Grant Cushman, 354-367. Auckland: Addison-Wesley, Longman New Zealand, 1998.

Goodlad, Douglas. "The Case for Two Hobbies." *Amateur Cine World* 16, no. 6 (1952): 531-558.

Harris, Percy. "The Editor's News-Reel." *Home Movies and Home Talkies* 1, no. 1 (1932): 7.

—. "Home Movie Cine Circles Leaders Wanted." *Home Movies and Home Talkies* 2, no. 4 (1933): 146.

—. "The Good Companions: More About Home Movies Cine Circles." *Home Movies and Home Talkies* 2, no. 8 (1934): 302.

Hill, Derek. "Amateur Feature Beats Professional Picture Hands Down." *Amateur Cine World* 23, no. 6 (1959): 560-562.

Hobson, Bryan. "Leisure Value Systems and Recreational Specialization: The Case of Trout Fishermen." *Journal of Leisure Research* 9, no. 3 (1977): 174-187.

Hogenkamp, Bert and Mieke Lauwers. "In Pursuit of Happiness? A Search for The Definition of Amateur Film." *CBG Nieuws* 24 (1993): 19-28.

Kattelle, Alan. *Home Movies: A History of the American Industry, 1897-1979*. Nashua, New Hampshire: Transition Publishing, 2000.

Le Neve Foster, Peter. "Amateur Film Maker." *Sight and Sound* 4, no. 13 (1935): 7-9.

"Lynx". "Why Not Try To Be Better Than The Professionals?" *Amateur Cine World* 19, no. 6 (1955): 541-542.

MacPherson, Don. "Part V: Amateur Films." In *British Cinema: Traditions of Independence* edited by Don MacPherson, 191-207. London: British Film Institute, 1980.

Malthouse, Gordon. "The Editor to His Readers." *Amateur Cine World* 1, no. 1 (1934): 5.

—. "The Editor to His Readers: In Defence of the Film Play." *Amateur Cine World* 5, no. 5 (1938): 225-226.

—. "The Amateur Story Film." *Amateur Cine World* 14, no. 2 (1950): 122-127.

—. "Just Among Friends." *Amateur Cine World* 15, no. 7 (1951): 628-672.

—. "Film Making and Film Judging." *Amateur Cine World* 15, no. 10 (1952): 990-1004.

—. "Cine Circle Rally." *Amateur Cine World* 21, no. 7 (1957): 672.

—. "The Story of Pathéscope Apparatus." [Parts 1-3] *Amateur Cine World* 24, no. 3 (1960): 249-252; 24, no. 4 (1960): 367-369; 24, no. 5 (1960): 472-474.

Mekas, Jonas. "8mm Cinema as Folk Art." *The Village Voice* (18 April 1963): 12.

Perry, Bliss. "Fishing With A Worm." In his *The Amateur Spirit*, 143-164. Boston and New York: Houghton, Mifflin and Company, 1904.

Rose, Tony. "First Performance." *Amateur Movie Maker* 1, no. 1 (1957): 15.

—. *Let's Make Movies*. London: New English Library, 1963.

Stebbins, Robert. "The Amateur: Two Sociological Definitions." *Pacific Sociological Review* 20, no. 4 (1977): 582-606.

—. *Amateurs on The Margin Between Work and Leisure*. London: Sage Press, 1979.

—. "Serious Leisure: A Conceptual Statement." *Pacific Sociological Review* 25, no. 2 (1982): 251-272.

—. *Amateurs, Professionals and Serious Leisure*. Montreal and Kingston: McGill-Queen's University Press, 1992.

—. "The Costs and Benefits of Hedonism: Some Consequences of Taking Casual Leisure Seriously." *Leisure Studies* 20, no. 4 (2001): 305-309.

—. "Erasing the Line Between Work and Leisure in North America." Unpublished paper presented to the "Leisure and Liberty in North America" Conference, University of Paris IV, France, 12-13 November, 2004. Available at: www.ucalgary.ca~stebbins/leisureliberty/innpap.pdf

—. "Project-Based Leisure: Theoretical Neglect of a Common Use of Free Time." *Leisure Studies* 24, no. 1 (2005): 1-11.

Stevenson, John. *British Society 1914-45*. Harmondsworth: Pelican Books, 1984.

Strasser, Alex. *Amateur Films: Planning, Directing and Cutting*. London: Link House Publications, 1937.

Todd, Elizabeth. "Amateur." In *Encyclopaedia of The Social Sciences*. Vol. 2, edited by Edwin R. A. Seligman, 18-20. New York: Macmillan, 1930.

Unruh, David R. "The Nature of Social Worlds." *Pacific Sociological Review* 23, no. 3 (1980): 271-296.

Watson, Ivan. "Experimental… A Word That Covers a Multitude of Junk." *Amateur Cine World* 26, no. 49 (1961): 1036-1037.

—. "How to Give Your Film a Better Chance to Win." *Amateur Cine World* 11, no. 4 (1966): 106-117.

Zimmermann, Patricia R. *Reel Families: A Social History of Amateur Film*. Bloomington and Indianapolis: Indiana University Press, 1995.

—. "Democracy and Cinema: A History of Amateur Film." In *Essays on Amateur Film: Jubilee Book*, edited by Nancy Kapstein, 73-80. Charleroi: Association Européenne Inédits, 1997.

Films Cited

All On A Summer's Day
  (Ian Ross, 1933) 16mm., 10 mins.
At Muriel's Wedding
  (Frank Marshall, 1955) 16mm., 8 mins. 49 secs.
Battleship Potemkin
  (Goskino, 1925) 35mm., 75 mins.
Before Time Came
  (Enrico Cocozza, 1958) 16mm., 18 mins.

Bicycle Thieves
  (PDS/ENIC, 1948) 35mm., 90 mins.
The Cabinet of Dr Caligari
  (Decla-Bioscop AG, 1920) 35mm., 71 mins.
Chick's Day
  (Enrico Cocozza, 1951) 16mm., 32 mins.
Christmas
  (Frank Marshall, 1937) 16mm., 10 mins. 20 secs.
Coming of The Camerons
  (Frank Marshall, 1944) 16mm., 10 mins. 34 secs.
Dream Holiday
  (Frank Marshall, 1970) 16mm., 5 mins. 27 secs.
Early Birds
  (Frank Marshall, 1956) 16mm., 12 mins.
Filters and Filtration
  (Frank Marshall, 1934) 16mm., 9 mins. 08 secs.
From Byre to Buyer
  (Frank Marshall, 1949) 16mm., 8 mins. 35 secs.
Joys of the Open Road
  (Frank Marshall, 1961) 16mm., 2 mins. 48 secs.
Mother
  (Mezhrabpom, 1926) 35mm., 90 mins.
Mower Madness
  (Frank Marshall, 1938) 16mm., 13 mins. 39 secs.
The Old Market Square
  (Nottingham & District Film Society, 1951) 16 mm., 13 mins. 19 secs.
Our Fifth Anniversary
  (Frank Marshall, 1932) 16mm., 16 mins. 19 secs.
Payment Deferred
  (Frank Marshall, 1941) 16mm., 9 mins. 59 secs.
Pitlochry Welcomes You
  (Frank Marshall, 1958) 16mm., 8 mins. 54 secs.
Twilight
  (Enrico Cocozza, 1955) 16mm., 15 mins.
A Very Fishy Tale
  (Frank Marshall, 1938) 16mm., 12 mins. 13 secs.
Weekend in Skye
  (Frank Marshall, 1962) 16mm., 10 mins. 35 secs.

PART I

ACTIVITIES

CHAPTER ONE

INNOVATION ON A SHOESTRING:
THE FILMS AND FILMMAKERS
OF THE SCOTTISH AMATEUR FILM FESTIVAL

RUTH WASHBROOK

"The most successful amateur film-maker is someone with a 'bee in his bonnet'..."
—Norman McLaren[1]

The Scottish Amateur Film Festival (SAFF) began life on Saturday, 14th October 1933 at the Athenaeum Theatre, Glasgow. The humble origins of what would become one of the most successful and well-respected of amateur film festivals, grew from an "open" competition organised by the Meteor (aka. Shooting Star) Film Producing Society. Members of this recently formed group were then meeting in a nearby rented studio, acquiring impressive filmmaking skills, and expanding their membership with remarkable speed. In order to maximise participation in the production process, it was decided by the Council of the Society that the best way forward would be to produce a cluster of short films, very much in a competitive spirit, and end the season with a small-scale gathering at which awards would be made to the most accomplished work generated.

With a view to promoting further interest in the group, and the encouragement of possible new members, Donald Sutherland, cinema correspondent for *The Glasgow Herald* newspaper, suggested to secretary Stanley L. Russell, that instead of limiting entries to Meteor Society members, the competition be opened up to filmmakers from the whole of Scotland. This resulted in a further four entries, including efforts from the Bearsden Film Club, Glasgow Amateur Ciné Club, Edinburgh Film Guild and Damyamount Picture Club. The quality of entry raised spirits high: as

---

[1] McLaren, in *Men with Bees in Their Bonnets*, 1.

the programme for the first festival states proudly, the initiative was to be experienced as "...a complete innovation in the annals of the Cinema World."[2] A sense of pioneering was to remain strong in the Festival's subsequent culture: Russell was still maintaining in 1963 that, "the Scottish Amateur Film Festival first held thirty years earlier was the first of the kind to be organised 'in the world'".[3] Certainly it was a close run thing: the Institute of Amateur Cinematographers (IAC) in London also held its first open festival in 1933, with the results being announced in November, "The Scottish" as it came to be known, having preceded it by just a month. Numerous other competitions soon followed, with the journal *Amateur Cine World* (1934-1967), for example, organising its first festival competition in 1936. Charles Oakley, then Chairman of the Scottish Film Council, could thus probably remark with some justification years later that "It can be fairly claimed, I think, that the Scottish Amateur Film Festival is not only the oldest but the finest amateur film festival held annually in Great Britain."[4]

Pre-War Development

From the outset, SAFF's organisers set precedents, which would differentiate "the Scottish" from other major amateur film competitions. With momentum building, and a total of seven submissions received for the first event, the decision, for example, to appoint a professional adjudicator to judge the competition, was a radical one, but a move clarifying SAFF's preferred image of the amateur filmmaker as struggling to refine his or her artistry, raise technical standards and even "match" the professional in terms of organisation and technique. As R. B. Macluskie reflected many years later, the policy of employing a sole adjudicator would remain:

> based on the belief that a professional will bring to his task a wide range of experience in production, independence of judgment, complete freedom from personal interest in the films or their makers and, above all, the ability, by his criticisms and commendations, to assist the amateur to raise the standard of his work.[5]

---

[2] *Scottish Amateur Film Festival Programme,* 1933.
[3] Russell, in *Men with Bees in Their Bonnets,* 2.
[4] Oakley, in *Men with Bees in Their Bonnets,* 3.
[5] Macluskie, in *Men with Bees in Their Bonnets,* 13.

In the event, identifying a suitable initial candidate proved far from easy. Sutherland however solved the dilemma when he suggested contacting film director Victor Saville, due in Glasgow to promote his new film *I Was A Spy* (1933), along with its leading lady, Madeleine Carroll. Saville agreed to take part. It was also decided early in the planning process that public screenings would form a key part of the Festival, exposing the work of amateur filmmakers to a ticket-buying audience.

With the first festival scheduled for a Saturday night, and Glasgow's commercial movie-houses unable to host the event, the Athenaeum Theatre was booked. However, with no projection facilities available at the venue, rented and borrowed machines were installed on the balcony, which otherwise had to be kept clear to adhere to fire regulations. Despite such technical challenges, the evening was a great success. Saville commented that a number of the films had "a professional touch"; Madeleine Carroll—at that time a major British screen idol—added glamour and charm to the event, and the show broke even financially.[6] Russell recalled later, "A packed house and a most enthusiastic audience witnessed an entertainment which at that time was completely new and unique not only in Glasgow, but in the country and the world."[7]

From the seven entries, Saville chose two films by the Meteor Film Society as joint winners. Selected in the "interest picture" class was *All On A Summer's Day* (1933). Described as a "Cinematic Presentation of a City Typist's Holiday", the film documents a young woman's recreational activities during an excursion, including golf, bathing, picnicking and dancing. In his review of the festival, the film correspondent of *The Glasgow Herald* commented favourably:

> I have no hesitation in saying that this modest little film was from every point of view, as cinema, as entertainment, as interest, very much better than nine out of ten professional shorts.[8]

With a simple narrative, what impresses most about *All On A Summer's Day* is its highly expressive direction, innovative camera angles and views, which lend the protagonist's day out a decidedly "artistic" treatment.

The other Meteor winner in the "story" class was *Hair* (1933), based on a "Grand Guignol" story.[9] The action focuses on a young girl, who

---

[6] Russell, in *Men with Bees in Their Bonnets*, 8.
[7] Ibid.
[8] Film Correspondent, "Amateur Film Festival", 20.

whilst staying with her aunt, has a nightmare about an escaped convict killing the maid. (see Fig. 1-1) The film is described as "A Tale of Imagination" and was made by a team featuring Russell and others. The same *Glasgow Herald* correspondent seemed less convinced of its merits:

> It was violent and infinitely more horrifying than any Ghoul of Frankenstein, so much so that one felt rather relieved that the producer did not have all the technical resources of the professional at their disposal.[10]

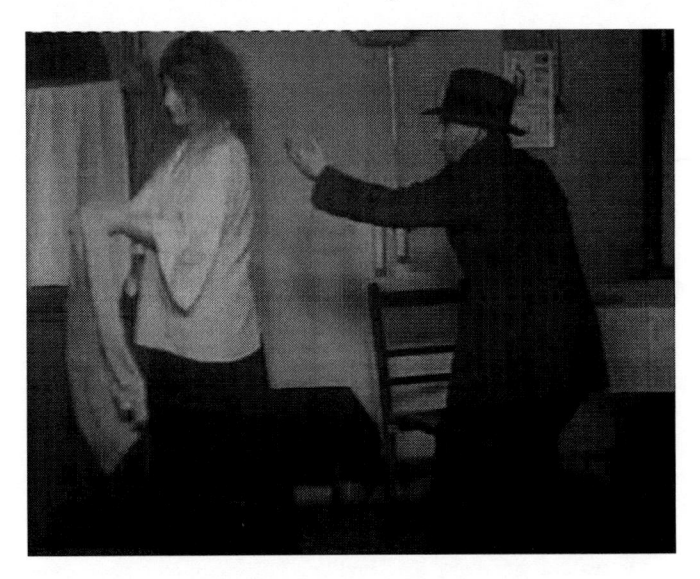

Fig. 1-1 frame enlargement from *Hair* (1933)
Source: Scottish Screen Archive

Other entries included *Fickle Fortune* (1933)—"An Episode in the Life of Rob Roy", *Maritime Moments* (1933)—"The Story of a Motor-Boat Cruise", *Nadia* (1933)—"The Story of What Happened When a Gipsy Girl Broke into Society", *Edinburgh* (1933)—"A Camera Impression of the Capital of Scotland" and *The Masked Rider* (1933)—"A Tale of Desperate Doings in the Wildest Woolliest West". Thus at its inauguration, the SAFF attracted work in a wide range of genres, employing diverse filmmaking

---

[9] The term "Grand Guignol" derives from a theatre of the same name in Paris, specialising in horror shows and now generically meaning graphic and amoral horror entertainment.
[10] Film Correspondent, "Amateur Film Festival", 20.

techniques, illustrating a range of participations, and endorsing Norman McLaren's comments in a later retrospective on amateur freedoms:

> The amateur's limitations... usually lie in his material means, but his great advantage over the professional is his greater freedom in choice of theme and approach to his subject. He has also the great asset of intimate contact with all sides of his craft, and he is spared the temptation to wallow in a welter of technical facilities and the deluding comfort of sheer spit and polish.[11]

Following the success of the first festival, it was decided to expand and widen the competition's reach, with the recognition and inclusion of films submitted from societies and clubs across the British Isles. Two new classes were established, and the now four entry categories re-defined as:

Class A:	Story Films open to clubs in Great Britain
Class B:	Interest Films open to clubs in Great Britain
Class C:	Interest Films open to individuals resident in Scotland
Class D:	Sound Films of any description open to clubs or individuals in Great Britain[12]

Classes A, B and C had no restrictions as to gauge of film; entries for class D were only accepted on 35mm however, for technical reasons. Perhaps more surprisingly, there were no restrictions placed on the length of films submitted. Amateur status was however monitored carefully. Conditions of involvement, circulated with entry forms, stipulated that films could only be submitted by amateurs or amateur societies. An amateur is defined as "one who does not earn his livelihood through the Photographic or Cinema Industry and Amateur Societies are composed of the same."[13] Caveats abounded however: sound and processing could be outsourced to a professional organisation, and special considerations would be given to amateur-produced titling, often a final arbiter in competition judging.

With the competition advertised nationally through the expanding hobby literature, and even a promotional 35mm trailer filmed by Russell to encourage support, the 1934 festival received 15 entries, with seven Scottish, and eight English, submissions received.[14] At this stage, the prize

---

[11] McLaren, in *Men with Bees in Their Bonnets*, 6.
[12] Entry form for the Second Scottish Amateur Film Festival.
[13] Ibid.
[14] Class A (Story Films) received 5 entries; Class B (Interest Films) received 6 entries; Class C (Interest Films – Scotland) received 2 entries; and Class D (Sound

money for the winning film in each category was £10, and winners included *Situations Vacant* (1934) from the Meteor Film Society in the story films class, and *Glasgow's Police* (1934) in the sound class, with the 35mm print being accompanied by sound-on-disc.[15] Other winners included *The Outer Isles* (1934) by the Modern School Club, Chesterfield, who won joint prize for best interest film, together with *Seven Till Five* (1934) filmed by Glasgow School of Art, Kinecraft Society (GSAKS).

The Kinecraft Society, formed as early as 1933, and heavily influenced by the avant-garde filmmaking regularly celebrated in writings around amateur cine, mixed styles, introducing animation and experimental editing techniques into their always innovative productions. Among the most active members of the society, which included staff and students, were Norman McLaren, Stewart McAllister, William J. McLean, Helen Biggar and Violet Anderson. Working with shoestring budgets and very limited equipment, it is unsurprising that McLaren would comment later that, "the successful amateur filmmaker has to learn the art of making virtues out of the necessities imposed on him".[16] *Seven Till Five* was shot by McLaren and McLean, and records "A Pattern of the Day's Doings" at the Glasgow School of Art, in a highly idiosyncratic manner.[17] One bibliography of McLaren recognises a "strong formalist attitude" in *Seven Till Five,* noting clear influences from Sergei Eisenstein.[18] With adjudication that year by Andrew Buchanan, well-known for his writings in *Amateur Cine World* magazine and elsewhere,[19] the 1934 festival was held on Saturday, 8th December at the Lyric Theatre, Glasgow. Violet Anderson later recalled that following their win with *Seven Till Five*, John Grierson arranged a trip for the filmmaking team to Pinewood Studios in Buckinghamshire, where they visited the set of Hitchcock's *The 39 Steps* (1935) featuring Robert Donat and Madeleine Carroll.[20]

No festival was held in 1935, perhaps due to financial or organisational difficulties. However, by 1936 the running of the event had been taken

---

Films) received 2 entries. The geographical scope of entries included London, Manchester, Middlesbrough, Derbyshire and Glasgow.

[15] McBain, "And the Winner Is....", 3.
[16] McLaren, in *Men with Bees in Their Bonnets*, 6.
[17] Opening credit to *Seven Till Five*.
[18] Sexton, *Biography of Norman McLaren*.
[19] Buchanan was at this point working professionally at the Gaumont-British Picture Corporation. He directed many short films, collaborated with Basil Wright and John Grierson on *O'er Hill and Dale* (1932), and frequently served as adjudicator at amateur film festivals. See Buchanan, "What I Look for in a Prizewinning Film", 475, and "Let The Film Help!", 87-88.
[20] Notes of a conversation with Violet Neish (Anderson), dated 14 October 1983.

over by the Scottish Film Council (SFC). Established in 1934 with the approval of the newly formed British Film Institute (BFI), the role of the SFC was to act as the national film body for Scotland, with a remit covering the "promotion of film and media culture, including production theory, media education, archiving, industrial development and exhibition."[21] Representatives on the Council included members from the cinema trade, industry, education, film societies and public interest groups including trade unions and amateur film societies. Within the Council, various panels were set up, including one for amateur cinematography. SFC involvement is indicative perhaps of the amateur movement's growing conspicuousness, and a feeling that supervision by a national body was needed in order to develop and maintain the prestige of the festival.[22] Certainly the Council's brief to encourage the "appreciation" of film beyond the commercial Hollywood experience, provided an ideal platform from which the SAFF could be supported, and the SFC would back the festival with remarkable loyalty until 1978.

Despite the involvement of the Council (who may have had some influence in procuring the services of John Grierson as adjudicator), there were relatively few entries in 1936, with just five Scottish and four English films received, and a certain familiarity about the participants and the character of their work: the Meteor Society again won the fiction prize with *Glencoe Legend* (1936). Of more lasting significance was the potential for "cross-over" suggested by the third festival: Grierson's adjudication this year would ultimately launch the careers of two talented amateur filmmakers in the professional sphere; Norman McLaren and Stewart McAllister, both members of the GSAKS. The Kinecraft Society entered *Camera Makes Whoopie* (1936), a lavish depiction of the staging of the Art School Carnival Ball, littered with "tricks" allowing the viewer to "tap into the aesthetic sensations supposedly produced by this event."[23] The other submission, entered by McLaren under his own name, was *Colour Cocktail* (1936). Whilst the film itself does not survive, the adjudicator's reaction to its screening was vividly recalled by film critic Forsyth Hardy, who described Grierson grasping his arm and declaring, "Who is that? ... Take me to him".[24]

Grierson subsequently offered McLaren and McAllister "apprenticeships" at the General Post Office (GPO) Film Unit. Access to such training was unprecedented, and soon set both filmmakers on highly distinguished

---

[21] Silverblatt et. al., *Dictionary of Media Literacy*, 170.
[22] Entry Form for Third Scottish Amateur Film Festival.
[23] Sexton, *Biography of Norman McLaren*.
[24] Hardy quoted by McBain in "And the winner is...", 99.

careers. McLaren went on to join the National Film Board of Canada, with McAllister finding long-term employment with British Transport Films. Looking back in later life, McLaren commented in 1963 that he was "deeply grateful to the Scottish Amateur Film Festival for the part it played" in establishing his career in filmmaking.[25]

By 1937 interest in the festival had increased, and there were 45 entries from all around Britain. The adjudicator this year was filmmaker Anthony Asquith. Classes had again been modified, and were now:

> Class A: Fiction (Story-films/Photoplays) open to the British Isles
> Class B: Non-fiction (Documentary/ Instructional) open to the British Isles
> Class C: Any Type of Film—open only to filmmakers resident in Scotland

The Victor Saville Trophy was reallocated as the overriding accolade for "Most Outstanding Film Shown" at the Festival, and The Andrew Buchanan Cup was introduced for the best film combining drama with realism, a "hybrid" mode widely advocated by Buchanan and others as an ideal model for amateur production in the 1930s.[26] Festival organisers also sought to keep pace with technical developments. Equipment for the amateur cinematographer had been innovated with remarkable speed, and "substandard" colour filmmaking was now more affordable and accessible. This new dimension was quickly recognised, with a prize created for best colour film, and the preface to the 1937 Festival programme confidently noting that:

> In the matter of colour films, the amateur is relatively better off than commercial producers, who require much additional and complicated equipment for natural colour filming, whereas the sub-standard gauges of film can now make colour movies without any extra apparatus and at only a slight increase in cost. The world of amateur cine is widening its borders daily.[27]

The unnamed film critic of *The Glasgow Evening News*, simply known as "Projector", also commented approvingly:

---

[25] McLaren, in *Men with Bees in Their Bonnets*, 6.
[26] Buchanan, "Fictional or Non-fictional Films?", 373-399. Over the years at SAFF, the Buchanan Cup would be awarded largely for films about Scotland and various family-centred projects.
[27] Preface to the Fourth Film Festival Programme.

The fact that the amateurs are now using colour intelligently and artistically... illustrates the progressive and ambitious ideas possessed by amateur cameramen.[28]

It seems then that the early ethos of the festival was shifting steadily on a range of fronts. The Meteor Film Producing Society entered only one film in 1937, *Fourth in Hand* (1937), which won the Andrew Buchanan Cup; Violent Anderson entered two films under her own name, *Pottery* (1936) and *A Glasgow Junior Instruction Centre* (1934), and although neither title won an award, her name would feature amongst future prize-winners. Other former members of the Kinecraft Society, filmmaker Norman McLaren and sculptor Helen Biggar entered *Hell Unltd* (1936). This highly experimental film utilised techniques mixing animation, live action, archival footage and graphics, to produce a powerful propagandist message, criticising arms sales, and associating the practice with the spread of fascism in Europe. Asquith was impressed by the technique but offered little on the politics, commenting that the film "shows a great deal of ingenuity and imagination... trick work models are very skillfully done and the cutting is incisive and effective."[29] Both filmmakers would preserve such aesthetic and political interests in their subsequent filmmaking, even as they moved away from the amateur scene.[30]

The big winner of 1937 was *The Day Thou Gavest* (1937), entered by Montague Pictures from Newcastle-Upon-Tyne. The film records typical activities undertaken on a Sunday, using a mixture of documentary and dramatised sequences, of which Buchanan would certainly have approved. Asquith considered it "The best film in the competition and one of the best films of its kind, amateur or professional I have ever seen" and went on to recommend that the filmmakers receive "the highest possible praise for a film which disproves the Wardour Street theory that entertainment cannot be reconciled with art".[31] The film duly received The Victor Saville Trophy for "most outstanding film" shown at the Festival.

A new category of Novice Class was also introduced this year, with novice being defined for festival purposes as "one who has not so far

---

[28] "Projector", "Scots Film Festival—Mr Asquith's Praise for Amateurs."
[29] Notes by the Honourable Anthony Asquith, Adjudicator.
[30] McLaren would next act as cameraman on *Defence of Madrid* (1936) a Spanish civil war documentary; Biggar would continue her political filmmaking with *Challenge To Fascism*, a 1939 film sponsored by Glasgow Trades Council and Burgh Labour Party, recording Glasgow's May Day parade and procession in support of "Arms for Spain" and an end to non-intervention policy. See Scottish Screen website: www.nls.uk/ssa—catalogue.
[31] Fourth Film Festival Programme, 11.

gained an award in any amateur film competition."[32] Apparently, the class had less to do with the newness of the filmmaker to the hobby, than with recognition within the movement. Ironically, it appears to accommodate an accomplished amateur filmmaker who might remain "unqualified" until winning a prize. In the event, Frank Marshall was to take the Novice Prize with his film *Just One Thing After Another* (1937), a figure who would feature heavily in later festivals, both as participant and later as organiser.

Internationalism and Interruption

Between 1933 and 1937, SAFF gradually consolidated its position as a reliable event in the amateur cine calendar. 1938 however marked perhaps a transition to a new phase of development. The year was an important one for Glasgow, with the hosting of the imposing Empire Exhibition in its Bellahouston Park. Grand pavilions in modernist art deco design were erected, with bold colours presenting a futuristic utopia of scientific innovation, economic regeneration and international co-operation. With the exhibition receiving over twelve million visitors during a six-month period, this celebration of Britain's international standing would become one of the Scottish highlights of the twentieth century, and a significant lure for amateur filmmakers. SAFF embraced the celebration, and championed the theme of international camaraderie, by opening up the competition to include entries from the Commonwealth countries. The name of the festival was also changed for this year to the British Empire Amateur Film Festival. With the 1938 festival arguably hosting one of the most significant competitions, it is interesting to note that this was the first year that the Meteor Film Producing Society, pivotal to the origination of the event, did not itself enter any films.

As the festival officially "attained the dignity of governmental status" senses of its ownership seem to have been in flux: it was now promoted under the auspices of the London-based BFI,[33] although practical organisation continued to be undertaken by the Amateur Cinematography Panel of the SFC.[34] Awards at the festival still included the Victor Saville Trophy, and the Andrew Buchanan Cup; new for 1938 however was a special trophy, initially referred to on entry forms as the "Empire

---

[32] Ibid.
[33] Ross, Programme for the Empire Amateur Film Festival, 1938, 5.
[34] Preliminary viewings of films entered for the competition were held on 26th and 27th May 1938, in the Educational Cinema constructed within the Scottish Pavilion at the Exhibition; final screenings and adjudication by Alfred Hitchcock took place at the Lyric Theatre, Glasgow, on Saturday 28th May.

Exhibition Cup" for best film.[35] By the time of the festival, the prize had obviously attracted sponsorship, and was thereafter referred to as the Associated British Picture Corporation Exhibition Cup, which could be retained by the winner indefinitely.[36] To reflect the international diversity of the festival this year a special prize was also awarded for films "From British Subjects Abroad". This attracted two entries from Australia, eight from India, one from Portugal, one from Siam (now Thailand) and one from Singapore. Many of these "foreign" entries clearly impressed greatly, although adjudicator Alfred Hitchcock, already a well-established director with strong links to the amateur movement, seems to have left a less positive impression: comments from *The Bulletin*'s film critic Melville Johnstone, are reiterated elsewhere:

> Hitch was rather a disappointment compared to other adjudicators in Scottish Amateur Film Festivals... Not for him the lashing criticisms of Mr John Grierson, who left Scottish amateurs punch-drunk, and made them wonder why they had not stuck to gardening. With an eye on the clock, he did not point out faults and give good advice in the Grierson style, just announced awards with a few brief words as to his reasons.[37]

Prize-winning films included Australian beach documentary, *Surf, Sand and Sunshine* (1938) which won the Andrew Buchanan Cup, and *Birds of the Reeds* (1938), a colour nature study which picked up the special First Prize "Inscribed Scottish Quaich" for colour film.[38] The prize for best film from British Subjects Abroad was awarded to *Tang* made by R. D. Pestonji from Bangkok, for a film depicting a day in the hard-working life of a young "Siamese" widow and her boy. Major awards were presented to the Stoke-on-Trent Cine Society, which received the Victor Saville Trophy for *Nancy's Garage* (1938), a comic film showing a day in the life of a female garage keeper, whilst the Associated British Film Corporation's Exhibition Cup was awarded to another Stoke-on-Trent filmmaker, Herbert J. Arundel for *The Smuggler's Cave* (1938), a melodrama featuring children on a holiday adventure.

Award lists such as these illustrate well the preoccupations of the amateur with mainstream conventions, whilst masking significant counter-

---

[35] British Empire Amateur Film Festival Entry Form, 1938.
[36] Ibid.
[37] Johnstone, "No Grouse About This Festival", 24.
[38] *Santa Passes Out* (1938), a tale of deception by a too hopeful father on Christmas morning, won the Second Prize Quaich, with the Third Prize Quaich being awarded to *The Fall of the Year* (1938), by Maurice B. Anderson from Newton Mearns, Scotland.

currents revealed through deeper research into submission lists. Violet Anderson's entry in the fifth festival, *Heil Osterreich* (1936), for example—whilst not a prize-winner—remains a significant film in the wider history of amateur film in Scotland. Documenting Austria from the perspective of the curious traveler in an era characterised by profound political and social change, the film represents a true "hidden" history. With the majority of films at this time depicting the official government perspective, it remains a unique social document, filmed through the eyes of a foreign female spectator.[39]

With the new plethora of prizes on offer at the 1938 Festival, confusion seems to have arisen as to definitions and functions. One unnamed correspondent for *The Glasgow Herald* summarised anxieties:

> The prize list in this festival is rather confusing. How is an adjudicator to distinguish between the "best" film and the "most outstanding" film? The multiplicity of awards reflects the high regard in which the donors hold the amateur movement, but it leads to anomalies.[40]

Related problems arose with success. With the volume of entries increasing, it had already become clear by 1938 that the adjudicator would be unable to view every entry, and that some method of pre-selection would be necessary.

1939 therefore saw the festival once again restricting entries to the British Isles, and a simplified classification for entries formalised thus:

Class A: Fiction	Alfred Hitchcock Cup
Class B: Non-fiction	Victor Saville Trophy
Class C: Colour Class	British Institute Cup
Class D: Scottish Class	Andrew Buchanan Cup
Class E: Novice Class	Bryce Walker Cup

With the Empire Exhibition providing—almost on the door-step—architectural spectacle, historical reconstructions, horticultural delights and exhilarating fairground rides, it is not surprising that the sixth SAFF included at least five films recording days out at the Exhibition. The adjudicator for that year was Alberto Cavalcanti, contemporary of Grierson at the GPO film unit, and already highly acclaimed for his work on *Night Mail* (1936). Triumphs at the festival included Frank Marshall's *Mower Madness* (1939), a comical tale of a lawnmower with a mind of its

---

[39] Notes of a conversation with Violet Neish (Anderson), dated 14 October 1983.
[40] Film Correspondent, "Amateur Film Festival: Success of English Entries", 20.

own, which won the Alfred Hitchcock Cup for best fiction film. The festival this year marked however something of an end to the suburban securities celebrated in Marshall's work, as the pleasures of amateur filmmaking were forced to give way to more urgent priorities. Like the hobby itself however, SAFF continued into the war years, albeit with significant modifications, and perhaps revised senses of purpose.

Festivals in 1940 and 1941, whilst still attracting significant entries, ceased to employ the services of a sole adjudicator. Instead, judgement was provided by a panel, which included local input from Oliver Bell, Forsyth Hardy, William Jeffery and Charles Oakley. Frank Marshall again won best fiction film in 1941 with *An Apple a Day* (1941), a story of two children who receive a dose of castor oil after eating too much stolen fruit. By the third year of the war in 1942, the scale of amateur filmmaking had dramatically diminished. This was due to a number of factors—film stock was rationed, restrictions were in force on the use of cameras, and many amateur filmmakers had been called up to aid the war effort. In this context, the SFC therefore decided that owing to the insufficient number of films available, they could no longer justify continuing the festival. Instead, in a fundamental break with tradition, the audience was asked to vote for their favourite films, from a selection of the festival's previous winners. The results of this initiative were screened as usual, with proceeds donated to the Navy League War Comforts Fund. Many amateur filmmakers however continued to make films related to the war effort. Filmed by Frank Marshall, *ARP: A Reminder for Peacetime* (1940), for example, records the impact of the war on family life, capturing children's reactions to necessities such as putting on a gas mask, or the mastery of First Aid skills. Marshall's familiar sense of fun is apparent nonetheless, shining through the adversities experienced during the early war years. By the darker days of 1943 however, with the war effort draining resources and the country on constant alert, the time and money needed for competitive filmmaking was more severely limited, and for many perhaps, harder to justify. Although amateur cine activity would continue under a range of guises throughout the war, no festival was held from 1943 to 1947, and prospects for its revival must have seemed bleak, even as the country emerged from conflict into the austerities of the post-1945 period.

Post-War Resurrection

Amateur cine recovered unevenly after 1945, as filmmakers de-mobilised, renovated equipment and gradually acquired reels of usable stock. After a slow start however, a new wave of enthusiasm for the hobby spread quickly, leading to the formation of many new clubs, and re-generating the organised movement's pre-war infrastructures. SAFF was resurrected in 1948, largely at the instigation of Donald Elliot, new Director of the SFC, and keen supporter of the amateur cine sector. Initially the Festival returned to tried-and-tested formulae and professional judging; adjudication that year was by industry all-rounder Michael Powell. A promotional trailer was made by Stanley Russell, which demonstrated how to make a film, for screening in commercial cinemas.[41] Such celebrity involvement and strong marketing generated 67 entries from the British Isles. In a decisive move, SAFF at last found a permanent home, taking up residence in the Cosmo Cinema, Glasgow, for the first time, a venue which would serve the event well for most of its remaining life. A new category of "classroom" films was also introduced, reflecting renewed interest in the moving image as an educational tool, and the spread of school-based production units, leaving classes defined thus:

Class A:	Fiction	Alfred Hitchcock Cup
Class B:	Non-Fiction	Victor Saville Trophy
Class C:	Classroom	Glasgow Cup
Class D:	Colour	British Film Institute Cup
Class E:	Scottish	Andrew Buchanan Cup
Class F:	Novice	Bryce Walker Cup
Class G:	Sound	Special Prize

The following year saw further reorganisation of infrastructures, with the creation of the Scottish Association of Amateur Cinematographers (SAAC)—a national body, within which all the cine clubs of Scotland were represented. The SAAC worked closely thereafter with the SFC in the organisation of the festival, and eventually ran the last few competitions, following withdrawal of public funding during the 1970s.

Something of the notoriety attending "the Scottish" by this point, is suggested by concerns published over its judging methods. Frustrations surface periodically in the surrounding hobby literatures, underlining the importance placed on festival recognition by the "serious" amateur, and anxieties in particular concerning definitional criteria relating to status. Prior to the festival taking place in 1949 for example, *Amateur Cine World* had criticised SAFF's policy of awarding prizes to films for specific aspects of their production, such as sound or colour. A typical article states

---

[41] Russell was by this time an established professional film director and producer, with his own company, Thames and Clyde films.

the magazine's stance on this system of adjudication in unambiguous terms:

> A film is an integration of a number of closely related elements, and to elevate one above the rest to the extent of awarding a prize for the film, irrespective of its other qualities, might well result in a picture which is good in one department but poor in the rest being placed above one which attains a higher average level of merit.[42]

The anonymous critic extends the critique in increasingly sarcastic tones, arguing that "formless" films have won prizes in national competitions, and questions the value of identifying single aspects of an entry as more prominent than others, or indeed the whole film:

> Why not give prizes for the film with the best produced titles, for the best film in which there are no titles, for the film which contains the best lit interiors...[43]

Further concerns are expressed over the possibility of one film winning all the prizes, which for this observer "surely defeats the purpose of an amateur film competition". Whatever this critic's underlying anxieties, and admissions of his or her "tetchy mood", final comment nonetheless admits that the Festival will still be well worth a visit if the standard matches preceding years.[44] Whether in response to such considerations or not, 1949 again saw tampering with SAFF classification systems, and the number of categories reduced from seven to four,[45] although specialist awards continued to be made for specific aspects of production, as circumstances dictated. Entries were also fewer than previous years, with the recorded number of submissions for this year being 57. It was felt though by at least one commentator, that the quality of filmmaking, which had received such a setback during the war years was beginning to make a recovery, with films that "showed skill, courage and imagination."[46]

The 1950s saw the festival growing steadily, with the number of entrants averaging from between 70 to 132. In part, this reflected the growing integration of Scottish competition culture with its European and North American counterparts. Certainly with the SAAC's growing

---

[42] Anon., "A Headache for the Judges at Scottish Amateur Film Festival", 742
[43] Ibid.
[44] Ibid.
[45] The categories were: Educational and Scientific, Fiction, General Interest (including Documentary, Travel and Family) and Novice.
[46] Anon., "Glasgow Amateur Film Festival", 60.

participation in UNICA (Union Internationale du Cinéma d'Amateurs) activity overseas, success at home increasingly opened doors to participation in competition elsewhere. Reflecting this new sense of international connection, the 10th UNICA congress was co-hosted in Glasgow in 1951, with the occasion recorded on film by members of the SAAC.[47] Such contacts clearly encouraged re-thinking of SAFF approaches, and by 1951 the Festival had put in place a pre-selection process mirroring the systems used in many international competitions. Two weeks prior to the competition, viewing panels would be established from members of the SFC, the Committees of the SAAC, and the Scottish Educational Film Association (SEFA). Members selected would be experienced in filmmaking techniques, with the panel viewing entries in the educational class comprised of teachers and educationists familiar with the use of film in the classroom.[48]

The 1950s and 1960s saw one of the most creative and innovative periods of amateur filmmaking represented at the festival. Amongst the most unusual of those emerging was Enrico Cocozza,[49] who made history in 1952 by winning all three major awards at the 14th Festival. The Victor Saville Trophy and the Alfred Hitchcock Cup, both went to his film *Robot Three* (1952), a dark tale of a scientist who creates two robots, which subsequently fall in love, with tragic consequences. (see Fig. 1-2) Whilst regarded as morbid, the film was highly commended for its bold and dramatic use of colour, and success in maintaining mood and tension.[50] Forsyth Hardy commented in *The Weekly Scotsman* that Cocozza's work "has all the confidence of professional filmmaking, and much more imagination than is normally shown there."[51] Cocozza's other winning film was *Nine O'Clock*, (1952) telling the story a young man's last few hours before he commits suicide. (see Fig. 1-3) This won the Humphrey Jennings Memorial Trophy for best abstract film with a sensitive and imaginative treatment, in which adjudicator Ralph Nunn May found "Imagination and skilful use of camera angles combined to create a strong

---

[47] Surviving footage records delegates arriving at the offices of the SFC, the reception dinner with Charles Oakley and Frank Marshall (by then Chairman of the SAAC) receiving the guests, and organised excursions, including a trip to the Hiram Walker Whisky distillery in Dunblane, and a cruise "doon the watter" aboard the Waverley paddle steamer.
[48] McBain provides an outline of the system in "And The Winner is...", 101-102.
[49] See Mitchell Miller's analysis of Cocozza's overall output elsewhere in this volume.
[50] The Adjudicator's Review of Entries. 1952.
[51] Hardy, *Weekly Scotsman*, 1952, typed draft sheets.

effect of frustration..."[52] Although Cocozza produced a variety of films, including travelogues, social dramas, and "poetic" landscape essays, he will undoubtedly be most remembered for his surreal, avant-garde work, often baffling audiences accustomed to more traditional forms of filmmaking.

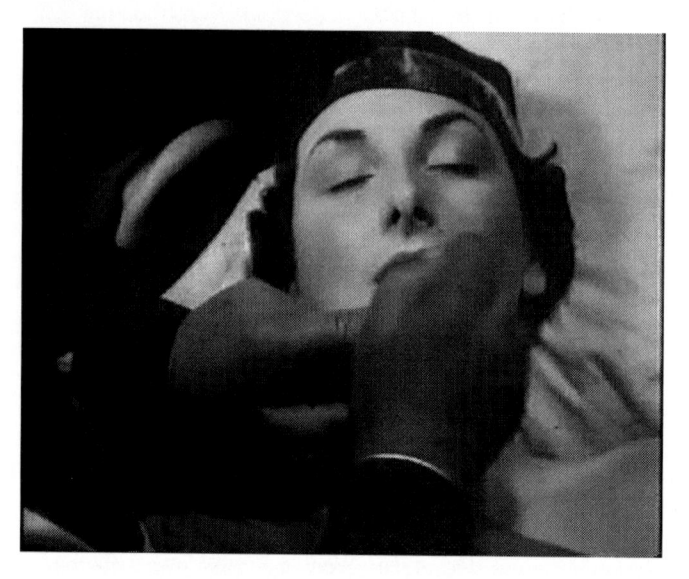

Fig. 1-2 frame enlargement from *Robot Three* (1952)
Source: Scottish Screen Archive

Controversy could be generated from a wide range of sources: in 1952 it had derived from Cocozza's films about mad scientists and suicide; in 1953 it arose from the comments of that year's adjudicator, Harry Watt. The experience of SAFF seems to have been a trying one for the celebrated documentarist: Watt's main criticism of most of the entries was that they were unduly protracted. Even when the amateur had mastered the technical aspects of filmmaking, he mused, the reluctance to edit out redundant or inappropriate material led to films which were "miles too long." He is quoted by Forsyth Hardy: "Any editor can cut out the bad stuff... It takes a good editor to cut out the good stuff."[53] Watt also went on to criticise the inadequacy of the performances in most of the films, and

---

[52] The Adjudicator's Review of Entries, 1952.
[53] Hardy, *Weekly Scotsman,* typed draft sheets.

suggested that amateurs draw on the talents of local dramatic societies to secure the quality of acting required for the ever more complicated stories that were emerging. Countering possible discouragement however, Hardy stresses though that Watt's criticism was presented in a spirit of assistance, and that his comments were "vigorously laced with humour" with there being "no danger of the audience feeling they were being lectured at".[54]

Fig. 1-3 frame enlargement from *Nine O'Clock* (1952)
Source: Scottish Screen Archive

1956 was to see the largest ever number of entries, as the festival moved towards something of a high-point.[55] The competition that year included noteworthy submissions from prize-winning regular Willam S. Dobson, from Edinburgh,[56] a figure heavily involved in amateur filmmaking throughout his life, taking on prominent roles as secretary of the Edinburgh Cine Society and Vice-Chairman of the SAAC. Dobson's films ranged from comedies such as *Pills for All Ills* (1956) a comic tale of

---

[54] Ibid.
[55] 135 films were entered in 1956, 108 on 16mm, 20 on 8mm, and 7 on 9.5mm.
[56] Dobson had already won the Victor Saville Cup and BFI Cup at the festival in 1955 with his film *Towards a Brighter Horizon* (1955), and he would continue to receive awards with prize-winning entries at the Festivals in 1956, 1957, 1958 and 1959.

a salesman selling "Dr Swindles Famous Zippo Vitality Pills", to essays including *How Would You Like It?* (1962) an "educational" short, dealing with the anti-social practice of dropping litter.

Other filmmakers featuring amongst the prize-winners, were Iain Dunnachie, Harry Birrell, and Elsie Cairns; Nettie McGavin and Louise Annand also made significant contributions. Dr Dunnachie from Glasgow won the Oliver Bell prize for a religious or moral film, with his entry *Who Is My Neighbour?* (1956), a documentary about community support for the elderly in Govan. Other awards followed.[57] Harry Birrell from Glasgow won his first prize in 1959, for *The Skimsters* (1959) a "hobby film" about water-skiing on Loch Earn, before going on to win prizes over the next thirteen years. Adjudicator, Clive Donner was so impressed by *The Skimsters* that he remarked:

> If I had seen this as a supporting film in a cinema programme, I would never have considered it to be the work of an amateur.[58]

Women filmmakers gained new prominence amongst the entrants and prize-winners in the 1950s and 1960s. Elsie Cairns from Gordon in the Scottish Borders won the Isabel Elder Cup for an educational film, and the Glasgow Scientific Film Society Prize of £2 for her nature film *Grey Seals* (1961), which left adjudicator Charles Frend, impressed by its simple story and delightful photography: "a first-class nature film…it was a wonderful film", he commented.[59] Once again early success seems to have created an appetite for further participation.[60] Nettie McGavin was another prolific filmmaker whose interest in film was perhaps no surprise, with her brother Frank Marshall also an active participant and regular prize-winner. McGavin, having married into the McGavin Tea family, regularly made films during business trips to tea-producing areas abroad. Her film *Italian Interlude* (1952) featuring scenes of the Mediterranean Coast, Lake Como,

---

[57] Dunnachie subsequently went on to win the Andrew Buchanan Cup for a family film with *Robin's Saturday* in 1958, and the Marshall Quaich for *Impressions of Skye* in 1960.
[58] Adjudicators comments for 1959 Film Festival.
[59] Adjudicators Comments for 1956 Film Festival.
[60] Cairns went on to win two awards in 1957, the Glasgow Cup for best educational film for *The Pool* (1957) and the prestigious Victor Saville Trophy for *Out and About* (1957). Whether Cairns was the only woman to win the Victor Saville Trophy is unknown at this point, although certainly she continued to be a presence: in the 1961 Festival she won the Glasgow Cup for a teaching film entitled *The Slovonian Grebe* (1961), focusing on the nesting habits of this particular bird.

Milan and the Italian Alps, won her the 1952 Scottish Film Council Prize of £10. A further film made with her husband Nat, entitled *Healing Hands in Nazareth* (1952) won the Oliver Bell Trophy for a religious or moral film at the 21st Festival the same year. Louise Annand too made a number of educational and teaching films throughout this period. *Arms and Armour Part 1* (1955), produced with Thomas Lindsay, demonstrating the use of different historic weapons housed at Kelvingrove Museum, won a prize at the 17th Festival. Another entry, *The History of Lighting* (1959), was highly commended in 1959. Already a respected amateur artist, who worked as Museums Education Officer in Glasgow, Annand's cine success would soon involve her in making films for SEFA.[61] She is also credited as producing the first film about Charles Rennie Mackintosh in 1965.[62]

1959 was a significant year for smaller gauge films. *Blind Faith* (1959) by Oscar Riesel from London, was the first 8mm film in twenty-one years of the SAFF to secure the Victor Saville Trophy for outstanding film of the competition.[63] The film also won the Hitchcock Cup for best fiction film and the Scottish Film Council Prize of £10. 1959 was, appropriately enough, also the first year that 8mm prize-winners were screened at the Cosmo Cinema. Prior to this, "bootlace" films were shown at the offices of the SFC, where the pre-selection panels would hold their initial viewing sessions. The majority of entries were still shot on 16mm however, with a decreasing number on the once popular 9.5mm gauge. Adjudicator, Clive Donner, reminiscing about his own early filmmaking, stressed his own credentials as an amateur schooled on the narrowest gauge:

> I am very pleased to be the first adjudicator to have been present when 8mm films were shown at the Cosmo for the first time. I myself started as an amateur with an 8mm projector. Later I graduated to an 8mm camera and was able to make some films for myself.[64]

---

[61] SEFA's objectives were to promote interest in and use of educational films in the classroom and the organisation was actively involved with the Scottish Film Council in the production of educational films in the post-war period. These films were held by the Scottish Central Film Library, which pioneered the loan of 16mm films and projectors to schools to encourage a new pedagogy for the classroom.
[62] Soroptomist International—A World Wide Organisation for Women in Management and the Professions.
[63] Only two 8mm films following *Blind Faith* went on to win the Victor Saville Trophy: *Psychose* (1966) by Warner Lepach from Germany in 1966, and *Rajada* (1971) by V. Branco from Portugal in 1971. There appear to be only two winners on Super 8mm format: *Giuseppe* (1972) by C. Satariano from Malta, and *One Coke Too Many* (1978) by Blantyre High School, Scotland.
[64] Adjudicators Comments for 1959 Film Festival.

By 1960 the Festival had again opened up the competition to entrants from overseas with an international entry, *Rhythm in Transit* (1960) by Antonio Cernuda from Cuba winning the Kodak Prize of £10.[65] The following year's Festival included films from Germany, Canada, Oslo, Belgium, New Zealand, Jersey and the USA. The adjudicator that year was the young Canadian film director, Sidney J. Furie. Striking from the records is the number of overseas entries which were awarded prizes. The Alfred Hitchcock Cup was won by an American entry, *Ten Cents* (1961) by A. Cernuda (now) from New York;[66] other overseas prize-winners included two films from Belgium, *Florea* (1961) by A. Leonard and *Quick Day* (1961) by L. Van Maelder. Other awards also headed for remote destinations.[67] Reflecting such trends, the Festival was officially renamed the Scottish International Amateur Film Festival (SIAFF) in 1969, and continued to receive a high level of foreign entries throughout the 1970s. Prize-winning films included entries from Switzerland, Belgium, Italy, France, the USA, Czechoslovakia, Canada, Spain and Ireland.

Conclusions

Against such an account of expansion, and innovation, the demise of the SIAFF seems perplexing, and a range of factors seem to have been involved. Certainly, with the SFC withdrawing funding in 1978, the beginning of the end had probably begun. This undoubtedly explains the lack of a festival in 1979 and 1980, and with the event now reliant on the resources of the SAAC, it is unsurprising that only three festivals followed. These took place in 1981 and 1983, followed by the final gathering, staged in 1986 with Cary Parker as adjudicator. It is unfortunate that no records survive of the entrants and prize-winners for this final festival. The minutes of the SAAC's AGM on 1 June 1986,[68] record only an apparent evaporation of interest, with only 30 SAAC members attending, and no members of the general public. Debate had certainly

---

[65] *Rhythm in Transit,* like many other SAFF entries, also went on to win awards at the IAC Festival in 1959.
[66] It is likely that Antonio Cernuda from Cuba is the same person as A. Cernuda from New York.
[67] The Marshall Sloan Prize was won by L. McLeod from New Zealand for *Nature's Day* (1961), the John Robertson Jnr. Prize was won by D. Davy from Canada for *Poison* (1961), and the Twentieth Century Movies Prize was awarded to *Golden Week in Kyoto* (1961) by O. H. Horovitz of Newton, USA.
[68] Minutes of SAAC AGM, dated 31 May 1987.

been ongoing concerning the chosen location—it would seem that the 1986 festival had been held at the Dowanhill headquarters of the SFC itself. Minutes from the AGM in 1987 record that the move from the Glasgow Film Theatre (re-developed from the Cosmo in 1974) was now regarded as a mistake, although a lack of ticket sales, thinner than usual publicity—and the fact that the receptionist at the Scottish Film Council knew nothing about the festival—all clearly impacted on the final collapse of the event.

Dr Norman Speirs, Chairman of the SAAC from 1977 to 1986 commented in a letter in 1996 to Janet McBain,[69] that he did not believe the demise of the Festival was due to the emergence of other competitions. The "Scottish 8" had after all been running since 1980, and was purely for 8mm films. Only after SIAFF had been closed down would the "8" widen its scope to include 16mm films and videotape—clearly an attempt to provide an arena in which to screen films which would formerly have been entered into SIAFF. However, unlike SIAFF, this competition did not accept entries from film schools, or projects which were sponsored. Dr Speirs suggests that the Scottish Film Council initially withdrew its funding due to financial restraints, but also because it saw no advantage in preserving such an event. The SAAC, following suit, finally discontinued running the festival, due to the huge amount of work involved, and the apparent lack of interest from Scottish filmmakers.[70] It seemed that whilst filmmakers no longer supported the event, neither did the public, with the attendance figures described as "abysmal". The collapse of such an influential amateur filmmaking event after fifty years, Dr Speirs contends, was "more a sign of the times and due to an increasing public apathy, rather than to any intrinsic fault in the administration or organisation."[71]

Before public enthusiasm waned however, the Scottish Amateur Film Festival was undoubtedly significant in the role it played within local, national and international film culture. The annual competition was highly regarded, both for the standard of films entered and the diversity of films shown, showcasing the best amateur talents to some of the most respected

---

[69] Letter from Dr Norman Speirs, Scottish Association of Moviemakers, dated 11 July. McBain was then curator of the Scottish Film Archive, now reconstituted as the Scottish Screen Archive, and currently part of the National Library of Scotland
[70] The SAAC changed its name in 1988 to the Scottish Association of Moviemakers (SAM), to reflect developments in technology, and the introduction of video cameras. SAM still maintains its operations as an umbrella organisation for film and video clubs in Scotland, and continues to hold its annual competition.
[71] Letter from Dr Norman Speirs, Scottish Association of Moviemakers, dated 11 July 1996.

filmmakers in the professional film business. The development of the festival over the years encouraged innovation in filmmaking standards, both technically and aesthetically, and offered incentives to investment and commitment crucial to the maintenance of a vital amateur culture. Two unique features of the festival—its sole professional adjudicator, and the showing of prize-winning films to a public audience—established the festival as a major event in the annual amateur cine calendar. Numerous adjudicators commented that they were extremely impressed by the quality, ingenuity and integrity of the prize-winning films and in Grierson's case went as far as to offer apprenticeships to several gifted winners. Moreover, many Scots filmmakers associated with the SAFF went on set up their own production companies, or to work professionally in the film industry.[72]

Of particular importance was the judging method applied to entrants, with a carefully constructed system of pre-selection by panels before a final adjudication. The festival's innovation and creativity during the years has certainly bequeathed a rich legacy of highly intricate, imaginative and influential amateur filmmaking, and it is now time to evaluate and analyse the filmmakers and their films, not only in the context of technical developments in filmmaking, but also in regard to the socio-political, cultural and aesthetic movements of the time. Norman McLaren's comments of 1963 about the qualities of a successful amateur filmmaker seem just as applicable today. Technologies may have changed, with the current amateur filmmaker using digital and high-definition formats, but the need to construct a narrative and tell a story remain paramount. The overarching qualities needed remain dedication, passion and a definite "bee in your bonnet...":

> the most successful amateur film-maker is someone with a "bee in his bonnet", who doesn't model his film on some other production he has seen, but who is excited about something close to him, which he knows well, something of his intimate environment, or his professional specialism, or his hobby, or his inner vision.[73]

---

[72] These include Stanley L. Russell (Thames and Clyde Films), Norman McLaren (National Film Board of Canada), Stewart McAllister (British Transport Films), W. J. McLean (Ferranti, Ltd), J. C. Elder and Isabel Elder (Elder Film Productions), Douglas Gray (Park Film Studios), Edward McConnell and Lawrence Henson (International Film Associates) and there are undoubtedly more.
[73] Norman McLaren, in *Men with Bees in Their Bonnets*, 6.

Works Cited

Primary Sources

Adjudicator's Review of Entries, 1952. Scottish Screen Archive Ref. 2/3/35.
Adjudicators Comments for 1956 Scottish Amateur Film Festival. Scottish Screen Archive Ref. 2/3/43.
Adjudicators Comments for 1959 Scottish Amateur Film Festival. Scottish Screen Archive Ref. 2/3/46.
Asquith, Anthony. Notes by the Honourable Anthony Asquith, Adjudicator. Scottish Screen Archive Ref. 2/3/13.
British Empire Amateur Film Festival Entry Form, 1938. Scottish Screen Archive Ref. 2/3/15.
British Empire Amateur Film Festival Programme, 1938. Scottish Screen Archive Ref. 2/3/16.
Entry Form for the Second Scottish Amateur Film Festival. Scottish Screen Archive Ref. 2/3/10.
Entry Form for the Third Scottish Amateur Film Festival. Scottish Screen Archive Ref. 2/3/11.
Fourth Scottish Amateur Film Festival Programme. Scottish Screen Archive Ref. 2/3/12.
Hardy, H. Forsyth. *Weekly Scotsman* (1952): Unpublished typed draft pages. Scottish Screen Archive Ref. 2/3/37.
Minutes of Scottish Association of Amateur Cinematographers AGM, dated 31 May 1987. Scottish Screen Archive Ref. 2/3/88.
Neish, Violet. Notes of a conversation with Violet Neish (Anderson), dated 14 October 1983. Scottish Screen Archive Ref. 11/1/121.
Ross, Ian S. Programme for the Empire Amateur Film Festival, 1938. Scottish Screen Archive Ref. 2/3/16.
Scottish Amateur Film Festival Programme, 1933. Scottish Screen Archive Ref. 2/3/8.
Speirs, Norman. Letter to Janet McBain from Norman Speirs, Scottish Association of Moviemakers, dated 11 July 1996. Scottish Screen Archive Ref. 2/3/88.

Secondary Sources

Anon. "A Headache for the Judges at Scottish Amateur Film Festival." *Amateur Cine World* 12, no. 11 (1949): 742.

—. "Glasgow Amateur Film Festival." *Amateur Cine World* 13, no. 1 (1949): 60.
Buchanan, Andrew. "Fictional or Non-fictional Films?" *Amateur Cine World* 3, no. 8 (1936): 373-399.
—. "Let The Screen Help!" *Sight and Sound* 8, no. 31 (1939): 87-88.
—. "What I Look For in A Prize-Winning Film." *Amateur Cine World* 11, no. 8 (1947): 475-477.
Film Correspondent. "Amateur Film Festival: Success of Glasgow Enterprise." *The Glasgow Herald* (16 October 1933): 20.
—. "Amateur Film Festival: Success of English Entries." *The Glasgow Herald* (30 May 1938): 8.
Johnstone, Melville. "No Grouse About This Festival: Amateur Films Provided Fine Entertainment." *The Bulletin* (30 May 1938): 24.
Low, Rachel. *The History of British Film 1929 to 1939: Films of Comment and Persuasion*. London: Unwin Brothers, 1949.
Martin, Andrew. *Going to the Pictures: Scottish Memories of Cinema*. Edinburgh: National Museums of Scotland Publishing, 2000.
Men with Bees in Their Bonnets—the Story Behind 25 Years of the Scottish Amateur Film Festival. Glasgow: The Scottish Film Council, 1963.
McBain, Janet. "And The Winner is…. A Brief History of the Scottish Amateur Film Festival, 1933-1986." In *Essays on Amateur Film: Jubilee Book*, edited by Nancy Kapstein, 97-106. Charleroi: Association Européenne Inédits, 1997.
"Projector". "Scots Film Festival—Mr Asquith's Praise for Amateurs." *Glasgow Evening News* (19 February 1937). Scottish Screen Archive Ref. 2/3/1.
Ross, David. *Biography of Glasgow Kinecraft Society*. Scottish Screen Archive website at: www.nls/ssa.
Sexton, Jamie. *Biography of Norman McLaren*. British Film Institute website at: www.screenonline.org.uk.
Silverblatt, Art and Ellen M. Enright Eliceiri. *The Dictionary of Media Literacy*. Westport, Ct.: Greenwood Press, 1997.
Soroptomist International—A World Wide Organisation for Women in Management and the Professions, website at: http://titan.glo.be/~bea/

Films Cited

A Glasgow Junior Instruction Centre
(Violet Anderson, 1934) 16mm., 10 mins.

All On A Summer's Day
  (Meteor Film Producing Society, 1933) 16mm., 10 mins.
Amateur Cinematography
  (Stanley Russell, 1948) 16mm., 3 mins.
An Apple a Day
  (Frank Marshall, 1941) 16mm., 10 mins.
Arms and Armour Part 1
  (Louise Annand and Thomas Lindsay, 1955) 16mm., 12 mins.
ARP: A Reminder for Peacetime
  (Frank Marshall, 1940) 16mm., 22 mins. 37 secs.
Birds of the Reeds
  (John Chear, 1938) 16mm., no running time available.
Blind Faith
  (Oscar Riesel, 1959) 8mm., no running time available.
Camera Makes Whoopee
  (GSA Kinecraft Society, 1936) 16mm., 18 mins. 25 secs.
Challenge to Fascism
  (Helen Biggar, 1938) 16mm., 29 mins.
Colour Cocktail
  (Norman McLaren, 1936) 16mm., no running time available.
The Day Thou Gavest
  (Anson Dyer, 1937) 16mm., no running time available.
Defence of Madrid
  (Ivor Montagu, 1936) 35mm., 34 mins.
Edinburgh
  (Edinburgh Film Guild, 1933) 16mm., no running time available.
The Fall of the Year
  (Maurice B. Anderson, 1938) 16mm., no running time available.
Fickle Fortune
  (Bearsden Film Club, 1933) 9.5mm., 15 mins. 30 secs.
Florea
  (A. Leonard, 1961) 16mm., no running time available.
Fourth In Hand
  (Meteor Film Producing Society, 1937) 16mm., 14 mins.
Glasgow's Police
  (Meteor Film Producing Society, 1934) 35mm., no running time available.
Glencoe Legend
  (Meteor Film Producing Society, 1936) 16mm., no running time available.

Golden Week in Kyoto
(O. H. Horovitz, 1961) 16mm., no running time available.
Grey Seals
(Elsie Cairns, 1961) 16mm., no running time available.
Giuseppi
(Cecil Satariano, 1972) 8mm., no running time available.
Hair
(Meteor Film Producing Society, 1933) 16mm., 11 mins.
Healing Hands in Nazareth
(Nettie and Nat McGavin, 1952) 16mm., no running time available.
Heil Osterreich
(Violet Anderson, 1936) 16mm., 26 mins.
Hell Unltd
(Norman McLaren and Helen Biggar, 1936) 16mm., 15 mins.
The History of Lighting
(Louise Annand for SEFA, 1959) 16mm., 9 mins. 17 secs.
How Would You Like It?
(William S. Dobson, 1962) 16mm., 9 mins.
I Was a Spy
(Gaumont British Picture Corporation, 1933) 35mm., 89 mins.
Impressions of Skye
(Iain Dunnachie, 1960) 16mm., no running time available.
Italian Interlude
(Nettie McGavin, 1952) 16mm., 17 mins.
Just One Thing After Another
(Frank Marshall, 1937) 16mm., no running time available.
Maritime Moments
(Glasgow Amateur Ciné Club, 1933) 9.5mm., no running time available.
Masked Rider, The
(Damyamount Picture Club, 1933) 16mm., no running time available.
Mower Madness
(Frank Marshall, 1939) 16mm., 13 mins. 39 secs.
Nadia
(Meteor Film Producing Society, 1933) 16mm., no running time available.
Nancy's Garage
(Stoke-on-Trent Ciné Society, 1938) 16mm., no running time available.
Night Mail
(General Post Office Film Unit, 1936) 35mm., 24 mins.

Nine O'Clock
   (Enrico Cocozza, 1952) 16mm., 20 mins.
One Coke Too Many
   (Blantyre High School, 1978) 8mm., no running time available.
Out and About
   (Elsie Cairns, 1957) 16mm., no running time available.
The Outer Isles
   (The Modern School Club, 1932) 16mm., 10 mins.
Pills for All Ills
   (William S. Dobson, 1956) 16mm., 15 mins. 18 secs.
Poison
   (Derek Davy, 1961) 16mm., no running time available.
Pool, The
   (Elsie Cairns, 1957) 16mm., no running time available.
Pottery
   (Violet Anderson, 1936) 16mm., 8 mins. 52 secs.
Psychose
   (Warner Lepach, 1966) 8mm., no running time available.
Quick Day
   (L. Van Maelder, 1961) 16mm., no running time available.
Rajada
   (V. Branco, 1971) 8mm., no running time available.
Rhythm in Transit
   (Antonio Cernuda, 1960) 16mm., no running time available.
Robin's Saturday
   (Iain Dunnachie, 1958) 16mm., no running time available.
Robot Three
   (Enrico Cocozza, 1952) 16mm., 12 mins.
Santa Passes Out
   (E. John Martin, 1938) 16mm., no running time available.
Seven Till Five
   (Glasgow School of Art Kinecraft Society, 1934) 16mm., 9 mins. 42 secs.
Situations Vacant
   (Meteor Film Producing Society, 1934) 16mm., no running time available.
The Skimsters
   (Harry Birrell, 1961) 16mm., 10 mins. 32 secs.
The Slovonian Grebe
   (Elsie Cairns, 1961) 16mm., 9 mins. 50 secs.

The Smuggler's Cave
   (Herbert J. Arundel, 1938) 16mm., no running time available.
Surf, Sand and Sunshine
   (J. A. Sherlock, 1938) 16mm., no running time available.
Tang
   (Ratanna Pestonji, 1938) 16mm., no running time available.
Ten Cents
   (A. Cernuda, 1961) 16mm., no running time available.
The 39 Steps
   (Gaumont British Picture Corporation, 1935) 35mm., 81 mins.
Towards a Brighter Horizon
   (William S. Dobson, 1955) 16mm., no running time available.
U.N.I.C.A
   (J. Barton, 1952) 16mm., 14 mins.
Who Is My Neighbour?
   (Iain Dunnachie, 1956) 16mm., no running
   time available.
The Young Ones
   (Associated British Picture Corporation, 1961) 35mm., 108 mins.

CHAPTER TWO

BABIES, KIDS, CARTOONS AND COMEDIES:
CHILDREN AND PATHÉSCOPE'S 9.5MM
HOME CINEMA IN BRITAIN

CLARE WATSON

In December 1922 in France, the Pathé Frères company launched the Pathé Baby, a miniature projector designed for amateur use, that employed a unique substandard gauge of film stock just 9.5mm wide.[1] As Gerald McKee has highlighted, in contrast with the rival 16mm format launched by Kodak in 1923, "9.5mm was intended primarily as a home entertainer and educator rather than as an amateur movie-making medium".[2] This primary purpose is expounded by slogans used in the early 1920s to promote the Baby in France and in Britain, respectively, as "Le Cinéma Chez Soi" and "The Ideal Home Cinema".[3] Soon after however, Pathé Frères did produce a 9.5mm camera, which first entered the market in France during the Christmas period in 1923. The 9.5mm gauge also quickly proved successful with British amateur cinematographers, particularly during the inter-war period. In 1936, the editor of a leading British amateur cine magazine claimed it to be the most popular gauge in the country.[4] The British subsidiary company, Pathé of France Ltd., had begun to commercially exploit the Pathé "Baby Ciné" outfit in its home

---

[1] In addition to the editor of this anthology, Ian Craven, I would like to thank the following people for their kind help in the preparation of this article: Pierluigi Ercole, Peter Kramer, David Cleveland, Brian Giles, John E. Lewis, Stéphanie Salmon and the Fondation Jérôme Seydoux-Pathé, and the staff of the Harrods Archive.
[2] McKee, *Film Collecting*, 73.
[3] Another common slogan used in early British promotional material was "Mirrors the World in Your Home". See advertisement in *The Amateur Photographer*, 30 September 1925, xxvi.
[4] Harris, "The Editor's News Reel", 313.

market in 1924.[5] Following the formation of Kodak-Pathé towards the end of the decade, 9.5mm was sold in Britain under the name of Pathéscope Ltd., the same trademark established in 1912 to exploit Pathé's forerunner to the 9.5mm gauge, the 28mm "KOK" drawing room cinematograph, or "Pathéscope" as it became known in this country.[6]

Pathé's 9.5mm gauge diffused quickly across the globe from France and Britain, to America, India, Sweden, Norway, Germany, Austria, Brazil, Italy, Java, Singapore, Siam, Indo-China, Spain and Portugal.[7] Specialist literatures soon accompanied the apparatus itself. In 1929, Englishman Harold B. Abbott authored *Motion Pictures with the Baby Ciné*, essentially a handbook for amateurs interested in projecting and filming with the new gauge. In its preface, the author justified his addition to "a bibliography which may be deemed to be already complete", thus:

> The Pathé Baby Ciné outfit, now also known as the Pathéscope, whilst broadly following general cinematograph principles, possesses many distinctive features which place it essentially in a class by itself, and as there are, in this country alone, many thousands of amateurs whose only acquaintance with the making and projecting of motion pictures comes through the medium of this remarkable miniature outfit, it seemed that there was need for a book which would deal with the practice of cinematography essentially from the Baby Ciné user's point of view.[8]

Although today primarily a collector's gauge, 9.5mm was used throughout Britain for over thirty-five years between 1924 and the early 1960s, both for the purposes of amateur filmmaking and for the projecting

---

[5] Prior to this, Pathé Frères had made at least three attempts to sell the Baby system in Britain through other agents. The deal with photographic retailers Houghtons Ltd would have provided Pathé Frères with an annual royalty of £2,000 for fifty years. The British Marconi company lost £30,000 upon cancellation of their contract in 1923. See Key industry duty: value of Pathé Baby cine projector, 1926, PRO, CUST 117/10. The frosty reception accorded to a Marconi agent in 1923 by Pathé's manufacturer, Continsouza, contributed to the termination of the agreement. An initial arrangement with Pathescope Ltd also fell through in 1923 due to manufacturing delays. See Salmon, "Le Coq Enchanteur".

[6] The name change was decided upon according to the terms of an agreement reached between Kodak-Pathé and Pathé Frères Cinema Ltd. The latter company exploited standard 35mm Pathé products in Britain and contested Pathé of France's use of the trade name "Pathé", for which it held the sole rights. Fondation Jérôme Seydoux-Pathé, Paris. Hereafter, I will refer to the British company as Pathéscope and use Pathé for the French.

[7] Salmon, "Le Coq Enchanteur", 608.

[8] Abbott, preface to *Motion Pictures with the Baby Cine*, iii.

of amateur- and professionally-produced films. The exact number of those engaged in the exhibition and production of films using the 9.5mm gauge during the period is unknown, and details as to the volume of equipment sales in this country are scarce.[9] It is likely however that only a minority of British cine enthusiasts spent their leisure-time engaged in 9.5mm related activities. Nonetheless, the Pathé Baby system emerged in the 1920s as one of the most successful home cinemas up to that time, and there is evidence to suggest that Britain was amongst the most profitable regions dealing in the gauge at the height of its popularity in the 1930s.[10]

This essay focuses on 9.5mm's use in Britain as a medium for projecting professionally-produced films, mainly in the pre-war period. More particular emphasis is placed upon relationships between the 9.5mm projecting technology and children, both as audience members and active operators and consumers of the gauge. Such relationships were well rehearsed: before the arrival of 9.5mm film in Britain in 1924, and since the late 1890s, a variety of projectors aimed at the home and amateur markets had been made available.[11] The first section of this chapter discusses the 9.5mm projector within this context, examining more closely some of the "many distinctive features", which, according to Abbott, placed it "essentially in a class by itself". Analysis of relevant promotional material (see Fig. 2-1) then posits some of the particular ways in which Pathéscope, in line with 9.5mm's marketing abroad, sought to target child consumers within a broader understanding of the technology as a product designed for the family market. Thirdly, evidence of children's engagement with the 9.5mm projecting technology evokes some of the most common genres of film viewed by juvenile audiences in the home. Lastly, a discussion of debates surrounding children's cinema-going in the 1930s indicates that group's film tastes more generally, as well as the

---

[9] British records show that at least 6160 projectors were imported into Britain between November 1924 and March 1926. Key industry duty, PRO, 1926, CUST 117/10.
[10] Records detailing the sales turnover for Pathé Baby equipment in France and in Britain between January 1935 and September 1938 show that the figures for Pathéscope far exceeded those of its French counterpart, la Societé Française du Pathé Baby. Across these years Pathéscope's total sales in terms of francs were at least 25% higher than those of the French company, and in the first nine months of 1938 this lead was as high as 46% with total sales amounting to 11,690,865 francs. See Fondation Jérôme Seydoux-Pathé, Paris.
[11] See Barnes, *The Beginnings of the Cinema in England, Vol. 5,* 125-142.

types of genres featured in film programmes designed by adults for children's consumption in the inter-war period.

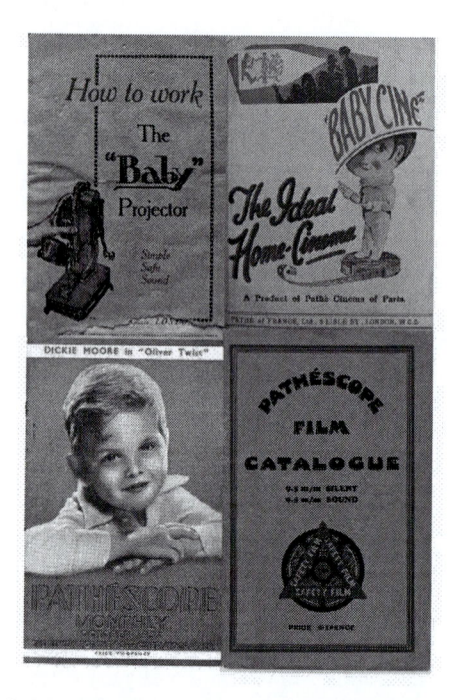

Fig 2-1 Pathéscope printed materials, 1920s-1930s
Source: Brian Giles Collection (upper images), and author's collection (lower images)

Pathé's 9.5mm in Context

Until the early 1920s, projectors designed for amateur or home use had met with varied, and in general, limited success. Various obstacles prevented their wider acceptance and sustained commercial viability, including issues of safety, quality and cost. Before 1912, the majority of films available for use with such projectors were manufactured using a highly flammable cellulose nitrate base, similar to that employed by the commercial film industry in Britain until the early 1950s. Press reports of accidents and fatalities caused by film fires continued to occur even after the introduction of the Cinematograph Act in 1909, legislation initially established to address issues of physical safety in cinemas.[12] Reports of such incidents could have done nothing to appease the concerns of consumers about bringing such a considerable fire hazard into their homes.

The cost and quality of home projectors was also troublingly variable. Cheaper home projectors were certainly available, but these often lacked durability and reliability. Stephen Herbert notes that low-cost tin projectors, doubling as magic lanterns, were widely manufactured up to the 1920s, and were produced primarily by German toy manufacturers.[13] Giving an idea of the reception of these "toys", Ben Singer quotes the following, from an article published in *The Moving Picture World* in 1911:

> There has been an idea prevalent for a number of years that the proper way in which to introduce cinematography as a home amusement would be to serve it up as some sort of a toy. Accordingly, along this line there have appeared and disappeared a number of dinky contraptions that burned the fingers, strained the eyes, tried the temper and warped the patience. These have been marketed under various names as home moving picture machines. It is no secret that they have all been dismal failures and found their ways into the scrap heap, simply because they were toys and not at all practicable.[14]

Ian Conrich's interview with his ninety–three year old grandfather, Samuel Conway, who, at the age of about ten, owned such a "toy" home projector in the 1910s, highlights anxieties about the safety of the technology. Samuel doesn't remember having any accidents with his projector, but does recall that: "one of the things I wasn't really happy about was the fire that the lamp was making. You see. I was only a young child and it used to worry me to some extent".[15]

A significant step forward in home cinema was therefore taken in 1912, when two of the largest names in the film industry released projectors into the amateur market, thereby creating the first home cinema systems to employ non-inflammable, or "safety" acetate, film. Singer has detailed the case of Edison's 22mm Home Projecting Kinetoscope in the US, which, despite its use of safety film, had a short and troubled history before it was abandoned in 1914. Singer suggests that, whilst "the cost of the projector [between $75 to $100] and films was probably a major obstacle to popular consumer acceptance", a range of factors, including

---

[12] A number of reports of film fires were reported in the press. See, for instance, Anon., "Fire at a Cinematograph Show", 8.
[13] Herbert, "German Home and Toy Magic Lantern-Cinematographs," 11-15.
[14] Anon., "Moving Pictures in the Home", 934, quoted in Singer, 39-40.
[15] Conrich, "Kitchen Cinema", 292.

technological imperfections and the lack of an aggressive marketing campaign, also played a part in the failure of the Home PK.[16]

In contrast, Pathé's 28mm Pathéscope projector met with a certain level of success in the US, which led to the adoption in that country of the 28mm gauge as the safety standard from 1918.[17] The projector does not appear to have enjoyed the same level of market penetration in Britain, although little trace remains of its exploitation in this country. Introduced into Britain by Pathéscope Ltd. in 1912, with photographic dealers Houghton's enlisted as its main wholesale retailer, the apparatus was also sold in department stores such as Harrods and Selfridges.[18] The 28mm Pathéscope's promotion, however, usefully anticipates methods later employed to sell the 9.5mm technology in the 1920s. Early publicity significantly claimed new standards for the apparatus:

> the coming of the Pathéscope, after many years of costly experimenting, at last raises the home Cinematograph from the realm of the Plaything to a scientifically perfect, yet simple instrument, absolutely complete in itself— easily portable, and of great durability.[19]

Although its designation as "Drawing Room Cinematograph" firmly established its primary market as a domestic one, the company also predicted that "the Pathéscope will appeal very strongly to educational authorities and the governing bodies of public and private schools throughout the country".[20] A pedagogical function for the apparatus was underlined by the types of films offered for use with the projector, which were described as "instructive, interesting and beautiful pictures".[21] To access such material, customers could join Pathéscope's subscription library, entitling them to receive a programme containing three spools of film, or about one hour's entertainment, which could be exchanged twice weekly.[22] Films of an instructional nature were heavily emphasised in

---

[16] Singer, "Early Home Cinema and The Edison Home Projecting Kinetoscope", 56-63.
[17] McBurn and Tepperman, "Resurrecting The Lost History of 28mm Film in North America", 137-151.
[18] Registration documents for Pathéscope Ltd, 1912, PRO, BT 31/14020/125579. Harrods continued to sell the Pathéscope into the early 1920s, see *The Times*, 17 November 1921, 7.
[19] *The Times*, 6 December 1912, 10.
[20] *The Times*, 12 December 1912, 17.
[21] *The Times*, 1 January 1913, 12.
[22] In 1914, a book of 125 or 50 coupons valid for one year could be bought for £7 or £3/10/- respectively. Each coupon could be exchanged for one reel, which could

early British film catalogues, which comprised two sections, the first and most prominent of which was labelled "Educational".[23] Although Pathéscope claimed that "by reason of [the projector's] low cost" it brought home exhibition "within the reach of all", most historians agree that its price of between 15/- and 17/10d was in fact prohibitive.[24]

With the launch of their 9.5mm Baby system in the early 1920s, Pathé again attempted to confront the issues of safety, cost and quality attending home projecting. Like the 28mm films before them, their 9.5mm counterparts were produced on non-inflammable stock: the importance of this to the British company was emphasised by Pathéscope's logo, which incorporated the words "safety film" on a triangular shape atop of a stylised film can. Affordability was also high on the agenda; early British promotional material stated that whilst "there are many types of miniature cinema apparatus now obtainable... the following facts will show how Pathéscope apparatus supersedes all in the most important factor: ECONOMY".[25] The company was also keen to point out the portability of the Pathé Baby, which "stands only 12½ins. high and weighs but 5½lbs.", and could be bought for £5.[26] Such economies were fundamentally dependent on the relatively small gauge of the film employed, and were stressed at every opportunity.

Reducing the width of the film to just 9.5mm meant that the cost of the films sold, and hired for use with the projector, was minimised. According to Barnes, "the idea of sub-standard gauge cinematography originated with Birt Acres, whose 17.5mm Birtac first appeared in 1898, closely followed by the 17.5mm Biokam manufactured by Alfred Darling of Brighton".[27] Like the Biokam films, a central sprocket hole was positioned between each frame of the 9.5mm film, instead of at the film's edges, as occurs with standard 35mm film. This ensured that a relatively greater picture area was retained despite the narrowed strip. Another cost-saving measure

---

be retained for up to two weeks. No more than six reels could be exchanged per week. *Harrods General Catalogue*, 1914, 421.

[23] All other films are collectively categorised under the heading "General Interest" in the latter part of the catalogue. Initially, all 28mm films were reductions of Pathé's own archive of theatrically released films. 28mm catalogues provided by collector Brian Giles.

[24] See, for instance, Kermabon, 206. Quotes from *The Times*, 9 December 1912, 8. Prices quoted in "Photographic Price List," Houghton's Ltd, 1914, provided by collector Brian Giles.

[25] Quoted from *The Pathéscope General Catalogue*, 1930.

[26] Quoted from promotional brochure, circa late 1920s. Price quoted in *9.5mm General Catalogue*, November 1926. Brian Giles collection.

[27] Barnes, *The Beginnings of Cinema in England, Vol. 5*,125.

was the "notching" of the earliest 9.5mm films, a device used to economise on the use of film for inter-titles and still pictures. Creating a notch on the side of the film activated a "claw" mechanism in the projector, which stopped the relevant frame for a time before it was set moving again automatically.

Economy was further achieved by limiting the length of the films offered for use with the 9.5mm system. The earliest titles, released in 1924, were only 30 feet in length, giving a running time of approximately one minute and twenty seconds, when projected at the official Pathéscope speed of 14 frames per second. In late 1925, Pathéscope introduced 60 foot reels, whilst 1927 saw the appearance of 300 foot "Super Reels". These ran for about four and seventeen minutes respectively, not including the time it took to wind through notched inter-titles. Individual films might be released on multiple reels, so that after 1927, film lengths could vary from a single 30-foot reel to five or more 300-foot super reels. The short lengths meant that the 9.5mm films were often heavily edited prior to release. An article published in the February 1934 issue of *Pathéscope Monthly*, a magazine issued by Pathéscope to its customers, reveals that such re-editing of films was clearly noticed by users of the gauge. One article, entitled "Does cutting spoil classical films?" typifies the company's response to concerns that the excision of material from classical and popular films detracted from their value. *Pathéscope Monthly* defended the practice, suggesting that the original length of some films was determined primarily by a need to "conform to a given time of showing in the standard size cinema", and that re-editing to produce 9.5mm versions eliminated scenes that bore an "insignificant relation to the principal interest". "Now why", the writer asked, "should you be subjected to viewing films as 'straight' reductions from 35mm to 9.5mm size?"[28]

Such design features and promotional rhetorics aimed at widening the "nine-five" home cinema's market, the supposed limitlessness of which was made explicit in a British 9.5mm general catalogue from 1930, which stated:

> the ideal cinema is now within the reach of *everyone*. For a small sum a compact and simple apparatus can be bought which projects in the average sitting room motion pictures equal in brilliance and precision to those of the picture house.[29]

---

[28] Anon., "Does cutting spoil classical film?", 3, and Anon., "The cutting of films," 14-15.
[29] *The Pathéscope General Catalogue*, 1930. My emphasis.

Pathéscope's strategy is very clear here: ie. to promote the quality of the 9.5mm system, and to counter senses of inferiority associated with previous versions of "substandard" motion pictures. Whilst the earlier "toy" projector had inherently connoted the idea of "playing at cinema", the 9.5mm projector would be presented as a miniature equivalent to, and an equal of, its theatrical counterpart.

Evidence of Pathéscope's growth, throughout the late 1920s, is registered through the transformation of its film lists and catalogues, which were distributed as early as 1925.[30] The first Pathé Baby film list contained over 200 titles. Most inclusions were non-fiction, and all were 30 feet in length. After 1925 however, the number of films represented in the catalogues increased steadily, and by 1955 over 800 titles were being identified. New additions were, for the most part, fiction films, and even by the end of the 1920s, fiction genres dominated the catalogues. In 1929, a new era of expansion was ushered in by the publication of a larger, and now illustrated catalogue. In the same year, Pathéscope also introduced its own magazine, *Pathéscope Monthly*, which contained articles on the latest 9.5mm film releases, the development of equipment, the opening of new dealerships, news from amateur clubs, and letters from readers. With reference to such evidence, commentators have justifiably described the period between 1929 and the late 1930s as the "Golden Age" of the 9.5mm gauge in Britain.

Films were made available at a variety of prices via a range of methods, either directly from Pathéscope, or from local independent dealerships and libraries. In the 1920s, the 30- and 60-foot reels could be bought outright for 3/6d and 6/- respectively.[31] Before 1939, Super Reels could be hired direct from Pathéscope, via a coupon system, for approximately 3/- per reel per week, roughly one-eighth the price of buying the reel outright. During World War Two, Pathéscope closed its lending library, but films continued to be hired through dealerships. By the mid-1950s, a network of over 200 such outlets spanned the length and breadth of Britain. Although 9.5mm home projection thus remained a minority practice in comparison with theatrical cinema going, it is clear from this analysis that not only was the 9.5mm home cinema commercially successful in Britain, but that it also enjoyed a widespread usage across the country, and provided a significant alternative means of viewing motion pictures, for many film enthusiasts.

---

[30] Details in this paragraph are taken from original Pathéscope film catalogues in the author's collection.

[31] These prices remained relatively stable with a slight increase to 3/9d and 6/6d in 1940. Figures provided in this paragraph are taken from Pathéscope catalogues.

Children in Pathéscope Marketing

Initially, all 9.5mm films and equipment were supplied by the French Pathé company, although film printing did get underway in Britain after 1932, following the construction of the Pathéscope factory in Cricklewood.[32] (see Fig. 2-2) Some differences existed however between the 9.5mm products offered in France, and those made available in Britain, including the number and titles of films. However, strong similarities between the advertising material produced in these and other countries indicate that the worldwide distribution of the 9.5mm home cinema system was to some extent standardised. Promotional material from different countries indicates broad, and international, marketing strategies.

Attempts to place 9.5mm home cinema within "the reach of everyone" fostered approaches developed to avoid alienating potential consumers of any age group or gender (although members of the white middle class seem to represent Pathéscope's notion of "everyone" in their advertising at this time!). One such method, echoing the promotion of the 28mm Pathéscope, presumably employed to attract adult consumers, was to present the miniature home cinema as a sophisticated piece of new technology. This involved disassociating the 9.5mm system from the types of small, low quality toy projectors alluded to above. In an early pamphlet produced in the 1920s to accompany the Pathé Baby projector, a "new era [in] Home Amusements" is heralded, whilst the consumer is advised that:

> Because the "Baby" Projector is constructed on a miniature scale for Home Use, one must not be misled into the belief that it is a Toy. On the contrary; built on the soundest principles, the "Baby" Projector is a machine in the perfecting of which Science, Mechanical Accuracy, Skilled Workmanship and Experience of over 25 years have been devoted.[33]

Aware that such dismissal of the projecting apparatus as a toy might alienate children, however, the statement is immediately followed by a more child-friendly qualification:

> The "Baby" Projector contains in its mechanism the greatest simplicity combined with the utmost efficiency and absolute safety. [...] the operating of the "Baby" Projector is a matter which a child of ordinary intelligence can learn in the course of an hour or two.[34]

---

[32] McKee, *A Half Century of Film Collecting*, 10.
[33] "How to work the 'Baby' Projector," early instructional pamphlet, circa late 1920s, 3. Brian Giles collection.
[34] Ibid.

Fig. 2-2 Aerial view of Pathéscope factory at Cricklewood, 1930s
Source: Collection Fondation Jérôme Seydoux-Pathé

Pathéscope thus found a way to distance the Pathé Baby system from concerns about the inefficiency or complexity of home projectors, simultaneously stressing the sophistication of the technology for adult consumption, and reassuring parents of its suitability for children, by emphasising its safety and simplicity.

The desire to appeal to everyone is equally apparent in the imagery used in many of the early advertisements for the 9.5mm projector. A French advertisement from 1926 contains an illustration depicting a group of children, and adults of diverse ages both male and female gazing up at, and reaching out to, a Pathé Baby projector. A common theme in both British and French marketing is the shorthand use of the familial tableau to represent both genders, and a broad demographic of ages. Phraseology also acts to promote the use of the technology by children and adults alike with statements such as "it charms, instructs and amuses both young and old".[35] British advertisements showed children both enjoying the spectacle of home projection and the pleasures of controlling the apparatus.[36] The on

---

[35] French advertisement in author's collection. For British example see, for instance, advertisement in *The Times*, 12 November 1924, 11.
[36] See, for instance, advertisements in *The Times*, 12 November 1924, 11, and *The Times*, 10 December 1925, 22, and "The 'Baby Cine' Projector and Camera'" and

76   Chapter Two

screen images depicted in such illustrations ranged from scenes of a more instructive nature to those referencing fictional genres. One image repeated in several early advertisements illustrates the exhibition of a comic scene by a child projectionist to a family audience. Evocative of the slapstick genre, the imagined film depicts a policeman chasing a jester, whilst a harlequin character in the background points the pursuing bobby in the wrong direction (see Fig. 2-3).[37] In keeping with earlier stresses on quality and value, promotional material did not exclude children from the enjoyment of films of a more instructive nature, as can be seen in an image provided in another British advertisement from 1926, where a child is seen projecting a sporting film to a predominantly adult audience.[38]

Fig. 2-3 Pathéscope advertisements for Baby and Kid projectors
Source: *The Guardian* (4th December 1925, and 12th December 1930, respectively)

"Les Appareils Pathé Baby et Leurs Accessoires"—both promotional pamphlets, circa 1920s, National Archives, file reference CUST 117/10.
[37] Promotional pamphlet, "The Ideal Home Cinema," Pathé of France, circa late 1920s. Brian Giles collection.
[38] Advertisement in *The Times*, 26 November 1925, 13.

Fig. 2-4 Pathéscope British Ace projector advertisement, c. 1935
Source: Gerald McKee, *A Half Century of Film Collecting*

Not all advertisements targeted children and adults collectively. Young children are routinely singled out in advertisements, both as spectators of a Pathé Baby show and as desirous owners of a Pathé Baby projector.[39] In publicity specifically targeting children (possibly through their parents), more youth-oriented fare, specifically comedies and cartoons, is usually emphasised. For example, a French advertisement, in which the audience consists exclusively of children and one small boy as the projectionist,

---

[39] See the French and Spanish advertisements from Christmas 1922 published in Kermabon, 378-379. The Spanish advertisement quite literally places the projector within the reach of the children, that is, of course, providing that their parents are as sagacious as the pictured wise King in offering the equipment to their offspring as a Christmas present.

depicts the on-screen image of a Felix the Cat cartoon.[40] A typical British advertisement from the 1930s, for the Ace projector (see Fig. 2-4), one of Pathéscope's later models, particularly associated with child consumers, presents images of Charlie Chaplin and Mickey Mouse, alongside the following dialogue:

> "Lights out", said Dad, and out they went, leaving a bright silvery beam cutting through the darkness. The children held their breath with excitement, then Dad began to turn—a soft, whirring hum—and then "Mickey Mouse!" The room was a bedlam of jolly noises. Dad could hardly turn for laughing. It was a grand programme. After Mickey Mouse came thrilling dramas, Wild West adventures and Charlie Chaplin. "I thought it was only a toy", said Mother, "but it's wonderful, and I'm glad the films are non inflammable".[41]

Adverts such as these suggest that certain genres, such as the cartoon and short comedy specifically, were promoted to juvenile audiences, and further evidence of this strategy can be found in the *Pathéscope Monthly* magazine. An article in the February 1934 issue entitled "Choosing Your Film Programme" reads:

> When choosing films regard should be paid to the tastes of the audience. Naturally, the same films that are used for juvenile entertainment cannot be shown to grown ups with any measure of success. [...] Sometimes the majority of an audience consists of children and hence comedy films are always well received. Charlie Chaplin and Felix the Cat are firm favourites with the kiddies, as also are Harold Lloyd and Snub Pollard.[42]

Whilst the advice given in "Choosing Your Film Programme" supports the notion that Pathéscope were promoting cartoons and comedies as suitable fare for juvenile audiences, it also suggests that comedies, specifically those featuring silent male comedians like Chaplin, were indeed well received by very young audiences.

---

[40] Ibid., 199.
[41] Reprinted in McKee, *A Half Century of Film Collecting*, 6. An advertisement placed by the Sheffield Photo Company describes the Ace as "not a toy, but a splendid projector for the juvenile", in *Home Movies and Home Talkies*, 1935, 274.
[42] Nicholson, "Choosing Your Film Program," 13.

Children and 9.5mm

Evidence confirming the popularity of these genres amongst children can also be found in the pages of cine club magazines, such as those published by Group 9.5. A national organisation, the Group was set up by two cine enthusiasts in 1962, following the closure of Pathéscope's operations at Cricklewood. The organisation's aim was to support, promote and further the 9.5mm gauge. With over five hundred members by the late 1960s, the 9.5 Group is still operational today. Most of the group's members are male, many of whom were first introduced to 9.5mm in the 1930s and 1940s, when they were young boys. Published accounts of these first encounters with home cinema in their quarterly magazine, entitled simply *9.5*, provide valuable insight into children's use of the gauge. In such memoirs, Chaplin is commonly recalled, alongside other silent comedians such as Snub Pollard, as well as Felix the cat cartoons in the 1930s, and the Mickey Mouse and other Disney and Max Fleischer cartoons, listed in Pathéscope's catalogues by the late 1930s.

Interestingly, some of the members' first encounters with 9.5mm came not through the official Pathéscope route, but via toy projectors manufactured by unrelated companies, aiming to cash in the popularity of the gauge. In addition to the Bing British, the Ray and the Bingoscope, was the Woolworth projector, which was sold in sixpenny parts because Woolworth's, then known as the "sixpenny store", sold its items for no more than sixpence each.[43] One group member, for example, recalls buying a toy 9.5mm projector from Woolworth's in the 1930s, when he was ten years old.[44] The Woolworth projector cost in total 2/6d, but was sold in several parts, each priced at 6d. Prefiguring the size of the television set, a 12 x 9 inch cardboard screen could also be bought for this outfit. Although produced by Pathéscope, the 6d films sold at Woolworths for use with the 9.5mm toy projectors were only 15 feet in length, and were not included in Pathéscope's film catalogues. With a running time of only about half a minute, such films clearly had very limited appeal. Importantly, however, they were cheap enough for a child to buy with his or her pocket money, and appear to have acted as a hooking device, introducing children to the 9.5mm gauge and the notion of projecting films, before they were able to gain access to a more sophisticated machine, such as the Pathé Baby.

---

[43] McKee, *The Home Cinema: Classic Home Movie Projectors 1922-1940*, 101-103. McKee's own first encounter with 9.5mm came via a Bing British toy projector, see McKee, *A Half Century of Film Collecting*, 15.
[44] Winpenny, "The Woolworth 9.5 Projector", 5-6.

Projectors like the Baby would have been beyond the budget of the average child's weekly pocket money, and were more usually purchased by parents at Christmas and on birthdays.[45] Pathéscope sold a variety of 9.5mm projectors between 1924 and 1960, many of which were more sophisticated and expensive than the original Baby models. Various versions of cheaper machines derived from the Pathé Baby were however also available across the period, and these included the aforementioned Ace, introduced in 1935.[46] Like the Pathé Baby, the Ace was originally designed for the projection of the shorter 30 and 60 foot reels, and was similarly hand cranked. In 1948, a motorised version of the Ace was introduced with a set projection speed of 19 frames per second, a compromise between silent and sound speeds, determined by the anticipated use of the machines to project mute versions of Disney cartoons. According to McKee, the Ace is one of the best remembered Pathéscope projectors, was sold for a longer period than any others, and "certainly must have introduced more youngsters to home movies than any other projector during its 25 years in production".[47]

Several accounts mention the shared experience of viewing 9.5mm films. Memories invoke the screening of Chaplin and Mickey Mouse pictures at a children's party, and the weekly film shows at a prep school during the winter term. One member recalls that "[t]hese shows were very much appreciated. [...] The Chaplin and other farces were immensely popular, as were the Disney and Popeye cartoons".[48] 9.5mm film shows were not however limited to children attending preparatory schools. In another article, a member reflects on his first encounter with the 9.5mm gauge in 1937, when he was age seven. The film show took place at his school, which he points out "was not some superior establishment but a small C of E elementary school in the Toxteth area of Liverpool".[49] This member recalls how his schoolteacher used his own 9.5mm projector to "put on a film show after school one evening a week and so I saw my first Chaplin films". The screen memory remains vivid many years later:

---

[45] Wordsworth, "A Personal Look Back", 12.

[46] The first 9.5mm projector produced in Britain in 1930 was the Kid, a cheaper alternative to the Baby. The Imp, an "improved" version of the Kid, was later introduced in 1934. A more expensive projector, the Lux, arrived in 1931. The Vox was the first 9.5mm sound projector issued in 1938. Before this date Pathéscope released silent versions of sound films.

[47] McKee, *The Home Cinema*, 66.

[48] Wordsworth, "A Personal Look Back", 12.

[49] Murray, "Flashback Part 1", 10.

I do remember that *Easy Street* (1917) was one of the Chaplin films he ran. Perhaps that is one reason why I still have a 9.5 copy of it today, and a 200B [projector] for that matter. That first viewing of *Easy Street* was memorable I suppose, because my father, a great Chaplin fan, had described it to me in some detail, but it was only those after school nine five shows which gave me the opportunity to see it. I found it every bit as funny as my father had.[50]

Not all school shows of course were put on by teachers. A letter written by a young boy, and published in the "Home Ciné Chats" section of the August 1930 issue of the *Pathéscope Monthly* entitled "The cinema at school" records early enthusiasm for self-projection:

> I am writing to tell you of a cinema show I gave at my school; the proceeds were to go to the school pavilion fund. It is the second I have given. The programme commenced at eight o'clock and included 5 Super reels, 7, 30ft. reels and one 60ft. reel. The Supers were *Carmen* (1926), *Easy Street*, *Good Dog* (1927) and [Mr.] Fry's film *A Voyage of Discovery* (c.1930). It lasted more than 2¾ hours and *Easy Street* was appreciated more than the others. Everyone was well pleased and wanted another show.[51]

It is evident then from promotional material surrounding the 9.5mm gauge, both in Britain and in other countries, that children were directly targeted as potential consumers of this new "substandard" cine technology. Specific types of films and equipment, notably cartoons and short comedies, and the cheaper forms of home projector specifically designed for projecting shorter length films, were promoted for juvenile consumption, and engaged with eagerness. Such films were not however restricted to child audiences, and it would be wrong to conclude that children were interested solely in these genres. A wide variety of films were available on the 9.5mm gauge including industrial, travel, documentary and sporting films, as well as many dramatic works and silent "classics" produced, for instance, by British International Pictures

---

[50] Ibid.
[51] Giles, "The Cinema at School", 6. Pathéscope commonly re-titled the 9.5mm versions of films. *Good Dog* was advertised as a "Rin Tin Tin" film, whose original title was *The Silent Avenger* (1927), starring in fact not his more celebrated counterpart, but "Thunder—The Dog Marvel", one of a number of canine celebrities featured in cine-series through the 1930s. The example illustrates well the scale of cutting involved in 9.5 distribution: *Good Dog* ran for 15 mins., whilst *The Silent Avenger* ran a little over 55 mins. on its theatrical release. *A Voyage of Discovery* (c. 1930) was a publicity film produced on behalf of J. S. Fry & Sons chocolate manufacturers, loaned out free of charge to 9.5mm customers.

and the German UFA studios.[52] Film historian Kevin Brownlow is perhaps only the most conspicuous child amateur whose interest in films of the silent era was fuelled by the 9.5mm home cinema, and catalogue coverage which extended far beyond the realm of cartoons and comedies.[53] It would appear, however, that cartoon and comedy films, and basic models of projector such as the Ace, were posited as staple products for children.

Films for Children at the Movie Theatre

Amateur exhibition activity such as that considered here takes on greater significance in relation to its professional counterparts. Studies of cinema going in Britain during the 1930s have affirmed the importance of this leisure activity to children, and one estimate suggests that some 4,610,000 children aged between five and fifteen were going to the cinema every week by the end of that decade.[54] However, before the establishment of special children's cinema clubs towards the mid-1930s, there was a lack of any widespread or systematic child-specific film programming in this country. Since at least the turn of the century, matinee shows for children had occurred in Britain. Yet prior to the 1930s, the films shown at such matinees (which often took place on Saturday afternoons) were little or no

---

[52] For more information about the subjects available on 9.5mm see McKee, *Film Collecting*, 73-102.

[53] During the Second World War, at the age of three, Brownlow's first experience of movies came via school shows of 9.5mm amateur films. School shows continued post-war and Brownlow recalls: "We grew up with Snub Pollard and Harold Lloyd and Chaplin, and I remember being struck by the crudity of the primitive comedians, with their huge moustaches and wondering why we were watching these... and I think it was Chaplin in *The Count* (1916) and Harold Lloyd in *Never Weaken* (1921) that awoke my fascination for cinema". Later, Christmas presents included a toy cinema that projected film-strips, followed by a 9.5mm Pathéscope projector. Here started a lifetime of film collecting and appreciation. See Robinson, "Interview with Kevin Brownlow".

[54] Jeffrey Richards has suggested that going to the cinema was "particularly important" to children during the 1930s, in "Cinemagoing in Worktown: Regional Film Audiences in 1930s Britain", 147-166. See also Richards, *The Age of the Dream Palace: Cinema and Society in Britain 1930-1939*, 12-13. The estimate, cited from the first book on children and the cinema published in Britain, equates to 67% of the number of children living in Scotland, England and Wales according to the Registrar-General for 1937. It is based on the assumption that no children from rural areas, half from urban districts, and all from County Boroughs and Greater London attend the cinema. See Ford, *Children in the Cinema*, 26.

different from those included on the general cinema programme and watched by adults.[55]

Considerable concern as to the ill effects, both physical and moral, of the cinema on children were strongly expressed by pressure groups and other moral guardians during the first few decades of the twentieth century.[56] Jeffrey Richards has suggested that the three main areas of concern dominating debates surrounding children and the cinema from the 'teens to the 1930s were, the physical effects of watching films, links between cinema and juvenile crime, and effects on children's behaviour and attitudes. Accounts of the molestation of, as well as a number of fatal accidents involving, children in cinemas also however marked out this public sphere as a dangerous space for children. As late as 1929, seventy children died in a crush when a minor film fire induced panic amongst the young audience attending an overcrowded and under supervised matinee at The Glen cinema in Paisley.[57] Anxieties over children's cinemagoing were articulated and examined in a number of inquiries into the effects of cinema on children, which were carried out in the 1910s and beyond.[58] Following its formation in 1912, the British Board of Film Censors had created the "U" (universally acceptable) and "A" (under 16s should be accompanied by an adult) categories of film. The Board's recommendations were not, however, legally enforceable. In 1922, the Home Office issued advice to exhibitors in England and Wales recommending the exclusion of under 16s from "A" films unless accompanied by an adult. But, by the end of the 1920s, these guidelines were not adhered to by 35% of local authorities, and did not apply at all in Scotland. Around 1930, five local inquiries into children's cinema going were undertaken across Britain.[59] At this time, A-rated films were still being shown in children's matinees, and the Edinburgh inquiry found that 93% of 649 teachers polled considered

---

[55] The earliest known record of a children's matinee in Britain is an advertisement for the Bioscope show at Mickleover, Derbyshire on 7 February 1900, republished in Staples, *All Pals Together,* 2. See also Agajanian, "'Just for Kids?", 395.

[56] See Ford, Richards, Staples, and Kuhn, "Children, 'Horrific' Films, and Censorship in 1930s Britain", 197-202.

[57] Staples, 25-28. On assaults in cinemas see "Children in Cinemas", *The Times* (7 February 1917), 9.

[58] This included an investigation conducted in 1917 by the National Council of Public Morals on behalf of the film industry into the "physical, social, moral and educational influence of the cinema, with special reference to young people". See National Council of Public Morals, *The Cinema: Its Present Position and Future Possibilities*, vii, reprinted in Herbert ed., *A History of Early Film, Vol. 3,* 65-529.

[59] Enquiries were carried out in London, Birmingham, Sheffield, Birkenhead and Edinburgh. See Richards, *Dream Palace,* 67.

the average film programme unsuitable for children, and 74% called for special children's matinees.[60] In 1939, Richard Ford concluded that, "[a]t the root of the problem was (and still is) the negative criticism that a very large proportion of films shown in cinemas are unsuitable for children".[61]

Around 1930, various attempts were made by a number of cinema owners, educationists and religious bodies to provide child specific film programmes, although these were mostly short lived ventures carried out on a local scale. Terry Staples' study of children and the cinema in Britain highlights a number of these efforts. In March 1928, Granada cinema chain owner Sidney Bernstein, introduced specially programmed children's matinees at four London locations where silent films were screened in an endeavour to provide "clean, healthy entertainment" for child audiences. A typical programme included a Felix the Cat or some other cartoon, an animal documentary or nature short, and a feature film from the last decade, such as Chaplin's *The Circus* (1928). In 1932, Marjorie Locket, education manager for Associated British Cinema, organised children's matinees in the London area. She lamented the unsuitability of most sound films, and stated: "If this venture fails […] it will be for lack of pictures. We shall soon exhaust the supply of suitable silent films…."[62]

In 1934, the art house Everyman Cinema in Hampstead formed the Children's Film Society, where programmes were comprised of shorts *only*, as it was felt that children tired when watching longer films. A typical programme featured Disney's Silly Symphonies, early Chaplin short comedies, newsreels, and documentary shorts. Non-theatrical film shows for children also reflected the preponderance of these genres and of older silent subjects. Lorimer Rees, minister of one East End mission, recalls showing 16mm gauge versions of westerns and Charlie Chaplin films to about three hundred children weekly. One travelling show in Yorkshire used 16mm equipment to put on ninety minute programmes made up of non-fiction shorts, and considered cartoons and short comedies to be a necessary, if somewhat regrettable, inclusion. These and other attempts were mostly undeveloped beyond initial experiments, and their success was limited.[63] According to Ford, this was, in part, due to the

---

[60] Statistics cited in Richards, *Dream Palace*, 48.
[61] Ford, *Children in the Cinema*, 2.
[62] Locket programmed a mix of silent films and talkies, and her matinees typically consisted of a two-reel Chaplin, a *Secrets of Nature* short, a Felix the Cat cartoon, a talkie newsreel, and a feature (silent or sound), Staples, 42-50.
[63] Other notable ventures include various Children's Cinema Councils run in close co-operation with Local Education Authorities. See Ford, 18-23.

educational imperatives behind the film shows: "Children do not want to recall association with the schoolroom on Saturday morning; they do not want films which adults imagine to be wholesome. They want action, excitement, suspense and comedy".[64]

A more successful form of children's cinema was represented by the special clubs for children organised by commercial cinemas, which began in Britain in 1934, when the Odeon cinema in Worthing established the first Mickey Mouse cinema club for children.[65] Soon, Mickey Mouse clubs spread throughout the Odeon circuit, and, in 1935, more cinema chains, such as Granada and Union, launched clubs featuring other cartoon characters, including Donald Duck and Popeye the Sailor. The clubs generally followed the format of those already in operation in America. Child members were given badges, they learnt a club creed and song that invoked patriotism, social responsibility and respect of parents, and watched a standard programme of films each Saturday morning, consisting of a feature, a serial episode, and, of course, a cartoon.[66] The films, however, were often older titles no longer shown on normal cinema programmes, and they could be in poor physical condition. Films shown at the clubs were required for one show only, and they were exhibited to a low-paying audience. In order to break even, exhibitors had to run the clubs on a limited budget, and this meant hiring older, cheaper films.[67]

A general idea of the age ranges and film preferences of children during the early 1930s can be gleaned from the aforementioned local inquiries, which generally concluded that children in towns attended the cinema more often than adults, and that adolescents went more often than young children. According to Richards, the London enquiry, which surveyed 21,280 children, found that "infants and young children preferred cartoons, that comic films were popular with all ages", and that, on the whole, non-fiction films did not rank among the most popular genres. War and adventure films were apparently favourites with boys, and romantic films with older girls; the enquiry also concluded that as the children grew, the more their interest declined in cartoons, war and cowboy pictures.[68] In

---

[64] Ibid., 21.
[65] Staples, *All Pals Together*, 51-61.
[66] The staging of competitions and other, sometimes fundraising, activities were common in the clubs, but were dependent on the regulations of the local licensing authorities. See Ford, *Children in The Cinema*, 154-185.
[67] For a discussion on the economics of running a children's matinee see ibid., 139-153.
[68] Richards, *Dream Palace*, 69. See also, Ford, *Children in The Cinema*, 28-32. Smith notes the unpopularity with child cinema-goers of educational films and

the late 1930s, Ford surveyed over one hundred cinema managers who ran children's cinema clubs. Not confident in the children's ability to answer his questions, he asked managers which films they considered popular amongst their young audiences. Within the typical feature serial cartoon format of the club programmes, Western, adventure, animal and comedy feature films, and Mickey Mouse followed by Silly Symphonies cartoons were thought the most popular. Over half of the respondents were in favour of including more short films on the programme, particularly two-reel comedies. One manager wrote: "The essential factor in entertainment for children is action, not dialogue – which in comedies must be fast, and in Westerns must have thrills".[69] Indeed, Ford concurred with other contemporary reports, stating that "action" was a key component in films popular with children, and was a quality found in both the Western and the slapstick comedy. In this respect he also highlights the parallel with silent features, which were "crammed with action", and were "far more suitable for children than the average slow-moving talkie". Nonetheless, he concludes that children preferred films with sound, although dialogue should be kept to a minimum. In this respect, it is interesting to note that early Chaplin shorts with added soundtracks were still shown at clubs in the late 1930s, and that 42% of 139 managers polled, considered the comedian still popular with child audiences.

To a limited extent, Pathéscope's 9.5mm home cinema can be seen as a non-theatrical answer to anxieties around children's cinema-going before the mid-1930s. Certainly, the home cinema allowed for the selection of films and the possibility, if desired, of parental supervision of the material watched by children. Moreover, the short lengths and age of the subjects of 9.5mm films anticipate some of the rationales underpinning attempts at child-specific film programming in the early 1930s, especially concerning the brevity of a child's attention span, and the appropriateness of silent films in general for child audiences. Of course, this view was influenced by a lack of suitable sound films and limited budgets. Similarly, the range of films offered by Pathéscope generally, and in marketing directed at children, aligns with the genres of films subsequently exhibited and deemed suitable, or at least "clean" enough, for children's consumption. By 1930, fiction titles dominated the 9.5mm film catalogue, yet a substantial range of instructional, travel and other non-fiction subjects

---

"sloppy stuff" as evidenced in the oral histories recorded by the "Cinema Culture in 1930s Britain" collection at the Institute for Cultural Research, Lancaster University. See Smith, "A Riot at the Palace", 280.

[69] For all information relating to Ford's findings about the films managers consider children to like, see Ford, *Children in The Cinema*, 103-138.

remained available until Pathéscope's closure in the early 1960s, and the use of 9.5mm in schools as an educational tool was consistently promoted in the *Pathéscope Monthly*.[70] Advertisements aimed at children frequently highlighted 9.5mm versions of cartoons and comedies, and included images of well-liked characters such as Charlie Chaplin and Mickey Mouse. In the context of debates surrounding children's cinema during the inter-war period, Pathéscope's marketing directed at children, through its invocation of comedy and cartoon genres, can be seen to be responding both to young children's film tastes generally, and to adult notions of suitable programming for children.

Conclusions

It is difficult to determine to what extent 9.5mm versions of cartoons and comedies were bought, borrowed and viewed, and whether their popularity exceeded that of other genres offered on the gauge. Both cartoons and comedies remain, however, prominent genres in the 9.5mm film catalogues, in terms of the number of films offered by Pathéscope. If we accept this as an indicator of the popularity of cartoon and comedy films, whilst it does not confirm that only children were viewing such films, it does imply that those films considered staple viewing for juvenile audiences were among the most prominent genres offered by Pathéscope.

Similarly, there is evidence to suggest that the cheaper forms of home projector, often linked to juvenile consumption, were amongst the highest selling models that Pathéscope offered. In an article published in *9.5* entitled "Tales from the Camera Shop, Ace Days", John E. Lewis, who was a shop assistant in a photographic retailer's in the 1950s, discusses the popularity of the Ace projector. He recalls a consistently high demand for such machines, especially the relatively high number of sales during the Christmas period, and remarks that employees at the Pathéscope factory endured compulsory overtime during autumn:

> from November onwards everybody was switched from their regular tasks to boost Ace production. As Christmas approached vans from Boots, Timothy Whites, Selfridges and even the prestigious Harrods would be queuing up at the Cricklewood plant to await trolley loads of Ace projectors".[71]

---

[70] See, for instance, "Education and 9.5mm Movies," 14.
[71] Lewis, "Tales from the Camera Shop, Ace Days", 5.

In actuality then, whilst promotional literature surrounding the 9.5mm system was keen to rule out the notion that the home projector was in any way a toy, this did not prohibit the use of the technology by children. Children's consumption of the 9.5mm projecting apparatus was neither accidental nor incidental. Whilst Pathéscope implicitly acknowledged children as potential consumers of the 9.5mm gauge through their use of the term "everyone", it also explicitly targeted children in its advertising, and through the provision of films specifically aimed at juvenile consumption. The popularity of the cartoon and short comedy films and high number of sales of the cheaper projectors most often associated with juvenile use, indicate the significant role played by children throughout the period of 9.5mm's commercial viability in Britain.

More research needs to be done to identify more fully the dynamics of amateur film shows run by or for children. Alongside the actual material screened, the viewing experiences available to 9.5mm audiences were also defined by the limitations of the technology and the individual choices made by the operator.[72] Projectors could be hand-cranked or motor-driven, and had variable running speeds. During the early 1930s, Pathéscope sold a range of screens of different sizes, from 24 x 18 inches to 5ft. x 4ft. 3 inches. Yet, to obtain a picture of just 3ft. in width, early Pathé projectors required a throw (the distance between projector and screen) of between 10ft. and 14ft. In confined domestic spaces, films may have been viewed, therefore, on screens 3ft. in width or less. Other variables need to be considered. Alongside the projector and films, Pathéscope sold a number of accessories that encouraged amateur exhibitors to customise their shows. Coloured gels were used to tint the projected image, and a transparent screen, usually employed in limited spaces, allowed the projector to be placed on the opposite side of the screen to the audience. In this case, however, images appeared back to front and intertitles could not be read—to correct the orientation of the pictures, Pathéscope sold the "Redressing Mirror". 9.5mm customers could also purchase the "Amplifier", which magnified the picture by up to 40%.

General information as to the screening practices of amateurs may be deduced from cine handbooks, such as the one authored by Harold B. Abbott, which offered programming advice. For musical accompaniment, the author suggested, in the probable absence of a piano or accomplished pianist, the use of a gramophone, whilst strongly discouraging the use of radio, because the projectionist had no control over the type of music being played. He recommended "bright and lively records" for comedies,

---

[72] I have elaborated this elsewhere. See Clare Watson, "Gauging Charlie: Pathé's 9.5mm Home Cinema in Britain and the Films of Charles Chaplin."

but advised using records of average suitability, as it would be impossible to change the music for every scene.[73] According to the *Pathéscope Monthly*, film programmes should last for two hours at most, including an interval, satiation should be avoided at all costs, whilst a mix of "printed" and amateur-produced films should provide adequate variation.[74]

Alexandra Schneider has recently argued for the private film collection's status as a significant source in the reconstruction of the history of non-theatrical film consumption and circulation. Schneider suggests that the private film collection constitutes an "archive of viewing practices", and that, alongside other documentation, its study has the potential to illuminate the ephemeral screening practices of the amateur cinéaste. As she remarks, "Little is known about program structures (e.g. sequencing, or the interplay between home-made and purchased films) or about which commercial titles found favor with which audiences."[75] One of the major difficulties hindering the study of the non-theatrical exhibition of professionally- and amateur-produced films is the relative scarcity of source material detailing such events. I hope to have shown here, that surviving material including company records, publicity, cine magazines, instructional documents, amateur cinema handbooks, and written and oral testimony, must play an important part alongside the private collection in the reconstruction of this forgotten pastime.

Works Cited

Primary Sources

Advertisement. *The Amateur Photographer and Photography* (30 September 1925): xxvi.

Advertisement. *Home Movies and Home Talkies* 4, no. 7 (1935): 274.

Key industry duty: value of Pathé Baby cine projector, 1926, PRO, CUST 117/10.

---

[73] Abbott, *Motion Pictures with the Baby Cine*, 106.
[74] Nicholson, "Choosing Your Film Program," 13.
[75] Schneider, "Time travel with Pathé Baby: The small-gauge film collection as historical archive", 353-354. Interestingly, in examining the private 9.5mm Pathé Baby collection of a Swiss family who lived in Italy during the 1930s, Schneider finds that "the surviving non-fiction prints are in better condition than the comedy prints, suggesting the latter were projected more frequently". The father screened programmes of animated films, comedy sketches and animal pictures mainly at functions with children, and his son particularly recalls the success of the many Felix the Cat sequels and of Chaplin. Schneider, 356.

Registration documents for Pathéscope Ltd, 1912, PRO, BT 31/14020/125579.

Secondary Sources

Abbott, Harold B. *Motion Pictures with the Baby Cine.* London: Iliffe & Sons, 1929.
Agajanian, Rowana. "'Just for Kids?': Saturday Morning Cinema and Britain's Children's Film Foundation in the 1960s." *Historical Journal of Film, Radio & Television* 18, no. 3 (1998): 395-409.
Anon. "Moving Pictures in the Home," *The Moving Picture World* 8, no. 17 (29 April 1911): 934.
—. "Fire at a Cinematograph Show." *The Times* (27 June 1911): 8.
—. "Children in Cinemas." *The Times* (27 February 1917): 9.
—. "Education and 9.5mm Movies." *Pathéscope Monthly* (June-July 1933): 14.
—. "Does cutting spoil classical film?" *Pathéscope Monthly* (February 1934): 3.
—. "The cutting of films." *Pathéscope Monthly* (April-May 1934): 14-15.
Barnes, John. *The Beginnings of the Cinema in England, 1894-1901, Vol. 5.* Exeter: University of Exeter Press, 1997.
Conrich, Ian. "Kitchen Cinema: Early Children's Film Shows in London's East End." *Journal of British Cinema and Television* 2, no. 2 (2005): 290-298.
Ford, Richard. *Children in the Cinema.* London: Allen & Unwin, 1939.
Giles, R. "The Cinema at School." *Pathéscope Monthly* (August-September 1930): 6.
Harris, Percy W. "The Editor's News Reel." *Home Movies and Home Talkies* 4, no. 8 (1936): 313.
Herbert, Stephen, ed. *A History of Early Film, Vol. 3.* London: Routledge, 2000.
—. "German Home and Toy Magic Lantern-Cinematographs." *New Magic Lantern Journal* 5 (1987): 11-15.
Kermabon, Jacques, ed. *Pathé: Premier Empire du Cinema.* Paris: Centre Georges Pompidou, 1994.
Kuhn, Annette. "Children, 'Horrific' Films, and Censorship in 1930s Britain." *Historical Journal of Film, Radio and Television* 22, no. 2 (2002): 197-202.
—. *An Everyday Magic: Cinema and Cultural Memory.* London: I. B. Tauris, 2002.

Lewis, John E. "Tales from the Camera Shop, Ace Days." *9.5* 108 (2002): 5-6.
McKee, Gerald. *Film Collecting*. London: Tantivy Press, 1978.
—. *The Home Cinema: Classic Home Movie Projectors 1922-1940*. Bucks, UK: Gerald McKee, 1989.
—. *A Half Century of Film Collecting*. Bucks, UK: Gerald McKee, 1993.
Mebuld, Anke and Charles Tepperman. "Resurrecting the Lost History of 28mm Film in North America." *Film History* 15, no. 2 (2003): 137-151.
Murray, Graham. "Flashback Part 1." *9.5* 123 (2005): 10.
National Council of Public Morals. *The Cinema: Its Present Position and Future Possibilities*. London: Williams & Norgate, 1917.
Nicholson, G. W. "Choosing Your Film Program." *Pathéscope Monthly* (February 1934): 13.
Richards, Jeffrey. "Cinemagoing in Worktown: Regional Film Audiences in 1930s Britain." *Historical Journal of Film, Radio & Television* 14, no. 2 (1994): 147-166.
—. *The Age of the Dream Palace: Cinema and Society in Britain 1930-1939*. London: Routledge, 1984.
Robinson, David. "Interview with Kevin Brownlow." Available at: www.bfi.org.uk/features/interviews/brownlow.html#interest.
Salmon, Stéphanie. "Le Coq Enchanteur: Pathé, Une Entreprise Pour L'industrie Et Le Commerce De Loisirs (1896-1929)." PhD diss., Université Paris I, 2007.
Schneider, Alexandra. "Time Travel With Pathé Baby: The Small-Gauge Film Collection As Historical Archive." *Film History* 19, no. 4 (2007): 353-360.
Singer, Ben. "Early Home Cinema and the Edison Home Projecting Kinetoscope." *Film History* 2, no. 1 (1988): 37-69.
Smith, Sarah J. "A Riot at the Palace: Children's Cinema-going in 1930s Britain." *British Journal of Cinema and Television* 2, no. 2 (2005): 275-289.
Staples, Terry. *All Pals Together: The Story of Children's Cinema*. Edinburgh: Edinburgh University Press, 1997.
Watson, Clare. "Gauging Charlie: Pathé's 9.5mm Home Cinema in Britain and the Films of Charles Chaplin." MA diss., University of East Anglia, 2005.
Winpenny, Brian. "The Woolworth 9.5 Projector." *9.5* 40 (1984-5): 5-6.
Wordsworth, Ken. "A Personal Look Back." *9.5* 40 (1984-5): 12.

Films Cited

The Count
(Mutual Films, 1916) 35mm., 34 mins.
Carmen
(Films Albatros and Sequana Films, 1926) 35mm., 110 mins. (released by Pathéscope Ltd on 9.5mm on two Super reels equal to 805ft., giving a running time of approximately 34 minutes, Pathéscope catalogue number S/627).
The Circus
(Chaplin Productions-United Artists, 1928) 35mm., 71 minutes.
Easy Street
(Mutual Films, 1917) 35mm., 19 mins. (released by Pathéscope Ltd on 9.5mm on one Super reel equal to 325ft., giving a running time of approximately 14 minutes, Pathéscope catalogue number SB/651).
Secrets of Nature
(British Instructional Films, 1922-1933) 35 mm., various durations.
The Silent Avenger
(Gotham Productions, 1927) 35 mm., 55 mins. (released by Pathéscope Ltd on 9.5mm as *Good Dog*, on one Super reel equal to 365ft., giving a running time of approximately 15 minutes, catalogue number S/639).
A Voyage of Discovery
(J. S. Fry & Sons. Ltd., c.1930), 35 mm., 15 mins. (released by Pathéscope Ltd on 9.5mm on one Super reel equal to approximately 300ft., giving a running time of approximately 12 mins.).

CHAPTER THREE

FRAMING THE VIEW: HOLIDAY RECORDING AND BRITAIN'S AMATEUR FILM MOVEMENT, 1925-1950

HEATHER NORRIS NICHOLSON

Holiday films occupy an intriguing position within traditions of travel representation. As what Derek Gregory has described as "spaces of constructed visibility",[1] they connect readily with earlier visual practices and cultures of travel.[2] This chapter examines the first twenty-five years of holiday recording on cine film, and charts such connections within that formative period.[3] Discussion considers how and why people were attracted to use their cine cameras to capture events and places, the cultural work involved in the sharing of holiday experiences, and the re-living of memories of travels with family, friends and wider audiences. Examples of amateur film footage, now held at the North West Film Archive and the Yorkshire Film Archive, help to situate this conspicuous strand of amateur cine practice within broader cultural, visual and social frameworks. The ideas explored form part of a wider interest in relationships

---

[1] Gregory, "Colonial Nostalgia", 111.
[2] Norris Nicholson, "Sites of Meaning", 182; see also Chard, *Pleasure and Guilt on The Grand Tour*.
[3] An earlier version of this discussion was presented at "Amateur Cinema in Theory and Practice", a conference organised by Ian Craven at the Centre for Screen Studies, University of Glasgow, 26th May 2006. Funding from the Krasna-Krausz Foundation and the British Council supported research discussed in this chapter; special thanks are owed to many patient and knowledgeable archive staff, in particular to those based at the North West Film Archive, Manchester Metropolitan University.

between visual and tourism histories, and connect more specifically with on-going research into Britain's amateur film movement.[4]

As this chapter spans the Second World War, some reference is made to day-excursions, and to longer holidays quite literally spent at home, but attention mainly focuses upon holidays involving an element of travel, and thus spent *away* from the participants' domestic settings. Formal and social questions are inescapably merged within these accounts of physical displacement. Not surprisingly, holiday films involving a journey often start and finish their narratives with scenes of departure and arrival. While it is easy to interpret sequences of returning home simply as a way of finishing the last reel of film after the holiday, the tendency to include opening scenes of half-packed bags, leaving the house, and even details of the journey to a destination, indicate more considered attempts to structure narrative. Such scenes hint at an aesthetic awareness of visual story-telling often marginalised within early academic discussion of amateur cinema.[5] At the same time, in their organisation of image, editing, point-of-view and camera movement, such films also disclose symptomatic family dynamics and gender roles on holiday, as well as broaching significant issues of authorship and control.

Holiday footage varies considerably in its depiction of destination locations. For some amateurs, local detail is the main focus, with camerawork capturing the distinctive characteristics of particular settings, and the holidaymaker's visual "reportage" geared firmly towards documenting the actuality of time and place. Such material may subsequently provide a wealth of socio-cultural, economic and historical "evidence", albeit mediated through the organising optics of the cinematic gaze, and the always inherently politicised process of representing other localities and lifestyles.[6] Finding opportunities to encounter and record such signs of difference may well prompt the organisation of travel arrangements by the cine enthusiast, particularly if the filmmaker's interests are driven by a desire to screen footage secured to public audiences. Charles Chislett, for instance, an employee and later manager of the Williams Deacons bank in Rotherham, South Yorkshire, a highly competent and prolific filmmaker, booked a ticket on the *Queen Mary*, so that he could record his own version of the liner's much awaited, and

---

[4] Norris Nicholson, *Visual Pleasures*, forthcoming; see also Norris Nicholson, "Through the Balkan States".
[5] Shand, "Worth Remembering", 54.
[6] Norris Nicholson, "Telling Travellers' Tales", and "Shooting the Mediterranean".

highly publicised, maiden voyage between Southampton and New York, in May 1936.[7]

Holiday footage confirms however that amateur interest often extended far beyond the mere "picturing" of places. Holiday *experiences* sometimes so predominate in the films, that any inclusion of setting seems largely incidental. As with still photography, visually distinctive locations often figure as extensions of domestic space, within which to "stage" a sequence showing family or friends.[8] Background details may hint at artistic effect and humour, or index other associations now possibly lost to interpretation, but their site-specific significance seems relatively unimportant to the overall ambition. Such distinctions may be interpreted in different ways: some holidays occur in places that may simply seem more interesting or possible to film, than others. It is also logical that family members and friends might feature more prominently when a filmmaker is travelling in company—perhaps, particularly, with children. Certainly it is likely that there is more opportunity to record the experience of sight-seeing when filming occurs alone or as a shared hobby with a partner although, inevitably, exceptions exist.[9]

During the years 1925-1950, self-produced footage brought personal and private holiday experiences into shared spheres of middle-class consumption in unprecedented ways.[10] Filmic records permitted the films' participants and others to join in re-living memories in a particularly intense manner, via a series of transformations, marking connections between memory, visualisation and identity which recur through much discussion of amateur footage. As suggested elsewhere, surviving holiday material from the period often discloses more about the person in charge of the camera, than the people and places framed by his or her viewfinder.[11] Subject to the protocols of filming, family experience can be manipulated in the same way that a filmmaker can compress time and miniaturise space.[12] No less than their "fictional" counterparts therefore, the text of the home movie involves a certain productivity: decisions about how to shoot, splice, caption and otherwise edit scenes of families on holiday, no less than family life in general, ascribe identities to the people and places portrayed on screen.

---

[7] Chislett's film was entitled *Maiden Voyage (*NWFA and Kingfisher Films).
[8] Chambers, "Family as Place", 96.
[9] see Norris Nicholson, "British Films of The Mediterranean", 114.
[10] Norris Nicholson, "At Home and Abroad With Cine Enthusiasts", 324-331.
[11] Norris Nicholson, "Telling Travellers' Tales", and subsequent works listed.
[12] Stewart, *On Longing: Narratives of The Miniature*, 69.

Stories about one's family told through moving pictures represent significant expressions of a filmmaker's own identification and positionality, and may thus usefully be understood as a form of autobiography.[13] While the filmmaker may be out of sight for much of a film's running time, typically appearing only in occasional—and loosely staged—walk-on parts, subsequent screening usually involves greater prominence, as all-in-one narrator, presenter and projectionist. Contrasting with the more private role occupied during shooting, where the camera may well function as something to hide behind, rather like a mask or screen, this public presentation invites interrogation and response. Where operating the camera prevents full participation, responsibility is usually assumed later for re-presenting "captured" experiences, when standing beside a turning projector in a darkened room. The minutiae of family dynamics sometimes evidenced by amateur holiday material permit us to explore therefore, relatively private processes of performing and constructing identities, whilst also speaking to more public histories. As Stuart Hall reminds us, stories told on camera about identities and memories are always, "in the end conditional [and] lodged in contingency".[14] If, as has been argued elsewhere, inherited assumptions and expectations about family relations and notions of selfhood profoundly lessened their influence upon personal behaviour and social practice during the interwar and post-1945 period,[15] the making and showing of amateur holiday and travel films certainly contributes to an understanding of these wider societal shifts.

Coincidental Opportunities

Emerging amateur interests in cinematography, from the early 1920s, coincided for many with unprecedented opportunities to see and be seen elsewhere, occasioned by a range of factors. Certainly the lifting of travel restrictions, after four years of limited movement, brought welcome stimulus to a tourist industry that had suffered greatly during the First World War.[16] Speeding recovery, hoteliers and travel operators re-established services as soon as upgrading or rebuilding could be completed, vying with each other to furnish a variety of planned itineraries

---

[13] Giddens, "The Trajectory of The Self", 255.
[14] Hall, "Who Needs Identity?", 17.
[15] Baumeister, *Identity, Cultural Change and The Struggle for Self*, cited in Giddens, 256.
[16] Brendon, *Thomas Cook: 150 Years of Popular Tourism*; Feifer, *The Ways of The Tourist*; Towner, *An Historical Geography of Recreation and Tourism*.

and attractive destinations suited to a broadening range of budgets.[17] Trains, steamers and increasingly, motorised public transport, played key roles, and as ownership of private vehicles increased, recreational driving gained popularity too, epitomising a widespread quest for non-work-related mobility, which could now be realised by those groups with sizable disposable incomes.[18] Publishing (assisted by new colour printing techniques) and advertising, further fuelled newfound desires to explore being somewhere—and perhaps, *someone*—else.

Technical possibilities of recording holiday experience in moving imagery combined then with new opportunities for recreational mobility and related leisure activities. A whole range of evidences suggest that new *ideas* about relationships between work, fatigue, and modernity were emerging too.[19] Uncertainties about identity and self, influenced by recent world events undoubtedly form an important part of the picture,[20] clearly indexed by the popularisation of new developments in psychology and philosophy.[21] Innovative attitudes toward sunshine and being outdoors, following the publication of Augustus Rollier's influential *Heliotherapy* (1923) also gradually helped to transform holiday behaviour.[22] This conjuncture of practical factors, and a range of changing ideas and attitudes, may usefully inform approaches to amateur film records of holiday experiences produced at this time.

Holiday-making and cine photography, two costly hobbies that came together in the mid-1920s, gradually became available to less affluent social groups through the 1930s. Initially, the manufacture of user-friendly 16mm cine cameras, offered a new travel accessory for well-heeled enthusiasts with sufficient time and money to indulge these interests. Typically, these early hobbyists were from the middle- or upper-classes of interwar Britain, individuals from moneyed backgrounds, often working as professionals or successful entrepreneurs, or holding influential positions. While some amateur enthusiasts still travelled purposefully with their cameras, in the course of overseas duty as missionaries, relief workers, doctors, government advisors and colonial administrators, others could already record their *tourist* experiences of being elsewhere.[23] Precedents had clearly been set by earlier technologies: Urry suggests, that the still

---

[17] Norris Nicholson, *Visual Pleaures*, forthcoming.
[18] Babcock, *Spanning The Atlantic*, 203-226.
[19] Rabinbach, *The Human Motor*, 274.
[20] Baumeister, *Identity, Cultural Change and The Struggle for Self*, see also note 14.
[21] Casey, *The Fate of Place*, 288.
[22] Brendon, *Thomas Cook: 150 Years of Popular Tourism*, 260.
[23] Norris Nicholson, "British Holiday Films of The Mediterranean", 116.

camera's invention welded together tourism and photography as "an irreversible and momentous double helix".[24] If so, successive, and rapid developments in amateur cine technologies, dramatically extended the historically-established links between visualisation, travel and memory at a critical phase in the rise of commercially-organised and mass-marketed holiday-making.

Lightweight, hand-cranked or clockwork cine cameras, could easily accompany filmmakers on a short excursion, or longer journeys further afield. In 1927, *The Amateur Photographer and Cinematographer*—an example of the burgeoning hobby literature aimed at the amateur filmmaker—organised a summer holiday competition specifically for "amateur photographers who are motorists".[25] A few weeks later, the same magazine published a short article entitled, "Car, Caravan and Camera" which recommended the suitability of caravan holidays for the cine enthusiast, noting that the caravan itself would allow ample space for developing film en-route![26]

Growing numbers of participants responded enthusiastically to the encouragements of such journal discourses. Amateur footage, for example—including numerous animation, fiction films, and documentaries, as well as holiday and home movies —comprises approximately seventy-five per cent of the material now held at the North West Film Archive.[27] Holidays clearly represented unparalleled occasions and subjects for filmmaking among amateurs, both for purely domestic purposes, and with a view to subsequent entry in cine club and film festival competitions. Inevitably, much of the content is predictable—children digging sandcastles, paddling and riding donkeys, playing cricket and other ball games, and families engaged in leisurely picnics, organised excursions and casual sight-seeing. Overseas material exhibits similar signs of convention, depicting well-established routes and "must see" destinations pre-identified by operators for tourists heading to the Mediterranean, landmark European locations and, occasionally, much further afield to North America, North Africa and the Middle East.[28]

---

[24] Urry, *The Tourist Gaze*, 149.
[25] Anon., "A Holiday Photographic Competition", 15; details were jointly promoted in its "sister paper" (sic), *The Auto Car,* and later extended to readers of *The Motor Cycle*.
[26] Anon., "Car, Caravan and Camera", 21.
[27] North West Film Archive (NWFA). Personal communication with director, Marion Hewitt, 15 February, 2007.
[28] Norris Nicholson, "At Home and Abroad With Cine Enthusiasts", 323-333.

Instances of cine film shot during extended visits to more distant locations, during the years 1925-1950, are relatively rare, and the motivations involved in its production decidedly mixed. Often such footage does not portray a holiday visit merely as recreational activity, as suggested by my interpretation elsewhere of *Gallipoli: a Pilgrimage Cruise, May 1934* (1934).[29] *Tour in the USSR* (1932) suggests more of an educational visit than sight-seeing trip, depicting an itinerary that was, at least in part, shaped by the Soviet organisers, without whose involvement tourists would have been unable to travel to such a destination.[30] Work-related travel is perhaps most clearly seen in *Go East, Young Man, Parts I-VI* (1927), although even here sight-seeing predominates to a remarkable degree.[31]

Significant conjunction therefore, between innovations in camera technology, a boom in leisure activity, and explorations of personal mobility, clearly prompted the innovation and recording of varied holiday experiences by amateurs. Changing circumstances however continuously influenced who, how, where and why amateur filmmakers travelled and filmed, during the years under consideration here. A periodisation distinguishing between interwar, wartime and immediate post-war phases, offers a useful means of clarifying more specific consistencies, ruptures and complications along a range of persistent axes.

Interwar Initiatives

Holiday and travel footage from the inter-war years often displays highly informed technique and practice, well illustrated by sequences in films made by two brothers, Harold and Sidney Preston from Stockport near Manchester, during the 1920s and 1930s.[32] Their footage of Mediterranean cruise holidays includes many well-composed scenes. As discussed elsewhere, close-up details of people and places combine visual competence with fascinating glimpses of lifestyles and landscapes that have now disappeared. Other amateur films may be technically poorer, but still valuable as visual histories, and testimony to different phases in the emergence of cine film practice. Dr John Barker Scarr, another enthusiast from the Greater Manchester area, includes experimental sequences of the French Riviera at night, semi-abstract images of waterfront scenes, illuminated buildings framed by garden vegetation, and offshore ships'

---

[29] Norris Nicholson, "Sites of Meaning".
[30] Norris Nicholson, "Journeys Into Seeing".
[31] Norris Nicholson, *Visual Pleasures*.
[32] Norris Nicholson, "At Home and Abroad With Homes Movies."

lights reflecting on water, in his films of a family cruise holiday in 1933—alongside less technically effective, over-exposed, and blurred camera-work.[33] During the early years of amateur film making, enthusiasts such as these clearly developed skills as they worked, and for some practitioners, almost any record of an unusual overseas experience was probably better than none. Rigorous editing tended to develop only with experience, and may help to explain the range of quality found in some filmmakers' work.

Camera-touting visitors frequently went southwards during the relatively short-lived flowering of more accessible tourist opportunities, across and beyond European frontiers, between the two world wars. Scenes of Paris and alpine regions in France, Italy, Austria and Switzerland, tend to predominate in footage of motoring holidays undertaken by the architects, doctors, chemists and other professionals who visited from Northern England. Much of their cine photography benefited considerably from the strong light of the southern sun and clear-air conditions of mountainous areas. Travel by train or by car, also helped to maintain the popularity, among English-speaking tourists, of longer-established destinations on the French or Italian Riviera. Members of the new middle-classes, including the Preston family mentioned above, whose wealth derived from commerce and industry, were also attracted by the newly available two- to four-week long Mediterranean cruises, that combined visits ashore with onboard entertainment.

From these cinematic records, we see how particular locales fade in and out of favour and enjoy shifting degrees of accessibility, for a variety of practical and political reasons. From around 1938, the swastikas on armbands and fluttering banners in pretty alpine settings recorded during continental motor tours,[34] tend to disappear from the holiday record, although interestingly—and perhaps not entirely unexpectedly—exceptions do occur. More holiday cruises and motoring tours in northern Europe also appear during this phase. Seasonal growth rings of additional hotels are evidenced by footage filmed in popular locations during successive visits, and the gradual metamorphosis from coastal community to resort is shown to be already well under way, within a few years. Even before 1939, land use changes and economic re-orientation brought about by tourism are apparent in films shot along Mediterranean coastlines.

---

[33] Barker Scarr, *Mediterranean Cruise. SS Arandora Star May 1933 (2)* NWFA, Accession no. RR229/13.
[34] See for example Riley, *On The Rhine*, NWFA, Accession no. 3272.

Portugal and Spain feature mainly as excursions ashore during cruise ship itineraries at this stage.[35] Holiday footage of Barcelona, for instance, frequently includes scenes of the Ramblas, bull ring and exhibition pavilions, but ignores the unfinished structures of the Sagrada Familia, and Gaudi's unique architectural contribution to the city.[36] Amateurs also seem to enjoy the chance to film unfamiliar animals in close-up during feeding and bathing time at Lisbon's zoo.[37] In a fascinating re-definition of the exotic, this may reflect restrictions against filming at some of Britain's zoos imposed during the inter-war years, as reported in *Amateur Cinematography*.[38] Perhaps filming opportunities of any sort provided welcome relief, after frequently rough conditions across the Bay of Biscay. Certainly, the initial flurry of filming during holidays afloat usually ceases during the outward leg of the cruise between the Channel and first landfall, often at Lisbon or Gibraltar.

Visible and material difference clearly prompts the impulse to expose film. The *urge* to capture on camera, how other people dress and go about their daily activities, or enjoy special occasions, and *access* to the technical means to do, both register the social inequalities dramatised in such travel and tourism. The opportunity to step voluntarily into someone else's world marks uneven social developments, and is definitive of differential histories inscribed in centre/periphery relations. Holiday-makers' visual encounters with difference thus turn them into time travellers of a sort, as their cine footage frames the objectified other in a separate time, despite the co-existence implied by the camera's and the operator's co-presence. Bhabha reminds us of the ambivalent nature of what he calls this post-colonial "prerogative": an image, he tells us, is always "spatially split—it makes *present* something that is *absent* and temporally deferred, (while also being) the representation of a time that is

---

[35] Barker Scarr, *Mediterranean Cruise: SS Arandora Star May 1933 (2)*, NWFA Accession no. RR229/8; Preston Brothers, *Preston Family—Cruise Holiday 1928*, NWFA Accession no. RR 116/88; *Royal Mail Line Cruise. M.V. Asturias (22,500 tonnes) to Spain, Madeira and the Canaries, Part I. Leaving Southampton June 22 1928*, NWFA Accession no. 1964D.

[36] Preston Brothers, *Barcelona*, NWFA Accession no. 1967D; *P & O Cruise of the Mediterranean May/June 1932*, NWFA Accession no. 1945D; *Peninsular & Orient Steam Navigation Co., Med. Cruise to Ceuta, Monte Carlo, Palma & Barcelona, Vigo, London by the turbo-electric ship Vice Roy of India. 20,000 tonnes*, NWFA Accession no. 1943D; *Orient Line Cruise: Leaving Lisbon we arrive in Gilbraltar*, NWFA Accession no. 1956.

[37] Preston Brothers, *Orient Line SS Orama*, NWFA Accession nos. 1960D and 1961.

[38] "Club Sec.", "Cinematography at the Zoo", 37.

always elsewhere, a repetition."[39] Sharing the framed image involves a temporal and visual split too: one individual's framing of a view provides its audience with a means to watch and understand a particular scene. Such dualities reinforce the nature of amateur cinema's relationship with modernity, since interwar holiday footage relies upon a cinematographic apparatus and a capacity to travel that are inherently modern. In unprecedented ways, cine film offers the possibility of making visible and consuming a past that belongs to somewhere, and someone, else.

For many filmmakers, the picture-making impulse also stems from a photographed scene's apparent articulation with conditions back home. *Through the Balkan States* (1934), made by Geoffrey Morey, a Lincolnshire doctor, suggests a fascination with the otherness of regional costume, history and material culture not dissimilar to that shown by many earlier western Europeans visiting the region.[40] Morey however searches beyond the visual tropes of an exotic and static past, for signs of evolution and negotiation with the present. While many interwar commentators lament the loss of regional distinctiveness, and the standardising effects of modernisation, Morey's imagery conveys a gradual transition within a liminal place—there's always a handbag, telegraph pole or a western suit before the camera eye. As a result, his footage offers a multi-facetted version of Balkan identities and cultures, which differs from much of the essentialising—often Orientalist—discourse about the region generated during the interwar years.[41]

Holiday footage emphasises time and again the serendipitous nature of gathering travel experiences, and the enduring value of the unexpected to the cine enthusiast. Although specialist literatures often urged rather formulaic approaches to shooting on holiday, unplanned opportunities frequently yield more interesting film. For subsequent audiences, chance encounters—laundry day beside a river,[42] a dead boar carried through the alley-ways of a North African medina,[43] uniformed guards flanking a busy

---

[39] Bhabha, "Interrogating Identity", 100.
[40] Norris Nicholson, "Through the Balkan States", 13-36.
[41] Such archival holdings have renewed contemporary relevance too, given the post-conflict debates about Balkan identities; destruction and ethnic conflict during the 1990s has given the footage new significance as some places in Morey's film no longer exist. See Torodova, *Imagining The Balkans*, and "What Is Or Is There a Balkan Culture?".
[42] Rigby, *On the Banks of the River Aude*, NWFA Accession no. RR 315/17; Behrens, *Italy*, NWFA Accession no. 1926 RR 16/24.
[43] Barker Scarr, *SS Mediterranean Cruise SS Arandora Star May 1934*, NWFA Accession no. RR229/8.

entrance into Rome's "Fascist Headquarters"[44] or earthquake destruction in Sicily[45]—undoubtedly enhanced the filmmaker's status as traveller, filmmaker and raconteur.[46] Such inclusions help viewers to briefly share the *frisson* of risk, excitement or recognition that derives from being in contact with someone who was "there" at a specific moment. They form part of a visual chain of association between original witness and subsequent spectator. Despite the increasing availability of contemporary newsreel coverage and other moving imagery for home screening from the 1930s, the personal connection established between the viewers and filmmaker/presenter remained a distinctive aspect of amateur cinema presentations to family, friends and more public audiences.[47]

When filmmakers ventured further afield, their imagery attracted even more curiosity back home. H. W. Taylor, a doctor from Bolton in Lancashire, repeatedly showed his black and white footage, following a visit to the USSR in 1932.[48] His diary details presentations given to local societies and organisations, following his return, as well as the occasional news report from the local press.[49] Although not notable for their technical excellence, the content of Taylor's films offers a rare glimpse of daily life inside the Soviet Union. Based upon a guided tour with companions from Manchester by boat and car, the footage covers visits to theatres, prisons, courts and hospitals, construction sites and factories—as well as to more routine sight-seeing locations. (see Fig. 3-1) Taylor's accompanying notes provide a telling commentary to his visual reportage, capturing both the tenor of the guide's version of State ideology, as well as his frank responses to travelling conditions and his own observations. Poor quality in some places may be due to filming covertly, and most institutions are only covered from outside.

Diary entries expand upon Taylor's visual evidence, offering more information than is possible in brief inter-titles—"Wireless is everywhere. In squares, parks, factories, railway stations—used largely for propaganda"— broadcast items include speeches by Bolsheviks, progress reports on five-year plans, lectures for students, workers' suggestions and

---

[44] Barker Scarr, *SS Mediterranean Cruise SS Arandora Star May 1934*, NWFA Accession no. RR229/16.
[45] Preston Brothers, *Orient Line Cruise*, NWFA Accession no. 1894.
[46] Norris Nicholson, "At Home and Abroad With Cine Enthusiasts".
[47] Norris Nicholson, "Telling Travellers' Tales", see also Harbour, "Holidays Afloat", 154-155 and Newens, "Exposures for your Colour Cruise Film", 119-121.
[48] Taylor, *Tour in the USSR,* NWFA Accession no. RR852.
[49] Taylor, *Tour in the USSRTravel Diary,* NWFA Accession no. D612.

complaints and news bulletins, he records.[50] As if to reinforce the State's technical omnipotence, the filmmaker repeatedly shows loudspeakers attached to telegraph poles or projecting from buildings, with and without anyone standing near. The problems of filming as an outsider also recur through his notes, as indicated by an entry concerning "a batch of prisoners" witnessed at Samara:

> They were a terrible depraved lot, 200-300 (sic). I was told they were mostly wealthy Kulaks who would not do as they were told which I did not believe. I think they were prisoners who were sympathetic to the old cause."[51]

Fig. 3-1 frame enlargement from *Tour in the USSR* (1932)
Source: North West Film Archive at Manchester Metropolitan University

Taylor's visit was clearly often uncomfortable, and included numerous encounters with the unfamiliar: women practising military drills, guards who share a cigarette with their prisoner, girls playing football, large wooden figures of state enemies cut out in fretsaw, and displayed for public ridicule in one of Moscow's parks. Whilst, the visual details may

---

[50] Taylor diary, 11.
[51] Ibid., 23.

offer nothing that is new to historians of Russia under Stalin, the circulation of such amateur footage contributes to a fuller understanding of mediated imagery about the USSR outside leftist circles during the 1930s.

Travel-related footage might combine a holiday record with other interests. *Gallipoli Revisited: A Pilgrimage Cruise* for example, brings together preoccupations with personal and shared acts of commemoration.[52] Made by James O'Grady, a Manchester doctor, and veteran of the Dardanelles campaign, the film records a return visit to Gallipoli made by survivors, family and friends in 1934.[53] (see Fig. 3-2) O'Grady himself was a commissioned officer, who interrupted his medical studies to serve at Gallipoli, before being invalided out in June 1915. His involvement with his regiment continued thereafter, and he subsequently filmed various aspects of regimental life. His footage creates a very detailed record of where the fighting took place almost twenty years earlier, indexing location imagery against hand-drawn plans and maps, and place names inserted on inter-titles. The grainy footage illustrates well the difficulties of trying to film landscape—how and where to focus, how to apply moving

Figure 3-2 frame enlargement from *Gallipoli: A Pilgrimage Cruise* (1934)
Source: North West Film Archive at Manchester Metropolitan University

---

[52] Norris Nicholson, "Sites of Meaning", 167-188.
[53] O'Grady, *Gallipoli*, NWFA Accession no. 1795.

image to the vastness of panorama, and how to cope with lighting contrasts over topography that remains a largely unknown territory.

O'Grady's material bears witness to a campaign that incurred severe loss for his regiment. Its representations are often conventional, including for instance, monuments to heroism and landscapes of remembrance.[54] But does the camera's sometimes erratic search over empty terrain hint at more complex subjectivities too? Do these jerky movements compelled by the recollection of specific places and their associations, trace a mind seeking to impose order and confer meaning upon remembered fragments of past experience? Trauma and loss affect both sides in the film's imaginary. O'Grady films Turkish cemeteries too, inserting a close-up of a small headstone inscribed in Arabic, whilst floral tributes, filmed on board ship before arriving at Gallipoli, include wreaths for the Turkish dead. Further cultural symmetries are possibly constrained however by the film's potential role back home, and likely incorporation as part of a visual regimental history. The hedonistic impulses of typical travel footage are however much in evidence: *Pilgrimage Cruise* is as much a record of the living, enjoying a Mediterranean holiday cruise, as a remembrance of the dead. O'Grady films other sightseeing visits ashore, and regimental survivors in playful mood raising their tankards in a toast in front of the camera with conspicuous relish. Commemorative reverence can scarcely sustain solemnity for over two weeks afloat. At home there would be a civilian audience too—perhaps comprising other members of the cruise, and very likely friends or descendants of those who fought at Gallipoli. Their need to be able to enjoy the film is anticipated, and the contrast in mood on the outward and return journeys is striking.

Links with work could also prompt a short holiday abroad or more extended period of travel. Two self-made entrepreneurs, who recorded experiences overseas, illustrate how amateur filmmakers shifted their focus as their own personal circumstances changed. The Preston brothers, mentioned earlier, worked for their father in the family tailoring business. Well-made films survive, documenting their father, Joshua Preston, in his role as mayor of Stockport, often accompanied by their sister Gertie, and many other aspects of family life at home and on holiday. Cine film shot at the International Colonial Exhibitions in Paris in 1931 and 1937, typically captures the lavish scale of pavilions and site layout, as well as the varied nature of popular visitor attractions.[55] (see Fig. 3-3) Footage of exhibition displays that feature various Francophone regions and Indo-China is

---

[54] Hanley, *Writing War: Fiction Gender and Memory*, 33.
[55] Preston Brothers, *International Colonial Exhibition in Paris 1931*, NWFA Accession no. 1895; *The Preston family in Paris*, NWFA Accession no. 1950.

testimony to past patterns of trade, colonial dominance and the objectification of race and culture. Scenes of animals at the exhibition zoo area remind us that wildlife, like cultural difference, is a variant of the exoticism on offer to visitors. Like the scenes of visitors riding elephants, and children in little carts pulled by llamas at Blackpool or Chester, zoo scenes recorded on overseas holidays, during the interwar years, exemplify how animals offer amusement and novelty to generations not yet exposed to the popular educational zeal of wildlife appeals and television natural history programmes.[56]

Fig. 3-3 frame enlargement from *International Colonial Exhibition in Paris* (1931)
Source: North West Film Archive at Manchester Metropolitan University

The mix of work and holiday during an extended period of travel may also be seen in a remarkable collection of cine films made by John Hindley of Southport in the late 1920s.[57] Orphaned during the First World War and brought up largely by an older brother, Hindley brought his first cine camera in 1927, prior to embarking upon a journey to East Asia, a trip

---
[56] See for example, Haffner, *Whipsnade Zoo*, NWFA Accession no. 688; Preston Brothers, *The Preston Family's Trip To The Zoo*, NWFA Accession no. 1917; Preston Brothers, *Isle of Man—for Holidays*, NWFA Accession no. 1923.
[57] Hindley, *Go East Young Man, Parts I-VI*, NWFA. Accession nos. 3638-3643.

seemingly prompted by a wish to learn more about competitive textile production in the Far East.[58] His resulting film, *Go East, Young Man, Parts 1-VI* documents his journey from Liverpool to China and other distant locations, via Australia, New Zealand and India. The surviving material includes extensive footage of street scenes and daily life in large and small settlements throughout the region. Again, as a male outsider's view of places and peoples encountered during a work-related journey that also included much sight-seeing, Hindley's material offers a visually rich perspective on late-colonial relations. As with H. W. Taylor's tour of the former USSR, Hindley kept a detailed notebook that accompanies the visual travel narrative.[59]

Holidays at Home

Family time spent together was precious for amateur filmmakers. Public holidays, festivals and school vacations structured domestic time in many households, and all were deemed key opportunities for the production of recreational records. Since this chapter's main focus is upon holidays that involve elements of travel, other vacation time spent within or close to home is not considered extensively. Moreover, in terms of subject matter alone, it might be hard sometimes to distinguish exactly what derived from holiday time, and what occurred at weekends. But the reality of spending holidays at home is too important to ignore completely within a survey that spans years of economic depression and war time, as well as the continuing effects of austerity and rationing during the late 1940s.

Employees' legal entitlement to one week's paid holiday from 1938 probably did not effect amateur film practice given the affluent backgrounds of early practitioners.[60] On the other hand, levels of car ownership and the ability to drive, indexing material wealth as well as the availability of opportunities for leisured activity beyond the home, clearly influenced how, where and how much time during holidays was spent at and away from home. Even before wartime control orders regulated where filming could occur, and restricted the availability of film stock, fuel and travel permits, the "home holiday" film had emerged as a staple amateur genre.[61] The Hindley family's footage shot on Blackpool Beach offers a

---

[58] Personal telephone conversation with filmmaker's daughter, Valerie Cutter, 22 May 2006.
[59] Cutter, *Go East Young Man: From Lancashire to Shanghai By Steamship*.
[60] Walvin, "'Dark Strangers' in Our Midst", 142-143.
[61] Malthouse, *"Cinematography in Wartime"*, 32, offered a précis of rulings issued by the War Office.

typical example from the mid-1930s: two small girls play in the sea with a parent, ride donkeys, pose with a puppet of Charlie Chaplin almost the same size as themselves, and delight in the distorting mirrors of the fair on the seafront.[62] For leisure historians, the visual details may merely confirm aspects of interwar seaside entertainment evidenced from other sources.[63] Yet, the use of colour film stock, scenes of John Hindley splashing with his daughters, filmed by his wife whilst standing in the water, and the length of the mirror sequence all enrich our understanding of amateur cine practice in the later 1930s, disclosing the effects of relative affluence and family circumstance upon filmmaking. Following his world trip in 1927, Hindley had married and continued to travel widely with his wife making films together. They maintained a shared hobby long after the birth of their children, hence the father's appearance in film shot by the mother.

In contrast, Charles Chislett rarely hands over the camera to another member of the family or friends.[64] His continuing use of colour footage through the wartime period and beyond, along with his organisation of regular touring holidays by car, despite the limited availability of petrol, reflect his financial status. Archive sources confirm his determination to share his enthusiasm, and reveal how he continued to make and show films as part of what his own publicity brochures described as "holidays at home", despite growing difficulties.[65] Although the title echoed the government's wartime campaign to discourage non-essential use of public transport—and to take part instead in locally organised events—Chislett's interpretation represented a wider endorsement of the value of holidaying in Britain, and perhaps, even an advertisement for the vicarious enjoyment of armchair travel, and of watching other people's home movies![66]

Chislett moved from giving informative lanternslide public lectures about his own travels in Europe, into presenting cine films accompanied by a scripted lecture, sometime during the 1930s. During the next forty years, his commitment to filmmaking resulted in over a thousand film shows, and mixed presentations of slides and cine film in venues across northern England and elsewhere. Very aware of the suggestive power of filmic imagery from early on, the educational imperative of his text and imagery is unmistakable, as he sought to provide "LIGHT HEARTED LECTURES which... tickle your imagination and your sense of humour

---

[62] Hindley, *Hindley family scenes and Blackpool*. NWFA Accession no. 3636.
[63] Walton, 2000, also *Histories of Tourism*, and *The Playful Crowd*.
[64] Chislett, Yorkshire Film Archive (YFA), Catalogue nos. 353-354.
[65] Norris Nicholson, *Visual Pleasures*, forthcoming; Chislett (c.1943) "Holidays at home and abroad leaflet", YFA files.
[66] Hughes, *Words on War: Memories on The Home Front*, 80.

[and...] help you to relive the joys and thrills of past holidays, or suggest ideas for future ones."[67]

Chislett's own children seem to have been the impetus, as with many amateur filmmakers, for starting to use a cine camera. Life cycle and status thus combine with the interplay of time, distance and cost to prompt a phase of more localised holiday activities, then prolonged by wartime circumstances into the early 1950s, when changing opportunities permit him to resume his pre-war enjoyment of overseas travel. His series of "holidays at home" films memorialise family life with its shared holidays, and offer a detailed picture of the excursions and changing leisure experiences of a northern middle-class household. The films are essentially domestic in their local and regional explorations, and discoveries of places that are enjoyable to visit with young children. Their titles promise nothing more: *Rachel Discovers England* (1937), *Scottish Holiday* (1939), *The Family Explores Lakeland* (1940) and *Dale Days* (1940). Chislett's holidays in Britain on film continue in the early post-war years with *Scottish September* (1948), *English Journey* (1950) and *Let's Go to Wales* (1952).[68] While the titles are evocative of contemporary publications, so too are many of the images of children at play as well as rural lives and landscapes untouched by war and daily austerities.

As discussed elsewhere,[69] Chislett's focus upon everyday experience and unchanging scenes and traditions forms part of what Chris Waters has described as a wider mid-century evocation of "commonsense ordinariness".[70] The filmmaker's affectionate presentation of "smoky towns and winding roads, green fields and red letter boxes" seems to offer nostalgic hope and reassurance to audiences in search of "the drowsy life of England" that was coming quite literally under enemy fire, and prone to the verbal assaults of more acerbic contemporary observers, including George Orwell.[71] *Dale Days* (1940), for instance, is a powerful evocation of the charms to be found in touring Wharfedale and Wensleydale in North Yorkshire by car with young children.[72] Picnics, messy ice-creams, playing cricket, clambering among rocks and visiting a farm and dairy offer an antidote to what Susan Sontag once called the "imperiled

---

[67] Norris Nicholson, "Telling Travellers' Tales".
[68] Chislett, YFA, nos. 101, 328, 451, 469, 500, 502.
[69] Norris Nicholson, "In Amateur Hands: Framing Time and Space in Home Movies."
[70] Waters, "'Dark Strangers' In Our Midst", 207-238.
[71] See for example, Orwell, "The Lion and The Unicorn", 77-80, and Baldick, *The Modern Movement*, 303-324.
[72] Chislett, *Dale Days* (1940), YFA Catalogue no. 328.

continuity and vanishing extendedness of family life" and, appropriately therefore, encroaching signs of modernity are omitted from Chislett's elegiac depiction of northern England's rural uplands.[73]

Perhaps the absence of pointers to material change and the indulgent portrayal of young children, express both sentimentality and future hope. This effacing of wider social and global changes may help to explain why these disingenuous scenes of simple pleasures were to remain so popular with Chislett's audiences for the next two decades. Like many other amateur filmmakers, Chislett himself went on to spend time during the 1940s producing wartime training films, preserving a leisure activity as a version of civil defence, before becoming involved in the war more directly. Later among one of the earliest groups of observers to witness atrocities first hand in the concentration camp at Belsen, he also experienced military service in Malaysia.[74] Against this background, perhaps the recurrence of his early "holiday at home" films within later screenings seems more understandable. They become increasingly vital reminders of times without cruelty and suffering.

Changing Habits, Changing Opportunities

The war years represent something of an anomaly in the history of Britain's amateur cinema movement. Although the Second World War affected, to varying degrees, life for everyone in Britain, the impacts upon civilian life are selectively recorded in amateur film footage. Some of the earliest filmmakers disappear from the record, for instance the Preston brothers; others appear to adopt the hobby for the first time in the later 1940s, perhaps as a result of serving with or encountering military personnel, particularly those from North America who had access to cine cameras. The relative prices of equipment begin to fall in the post-war years too.[75] Large numbers of new enthusiasts increasingly joined the

---

[73] Sontag, *On Photography*, 9.
[74] Norris Nicholson, "As if by Magic: Authority, Aesthetics and Visions of The Work Place in Home Movies", 221.
[75] For instance, in 1939, Bolex G3 (8mm., 9.5mm and 16mm) all cost approx. £52 10s 0d (£52.50); Kodak offered Kodak f/35 (8mm) K. f/1.9 Model B (16mm) at £10 and £30 respectively, while Pathé advertised 9.5mm from £6 6s (Pathé f/3.5 Motocamera) to £16 (Ditmar f/1.8 Super Camera), see Advertisements, *Amateur Cine World* advertisements, 1939, 104. In 1963, a Eumig S2 cost £27 18s (£27.90) while a Sankyo 8CM Zoom cost £49 (see Campbell, "Almost Universal Hobby", 1963, 33). Prices for all ranges of camera equipment varied considerably between dealers and manufacturers, and the abolition of wartime price controls in 1949

ranks of Britain's amateur film movement in the decades following 1945, as attested by *Amateur Cine World* carrying regular reports of new clubs being opened and extended.[76]

Opportunities to resume peacetime travel came slowly as restrictions were lifted, infrastructure was repaired and, after years of disruption at individual, family and collective levels, people gradually regained the means and the desire to make journeys. Amateur cine too recovered only gradually. Rationing had reduced supplies of film stock and essential equipment, as well as the more basic requirements of clothes and food. For most people, after the end of hostilities, it was enough simply to get on with the practical and psychological challenge of, in the words of one book title, *Living Together Again*.[77] Holidays were often out of the question for financial reasons, although for the more affluent, family excursions gradually resumed either by car, or public transport.

Generally restricted to black and white filmstock, records of countryside and seaside holidays occur from the later 1940s in increasing numbers. *Sykes family holiday in the Lake District* (1949) is indicative of post-war holiday activity, and representative of a camera practice that, in some ways, echoes pre-war leisure patterns.[78] (see Fig. 3-4) The holiday group comprises several young couples and older people sharing cars, staying together at a country hotel. They enjoy picnics by the sea at Ravenglass, travel on the Ravenglass and Eskdale miniature railway, watch a farmer making hay, and spend time together in the grounds of the hotel where they are based. The antics of young children and waddling ducks prompt much amusement and filming. Camera work is straightforward, in its recording of shared enjoyment and relaxation. There are no inter-titles. Unfortunately, over-exposure and unfamiliarity with the camera, detracts from a lengthy sequence that documents some of the

---

allowed sales of pre-war cameras on the open market (rather than at their original pre-1939 purchase price) thus boosting the post-war second market (see Sowerby, "End of Price Control", 685). Price and other changes for the 9.5mm Pathéscope Ace hand-turned projector between its first appearance in 1935, priced 37 shillings and sixpence (£1.00) and its £7 17s 0d (£7.00) price tag in 1961, are summarised by Graeme Newnham (2006), see his website, www.pathefilm.freeserve.co.uk/nine five.htm. The Photographic Information Council reported that c. 200,000 cine cameras were sold annually in 1964-66, although sales of projectors rose only from 170,000 to 190,000 over the same period; overall spending by amateur photographers (still and cine) probably doubled in the years 1960-66; see Anon., *The Guardian*, 26 January 1966, 12.

[76] See note 33.
[77] Bendit and Bendit, *Living Together Again*.
[78] Sykes, *Sykes family holiday to the Lake District*, NWFA, Accession no. 4380.

adults as they go hill-walking. Dress codes hint of an earlier era of outdoor pursuits; canvas, leather, wood and tweed predominate. Panoramic views extend over the fells of the southwestern Lake District, and stretch to the dunes of the Cumbrian coastline. The distant shoreline remains untouched by the development of the world's first industrial nuclear power station at Calder Hall, and the Windscale nuclear fuel reprocessing plant, and the village of Seascale has not yet undergone residential expansion.[79]

Fig. 3-4 frame enlargement from
Sykes family holiday in the Lake District (1949)
Source: North West Film Archive at Manchester Metropolitan University

Cine holiday footage captures transitional moments further from home too. Correspondence and script-notes exist for an intriguing family holiday that involves the Chisletts taking their car by air to Syria in the early 1960s.[80] The use of war-time transporter planes for civilians to travel with their own cars reflects a brief phase in the converging histories of post-war commercial aviation and tourism, prior to the introduction of organised air travel as part of all-inclusive package holidays. Occasionally these planes

---

[79] Powell and Wood, *Ordnance Survey Leisure Guide*, 56.
[80] Chislett, YFA, Catalogue no. 458. Orange correspondence file. See also Chislett, "Air Cruise to The Lebanon, Syria and Jordan", 15.

also occur in footage of motoring holidays to mainland Europe. Detailed sequences of the family car being driven into and out of a plane, filmed from the tarmac near the parked aircraft, or from an observation terrace at the terminal building, capture a now remote phase of holiday culture. Indeed, the amateur's enthusiastic record of the experience of air travel continues for another ten to fifteen years, as successive new converts to the hobby delight in capturing and sharing the excitement and novelty of going on package holiday by air. Instances of holiday footage that focus longer on travelling to the destination than the rest of the holiday occur well into the mid-sixties. The sheer scale and unfamiliarity of terminal buildings, escalators, check-in desks, departure boards and boarding arrangements prompt enthusiasts to record the minutiae of departing, unrestricted by modern airport security.[81]

Further signs of changing travel trends are detectable in holiday footage from the immediate post-war years. Short flights between Britain and mainland Europe occur from small airfields that remained in operation for a few years after the Second World War, prior to the rationalisation of the airport sector in accordance with planned development for large-scale, commercial travel.[82] Two- to four-day air trips also hint at the origins of the modern weekend city break dating to the late 1940s.[83] Intriguing as they are, films involving air travel continue to be the exception—even for many cine camera users—during the 1950s, and their presence in the regional film record should not be overestimated. Generally, where people could afford overseas travel at the end of the 1940s, their journeys involve a ferry crossing, with or without a car. Films made by the Haffner family however, illustrate the trend towards more ambitious holidays, and more adventurous aesthetic techniques. *Charming Switzerland* (1949), *2400miles Continental Journey/The Car/The Mayflower* (1948-1952) and *Norway June 1950*, record scenes of the family on holiday, their car being loaded to and from boats, and a mix of footage that depicts the landscapes and local life passed en route.[84]

Stylistically, much of the holiday footage from this period contrasts with the pre-war years. The films tend to be longer, perhaps the result of numerous reels being edited together, and are increasingly made on

---

[81] Consultation role on films from the Ramsden Collection, YFA, and films by Linda and Michael Gough (Newcastle Amateur Cine Association and Video Group) for "Package Holidays", *Nation on Film*, fourth series BBC/OU, BB4, tx. November 2006, and February 2007, BBC2.
[82] YFA, Ramsden Collection.
[83] Senat, *Weekend in Italy*, British Film Institute, no. 650558.
[84] Haffner, NWFA, Accession nos. 669-671.

smaller gauge film—9.5mm or 8mm—relatively cheaper to use, and then helping to widen cine photography's social appeal to a new generation of enthusiasts. Holiday films from fresh converts also tend to represent an ever-widening spectrum of interests and levels of competence. At the one extreme, there are cine society specialists whose productions are carefully crafted, and critically informed through regular contact with other practitioners, and a hobby press aimed at a discerning readership. Holiday and travel-related films, shaped under such influences might include increasingly elaborate opening sequences that use lettering and images assembled from fabric collage designs, montages from holiday brochures and simple animations. Staged narrative openings seem to become more popular too from the early 1950s, as people become imaginative in handling the evolving technical capabilities of cine equipment.

At the other end of the continuum are the visual diaries, comprising numerous scenes from different occasions, simply edited together for convenience. These often lack titles, credits and pose many interpretative challenges, since little or nothing may be known about the people and places included in the footage, and even knowledge of the filmmaker's identity may have been lost over time. As what Streible has usefully termed "orphan film",[85] the serendipitous character of its subject matter may still yield gems of visual history, and proves of ever-increasing fascination to both scholars and experimental filmmakers.[86]

Conclusions

Over time, the use of cine cameras, initially available only to Britain's middle- and upper-classes, gradually extended to other social groups. In combination with new opportunities for travel, the diffusion of these new "substandard" visual technologies, encouraged the growth of a tourist filming which assumed a variety of distinctive generic forms. As more of the population gained legal entitlement, and later the financial means, to enjoy holidays at home and overseas, the widening record of holidays on cine film generated, provides a unique "evidential" perspective upon interrelated aspects of leisure consumption and behaviour during the middle years of the twentieth century. Analysis of holiday footage shot

---

[85] Stone and Streible, "Small Gauge and Amateur Film", 125.
[86] "Found" material, free of direct associated contextual evidence has paradoxically accrued new meaning and value through re-contextualisation in the work of contemporary visual artists. See Forgács, "Wittgenstein Tracatus", 47-56; Fung, "Remaking Home Movies", 29-40; Abraham, "Deteriorating Memories", 168-184; Nakamura and Ishizuka, "Something Strong Within", 98-106.

between 1925 and 1950 now readily connects to issues of class relations and social formation, as well as changing patterns of work and recreation. Family holiday films also strengthen our understanding of domestic relations, family culture and the daily routines of patriarchy. Cine film emerges primarily as a middle-class male pursuit that often occurred within a family setting, where the filmmaker also frequently expected family involvement as subject matter or subsequent audience member.

Largely overlooked until recently because of its sheer ubiquity, the holiday film's frequently clichéd content has become worthy of analysis, and its distinctive formal characteristics understood in increasingly aesthetic as well as instrumental terms. Often mocked for being of poor quality and of limited wider interest, such amateur film's typically informal, unofficial focus upon past worlds of personal and private experience, now valorises its record as a window upon particular ways of seeing and being seen, and the processes of identity-formation implicit in these processes. Long neglected within studies of visual history, the formerly derided subjectivities and clichéd scenes of holiday films now attract attention from geographers, anthropologists, and sociologists as well as from historians with interests in media, tourism, leisure, landscape and social and cultural change.[87]

Holiday film offers much more than a socio-cultural history constructed through moving pictures. Rather, these individual visual stories offer ways of building more inclusive, multi-voiced and multi-visioned interpretations of past experiences, in the demand that they make for synthetic approaches drawing on a broad range of disciplines. Where sequences feature activities and experiences shared between parents, siblings, or as part an extended family group, the analysis may benefit from insights derived from studies of gender, psychology, autobiography,

---

[87] Zimmermann's *Reel Families*, and Odin's *Le Film De Famille*, gave significant impetus to critical writing on amateur cinema on both sides of the Atlantic. See also Kapstein, ed. *Jubilee Book* and Kattelle, *Home Movies: A History of The American Industry*, for invaluable surveys. Liz Czach compiles a useful range of publications on amateur film and home movies in "Selected Bibliography", 299-307; a bibliography by Compton, 252-27, formed the basis for a regularly updated bibliography for the Small Gauge and Amateur Film Interest Group within the Association of Moving Image Archivists (AMIA), now available at www.amianet.org/groups/interest/smallgauge/about.php. Within Europe's own expanding body of literature, see Tousignant, *Le Film De Famille*; Aasman, *Ritueel Van Huiselijk Geluk*; Enticknap, *Moving Image Technology*; Tenkanen, "Cine Films in Youth Work" and "Searching for a 9.5mm Family", also contain useful bibliographies.

and the politics of identity.[88] Footage that involves being elsewhere may also connect with issues of post-colonialism, travel narration and representation.[89] Indeed amateur cine footage is such an expression of twentieth century touristic behaviour, so closely connected to continuing trends in personal image-making via camcorders, mobile phones and other digital technologies, that it has a formative role in what Mazierska and Walton have called the emergent world of "liquid modernity".[90]

The amount of attention devoted to holiday-related films within amateur cine's hobby literature, indicates that travel-related genres did not develop within a visual vacuum. Its makers and viewers seem unlikely to have been isolated from real and fictive place identities mediated by other visual, written and cinematic sources including newsreels, documentary, promotional, educational, and commercial feature films. Home-produced travelogues and the sharing of holiday footage were produced and consumed within a wider visual context that was much influenced by prevailing professional, commercial and technical debates elsewhere. As the mapping of links, participants, and areas of shared debate continues, the interplay of similarities and differences between professional cinematic activity and the early enthusiasts become clearer too.[91] Such links help to place understanding of holiday films within a more nuanced reading of cinematic histories elaborated at national and international levels.

The aesthetic dimension of amateur travel-related films, despite the obvious opportunities for experimenting with light, materials and visual form in different localities, has attracted rather less academic attention so far than their apparent testimony to past realities. Arguably, the visual aesthetics of place representation in still photographs, as discussed by Schwartz and Ryan, and Gregory, readily transfer to the interpretation of travel-related cine film dating from the early decades of the last century.[92]

---

[88] See for example Chalfen, *Snapshot Versions of Life*; Irurralde, "Amateur Filmmaking, Collective Memory and Cultural Identity"; Citron, *Movies and Other Necessary Fictions*; Szczelkun, "Amateur Film/Home Movies/Underground Film".

[89] Norris Nicholson, "Telling Travellers' Tales", Abraham, "Deteriorating Memories", 168-184; Odin, *Le Film De Famille*. Comparative perspectives are offered by Motrescu, "British Colonial Identity in Amateur Films", and also by her work with material at The British Empire & Commonwealth Museum, Bristol, England, available at: www.imagesofempire.com.

[90] See Mazierska and Walton, "Tourism and The Moving Image", 10; see also Urry, *The Tourist Gaze*, 142.

[91] See Norris Nicholson, "Floating Hotels: Cruise Holidays and Amateur Film-Making in the Interwar Period".

[92] See Schwartz and Ryan, "Photography and The Geographical Imagination", and Gregory, "Emperors of The Gaze".

Many post-colonial issues associated with the politics of late-imperial travel encounters,[93] and picture-making impulses apply to both still and moving imagery.[94] Yet, the very nature of moving imagery, and its capacity to replicate successive moments of action and visual encounter, extends the gaze beyond the limits of the single frame.

Amateur cine users were pioneers in their use of the new medium and, like the professionals that they sometimes sought to emulate, their holiday output reflected their explorations of what was possible and interesting to film and screen. Perhaps their collective records of holiday experiences helped to democratise the process of travel itself; certainly they helped to establish principles of holiday recording in moving imagery that inform the use of today's visual technologies in making and shaping holiday memories and tourist behaviours. Undoubtedly cine films have played a part in the cultural consumption of landscapes and lifestyles by tourists, and perhaps even in the rising popularity of particular destinations in the second half of the last century. Could these distinctive media histories of past touristic practice help to uncover the earlier identities of settlements and communities now transformed by tourism? Have the informal visions of people and places captured in outsiders' holiday memories also a value in being repatriated as part of visual histories that belong elsewhere? This chapter set out to make a case for the inclusion of holiday footage within the critical study of amateur film. I conclude by restating my belief that the holiday imagery of Britain's twentieth century amateur cinema is an important archive still ripe for further exploration.

Works Cited

Aasman, S. *Ritueel Van Huiselijk Geluk: Een Cultuurhistorische Verkenning Van De Familiefilm*. Amsterdam: Spinhuis, 2004.
Abraham, A. "Deteriorating Memories. Blurring Fact and Fiction in Home Movies in India." In *Mining the Home Movie: Excavations in Histories and Memories*, edited by Karen L. Ishizuka and Patricia R. Zimmermann, 168-184. Berkeley: University of California Press, 2007.
Advertisements. *Amateur Cine World* 6, no. 2 (1939): 104.
Anon. "A Holiday Photographic Competition for Motorists." *The Amateur Photographer and Cinematographer* 64, no. 2017 (1927): 15.

---

[93] See Pratt, *Imperial Eyes: Travel Writing and Transculturation*, and Sharp, "Writing Travel/Travel Writing".
[94] See Ryan, "Imperial Landscapes", 1997, and Doherty, "The Age of Exploration: The Hollywood Travelogue Film".

Anon. "Car, Caravan and Camera." *The Amateur Photographer and Cinematographer* 64, no. 2020 (1927): 21.
Anon. "£7m. Increase in Amateur Photography Expenditure." *The Guardian* (26 January 1966): 12.
Babcock, F. Lawrence. *Spanning the Atlantic*. New York: Alfred H. Knopf, 1931.
Baldick, Christopher. *The Modern Movement, 1910-1940. The Oxford Literary History, Volume 10.* Oxford: Oxford University Press, 2000.
Baumeister, Roy F. *Identity, Cultural Change and the Struggle for Self.* New York: Oxford University Press, 1986.
Bendit, Phoebe D. and Laurence J. Bendit. *Living Together Again*. London: Gramol, 1946.
Bhabha, Homi K. "Interrogating Identity: The Post-Colonial Prerogative." In *Identity: A Reader*, edited by Paul du Gay, Jessica Evans and Peter Redman, 95-10. London: Sage, 2000.
Brendon, Piers. *Thomas Cook: 150 Years of Popular Tourism*. London: Secker and Warburg, 1991.
Campbell, B. "The Almost Universal Hobby", *The Observer* (1 December 1963): 33.
Casey, Edward S. *The Fate of Place: A Philosophical History*. Berkeley and Los Angeles: University of California Press, 1998.
Chalfen, Richard. *Snapshot Versions of Life*. Bowling Green, Ohio: Bowling Green State University Popular Press, 1987.
Chambers, Deborah. "Family as Place: Family Photograph Albums and the Domestication of Public and Private Space." In *Picturing Place: Photography and the Geographical Imagination*, edited by Joan M. Schwartz and James R. Ryan, 96-114. London: I. B. Tauris, 2003.
Chard, Chloe. *Pleasure and Guilt on the Grand Tour: Travel Writing and Imaginative Geographies, 1600-1830*. Manchester: Manchester University Press, 1999.
Chislett, Charles J. "Air Cruise to the Lebanon, Syria and Jordan." *Rotary in the Ridings* 35, no. 3 (1964): 15-18.
Citron, Michelle. *Home Movies and Other Necessary Fictions*. Minneapolis: University of Minnesota Press, 1998.
—. *Loneliness and Time: British Travel Writing in the Twentieth Century*. London: Secker and Warburg, 1992.
"Club Sec." "Cinematography at the Zoo." *Amateur Photographer and Cinematographer* ["Correspondence" Section] 64, no. 2020 (1927): 37.
Compton, Margaret, ed. "Small Gauge and Amateur Film Bibliography." *Film History* 15, no. 2 (2003): 252-271.

Cutter, Valerie. *Go East Young Man: from Lancashire to Shanghai by Steamship*. London: Regency Press, 1985.
Czach, Liz. "Selected Bibliography." In *Mining the Home Movie: Excavations in Histories and Memories*, edited by Karen L. Ishizuka and Patricia R. Zimmermann, 299-307. Berkeley: University of California Press, 2007.
Doherty, Thomas. "The Age of Exploration: The Hollywood Travelogue Film." *Cinéaste* 20, no. 2 (1993): 38-40.
Enticknap, Leo. *Moving Image Technology: from Zoetrope to Digital*. London: Wallflower Press, 2005.
Feifer, Maxine. *Going Places. The Ways of the Tourist from Imperial Rome to the Present Day*. New York: Stein and Day, 1985.
Forgács, Péter. "Wittgenstein Tractatus: Personal Reflections on Home Movies." In *Mining the Home Movie: Excavations in Histories and Memories*, edited by Karen L. Ishizuka and Patricia R. Zimmermann, 47-56. Berkeley: University of California Press, 2007.
Fung, Richard. "Remaking Home Movies." In *Mining the Home Movie: Excavations in Histories and Memories*, edited by Karen L. Ishizuka and Patricia R. Zimmermann, 29-40. Berkeley: University of California Press, 2007.
Giddens, Anthony. "The Trajectory of the Self." In *Identity: A Reader*, edited by Paul du Gay, Jessica Evans and Peter Redman, 248-266. London: Sage, 2000.
Gregory, Derek. "Colonial Nostalgia and Cultures of Travel: Spaces of Constructed Visibility." In *Consuming Tradition, Manufacturing Heritage: Global Norms and Urban Forms in the Age of Tourism*, edited by Nezar Alsayyad, 111-151. London: Routledge, 2001.
—. "Emperors of the Gaze: Photographic Practices and Productions of Space in Egypt, 1839-1914." In *Picturing Place: Photography and the Geographical Imagination*, edited by Joan M. Schwartz and James R. Ryan, 195-225. London: I.B. Tauris, 2003.
Hall, Stuart. "Who Needs Identity?" In *Identity: A Reader*, edited by Paul du Gay, Jessica Evans and Peter Redman, 16-30. London: Sage, 2000.
Hanley, Lynne. *Writing War: Fiction, Gender and Memory*. Amherst: University of Massachusetts Press, 1991.
Harbour, R. H. "Holidays Afloat." *Amateur Cine World* 1, no. 4 (1934): 154-155.
Hughes, H. *Words on War: Memories of the Home Front during the Second World War from the People of the Kirklees Area*. Huddersfield: Kirklees Cultural Services/Kirklees Sound Archive, 1991.

Irurralde, E. Rebello. "Amateur Filmmaking, Collective Memory and Cultural Identity" (first published as "Cine Amateur, Memorias Colectivas e Identidades Culturales." *EnteleQuia* Catholic University of Uruguay, July 1995). Available at : http://www.wacc.org.uk/wacc/publications/media_development/archive/1996_4/amateur_film_making_collective_memory_and_cultural_identity

Kapstein, Nancy, ed. *Jubilee Book: Essays on Amateur Film.* Charleroi: Association Européenne Inédits, 1997.

Kattelle, Alan. *Home Movies: A History of the American Industry 1897-1979.* Nashua, New Hampshire: Transition Publishing, 2000.

Malthouse, Gordon. "Cinematography in Wartime." In *Amateur Cine World Diary,* edited by Gordon Malthouse. London: Link House Publications, 1941.

—. "Equipments, Materials, Technical Developments, Services." *Amateur Cine World* 19, no. 1 (1955): 40-43.

—. "Quantity and Quality." *Amateur Cine World* 23, no. 4 (1959): 326-329.

Mazierska, Ewa and John Walton. "Tourism and the Moving Image." *Tourist Studies* 6, no. 1 (2006): 5-11.

Motrescu, Annamaria. "British Colonial Identity in Amateur Films from India and Australia, 1920-1940s." Ph.D. diss., Department of Drama, University of Bristol, 2007.

Nakaruma, R. A. and Karen L. Ishizuka. "Something Strong Within: A Visual Essay." In *Mining the Home Movie: Excavations in Histories and Memories,* edited by Karen L. Ishizuka and Patricia R. Zimmermann, 98-106. Berkeley: University of California Press, 2007.

Newens, Frank R. "Exposures for your Colour Cruise Film." *Amateur Cine World* 6, no. 3 (1939): 119-121.

Newnham, Grahame. "The Pathéscope Ace 9.5mm Cine Projector." *9.5 Magazine* (2006): 125. Available at: http://www.pathefilm.freeserve.co.uk/95ninefive.htm

Norris Nicholson, Heather. "In Amateur Hands: Framing Time and Space in Home Movies." *History Workshop Journal* 43 (1997): 198-212.

—. "Seeing It How It Was? Childhood, Memory and Identity in Home-Movies." *Area* 33, no. 2 (2001): 128-140.

—. "Picturing the Past: Archival Film and Historical Landscape Change." *Landscapes* 3, no. 1 (2002): 81-100.

—. "Telling Travellers' Tales: Framing the World in Home Movies, c.1935-1967." In *Engaging Film: Geographies of Mobility and*

Identity, edited by Tim Cresswell and Deborah Dixon, 47-68. Lanham, ML.: Rowman & Littlefield, 2002.
—. "British Holiday Films of the Mediterranean: At Home and Abroad with Home Movies, c. 1925-1936." *Film History* 15, no. 2 (2003):102-116.
—. "At Home and Abroad with Cine Enthusiasts: Regional Amateur Filmmaking and Visualizing the Mediterranean, c.1928-1962." *Geo Journal* 59, no. 4 (2004): 323-333.
—. "'Through the Balkan States: Home Movies as Travel Texts and Tourism Histories." *Tourist Studies* 6, no. 1 (2006): 13-36.
—. "Sites of Meaning: Picturing Mediterranean and other Landscapes in British Home Movies, c.1928-1965." In *Landscape and Film*, edited by Martin Lefebvre, 167-188. London: Routledge, 2006.
—. "Shooting the Mediterranean: Conflict, Compassion and Amateur Filmmaking in the Mediterranean, c.1925-1939." *Journal of Intercultural Studies* 27, no. 3 (2006): 313-330.
—. "'As if by Magic': Authority, Aesthetics and Visions of the Work Place in Home Movies". In *Mining the Home Movie: Excavations in Histories and Memories*, edited by Karen L. Ishizuka and Patricia R. Zimmermann, 214-230. Berkeley: University of California Press, 2007.
—. "Floating Hotels: Cruise Holidays and Amateur Film-Making in the Inter-War Period." In *Moving Pictures/Stopping Places: Hotels & Motels on Film*, edited by Dave Clarke and Valerie Crawford Pfannhauser. London: Wallflower, 2008/9. (in progress)
—. "Journeys into Seeing: Russian and Soviet Encounters and Footage from the North West Film Archive, 1932-1965." *New Readings*. School of European Studies, Cardiff University, 2008/9. (forthcoming)
—. *Visual Pleasures: Leisure, Society and Britain's Amateur Film Movement c.1923-1977.*" Manchester: Manchester University Press, 2009. (forthcoming)
Odin, Roger. *Le Film de Famille: Usage Privé, Usage Public.* Paris: Editions Méridiens Klincksieck et Cie, 1995.
Orwell, George. "The Lion and the Unicorn: Socialism and the English Genius. Part One: England, Your England." In *The Collected Essays, Journalism and Letters of George Orwell Volume 2: My Country Right or Left 1940-1943*, edited by Sonia Orwell and Ian Angus, 74-133. Harmondsworth: Penguin, 1968.
Powell, R. and D. Wood. *Ordnance Survey Leisure Guide. Lake District. Basingstoke and Southampton.* London: Automobile Association and Ordnance Survey, 1984.

Pratt, Mary-Louise. *Imperial Eyes: Travel Writing and Transculturation.* London and New York, Routledge, 1992.

Rabinbach, Anson. *The Human Motor: Energy, Fatigue, and the Origins of Modernity.* Berkeley and Los Angeles: University of California Press, 1992.

Rollier, Augustus. *Heliotherapy.* London: Henry Frowde and Hodder & Stoughton, 1923.

Ryan, James R. "Imperial Landscapes: Photography, Geography and British Overseas Exploration, 1785-1872." In *Geography and Imperialism, 1820-1940,* edited by Morag Bell, Robin Butlin and Michael Heffernan, 53-79. Manchester: Manchester University Press, 1995.

—. *Picturing Empire: Photography and the Visualization of the British Empire.* Chicago: University of Chicago Press, 1997.

Schwartz, Joan M., and James R. Ryan. "Photography and the Geographical Imagination." In *Picturing Place: Photography and the Geographical Imagination,* edited by Joan M. Schwartz and James R. Ryan, 1-18. London: I. B. Tauris, 2003.

Shand, Ryan. "'Worth Remembering': Why *Around Wick Harbour 74/75* is Important." *The Drouth* 15 (2005): 53-56.

Sharp, Joanne P. "Writing Travel/Travelling Writing: Roland Barthes detours the Orient." *Environment and Planning D. Society and Space* 20 (2002):156-166.

Sontag, Susan. *On Photography.* Harmondsworth: Penguin, 1979.

Sowerby, Arthur Lindsey McRae. "End of Price Control." *Amateur Photographer* 3177 (28 September 1949): 685.

Stewart, Susan A. *On Longing: Narratives of the Miniature, the Gigantic, the Souvenir, the Collection.* Durham, North Carolina: Duke University Press, 1993.

Stone, Melinda and Dan Streible. "Small-Gauge and Amateur Film." *Film History* 15, no. 2 (2003): 123-125.

Szczelkun, Stefan. "Amateur Film/Home Movies/Underground Film." *Oral History Society Journal* 28, no. 2 (2000): 94-98.

Tenkanen, Salla. "Cine Films in Youth Work." In *Swings, Films, Clubs and Tattoos. An Ethnologic Approach to Youth Culture,* edited by Minna Heikkinen, 55-74. Turku: Turku Provincial Museum Publication Series 11, 2006.

—. "Searching for a 9.5mm Family—Aspects on the Privacy of Home Movies." *Ethnologia Fennica* 26, no. 3 (2006): 24-31.

Todorova, Maria. *Imagining the Balkans.* New York: Oxford University Press, 1997.

—. "What Is Or Is There A Balkan Culture, And Do Or Should The Balkans Have A Regional Identity?" *Journal of South East European and Black Sea Studies* 4, no. 1 (2004): 175-185.

Tousignant, Nathalie. *Le Film De Famille: Actes de la Rencontre Autour des Inédits tenue a Bruxelles en Novembre 2000*. Brussels: Facultés Universitaires Saint-Louis, 2004.

Towner, John. *An Historical Geography of Recreation & Tourism, 1540-1940*. Chichester: John Wiley, 1996.

Urry, John. *The Tourist Gaze*. London: Sage, 2002.

Walton, John. *The British Seaside: Holidays and Resorts in the Twentieth Century*. Manchester: Manchester University Press, 2000.

—. *The Playful Crowd: Pleasure Places in the Twentieth Century*. New York: Columbia University Press, 2005.

Walton, John, ed. *Histories of Tourism: Representation, Identity and Conflict*. Clevedon: Channel View Press, 2005.

Walvin, James. *Leisure and Society, 1830-1950*. New York: Longman, 1978.

Waters, Chris. "'Dark Strangers' in Our Midst: Discourses of Race and Nation in Britain, 1947-1963." *Journal of British Studies* 36, no. 2 (1997): 207-238.

Zimmermann, Patricia R. *Reel Families: A Social History of Amateur Film*. Bloomington and Indianapolis: Indiana University Press, 1995.

Films Cited

NB: Titles in square brackets have been assigned during cataloguing by archive staff, and refer primarily to locations filmed. Film dates indicate the age of the film stock, where shooting date is uncertain.

[*Arandora Star Cruise 1931—Tangier and Oporto*]
    (John Barker Scarr, 1931) 16mm., 14 mins. 24 secs.
[*Arandora Star Cruise 1931—North Africa*]
    (John Barker Scarr, 1931) 16mm., 14 mins. 57 secs.
Barcelona
    (Preston Brothers, 1928/35) 16mm., 17 mins. 43 secs.
[*Casablanca and Shipboard Scenes*]
    (John Barker Scarr, 1931) 16mm., 14 mins. 57 secs.
Charming Switzerland, 1949
    (J. H. Haffner, 1949) 16mm., 22 mins. 13 secs.
Dale Days
    (Charles Chislett, 1942) 16mm., 70 mins.

English Journey
(Charles Chislett, 1950) 16mm., 70 mins.
Europe as we saw it—June 1938 [Parts 1 & 2]
(John Barker Scarr, 1938) 16mm., 29 mins. 08 secs.
The Family Explores Lakeland
(Charles Chislett, 1940) 16mm., 70mins.
Gallipoli: A Pilgrimage Cruise, May 1934 [Parts 1 & 2]
(Lt. Col. James Fitzwilliam O'Grady, 1934) 16mm., 22 mins. 31 secs.
[*Go East Young Man*—Parts 1-6]
(John Hindley, 1927) 16mm., 66 mins.
Hindley family scenes and Blackpool
(John Hindley, 1934/36) 16mm., 13 mins. 30 secs.
Holiday in Italy, September/October 1926
(Leonard Behrens, 1926) 16mm., 5 mins. 45 secs.
International Colonial Exhibition in Paris 1931
(Preston Brothers, 1931) 16mm., 10 mins. 29 secs.
Isle of Man—For Holidays
(Preston Brothers, 1933) 16mm., 14 mins. 49 secs.
Lakeland Holiday, Borrowdale, September 1948
(Peter Sykes, 1948) 16mm., 11 mins. 49 secs.
Las Palmas: The Capitol of Grand Canary [Part 3]
(Preston Brothers, 1928) 16mm., 14 mins. 44 secs.
Let's Go to Wales
(Charles Chislett, 1952) 16mm., 35 mins.
Maiden Voyage
(Charles Chislett, 1936) 16mm., 40 mins.
Mediterranean Cruise; SS Arandora Star May 1933 [Parts 1-3]
(John Barker Scarr, 1933) 16mm., 33 mins. 13 secs.
Mediterranean Cruise; SS Arandora Star May 1934 [Parts 1 & 2]
(John Barker Scarr, 1934) 16mm., 36 mins. 08 secs.
Mediterranean Cruise; SS Arandora Star May 1935 [Parts 1 & 2]
(John Barker Scarr, 1935) 30 mins. 15 secs.
Norway, June 1950
(J. H. Haffner, 1950) 16mm., 18 mins. 09 secs.
On Holiday in Germany and Switzerland
(George Higginson, 1937) 16mm., 28 mins. 57 secs.
On the Banks of the River Aude
(Reginald Rigby, c.1930s) 9.5mm.,11 mins. 10 secs.
On The Rhine
(Arthur Riley, 1934/5) 16mm., 11 mins. 28 secs.

Orient Line Cruise [on board the Orama]
(Preston Brothers, 1932/33) 16mm., 16 mins. 40 secs.
Orient Line SS Orama Cruising Lisbon
(Preston Brothers, 1932/33) 16mm., 14 mins. 26 secs.
Orient Line Cruise: Leaving Lisbon, We Arrive in Gilbraltar
(Preston Brothers, 1933/35) 16mm., 16mins. 59 secs.
[Orient Sea Liner SS Orama at Sea]
(Preston Brothers, 1932/4) 16mm., 12 mins. 35 secs.
Orient Line Cruise Tatuan and Ceuta
(Preston Brothers, 1933) 16mm., 13 mins. 39 secs.
[Palma and Mallorca]
(Preston Brothers, 1933) 16mm., 15 mins. 39 secs.
P & O Cruise of the Mediterranean May/June 1932
(Preston Brothers, 1932) 16mm., 16mins. 55 secs.
Peninsular & Orient Steam Navigation Co. Mediterranean Cruise to Ceuta, Monte Carlo, Palma & Barcelona, Vigo, London, by the turbo-electric ship Vice-Roy of India, 20,000 tonnes.
(Preston Brothers, 1932) 16mm., 13 mins. 07 secs.
Preston Family—Cruise Holiday 1928
(Preston Brothers, 1928) 16mm., 10 mins.
[The Preston Family In Paris]
(Preston Brothers, 1937) 16mm., 11 mins. 07 secs.
[The Preston Family's Trip To The Zoo]
(Preston Brothers, 1933/35) 16mm., 11 mins. 15 secs.
The Preston Family Visit Naples and Pompeii
(Preston Brothers, 1932/33) 16mm., 16 mins. 48 secs.
Rachel Discovers England
(Charles Chislett, 1937) 16mm., 35mins.
Rachel Discovers The Sea
(Charles Chislett, 1939) 16mm., 17 mins.
Royal Mail Line Cruise. M.V. Asturias (22,500 tonnes) to Spain, Madeira and the Canaries Part 1. Leaving Southampton June 22 1928
(Preston Brothers, 1928) 16mm., 15 mins. 53 secs.
Scottish Holiday
(Charles Chislett, 1939) 16mm., 70 mins.
Scottish September (Charles Chislett, 1948), 16mm., 70mins.
Southern Railway Depart London, Victoria. Golden Arrow [for the 1931 International Colonial Exhibition in Paris] (Preston Brothers, 1930-31/39) 16mm., 10 mins. 12 secs.
[Sykes family holiday in the Lake District]
(Peter Sykes, 1949) 16mm., 5 mins. 57 secs.

The Story of an Air-Cruise to Syria, Lebanon and Jordan
(Charles Chislett, 1963) 16mm., 75 mins.
Touring Europe By Car—June 1937 [Parts 1 & 2]
(John Barker Scarr, 1937) 16mm., 33 mins. 39 secs.
Tour in the USSR [Parts 1 & 2]
(H. W. Taylor, 1932) 16mm., 19 mins. 38 secs.
2400 Miles Continental Journey/The Car/The Mayflower
(J. H. Haffner, 1948-52) 16mm., 28 mins. 32 secs.
[*A Visit to The Paris International Colonial Exhibition, 1931*]
(Preston Brothers, 1931) 16mm., 15 mins. 08 secs.
Weekend in Italy (also called *Senator Films presents Florence and Milan, August 1949*)
(A. Senat, 1949) 16mm., 10mins. 23 secs.
[*Whipsnade Zoo*]
(J. H. Haffner, 1934/36/44/52) 16mm., 8 mins. 21 secs.
Whitby—Family On The Sands
(Charles Chislett, 1935) 16mm., 12 mins.
Zoological Gardens
(Preston Brothers, 1934) 16mm., 8 mins. 18 secs.[3]

PART II

CONTROVERSIES

CHAPTER FOUR

PUTTING FILM ON NOTTINGHAM'S CULTURAL MAP: FILM PRODUCTION AND THE FESTIVAL OF BRITAIN

MELANIE SELFE

This chapter explores some of the issues and motivations involved when amateur films are produced under the umbrella of an exhibition-centred organisation. Its main focus is on the production section of the Nottingham and District Film Society (NDFS), a provincial group founded in 1945 at the start of the British film society movement's post-war boom. In particular, it explores the ways in which a film made for the local Festival of Britain (FOB) celebrations was used to try to secure a position for the NDFS—and for the medium of cinema—within the officially sanctioned cultural life of the city. To this end, analysis of the film, *Old Market Square* (1951), is framed within a number of layered contexts: the aims of the film society movement, the multiple meanings of the FOB, and the spectrum of film and non-film related activities planned as local festival events. Mapping what Doreen Massey has termed the "relational geography" of this highly regionalised amateur cine culture,[1] *Old Market Square* is located within a complex network of perceptions of place and power—from the national to the most local—seen as affecting both the choice of subject for the Nottingham film, and the way in which it was portrayed and presented for the local audience.

The story of the amateur-run film society movement in the UK remains a largely unwritten history, running parallel to the trajectory of amateur cine production. In common with the latter tradition, it encompasses a small number of politically and/or aesthetically radical elements, which

---

[1] Massey, *Space, Place and Gender*, Allen et. al., *Rethinking The Region*.

have received perhaps disproportionate academic attention—whilst the normative and less radical activities of the broader film society movement remain largely neglected by current scholarship. Within this volume, Richard MacDonald's chapter provides an illuminating introduction to the aims and practices of the movement in the post-war period, which for the purposes of this essay, can be well and quickly characterised by the Federation of Film Societies' (FFS') own published list of "objects":

> 1. To encourage interest in the film as an art and as a medium of information and education.
> 2. To promote the study and appreciation of films by means of lectures, discussions, and exhibitions.
> 3. The Society shall be non-political and non-profit-making.[2]

In practice, this meant that the monthly Sunday meetings of the NDFS and its like filled in gaps left by the local commercial exhibition sector. Within an ethos of cultural enrichment, the group provided its members with access to contemporary foreign cinema, documentaries, silent classics and older sound titles. Through regular programme notes, these selected "cultural films" were framed within a narrative of the historical development of the medium as an art form: "masterworks" were defined, reading was recommended, and debate and discussion of key topics was encouraged. Although the group followed FFS guidelines, and constructed itself as pointedly apolitical, members shared with the broader movement a sense that the viewing and discussion of cinema from other nations (at the time, still overwhelmingly European) could help to foster a positive humanitarian climate of international understanding.

Early Production and Festival Preparation

The NDFS Film Production section emerged naturally from the personal interests of a small sub-set of existing film society members. Although the numbers actively involved were few,[3] through their involvement in

---

[2] Cottrill, *The Handbook of the Federation of Film Societies*, 15.
[3] Although in 1947, thirty-seven film society members had signed up for the production section, the group secretary noted that "the number of really enthusiastic members is rather less than this figure". Report of the Activities of the Amateur Film Production Section of the Nottingham & District Film Society (NDFS), 1947, M12 390, Nottinghamshire County Archive (NCA). Anecdotal reports support this, and those who were actively involved in production numbered less than a dozen.

council-sponsored civic events the section was able to make a major contribution to the public visibility of the society. Examination of their projects provides a remarkable insight into the amateur spirit of the film society as a whole, and a particularly clear expression of their combined ideals of active leisure and public service.

As Jamie Sexton's work on films produced by individuals involved with the pioneering [London] Film Society (1925-1939) has demonstrated, the filmmaking practiced by those active within exhibition-centred societies can be understood as an extended forum for critical debates taking place within the larger group. Similarly, the films produced in such contexts can be seen to share and advance the same priorities and cultural ethos as the film exhibition agenda.[4] But where the main aims of the artists/writers and "off-duty" film professionals considered by Sexton (Ivor Montagu, Adrian Brunel and the like), were to influence the future aesthetic evolution of film form, the priorities of the Nottingham & District filmmakers—and indeed much of the post-war film society movement—went beyond merely artistic concerns, and also expressed clear social preoccupations. As a result, rather than making films that were essentially cine-literate "burlesques"—aesthetic experiments which commented critically on current filmmaking conventions—the filmmaking of the NDFS was heavily influenced by the socially-responsible British documentaries which they also favoured as viewers. In the case of the film they made for the FOB, this influence was combined with that of another staple of international, and internationalist film culture: the dawn-til-dusk "city symphony" picture.

The Production section of the Nottingham and District was established in 1947, a year in which the film society grew rapidly and was filled with optimism and ambition.[5] In their first season, a number of different projects were considered for development, each locally specific and containing some element of social purpose. Histories were proposed on lace manufacture in Nottingham, and on the Old City itself. A documentary about the River Trent was also considered, as were two titles engaging explicitly with questions of public provision and private responsibility in local civic life. "The Municipal Services" and "The Abuse of Amenities in

---

[4] Sexton, "The Film Society and the Creation of an Alternative Film Culture in Britain in the 1920s", 292-294.

[5] It was the securing of a larger venue in 1947 that enabled the membership to rise rapidly to a high of 600 in 1950. As well as the production section, and short-lived junior section, a study and discussion group was launched the same year.

the County".[6] Finally a topic was settled upon; the first film was to be a documentary simply entitled *Rural Blacksmith*.

Although no copy of *Rural Blacksmith* (1947) remains available for examination, it is clear from the group's production notes and surviving still images, that the film was heavily influenced by the professional documentary movement of the inter-war years. Moreover, the themes which would soon emerge as central to the national FOB celebrations—time and place—were already visible within this insistently local project.[7] Through the treatment of the two central characters, an old blacksmith shoeing a horse and a young blacksmith repairing a tractor, they planned to emphasise the contrast between traditional forms of 'smithing and the more modern breed of blacksmith/engineer. The final sequence was outlined thus:

> The tempo of the film will decelerate as the final sequence follows—the operation of the forge by the young 'smith. This will serve to indicate that while the modern 'smith is capable of high precision machine operation he still plies the older aspects of his trade with undiminished skill.[8]

Clearly the group wished to create a deliberate message: the film would work to express not only contrast but also continuity. Although much of the appeal of this production had lain in the picturesque filming possibilities of rural Papplewick,[9] the location also suggested thematic potential—through the harmonious embodiment in the younger blacksmith of both old and new skills, the past would not be sectioned-off, nor nostalgically lamented, but carried forward into a new and improved future. This sense of the post-war present as an optimistic meeting point between a noble, traditional past and a technologically enhanced future, would provide a core structuring theme within the national FOB celebrations of a few of years later, and would be equally visible in other local films produced for the event.[10] Following *Rural Blacksmith*, the

---

[6] NDFS Amateur Film Production Section, Notes and Agenda for March Meetings, 1947, M12 389, NCA.

[7] These are identified as core to the FOB project by Conekin, *'The autobiography of a nation': The 1951 Festival of Britain*, 80, and Hewison, *Culture and Consensus: England, Art and Politics, Since 1940*, 40.

[8] NDFS Amateur Film Production Section, Notes and Agenda for 31 October Meeting, 1947, M12 389, NCA.

[9] Papplewick is a village a few miles north of Nottingham. Its photogenic potential is discussed in NDFS Amateur Film Production Section, Notes and Agenda for 17 October Meeting, 1947, M12 389, NCA.

[10] Conekin, *'The autobiography of a nation': The 1951 Festival of Britain*, 80.

group honed their skills shooting basic record footage of local events, before the next documentary proper to be undertaken, entitled *Nottingham: Variations on a Theme*, was completed in 1949.[11] This was shot in and around the city itself, and included a sequence showing the film society at work. The result enabled the group to gain local press attention that could subsequently be used to frame the work of the film society.

Whilst the NDFS production section was learning its craft, the city of Nottingham Corporation (latterly the City Council) was also gaining valuable expertise, specifically in the management of large civic events. With the FOB in 1951 and the Coronation in 1953, the early 1950s were a boom period for symbolic national celebrations. However, in 1949, the City of Nottingham had already had the advantage of a local practice run. That year had marked the city's Quincentennial, with a special committee formed to plan a wide range of festive and cultural events.[12] Although records mark a desire to include some sort of film element within this programme, in contrast with the case of music and theatre, little automatic or obvious sense of the form this should take seems to have emerged.

Following an approach by a professional filmmaker, a commercially-made production was considered, but the price quoted for the preferred choice—a film depicting Nottingham—proved prohibitively expensive (£1,500). As an alternative, the cheaper option of a short film of the Lord Mayor giving an interview was eventually commissioned. Although probably rather drier in flavour, this cost less than £90, including prints.[13] The desire to screen archive footage of Nottingham was also discussed by the committee, but although members were aware that the Lord Mayor's secretary had been filming civic occasions on an amateur basis over a number of years, no action arose from this information.[14] The Quincentenary Committee did however approve filming requests from two outside bodies: an offer from Gaumont British News to make a film of the celebrations for commercial exhibition at the local News Theatre—

---

[11] The survival of this title is uncertain, and no archive copy is currently available.
[12] Nottingham City Corporation Records, Special Committee Reports. Minutes of the Quintcentenary Executive Committee meetings 19 November 1948-19 July 1949, CA/CM/60(misc)/13, NCA,
[13] Nottingham City Corporation Records, Special Committee Reports. Minutes of the Quintcentenary Executive Committee meetings, 23 February 1949, CA/CM/60(misc)/13, NCA. I have not managed to locate this film but cannot imagine it was an entertaining success.
[14] Nottingham City Corporation Records, Special Committee Reports. Minutes of the Quintcentenery Executive Committee meetings, 28 January 1949, CA/CM/60(misc)/13, NCA.

eventually released as *Quincentenary Celebrations* (1949), and a request from the Nottingham Amateur Cine Society to film the River Carnival. Clearly, the committee were open to such film-related suggestions, but perhaps lacked the knowledge or the means to shape them. As a result the medium's actual presence within the celebrations was somewhat *ad hoc* and uncoordinated.

The Festival of Britain in Nottingham

The Festival of Britain was a far more complex celebration than either the Nottingham Quincentennial or the subsequent Coronation. Spanning the summer of 1951 (May-September) its centrepiece was the main London South Bank exhibition site, where achievements in industry and culture were showcased for the nation and the visiting world. The representations of region visible within the main site were somewhat predictably confined however to celebrations of landscapes, landmarks and the goods produced by a particular area.[15] Outside London however the picture was inevitably more complex. A centrally organised touring exhibition visited the major industrial cities of Manchester, Leeds, Birmingham and Nottingham, and locally organised celebrations were planned and executed in cities, towns and villages all over the country. This combination of nationally and locally organised elements meant that a more layered representation of place became visible within each locale. As the final destination for the touring exhibition and the nearest city to the officially designated "Festival Village" of Trowell, Nottingham was something of a FOB hotspot at the end of the summer, and it is as part of this overall mix that the locally planned events must be considered.[16]

Unlike the Great Exhibition a hundred years before, which had functioned as an expression of the might and reach of the British Empire, the 1951 celebration looked inward, aiming to be "an act of national autobiography". In her social history of the festival, Becky Conekin assesses the complex relationships between place and power that this ambitious brief threw up. She argues that although the local was conceived at a central level as being essential to the festival's success, some members of the organising committee soon found it a cause for concern. While the director of the Science Dome feared, for example, that the local events might undermine the message of the festival, others worried that left to

---

[15] These priorities were reinforced by a series of thirteen books brought out to coincide with the festival, entitled *About Britain*. See for example volume 8; Hoskins, *East Midlands and The Peak*.

[16] The Travelling Exhibition's Nottingham run was 15 September to 6 October.

their own devices, the regions would simply not come up with anything. This belief was fuelled in part by anxieties concerning the levels of indigenous culture and civic pride in provincial towns and cities.[17] Conekin quotes Jacquetta Hawkes, the "theme convener" for the South Bank's "People of Britain" displays, who worried about the paucity of (already) post-industrial provincial culture, describing it as an "urban culture which is highly complex, yet not creatively embodied in the people themselves", before adding, of the provincial citizenry:

> Everything is supplied for them from outside, whether by the State, the merchant or the purveyor of entertainment. The individual, especially the man, does not possess culture, cannot express it, but merely receives it in a spoon, paid for from his purse.[18]

In this, it is possible to see the rationale for encouraging a "handmade" festival, crafted at local level to express a myriad of different British places—and to express them differently. However Hawkes' longing for a pre-industrial age was not representative of the festival as a whole, which as Conekin argues, achieved a more sympathetic and "mutually reinforcing" synthesis of past and future, similar to that already evident in the production notes for *Rural Blacksmith*.[19] This was certainly appropriate to inscriptions of Nottingham and its environs. As a textile production area, busily developing new and desirable fabrics, Nottingham was well represented in the trades' shows, and justifiable industrial pride was reinforced at cultural levels. Trowell's selection as festival village was based not on it being a Cotswolds-style "show village" of perfectly preserved rural beauty, untouched by industrialisation; instead it was to be "a representative of English community", firmly located in 1951, not 1851.[20] Likewise in Nottingham itself, the focus was on creating a history of the contemporary city and its people rather than, for instance, focusing in a dislocated way on Robin Hood and the pageantry of Merrie England. In particular, through its emphasis on the previous one hundred years, the City's celebrations embraced its industrial past, recognised its manufacturing present and pointed forward towards an optimistic future.

---

[17] Conekin, *'The autobiography of a nation': The 1951 Festival of Britain*, 155-156.
[18] Quoted in Conekin, 156.
[19] Ibid., 80.
[20] Trowell Official Festival of Britain Programme, 3.

Placing Film within the Local Festival Celebrations

Towards the end of the 1949 Quincentennial, a more coherent strategy to utilise some of the film footage of the main celebrations had finally begun to emerge from the sub-committee responsible for the organisation of the very last event: a garden party at the castle, held to thank all the volunteers for their hard work. This sense of direction may have been due, in part, to the vocal presence of Jesse Boydell—city treasurer and a founding NDFS committee member. Boydell was not the only film society enthusiast who happened to be involved in the various special committees for civic celebrations. An examination of some of the other names on the planning committees of both the Quincentennial and the FOB celebrations reveals more film society activists, often present in their capacity as spokespersons for their other voluntary and professional involvements. Most notably, W. C. Boswell appeared as a representative of the Rotary Club, and the NDFS president, Vice-Chancellor Hallward, was there to represent the University. Given this unofficial film society presence, it is perhaps unsurprising that when, little more than a year later, the FOB committee came to consider their film options, the clamour of offers for piecemeal commercial enterprises were rejected, and that the NDFS was this time invited to submit a plan.[21]

It is hard to pin down quite where the impetus for this invitation originated; gaps in the chronology of the recorded discussions perhaps suggest that more informal negotiations were taking place, and that the film society did not sit back and wait to be called. Moreover, although the FOB film sub-committee which was eventually formed was composed of representatives of three local film groups—the NDFS, the Nottingham Amateur Cine Society and the Nottingham Scientific Film Society—the leading role the NDFS played in all the film events also attests to their pro-active nature. The planning and production of the filmmaking and screening events seem to have been completely dominated by NDFS personnel.

The most telling difference between the first internal Nottingham & District account of their FOB plans, and the version submitted to the FOB Special Committee, is the order in which the proposed film events are listed. In the minutes of the NDFS discussion, recorded on the 8th November 1950, the emphasis was placed on "showing films", and the plan to screen a series of titles illustrating the historical development of British cinema (to be supplied by the BFI) was more clearly articulated

---

[21] Executive Committee Minutes, 8 November 1950, point 4, M12, 342/18, NCA.

than any film production element;[22] in the proposal which moved forward to be approved by the FOB Special Committee, the emphasis had shifted somewhat, and the plan was structured as follows, to include:[23]

1. The viewing, appraisal, and editing of films of local interest held by the City Authorities, with a view to exhibition during the festival. [eventual agreed budget £60]
2. The making of a film of local interest of ten to fifteen minutes duration. The cost of film stock, materials and the necessary extra prints would be in the region of £100-£150. [eventual agreed budget for *Old Market Square*, £150]
3. The making of a record film of local activities during the Festival. The authorities to purchase the necessary film stock [eventual agreed budget, £100]
4. The organising, booking and exhibition of a Festival of British Films (16mm) upon the theme "The History of the British Film" consisting of six programmes (i.e. two programmes per week for a period of three weeks). [total agreed budget including hall hire and printing costs, £89]

In putting its case to the City, the NDFS moved the three Nottingham-specific elements to the fore. In doing so, they answered each of the film-related omissions of the earlier Quincentennial celebrations, positioning themselves as custodians of the city's film record, producers of an affordably low cost Nottingham documentary, chroniclers of the event, and then—*and only then*—as educators in the art of "film appreciation". Set out in this way, the "cultural" film exhibition which usually formed the core of the film society's work became a more minor element, piggy-backed into the festival on the more populist projects promising films of local interest. This gives some indication that the Film Society may have had concerns about the potential appeal of their usual work. As part of a wider film movement with a more highbrow and metropolitan image, they may have feared being viewed as part of the kind of centrist cultural imposition that had worried Jacquetta Hawkes. In rearranging the emphasis, they chose to demonstrate their *local* relevance and an egalitarian devotion to *local* public service.

Nottingham's total FOB film budget came to £400. Although far larger sums were reserved for the main festival site (£25,000), the publicity

---

[22] NDFS Executive Committee Minutes, 8 November 1950, point 4, M12, 342/18, NCA.

[23] Plan proposal taken from FOB Special Committee minutes, 14 November 1950. Approved budget figures taken from Scheme for Financial Control, FOB Special Committee minutes, 17 January 1951, both CA/CM/60(misc)/13, NCA.

(£2,000), and the fireworks (£1,000), the film total compared well with a music budget of £500, an education budget of £200, and a historical exhibition (museums) budget of just £160.[24] The film sub-committee had apparently been allocated funding appropriate to a significant culturally-sanctioned entertainment, almost on a par with music. However, the strongest allegiance the film unit proceeded to form within the festival celebrations was expressly social and educational in purpose. Through the topic, treatment and screening of their Nottingham films, they effectively added their weight to the museums and exhibition agenda.

One of the major selling points of the national festival was its potential to create a lasting cultural legacy. On the main South Bank site in London, this took the concrete form of the Royal Festival Hall, and the Telecinema (which was soon to become the first incarnation of the National Film Theatre). In Nottingham, there were no new buildings to exploit, but the idea of using the festival to create long-term cultural momentum was nonetheless embraced by the Nottingham Council of Social Service (NCSS). As part of the festival, the NCSS arranged the "People of Nottingham 1851-1951 Exhibition", sub-titled "The Social History of a City which has Changed Beyond Belief", and through a variety of means—the local press, advance publicity, the exhibition programme booklets, talks and accompanying events—they campaigned to create a permanent folk museum, devoted to the history and experiences of the people of Nottingham.[25] The film unit's productions fitted the folk museum brief perfectly. Moreover, both the edited collection of archival footage—*The Crowded Years* (1951)—and the film unit's new FOB film—*Old Market Square*—were screened within the frame of the "People of Nottingham" exhibition, and so it is in light of the priorities of that event that the themes and content of the films must be considered.

The "People of Nottingham Exhibition" placed a heavy emphasis on the radical and reforming role of grass-roots voluntary organisations, both past and present, in improving the quality of local life and driving legislative change. As such, it represented a direct counter to Hawkes' formulation of a provincial culture waiting to be spoon-fed. Instead, in an early public document, its organisers proclaimed:

---

[24] "Scheme for financial control", FOB Special Committee minutes, 17 January 1951, CA/CM/60(misc)/13, NCA.
[25] NCSS 1950; NCSS et al. 1951; Anon., "Nottingham Project Needs Aid"; Anon. "'People' Exhibition Opened in Nottingham". Although it would be decades before the Museum of Nottingham Life at the Brewhouse Yard would open its doors, a line can be traced all the way back to this campaign.

Since 1851, the men women and children of Nottingham have been faced with many problems of living. They have desperately needed help and in many cases an individual has seen that need, banded first his or her friends together to meet it and then gained the help of other citizens in Nottingham and formed a voluntary organisation. [....] Today the individual citizen, the voluntary organisation and the statutory authority work together as partners to overcome many of the problems of living which 100 years ago meant misery, hardship, suffering, death or loss of opportunity to so many.[26]

Here the focus is on the life-and-death aspects of social progress; however, the idealised synthesis of individual endeavour, voluntary group activity, and official sanction presented could also describe the organisation of the "People of Nottingham" exhibition itself, the film sub-committee, and the planning of various other cultural events within Nottingham's festival. This structure, with relatively few individuals, operating within small teams, actively involved in planning the direction of the celebrations, has also been observed within the organisation of the London festival. Conekin, amongst others, reads this as signifying the rise of a new technocracy—a move away from "the great and the good" model of civic government, towards a more professionalised (although equally undemocratic) model, based on ideas of specialist knowledge.[27] Noticeably, in the NCSS's narrative, the local version is given greater democratic legitimacy through the positioning of *voluntary* workers as unusually prescient examples of the ordinary citizen, emerging from within, rather than imposing their beliefs upon, the people of Nottingham.

Given that this part of the festival was organised by the Nottingham Council of Social Service—the "statutory authority" part of the equation—this emphasis on the voluntary is particularly interesting. By invoking their heritage of "folk" legitimacy, and stressing connections between a past of amateur volunteer spirit and a present of professional social provision, the NCSS sought to construct themselves as also being "of the people", despite their now patently secure professional status. Within the exhibition, lectures were included from other representatives of the modern professional classes—including Dr J D Chambers, an economic and social historian from the University College (now The University of Nottingham).[28] In light of this, the film society's involvement can be seen as key to the assertion of the continued relevance of the voluntary sector. However, although the films made by the Nottingham & District-led

---

[26] NCSS, 1950.
[27] Conekin, *'The autobiography of a nation'*: *The 1951 Festival of Britain*, 34.
[28] Chambers lecture is included in NCSS et al. 1951.

Festival Film Unit clearly attempt to place "the people" centre stage, within their content, form and structure, they simultaneously evidence a continuing tension, for example, between the officially-sanctioned use of the city's main public space, the Market Square, and Nottingham life as lived within it by the local population.

Filming Place: Nottingham's Festival Films

The souvenir brochure of the "People of Nottingham" exhibition proclaims insistently that "It is not the building and machines which make the city of Nottingham but the people...", however, the presentation of the Council House, which had been completed and opened in 1929, suggested something of a qualification of such sentiments. Within the festival, and particularly within the local films, the building was presented as more than a physical structure, and would be called upon to embody the very spirit of the modern city. This tendency had been apparent early in proceedings: a supplement in the *Nottingham Journal*, published at the start of the national festival in May, had heralded the local events to come and picked out an image of the Council House, heading it in bold simply as "symbolic". The accompanying text read:

> Nottingham's modern council house towering over the Old Market Square, hub of the city's life for centuries, symbolises the outlook of a community whose ancient traditions are a foundation on which to build from new ideas.[29]

Amidst such stress on "ancient traditions", it is important to note that the Council House building, and the formal landscaping of the Market Square which accompanied it, were not only recent additions to the cityscape, but had also been hotly contested. A particular bone of contention was the displacement of the regular market and the annual Goose Fair to other sites. According to John Beckett and Ken Brand, the Council House was designed to be a bold statement of civic pride, and the presence of these less grand aspects of city life were seen as being at odds with this. City centre shopkeepers had opposed the Goose Fair since the previous century, branding it an unruly disruption to respectable business; a 1927 report by the General Purposes Committee had also attacked the regular market, as

---

[29] Anon., "Century of Industrial Progress Makes a Story We Are Proud to Tell".

"no credit to the city" and as "nothing more than a conglomeration of unsightly stalls."[30]

Following the council debate on the report, the *Nottingham Evening Post* had stressed opposition to the document's findings, and cast itself as popular champion, claiming "the market belonged to the people, whose voice had been heard in the press." It reported further, with some indignation that, with the exception of two Labour councillors, those present were unanimously in favour of its abolition, and gave space to voices of dissent, including Alderman Ward's suggestion that re-development would harm the prosperity of the city, and that the New Exchange would prove a "white elephant".[31] Countering these fears in September 1927, the architect, Cecil Howitt, stressed the importance of the "value of simple, large open spaces", citing prestigious European examples to which the City should aspire: St Peter's in Rome, St Mark's Square in Venice, and the Plaçe de la Concorde in Paris.[32] The eventual design removed the ramshackle stalls from the front of the Council House site, and a new covered shopping arcade at the rear of the building (modelled on a similar feature in Milan) replaced their English "market town" connotations with far grander aspirations. Through such redefinition of space, Nottingham was staking its claim as a provincial centre of stature, and was doing so, not through reference to London, but by claiming a kinship with the architectural treasures, and the commercial and civic spaces of Europe. Both the European architectural influence, and the fact that the Council House had been "once the subject of much controversy", would be directly acknowledged by the voice-over to *Old Market Square*. Overall, however, the filmmakers' stance was in line with the *Nottingham Journal* when they sought to reinforce and consolidate the building's official status, with the finished commentary declaring it "a familiar and comfortable landmark, whose impressive beauty dominates the city centre."

The festival's depiction of Nottingham through the archival film *The Crowded Years* was always going to be somewhat more limited in content. Constructed from the available footage shot by the Lord Mayor's Secretary, H. S. Sherwin, throughout the 1920s and 1930s, its source material displayed a heavy bias towards pomp and ceremony, capturing

---

[30] Quoted in Beckett and Brand, *The Council House Nottingham and the Old Market Square,* 32.

[31] Clipping from the *Nottingham Evening Post*, 5 July 1927, held in the Old Market Square subject file, Nottingham Local Studies Library.

[32] Quoted in Beckett and Brand, *The Council House Nottingham and the Old Market* Square, 34.

many civic processions and royal visits, and focusing inevitably on the central civic space of the Old Market Square itself. Its title usefully suggested the film's condensation of time—covering two decades, in a little over seventeen minutes,[33] but in putting it together, Basil Harley (an active committee member of both the main NDFS and production group, and local Ministry of Information officer) also ensured that from the opening shot, there were plenty of images of crowds themselves, more specifically, of the massed people of Nottingham present at each event.

Although it began with a particularly bustling scene, the first main section of *The Crowded Years* dealt with the building of the city's Council House during the late 1920s, and utilised still images to show the new centre of local government at different stages of its construction. This may have been meant to summarise the recent narrative of the square, referencing the people who had gathered in protest (although this did not look to be footage of the actual protesting throng) and the imposition of order on the space, via a montage illustrating the construction process, followed by footage of subsequent civic use. In the latter sequences of royal visits and ceremonial processions, within the now more ordered and formal physical environment, the crowd was certainly still present, but now confined to the sidelines and contained behind barriers. If this was a depiction of progress, the choice to end the segment with extensive footage of the city at play during the 1930 Goose Fair is an interesting one. This showed the activities which had characterised the square at its most riotous, but although not obvious from the framing of the shots, the footage is clearly dated as being from 1930—a year in which (as most Nottingham residents would know) the fair took place in its new location at the Forest Recreation Ground, far away from the Market Square itself.

The conflicting versions of the life of the square that the new film, *Old Market Square* needed to be able to represent, threw up a number of stylistic tensions. These were already visible in the early story treatment for the film which was drafted by Roy Corden (a local headmaster and the overall writer and director of the film), and submitted to the main festival committee for approval on 16th March 1951 by Basil Harley.[34] Within this

---

[33] Given that Nottingham, like most places, was addressing a post-war housing shortage, it also carried a second meaning: the bad old days of overcrowding, see Anon., "Nottingham of 'Bad old Days'".

[34] Corden, "Suggested story treatment for the film on Old Market Square". This has not been archived, but a copy of this survives in cameraman Geoff Spencer's personal collection. The precise date is illegible, however, although the specific receipt of this document is not mentioned, dating is corroborated by the presence

document, the basic structure of the film is laid out. The first paragraph summarises ambitions:

> The film will try to present the Old Market Square in such a way as to make it more interesting to even those who are already familiar with it, by picking out points of special or unusual interest, by highlighting items which might be unknown to, or not noticed by, the casual passer-by, and by presenting all these against the background of the square as it probably appears to most people—chiefly as a place to change buses.[35]

These two aspects—the highlighting of interesting facts, and the background use of the square in daily life—lent themselves most readily to different documentary styles. On one hand, the film was to function informatively, beginning by illustrating the history of the square with maps, and later explaining the civic role of the Council House. However, woven through this account was to be the more lyrical story of the square as the bustling centre of daily life, told from the first morning buses to the last nightly chime of Little John (the bell on the Council House clock). Within the shooting script (again by Roy Corden) these aspects crystallised into seven sections. Section One began outside the focal day with the factual history of the site, and was followed, in Section Two, by the city waking up and hurrying to work.[36] Sections Three to Seven were titled as follows: "The Shoppers", "The People of the Square", "Ceremonial", "Civic" and "Evening".

Where the historical aspects and the representations of the city's bus exchange sat comfortably within the conventions of British expository documentary, and some elements of the ceremonial and civic sections resembled advertising films, both the overall structure and some of the later sequences seemed from the outset to belong to rather different traditions. The extended and overhead shots of human movement within the square (see Fig. 4-1), the gentle passages dwelling on the citizens of Nottingham going about their ordinary business (window-shoppers, older people taking in the afternoon sights and catching up on gossip, young

---

of film society representative W. B. Harley recorded in the committee minutes for the 16 March 1951, CA.CM/60(misc)/13, NCA.

[35] Ibid.

[36] Again no copy has been archived, but Geoff Spencer has an almost complete copy. Page one has been lost, but from comparison of the treatment and the finished film it is likely that "Section One" would have contained a version of the eventual intro. "Section Two" is given no other title, but all the subsequent chapters are given specific titles, which I have listed.

people hurrying towards or anxiously awaiting their dates) all clearly bore a debt to a more European non-fiction form: the "city symphony" film.

Templates for this style of filmmaking had been established by Walter Ruttman's *Berlin: Symphony of a City* (1927) and Dziga Vertov's *Man with a Movie Camera* (1929) in the 1920s, and had recently been revisited and revived by Arne Sucksdorff with his study of Stockholm, suggestively entitled *Rhythm of a City* (1948). Sucksdorff's film had met with particular success on the international film festival circuit, gaining the director substantial feature articles in both *Sight and Sound* and *Sequence*.[37] In the latter, Peter Ericsson had celebrated Sucksdorff (who wrote, directed, shot and edited his own films) as an inspiration for ambitious amateur filmmakers. Many responded to the incentives the film offered, and *Rhythm of a City*'s influence was also rapidly felt within a professional British production—John Eldridge's *Waverley Steps* (1948)—an Edinburgh-based variation of the genre which was soon warmly welcomed by film societies right across the country. NDFS members got a chance to see it in November 1948, as part of a special joint presentation held with the Leicester Film Society at Sanford Hall, Loughborough.[38]

In visual sequences which owe a clear debt to the "city symphony" model, *Old Market Square* sketches the pattern of human activity around the edges of the square: the rush to work, the bustle of shoppers, and the long queues to return home. As the urgent flow of passengers depart on buses at the end of the working day, the voice-over reports that around 25,000 people are transported home to surrounding districts and suburbs that chart the spread of the city. These places (which it lists) "even at the beginning of the last century were country villages sending produce and not people to this market place", we are told. The film then reflects on the effect of these changes for popular memory; as we watch elderly citizens (see Fig. 4-2) on the ornamental walls and park benches, the narrator muses upon what they might be thinking:

> It is a favourite resort of many people who come here, not to go on to somewhere else, but to sit, to gossip, [pause] to study their fellows [pause] or to remember old times; times when this really was a market place, when within its five and a quarter acres were sold pots and poultry, boots and butter, cloth and corn cures; times when the Square and the neighbouring streets were filled with the booths and roundabouts of the great Goose Fair.

---

[37] Hardy, "The Films of Arne Sucksdorff"; Ericsson, "Arne Sucksdorff".
[38] NDFS and Leicester Film Society, Programme for the Joint Meeting at Stanford Hall, 27 November 1948, NCL. LSC.

Fig. 4-1 frame enlargement from *Old Market Square* (1951)
Source: Media Archive of Central England

Fig. 4-2 frame enlargement from *Old Market Square* (1951)
Source: Media Archive of Central England

Although the notion of an ordinary day implies a regular and repeatable cycle, onscreen, the passage from dawn to dusk is presented but once. This linear progression reinforces within the very structure of the film the notion of evolution over time that the voice-over draws attention to. We are offered here a version of place which rejects stasis, and embraces the naturalness and inevitability of transformation: changing relationships between city centre and suburbs, between spaces of work and leisure, between destination and transitional space, mapping both the flow of people through the city, and the flow of the city through time. This, once more, plays into the FOB's grand themes of past and future, visible through, and embodied within its organising conceptions of place. However, through the contrast between the constant movement at the edges of the square and the relative stasis within it, and more pointedly in the juxtaposition of images against words, it also introduces something of a lament for the more active bustling space that the square itself had been—notes in a minor key which gently undermine the celebration of the Council's 1927 decision to re-develop the space.

In the finished version of *Old Market Square*, the different styles are held together by a voice-over, which leaves almost no aural space. Although, this "voice of god" commentary enables a reflexive consideration of the past during the sequences depicting the present use of the square, it is somewhat overbearing, and in terms of the usual framework of a "city symphony" picture, this wall-to-wall explanation might well be considered something of a compromise. There is one sequence, however, lasting a little over a minute, where the voice-over is completely absent. Ironically, this depicts public debate within the square, and in conjunction with the sequence addressing aspects of civic process, which directly precedes it, this raises interesting questions about attitudes towards the public sphere depicted.

In the "civic" sequence, the key external architectural features of the Council House are shown and admired, and their symbolic significance underlined by framing and commentary. Although the camera briefly enters the building itself, to observe a statue, named "Welcome", set half-way up the entrance hall's grand staircase, it does not however move beyond it. Instead we are returned to the exterior, to witness people, who the voice-over informs us are councillors, arriving for a meeting. A strict protocol seems to have regulated exploration of the inner areas of the Council House, and although the official status of the Festival Film Unit ensured access right through the building to the roof, enabling shots over the square to be secured,[39] permission to film the interior may have been more limited. Whatever the reason, the deliberations of the council, and the spaces in which they take place, remain hidden from view.

Scenes depicting the arrival of the councillors are followed by a cut to an overhead shot of people gathering in the square (see Fig. 4-3), and then to a wide shot of a young man, without formal props, holding the attention of a small crowd (see Fig. 4-4), framings accompanied by voice-over:

> ... and while the formal debates on civic affairs take place within the Council House, the old Market Square provides a forum for the free expression of all shades of opinion, both religious and political.

Fig. 4-3 frame enlargement from *Old Market Square* (1951)
Source: Media Archive of Central England

At which point, the voice-over ceases, as we are offered a series of further examples of this public forum in action: the Salvation Army find some favour with the crowd; an older man atop one of the ornamental walls finds none; a man with Bevanesque mannerisms fares little better; and the

---

[39] Geoff Spencer has retained two rather formal letters of authorisation signed by the Town Clerk, T. J. Owen, but the one relating to *Old Market Square* (dated 25 May 1951) does not specify how much access the filmmakers were to be granted.

lack of interest attracted by a sandwich-boarded bible-waver is emphasised with a second shot of indifferent passers by, taken from a different angle.

Fig. 4-4 frame enlargement from *Old Market Square* (1951)
Source: Media Archive of Central England

From here the sequence moves on to the more organised and formal speakers, elevated on platforms within the square, and using amplified sound for better projection. A trade union speaker's flatbed truck, proclaiming the legend "a Union card is your safeguard", is framed first behind a man in military uniform who turns away, and then behind a young girl blowing bubbles towards the camera. If the Union speaker has succeeded in drawing a crowd, this is not shown, as the next shot quickly moves to a position behind a different elevated speaker, who addresses a sizable audience. This soon centres on a working-class man who takes the speaker to task. He jabs his finger to make his point, and following the cut back to the emphatic speaker—visually constructing the appearance of a direct response—the angry man is shown again (from a slightly different angle), this time forcefully gesticulating in a manner which suggests that he is telling the speaker to "sling his hook".

As Heather Norris Nicholson has suggested in relation to contrasting amateur films of Salford in the 1960s, the position of non-professional filmmakers within the communities they film, is reflected in what they choose to capture, and how they frame their chosen views.[40] With *Old Market Square*, the Festival Production Unit's cultural authority and official status is visible from the image stream, but in attempting to pin down the meaning of the Square as a serious democratic space, a core contradiction within the film society's values, is also exposed.

Within Corden's original shooting script, the Square was presented as an expression of a true public sphere, and a point of contrast with the councillors' zones of deliberation:

> Do they ever leave the claustral calm of the Council Chamber to walk in the square, listening not telling? For life in the square goes on, heedless of councils and councillors... [41]

In the event, this early written version promises a more critical take on the Council Chamber than the film actually achieves. While the principle of a free and open public sphere—equally available to all—is trumpeted in the finished film, and the absence of voice-over in the sequence means that the speakers are neither "spoken for" nor "talked over", something is still lacking; in a very literal sense, their opinions remain unvoiced.

Within a silent sequence it is possible for the heckler to function as a heroic everyman, unconvinced by, and visibly critical of, the elevated speaker before him. Although in wide shot, frontal framing and his dynamic movement relative to those surrounding him, afford him greater screen presence than the official speaker (held in a closer framing, partially obscured and shot from the side) in this case. The medium of film without sound permits here an artificial parity, where all can engage in an ideal democratic sphere, and position is not a barrier to participation and effective communication. In this form, audible markers of power are concealed; we cannot hear the difference in volume between those with amplification and those without, and we cannot discern if there are any differences in articulacy or credibility.

In the present context, the sequence functions somewhat as an ode to the value of the amateur sphere, and in the climactic exchange, the heckler

---

[40] Norris Nicholson, "Two tales of a city: Salford in regional filmmaking, 1957-1973".

[41] Cordon, "Shooting script". Although some aspects of professional production practice are followed, it is interesting to see how these are interpreted by the amateur group. The "shooting script" contains many descriptions of moods and meaning which the filmmakers wished to convey, but it is often unclear how these could be created through filming and editing.

is portrayed as the visual winner, defeating the professional speaker with his final gesture. However, although the viewer is invited to enjoy the humour of a challenge to authority, [42] the opening shot of the sequence (from a privileged vantage point atop the Council House), and the "voice of god" which introduced it, position the film—and by implication, its audience—somewhere above the fray. It is doubtful if the heckler would have been so attractive to the filmmakers with his voice restored. Whilst the absence of synchronised sound may have been matter of practical constraint, it nonetheless allows the filmmakers to champion the *image* of free and equal democratic debate, without having to actually engage with the messy business of conflicting opinions and the ordering of discourses.

Conclusions

The Nottingham & District Film Society's Festival of Britain contribution articulated complex and negotiated relationships both to place, and to the film society's status as a voluntary body within the local cultural establishment. Facilitated by the BFI, the historical significance of British film was championed within the film exhibition and lecture side of proceedings, and given that this element was ultimately missing from London's programme of film events,[43] this certainly deserves some recognition. This is particularly pertinent given the degree to which film society culture and a middlebrow critical consensus have been held responsible for the critical neglect of British cinema to this point. However, within the spectrum of local film events this "film appreciation" aspect stood apart, screened at a separate venue—the YMCA Hall. This marked out the film-as-art component of their work from their film-as-social-service contribution to the "People of Nottingham Exhibition", and it was the latter that gathered greater press attention, including reports of repeated praise from the mayor, who urged all citizens to see *Old Market*

---

[42] It was interesting to see this screened to a predominantly older audience recently (at a busy screening of local films at the Broadway Media Centre, 11 March 2007). The passage in question seemed to be received as a humorous narrative moment.
[43] The BFI programme was announced in the press in February 1951, and should have taken place at a West End cinema between 4 and 17 June 1951. Its cancellation, due to an inability to obtain exemption from Entertainment Duty, was announced on the 11 May 1951. Film societies running the same programme did not appear to face this problem, although, contrary to normal Entertainment Duty rules, non-members were permitted to buy tickets. A variety of memos and press clippings are held in British Film Institute subject file: FOB vol. 1.

Square.[44] Such official endorsement of the film highlights its most problematic aspect. Perhaps there is a question to answer as to whether the film really champions the square as a more authentic public forum than the council itself, or simply offers it up as a substitute, whilst colluding in keeping the processes of local government closed to view. The failure of the film to enter and explore the Council House is all the more pertinent in light of the fact that public access to the building had been controversially discontinued in 1929, following accusations of vandalism.[45]

The NDFS itself actively pursued official status within organisation of local FOB events, and its contribution readily celebrated the City Corporation, and the development choices that it had made concerning the use of the Old Market Square. This was neither surprising nor contradictory, given the fact that many key film society committee members were themselves part of the professional/managerial classes and active within the local establishment. Such official status won funding, privileged access for filmmaking, and a platform for exhibition that they would not otherwise have achieved. In return, their voluntary status lent a degree of populist authenticity to the "People of Nottingham Exhibition", as well as providing a cut-price alternative to professional production, which was free from any commercial taint.[46] However, the curious omissions in the depiction of democratic space in *Old Market Square* begin to illuminate more fundamental contradictions between the nature of the film society's ideal of democracy and its distaste for the messy reality of democratic debate.

Within their films, the NDFS-led Festival Film Unit presented a version of Nottingham that was broadly in sympathy with the main festival

---

[44] Anon., "City Film Surprises Viewers".

[45] Jancovich et al., *The Place of the Audience: Cultural Geographies of Film Consumption*, 101. In one respect this spoke directly to issues of public ownership of the building, as one complaint was that members of the public had scratched their names into the woodwork, see Beckett and Brand, *The Council House Nottingham and the Old Market Square*, 50.

[46] It should also be noted here that the local FOB committee had rejected an approach by the Disney Corporation to organise a historical tableau (presumably free of cost) with the film stars of their latest Robin Hood adventure, *The Story of Robin Hood and His Merrie Men*, (1952): see letter from Mr Cyril H. Eagar, discussed at meeting, 23 May 1951, CA/CM/60(misc)/13 cont, NCA. This would perhaps have been seen not only as insufficiently British, but also as presenting a version of the past that conflicted with the socially progressive one the local festival wanted to project. Commerce was a point of pride within the industrial rather than the cultural aspects of the events, however, suggesting that manufacturing and entertainment industries were viewed rather differently.

themes, and with the specific local focus on "people" and their place within the industrial and social progress of the city. Ultimately the Nottingham FOB filmmaking was successful because it responded not just to a national media event, but also to its local moment, however compromised that might have been by tensions between the official and the popular uses of the square. The NDFS-led production unit made their festival films relevant by becoming a part of the wider local campaign for a folk museum for Nottingham. In doing so, they drew on multiple influences, including the British documentary tradition, which went some way to presenting the film society as more than purveyors of European fare. Although few commentators seem to have noted that, in producing the film's most successful expressions of local life—the images which undercut official positions on the use of square—they drew heavily on the distinctly European "city symphony" format. If the inexpert blending of styles resulted in a film that was less coherent than it might have been, it is this very dissonance which allows such a rich insight into amateur cine's role in contesting the history of Nottingham's central public space.

Works Cited

Primary Sources

British Film Institute, Festival of Britain, subject file vol. 1, BFI Library.
Corden, Roy. "Suggested story treatment for the film on Old Market Square", n.d., ca. March 1951, personal collection of Geoffrey Spencer.
—. "Shooting script for *Old Market Square*", n.d., ca. spring 1951, personal collection of Geoffrey Spencer.
Nottingham City Corporation Records, Special Committee Reports, 1947-1951. CA/CM/60(misc)/13, Nottingham County Archive (NCA).
Nottingham Council of Social Service (NCSS). "A Social History of The People of Nottingham and District" [a special leaflet replacing the quarterly issue of "Community Service"] Nottingham: Nottingham Council of Social Service, 1950. FOB collection, Nottingham Local Studies Department (NLS), Nottingham Central Library (NCL).
Nottingham Council of Social Service (NCSS), in collaboration with The City Corporation and the City Festival Committee. "The People of Nottingham 1851-1951 Exhibition: A Souvenir of the Exhibition", Nottingham: Nottingham Council of Social Service, in collaboration with the City Corporation and the City Festival Committee, 1951. FOB

collection, Nottingham Local Studies Department (NLS), Nottingham Central Library (NCL).

Nottingham & District Film Society, Administrative Records, M12, 334-94, NCA.

Nottingham Old Market Square, subject file, Nottingham Local Studies Library.

Owen, T. J. Letter of authorisation from the Town Clerk to the Festival Film Unit, 25 May 1951, personal collection of Geoffrey Spencer.

Trowell Official Festival of Britain Programme, 1951, 3. Parish Pamphlets, Box T-W, 90.2, NCA.

Secondary Sources

Allen, John, et. al. *Rethinking The Region*. London & New York: Routledge, 1998.

Anon. "Nottingham Project Needs Aid." *Nottingham Guardian* (3 May 1951): 4.

—. "'People' Exhibition Opened in Nottingham: Folk Museum Plea." *Nottingham Guardian* (26 September 1951): 3.

—. "Century of Industrial Progress Makes a Story We Are Proud to Tell." *Nottingham Journal* (3 May 1951): 3.

—. *Nottingham Journal* (24 September 1951): 2.

—. "Nottingham of 'Bad old Days.'" *Nottingham Journal* (26 September 1951): 2.

Beckett, John, and Ken Brand. *The Council House Nottingham and the Old Market Square*. Nottingham: Nottingham Civic Society, 2004.

Conekin, Becky. *'The autobiography of a nation': The 1951 Festival of Britain*. Manchester: Manchester University Press, 2003.

Cottrill, J. R. ed. *Forming and Running a Film Society*. Leicester: The Federation of Film Societies, 1950.

Ericsson, Peter. "Arne Sucksdorff." *Sequence* 7, (1949): 24-29.

Hardy, Forsyth. "The Films of Arne Sucksdorff." *Sight and Sound* 17, no. 66 (1948): 60-63, 89.

Hewison, Robert. *Culture and Consensus: England, Art and Politics, Since 1940*. London: Methuen, 1997.

Hoskins, W. G. *East Midlands and The Peak*. London: Collins, 1951.

Jancovich, Mark, Lucy Faire and Sarah Stubbings. *The Place of the Audience: Cultural Geographies of Film Consumption*. London: British Film Institute, 2003.

Massey, Doreen. *Space, Place and Gender*. Cambridge: Polity Press, 1994.

Norris Nicholson, Heather. "Two tales of a city: Salford in regional filmmaking, 1957-1973." *Manchester Regional History Review* 15 (2001): 41-53.

Sexton, Jamie. "The Film Society and the Creation of an Alternative Film Culture in Britain in the 1920s." In *Young and Innocent? The Cinema in Britain 1896-1930*, edited by Andrew Higson, 291-305. Exeter: University of Exeter Press, 2002.

Films Cited

Berlin-Symphony of A City
(Deutsche-Verenis-Film, 1927) 35mm., 53 mins.
The Crowded Years
(Nottingham Festival Film Unit, 1951) 16mm., 26 mins. 32 secs.
Man With A Movie Camera
(VUFKU, 1929) 35mm., 68 mins.
Nottingham: Variations On A Theme
(Nottingham & District Film Society, 1949) 16mm., no running time available.
Old Market Square
(Nottingham Festival Film Unit, 1951) 16mm., 14 mins. 30 secs.
Quincentenary Celebrations
(Gaumont British, 1949) 35mm., 9 mins. 39 secs.
Rhythm of A City
(Svensk Filmindustri, 1948) 35mm., 20 mins.
Rural Blacksmith
(Nottingham & District Film Society, 1947) 16mm., no running time available.
The Story of Robin Hood and His Merrie Men
(Walt Disney Productions, 1952) 35mm., 84 mins.
Symphony of A City
(Svensk Filmindustri, 1948) 35mm., 20 mins.
Waverley Steps
(Greenpark Productions, 1948) 35mm., 31 mins.

CHAPTER FIVE

AMATEUR CINEMA RE-LOCATED: LOCALISM IN FACT AND FICTION

RYAN SHAND

While the study of amateur cinema has understandably been frustrated by practical considerations, such as archival access, and the poor condition of surviving footage, a range of other factors help to explain why this remarkable cine movement has so often escaped the scholarly agenda. Associations with the technically "substandard" have certainly coloured aesthetic expectations of the mode; instinctive assimilations of amateurism with a range of socio-cultural conservatisms have implied little in the way of experimentalism and thus critical interest; the "personal" dimensions of much amateur filmmaking have seemed to distance it from the "master" narratives of history-proper, marking an essential inscrutability resistant to translation from elsewhere, etc. A particularly marginalising role has also been played by emphasis upon the cultural geographies of the nation. Since developing from its primal formulations in the study of genre and authorship, the focus of Film Studies has often been on national cinemas, a paradigm proving remarkably resilient, even when re-worked by post-structuralism in its "trans-national" and "cross-border" variants. With its persistently *local* representational emphases, demand for "*local* knowledge", and assertion of very *local* "priorities", amateur cinema has seemed to fall beyond the scope of this crucial paradigm at a series of levels. Advancing from very different points of departure, a range of pioneering studies have however now begun to shift attention away from such national preoccupations. This chapter seeks to locate a small sample of Scottish amateur film production in relation to some of this emerging work, and to sketch the lines of possible future enquiries.

With a special issue on "Local Film" published in 2005, the journal *Film History* acknowledged the increasing influence which localism seemed to be having on contemporary debates.[1] Whilst local exhibition histories were the primary concern for most contributors, more relevant issues, in the present context, are explored in one particular essay, which examined the ways in which spectators recognised themselves in the "local topical" films staple to early cinema exhibition, and the significances attributable to those acts of recognition.[2] A useful and timely excursion into localist questions, emphasising the importance of very immediate senses of placement in identity-formation, it is nonetheless suggestive that the article's focus is confined to commercially-produced fare, exploiting local audiences' fascinations, but in formats with little direct connection to local issues or histories. The neglect of amateur film production in general from the special issue is perhaps striking, given that an earlier number of *Film History* had been dedicated to "small gauge" equipment largely marketed towards non-professionals.[3]

As enthusiastic purchasers of small gauge stock and cameras, amateur filmmakers have perhaps been most active in the exploration of both actual and imagined local worlds, enjoying a particular intimacy with geographies close to home, and a characteristic sensitivity to often highly nuanced aspects of localised social practice. Where the professional filmmaker's relationship with such milieus has often seemed tentative and temporary ("on location" implies a sojourn away from a production "base") arguably shading towards the exploitative ("asset-stripping" the local of scenes and behaviours for commodification elsewhere?), amateur filmmaking connotes longer-term investment, a continuity of engagement and a sharing of filmic outcomes, involving a kind of re-investment of significance within the local community. Whilst a range of initiatives clearly characterise such amateur involvement on the local scene, focus here is placed on questions of production, and more particularly upon a specific question: what precisely is the "local" inscription of place characteristic of amateur film production?

Suggestive comparison might be offered between one commercially-sponsored film, produced professionally, *Seawards the Great Ships* (1960), and two amateur pictures, *Fit O' The Toon* (1978) and *Seven Ages* (1957), an amateur documentary film, and an amateur fiction film, respectively. Juxtaposition of the works helps both to demonstrate ontological differences between non-fiction and fiction amateur films, and to establish the amateur filmmaker's often *divided* relationship with the local. Analysis of these works suggests possible starting points for a

---

[1] Fullerton, *Film History*, 2005.
[2] Toulmin and Loiperdinger, "Is it You?", 7-18.
[3] Stone and Streible, *Film History*, 2003.

theorisation of "local" film production within national film culture, with implications for future historians of Scottish and other national cinemas.

Resistance to Nationalism

Encouragements to the exploration undertaken here might be identified in a range of existing writings, which sense local tensions within the national, and hint at the unique potential of the amateur as local filmmaker. John Hill's contribution to the edited collection *Scotch Reels*, for example, "Scotland doesna mean much tae Glesca: Some notes on *The Gorbals Story*", as the title suggests, examines the "local" within professional cinema, at least implicitly.[4] Hill argues that, according to the chosen example's narrative, working-class Glaswegians seem not to share the same vision of the nation associated with the rest of the country, due to the uneven social and economic development of life in Scotland's urban centres. Localist "Glesca" sensibilities are apparently "out of sync" with an officially sanctioned national imaginary. Very much in keeping with the priorities of the Film Studies of its moment however, the main focus of the essay rests on assessing the ideological progressiveness of the narrative for a spectator conceived very largely as textual- rather than social-subject. Indexing broader disciplinary shifts however, it is to the restoration of such social subjectivity which much of the work of influence upon the present analysis attends, a move made peculiarly urgent by the case of amateur cinema. Patricia Zimmermann's article, "Morphing History into Histories: From Amateur Film to the Archive of the Future", for example, is suggestive of several ways in which localism might prove a useful framework for the future study of amateur movie-making.[5] It begins:

> In this essay, I will propose a tentative, provisional strategy for how we can begin to theorise a historiography of the amateur film imaginary by tracing how the visual structures of these works map localised microhistories rather than nationalised phantasmatic representations. These microhistories are not simply local, but are crisscrossed hybrids between the local and the global, between the psychic and political terrains.[6]

Contrast between such "localised microhistories" and their "nationalised phantasmatic" counterparts structures the rest of her essay. Zimmermann's conceptual categories are grounded with reference to three amateur films,

---

[4] Hill, "Scotland doesna mean much tae Glesca", 100-111.
[5] Zimmermann, "Morphing History into Histories", 108-130.
[6] Ibid., 109.

and in relation to academic debates around the commercial art cinema, without reference to any particular example. The amateur films scrutinised are seen as staging an ideological critique of nationalism—via what might be termed elsewhere as a *failure* of realisation—which constantly emphasises alterity:

> If professional film poses as the pinnacle, then amateur film represents the nadir of art. If professional film is slick and seamless, then amateur film is sloppy and filled with gaps and jump cuts.[7]

The article is an ambitious combination of geography and aesthetics, absorbing and responding to debates advanced since the publication of her monograph, *Reel Families: A Social History of Amateur Film*, in 1995.[8] Interestingly, the analysis emerged in its original form as a paper presented at a conference organised by Karen L. Ishizuka, titled "The Past as Present: Home Movies as a Cinema of Record". A filmmaker and curator of the Japanese American National Museum in Los Angeles, Ishizuka has written widely on home movies.[9] As the theme of the conference suggests, participants were interested in looking at home movies from what, elsewhere, I have termed the *evidential* perspective.[10] While this once again reinforced common perceptions about the function and value of amateur cinema as memory text or record, it is interesting that Zimmermann does discuss one early amateur fiction film, *A Study in Reds* (1927) in her article. Typically relegated to second-class status even within archive culture, it is welcome that amateur fiction films are now beginning to receive long overdue attention, and in doing so, to unsettle understandings of amateur film's value.[11]

Zimmermann's focus moves on from a consideration of localism as impulse to record, to suggesting how the valuation of amateur film in these terms challenges established forms of film history. "What happens when we move from a unified concept of film history toward ever morphing, evolving, contradictory processes of overlapping film histories?" emerges as a key question.[12] In her ensuing attempt to re-write dominant versions

---

[7] Ibid., 114.
[8] Zimmermann, *Reel Families*.
[9] Ishizuka, "Artifacts of Culture", 15-20, and "The Home Movie: A Veil of Poetry", 45-50.
[10] Shand, "Theorising Amateur Cinema: Limitations and Possibilities", forthcoming.
[11] The conference, "Amateur Fiction Films" at the Northeast Historic Film Archive, Maine, U.S.A, 21-23 July 2005, was a notable exception to the focus on non-fiction amateur film.
[12] Zimmermann, "Morphing History into Histories", 110.

of film history, she invokes writers such as Keith Jenkins and Michel Foucault, identified elsewhere with moves towards a New Historicism, sceptical of "classical" historiography's unifying impulses.[13] Where a once highly selective film canon structured the historical narrative, she argues, analysis can now only recognise an infinite network of multiple texts, defying attempts to establish hierarchies, isolate auteurs or map genres. "Variegated practices" representing a limitless diversification of filmic forms, displace more binary formulations of the mainstream and counter-practice. As she notes, "Rather than finishing, this essay is perhaps, in the end, only an invocation for a beginning: to write the archive differently, and with difference and plurality as its major criteria for selection."[14] In keeping with the instincts and uncertainties of what slowly emerges as a post-history perspective, a search for *difference* and *fragmentation*, rather than consistency and continuity, structures this approach.[15]

Stress on the "variegation" of film history generated through attention to amateur film, need not be incompatible with recognition of this peculiarly "alterior" cinema's own strong commitment to convention, formula, and the standardisation of its own practices. Such an impulse was a very self-conscious one within the amateur cine "movement" from its origins. A range of organisations emerged quickly to define and disseminate "norms", and films made within, what I have termed elsewhere, amateurism's "community mode" remained surprisingly unified and consistent between 1930 and 1980.[16] Like those of the mainstream cinema it so often modelled itself upon, the aesthetics of amateur cinema changed only in small ways over these years, shaped by definitional discourses with remarkable resilience, which often involved an uncanny echo of those patterning the professional sector. From this perspective, the community mode of amateur cinema might be seen more as a homogenous and *parallel* film practice than has been acknowledged up until this point, existing not necessarily to challenge the mainstream, but to stage a *dialogue* with it.

---

[13] Jenkins, *Re-Thinking History*, and Foucault, *The Archaeology of Knowledge*.
[14] Zimmermann, "Morphing History into Histories", 128.
[15] Southgate, *History: What and Why: Ancient, Modern and Postmodern Perspectives*. 115-147.
[16] This formulation, "community mode", addresses and acknowledges the limited public profile enjoyed by these filmmakers, without implying that they are simply home moviemakers, or attempting entry into what Richard Chalfen (1975) termed the "mass mode"; it is defined rather by the ambivalent exhibition space it occupies *between* the home and mass modes. See Shand, "Theorising Amateur Cinema: Limitations and Possibilities".

Framing amateur cinema as "dialogue" rather than "resistance" concedes little of its critical potential, and perhaps gets somewhat closer to the mode's characteristic acknowledgements and transformations of the professional. As Zimmermann notes, the amateur film movement did, for example, introduce a number of genres that modelled themselves on professional templates:

> ... we begin to define amateur film itself as a range and plurality of practices: home movies, surveillance, fantasies, narratives, experimental works, travelogues, documentaries, industrials, hobbies, practice zone for Hollywood style, places for emergent subjectivities, sites of *resistance to nationalism and hegemony* (my emphasis).[17]

But how are constructions of amateur film as "practice zone" to be reconciled with its construction as "resistance"? Despite the opening assertion that "These microhistories are not simply local, but are criss-crossed hybrids between the local and the global...", it seems finally that localism is to be seen unilaterally as a form of cultural *resistance* to forces such as nationalism.[18] Following allusions to "plurality" and "diversity", this seems perhaps a defensive way of formulating a localist approach to amateur cinema. Rather than deconstructing the hegemonies of nationalism and professionalism therefore, by isolating internal contradictions or "local" moments of resistance to them, the aim here is to give attention to the local itself as a more self-sufficient imaginary, not untouched by the national or unaware of it, but filtering the national in its own distinctive ways for its own often strategic or narcissistic ends. In this respect, the argument below suggests that non-fiction and fiction amateur films provide somewhat different perspectives on localism, articulating visions that in their failure to overlap, say much about the "variegated" definition of amateur cine long shared by actual filmmakers.

Sponsored Film and the Unfamiliar Gaze

Scotland enjoyed a particularly dynamic and integrated documentary film movement from the 1950s to the 1980s, in no small measure thanks to initiatives undertaken by Forsyth Hardy and the second Films of Scotland (FOS) Committee, the national public body re-established in 1954 to "promote Scotland's social, cultural and industrial attributes both

---

[17] Zimmermann, "Morphing History into Histories", 110.
[18] Ibid., 109.

nationally and internationally."[19] As Director of the organisation from 1955-1974, Hardy oversaw projects on various aspects of Scottish life, including fishing, the operation of new industries, and the rich cultural and artistic traditions of the nation.

Films such as *Seawards the Great Ships*, were commissioned to exhibit Scotland as self-confident, and as contributing to the industrial and cultural progress of Britain and the wider world. Typical FOS positivism is audible in the commentary accompanying the film's opening sequence (see Fig. 5-1), describing the geographical location, at the mouth of the River Clyde, of the shipyards which will form its subject:

> Britain is an island nation, a nation of islanders and shipbuilders. On its shores generations of craftsmen have made great ships for the world, but nowhere in such profusion as on the River Clyde in Scotland. The estuary of the Clyde is a place for pleasure, people write songs about its green hills and lochs and islands, and they come to find peace and enjoy the scenery...
>
> ...Greenock is a town on the Clyde, down these waters Clyde-built clippers like *The Cutty Sark* once sailed to the China seas. It was then too that James Watt of Greenock was working on a steam engine that would change the face of the world. Up river, the ancient landmark of Dumbarton Rock has looked down on long ago battles. Today a voyage up this river is a voyage into the industrial age. There are still green fields on Clydeside but they have shrunk as the industry of the Clyde has spread. A river of shipyards. And of all shipbuilding rivers the Clyde is the most versatile in the world. It makes every kind of ship; cargo ships, the bread and butter traders that feed and clothe the world. Ships that cross all the waters of the globe...

The narration is thus keen to stress inter-relationships between local industrial activity, and wider global impacts. The Glasgow shipbuilders, who will remain the focus of the film are prized highly, although in somewhat instrumental terms, valued not in and of themselves, but rather for their contribution to Britain's developmental role on the world stage. Such a perspective persists in the main, as the film places a characteristically FOS emphasis upon mechanistic process and outcome. A token attempt is made however, halfway through the film, to give hitherto anonymous workers a voice of their own. (see Fig. 5-2) In one short sequence, over shots of seagulls, the river and the shipyard, disembodied voices attempt to recreate lunchtime banter between three workers:

---

[19] Sherington, "To Speak Its Pride", 10.

Fig. 5-1 frame enlargement from *Seawards the Great Ships* (1951)
Source: Scottish Screen Archive

—I must have welded about a million tons of plate this morning
—The boy's got hallucinations again; it's the sun that gets him
—Oh look who's talkin', you couldnae weld a spoon to a tea can
—Oh is that your trade? I never tried it
—Come on… there's a ship to be welded
—Oh aye, work, work, work…

The "staged" informality of this scene contrasts sharply with the impersonal coverage of industrial process occupying the rest of the film. Perhaps the spectator is left with a lingering suspicion that these were not actual recordings of workers, but of directed actors, effectively "performing" the working-class. Even here, where their labours are finally the focus of direct attention, the men scarcely speak for themselves; someone else—the narrator—speaks for them.

Fig. 5-2 frame enlargement from *Seawards the Great Ships* (1951)
Source: Scottish Screen Archive

Certainly the film's "translation" of the local for the global proved a successful instance of cultural transfer: *Seawards the Great Ships* went on to win an Academy Award for best live-action short in 1961. Yet whilst its decidedly poetic sensibility, evident in the camerawork and editing of American director Hilary Harris immediately impresses, the film has attracted critical concern. Colin McArthur has chastised *Seawards the Great Ships* for presenting a misleading image of life in the shipyards, seeing it as mythologising the industry, and indulging the potential fascinations of the image stream at the expense of a more thorough analysis of history and class relations:

> the elementalism and gigantism of the visual and verbal imagery seem shabby and hollow in the light of what has become of the upper Clyde. Starkly in retrospect, the breast-beating and tub-thumping of *Seawards The Great Ships* offers no comfort to Clydeside workers or guidance to the historical processes which have put them out of work.[20]

It is less surprising however that *Seawards the Great Ships* presents a romantic view of shipbuilding on the Clyde (the film might be seen as a

---

[20] McArthur, "Scotland and Cinema: The Iniquity of the Fathers", 63.

typical example of the FOS sponsored documentary in this respect) than that it makes some gesture towards the articulation of local "accent", and associates that endeavour with a shift in artistic register—the "performance" of working class life introduced resembles in fact, nothing less than a brief amateur "interlude" within a professionally-produced meta-narrative.

Seawards the Great Ships illustrates especially well then the condition of the professional filmmaker "on location", shaping an uncertain grasp of the local to meet remote national (or international) requirements. The role of the sponsor in this process is also very apparent. The co-financing of the project by the Clyde Shipbuilders Association clearly had considerable influence upon the finished film, dictating its stresses on efficient working practices, reputation for quality, and a professional expertise unparalleled thanks to its long cultivation. Conceived as *products* to be consumed within the marketplace via mainstream exhibition, *Seawards the Great Ships* and other films of its type seek commercial distribution, and must prioritise distant spectators, or so McArthur argues, at the expense of the local audience. The centrality of voice-over to this "appropriation" of the local is seen as particularly indicative of the need to mediate between the spheres. In this case, the problems surrounding acknowledgement of the implied addressee, are made explicit by the commissioning of two different voice-overs, one with a Scots accent for the local audience and one in Received Pronunciation for prints destined for international distribution.[21] Whatever the accent of the voice-over however, McArthur would argue that the local is made "strange" and exotic here for the benefit of the *unfamiliar* gaze. Such estrangement remains a characteristic of the professionally-made film as it comes to terms with the local.

Amateur Film and the Familiar Gaze

In 1949, documentarist John Grierson was interviewed by *Amateur Cine World*, and invited to discuss the possibilities of the rapidly-expanding amateur cine sector. He used the opportunity to address non-professional filmmakers, in terms of their potential "public service" role, interestingly setting out key responsibilities, in specifically *local* terms:

> General information from a national point of view does not fill the gaps. It is up to the local amateur cinematographer to play his part and provide a local information service. You have a great power in your hands. It will be

---

[21] Bryden Murdoch provided the Scottish commentary, while Kenneth Kendall's voice was used in the English version.

seen during the next decade that the amateur has a great duty to the people, since he can reach them in a way the national information film makers cannot hope to do. We have not the right sort of money at our disposal, and we do not know local conditions. The small film dealing with local interests is your medium.[22]

For Grierson, the amateur's combination of local knowledge and immediate access to local audiences, places him or her in a unique position to "fill the gaps" in a way impossible for nationally-obligated filmmakers. So while sponsored films such as *Seawards the Great Ships* may be seen to project a national perspective whilst suppressing localism, the amateur filmmaker can apparently reconcile the local interest with national responsibility, i.e. contribute to the national record by focusing on the enriching detail of the local environment. For Grierson, amateur filmmaking is only legitimised to the extent that it plays such a role in encouraging active national-local citizenship.

It is hard to know what Grierson would have made of *Fit O' The Toon* (1978), put together by Scottish amateur filmmaker Enrico Cocozza, former FOS employee, and prize-winning presence on the amateur cine scene for many years.[23] Certainly its function as "local information service" seems oblique, and its engagement with "local interests" confined, even within Grierson's narrowed definitions, straying no more than a few hundred yards in any direction from the filmmaker's own front door. Its access to "local" audiences also seems to have been limited: *Fit O' The Toon* won no competition recognition, nor did it even reach the "sub-local" audiences of the Scottish amateur film movement. The ambitions involved seem altogether more "microhistorical" as Zimmermann might put it. In an almost two-hour film, Cocozza creates an impression of daily life along a couple of roads in his home town of Wishaw in Lanarkshire, stringing together scenes of everyday activity, and interviews with passers-by, usually neighbours or locals well-known to himself. The film's title translates roughly as "at the foot of the town", the setting within which Cocozza shoots most of the incidents included in the film, many from his own living room window. (see Fig. 5-3) Immediately striking is the film's introduction of Scots dialect in the title, and in its intense sense of location: focus is placed relentlessly on a non-descript road junction with apparently little historical significance, rather than a site making more of a claim to Wishavian, or perhaps even Scottish fame. The film seems

---

[22] Malthouse, "John Grierson Discusses the A.C.W. 'Commended' Films", 150.
[23] For more information on Enrico Cocozza, see Mitch Miller's chapter in this collection.

conscious of restricted ambitions and narrowed perspectives, whilst remaining unashamedly content with them. Cocozza's voice-over sets an appropriately semi-ironic scene:

> This film is an impression of the fit o' the toon in Wishaw, in the course of a day in late summer 1978. And you are going to see the following interesting people... [Cocozza then goes on to list a long litany of everyone who will appear in his film, recognising the importance of each individual by doing so]... not to mention many other charming people who live, work, serve, gamble, drink or play at the fit o' the toon...

Fig. 5-3 frame enlargement from *Fit O' The Toon* (1978)
Source: Scottish Screen Archive

Here, in contrast to the introduction in *Seawards the Great Ships*, the location seems to need little mythologisation or explanation: an assumption is marked in the voice-over that the spectator already knows these people and places well, and can readily position them within the frame of his or her own experience. From the outset the film focuses on lives and locations in terms of such potential for recognition, rather than in relation to any narrative service they might render: in his interviews, Cocozza asks random Wishavians how they spend their days, when they go shopping and so on. (see Fig. 5-4) After a sequence showing bread and rolls being delivered to the bakery—curiously accompanied on the soundtrack by seventies funk music—he halts a sceptical-looking pensioner:

> Cocozza: Are you always the first customer in the morning?
> Man: Well yes
> Cocozza: What time do you get up?
> Man: We're out seven o'clock
> Cocozza: Seven o'clock? You're not up nearly as early as me then?
> Man: Oh no
> Cocozza: No, and you're always down here first thing?
> Man: About first thing…
> Cocozza: For your rolls is it?
> Man: Rolls
> Cocozza: Very good. Do you enjoy your rolls then?
> Man: Certainly do
> Cocozza: That's lovely
> Man: (man tries to say something but Cocozza talks over him)
> Cocozza: Fine, fine. Oh well, we'll let you get your rolls then
> Man: Yes
> Cocozza: Fine

Fig. 5-4 frame enlargement from *Fit O' The Toon* (1978)
Source: Scottish Screen Archive

Immediately following this short exchange, the film cuts inside the bakery, where Cocozza asks the owner how his day tends to pan out. Connection is subtly drawn between the owners and the customers of the shop, with quiet emphasis placed on the comforting routines of the everyday, and an overall impression created of dignity in the lives and exchanges encountered on one's doorstep. In stark contrast with *Seawards the Great Ships*, the filmmaker interacts with people as a matter of course (rather than hiatus) and allows them to speak for themselves, in ways which contribute or not to the onward movement of the account. A sense is retained here of the protracted nature of the production, and of incidental detail accumulated over time, signalling long-term investment in both community and film that creates a strong effect of local connection.

A relaxed, meandering style and unhurried pacing characterise the film as a whole, which are perhaps too easily dismissed as "slowness" or "redundancy". In *Fit O' The Toon* scenes and interviews are not asked to secure motivation in terms of an organising dominant of any kind: collages of places and people become important not for what they contribute to national or international culture, but for what they contribute to imaginary investment in the local space. Personal, local narratives are referenced and validated, creating an imaginary Wishaw within which the lives of those depicted on screen, and recognising in the audience, are endorsed and appreciated. Where Benedict Anderson has famously described the nation as an "imagined political community", imagined because:

> the members of even the smallest nation will never know most of their fellow members, meet them, or even hear of them... yet in the minds of each lives the image of their communion...[24]

what *Fit O' The Toon* makes clear is that the local community can offer more concrete "communion", dependent less on acts of faith sponsored by remote discourse, than on everyday contact between its participant membership. Cocozza thus shows us not only a small-scale version of an "imagined community" in Anderson's illusionary sense, but the means of its confirmation in the routines played out by the group of individuals introduced at the beginning of the film.

This very different way of looking at an apparently everyday world is made possible by the *parallel* film production and exhibition culture that helps to define amateur cinema. *Fit O' The Toon* was made with a small Super-8 camera, edited at home, and shown in community spaces such as town halls, and at screenings organised by other film societies and amateur

---

[24] Anderson, *Imagined Communities*, 6.

cine clubs. This active and highly localised exhibition network ensured that the film could be seen by many people who would be interested in how it represented their own and neighbouring towns, without ever being recognised by an international audience: this film was never mentioned in national or international newspapers or magazines, something often used as an indicator of a film's importance. Undoubtedly the film has posterity value: Cocozza has certainly preserved a time, a place, a way of life and a people now inevitably changed or disappeared altogether. Perhaps more importantly however the film preserves the filmmaker's relationships with his subjects, and a sense of his own participation as a kind of everyday "contacting" of his community. For all its stress on observation, *Fit O' The Toon* involves little sense of "looking in" at these people and places from an external perspective. A film such as this is not a *product* to be consumed by a remote audience, but a *process* to be relished by filmmaker and subject: it need not mediate between local and national—let alone international—concerns: the local is made "strange" and perhaps even marvellous here, for the *familiar* gaze.

According to this argument, non-fiction films such as *Fit O' The Toon* ultimately offer an inward-looking vision of the nation, which escapes most existing conceptions of national cinemas, precisely because it does not address issues of national significance, and is not viewed by a national audience. As Andrew Higson comments, upon the limitations of nationalistic surveys:

> Historical accounts of national cinemas have too often been premised on unproblematised notions of nationhood and its production. The search for a stable and coherent national identity can only be successful at the expense of repressing internal differences, tensions and contradictions—differences of class, race, gender, region, etc.[25]

As we have seen, the articulation of local specificity, championed by amateur filmmakers—sometimes with the encouragement of professionals such as Grierson—has largely been repressed by accounts of the nation insensitive to internal contradictions. Rather, such accounts have favoured a narrowed sample of locations and images, determining moments, and the symbolic work of a particular range of canonical texts. The great strength of amateur film production was however that it could happen anywhere, with scant concern for centralising logics and demands. Localism may be understood in this sense as a quite literally *de-centring* process, where location can become vital, or just as equally, completely unimportant.

---

[25] Higson, "The Concept of National Cinema", 43.

In these non-fiction films, place "authorises" filmmaking; focus is given insistently to setting and the individuals who occupy it. In *Fit O' The Toon*, the people found moving through its highly focused zone of action are merely transitory passers-by, caught up in a process of passing time that will exceed the duration of their own lives. While many of the participants in *Fit O' The Toon* may no longer live there, or remain alive, Wishaw still exists to be filmed by today's amateur filmmakers. Once completed, this hypothetical contemporary documentary would exist to be screened alongside earlier films about Wishaw, films where its status as "A Film By Enrico Cocozza" takes on less importance than the fact that is a film *about* the Wishavian community.

In writing about British feature films in the context of both increasing European harmonisation and globalisation, Mike Wayne outlines four categories of contemporary national film production: embedded films; disembedded films; cross-border films; and anti-national national films.[26] Amateur variants of these categories are certainly discernible. The travel films examined by Heather Norris Nicholson, for example, could well be seen as amateur cross-border films,[27] however the first two categories have direct and immediate usefulness in relation to questions of localism and amateur filmmaking. Embedded films:

> are pitched primarily (although not exclusively) for the national market, either because the budgets (including the marketing budgets) for the films are not sufficiently high for there to be a reasonable expectation that they will gain profile abroad, and/or because the cultural material which the film is dealing with has not had sufficiently successful prior circulation in the international market.[28]

While in the context of professional feature filmmaking, embedded films tend to be comedies or small-scale dramas, the low- or no-budget amateur filmmaker will mostly gravitate towards newsreel and documentary projects. Bert Hogenkamp and Mieke Lauwers explain this is the case:

> because making them does not involve the organisational, financial and technical problems that are inherent in the feature film and the animated movie. In addition they are the most direct form of expression the amateur filmmaker can have.[29]

---

[26] Wayne, *The Politics of Contemporary European Cinema*, 33-72.
[27] Norris Nicholson, "British Holiday Films and The Mediterranean", 152-65.
[28] Wayne, *The Politics of Contemporary European Cinema*, 41.
[29] Hogenkamp and Lauwers, "In Pursuit of Happiness", 114.

While the low-budget comedies and dramas often fail to travel beyond national boundaries, amateur newsreels and documentaries often fail to travel beyond the local space. In this sense a film such as *Fit O' the Toon* might represent a kind of *embedded localism*—a localism that is not necessarily insular, but not yet found the distribution needed to reach audiences elsewhere. As a filmmaking strategy, non-fiction reinforces the link between location and representation. However, this is *not* the case for amateur fiction films, as will become clear in the next case study.

Mediating the Local and the National

While the amateur non-fiction films discussed above are defined by a strong sense of place, the fiction films commonly produced by cine clubs often work against this form of localism, and were therefore only rarely embraced by figures such as John Grierson. This is no accident, given that amateur film festivals encouraged entrants from outside national boundaries. In addition to the introspective non-fiction films discussed above, amateur filmmakers were usually simultaneously keen to produce works that could potentially interest audiences from beyond their immediate surroundings. More outward-looking variants of localism seem to be associated with the amateur fiction film in particular, and are explored here in relation to one suggestive example, the Edinburgh Cine Society (ECS) production, *Seven Ages*.

The Edinburgh Cine Society, which still exists at the time of writing, is one of the oldest of such clubs in Britain.[30] Unlike other groups, which were often dominated by a few strong personalities, the ECS seems to have been able to practice a more collective form of filmmaking over a long period of time. Certainly its survival after the general decline of the amateur cine movement in the 1970s is due to the dedication of a number of individuals committed to this group ethos. The case of Edinburgh illustrates well the qualifying perspectives of local knowledge and their ambivalence towards the making of "master" narratives in a particularly apposite way. The example may also illustrate some significant geographical variations beyond the local: Zimmermann, for example, romanticises European cine clubs as being more overtly "political" than

---

[30] Originally designated The Waverley Cine Society, formed in 1936, the club was re-named The Edinburgh Cine Society, only a year later, on the occasion of moving from rented rooms to newly purchased premises at 23 Fettes Row. This name was retained for over fifty years, until the advent of newer technologies eventually had to be recognised. The acronym ECS is retained here for clarity. See Speirs, "A Brief History", 6-8.

their American counterparts, contrasting them favourably with the conservatisms of the American Cinema League:

> The league ran yearly contests, circulated amateur films, and held exhibitions of work, a sort of Americanised, depoliticised, hobbyist version of the more avant-garde and politically orientated European cine clubs.[31]

However, newly conducted research indicates that agitational amateur filmmakers were usually in the minority within cine societies, certainly in Scotland, and probably elsewhere.[32] Certainly, the ECS sat firmly in the mainstream of the amateur film movement, producing documentaries on local events, as well as animations, experimental pieces and many short fiction films. While general conclusions about the club are beyond the reach of this article, the example of *Seven Ages* is suggestive of particularly complex attitudes towards the localism endorsed in a film such as *Fit O' The Toon*.

Seven Ages is a short comedy based around much-quoted lines from Shakespeare's *As You Like It*, from which the film takes its inspiration and structure, describing in sketch-like scenes seven life-stages characterised as those of the: infant, schoolboy, lover, soldier, justice, pantaloon, and second childhood. Such stages describe a supposedly universal journey, between birth and death, which in its consideration of mortality and the circular nature of history, could potentially make for sober drama. However, directed by Ian Brock, the ECS *Seven Ages* manages to find much comedy in the material it is loosely based on. By drawing on Shakespearian references, the film has resonance for viewers well beyond Edinburgh, or even Britain, and clearly aspires towards them. Here, the location of the film exists as a setting for other explorations; unlike *Fit O' The Toon*, location is not important in and of itself. *Seven Ages* really could have been made anywhere.

Following the credits, the satiric tone of the film is set unambiguously. *Seven Ages* opens on a shot of a globe spinning on its axis. Already it is clear from the use of this image, rather than a map of Edinburgh, that this is not to be a film about the Scottish capital city. When this movement is halted by the sudden intrusion of a hand into the frame, the story begins. The camera tilts up, and through smoke we see a figure costumed as William Shakespeare, who delivers probably over-familiar lines: "All the world's a stage, And all the men and women merely players", establishing

---

[31] Zimmermann, "Morphing History into Histories", 119.
[32] Shand, *Amateur Cinema: History, Theory, and Genre*.

a ready-reference for the scenes that follow.[33] (see Fig. 5-5) *Seven Ages* then stages the key moments in an everyman's life, in a humorous way.

The first scene offsets literary pretensions by showing an old man being thrown out of a pub as the narrator, John Piper, intones with mock profundity "They have their exits"... and ... "their entrances", as the man stumbles into a nearby public toilet. The cultural elevation of Shakespeare is set against the bodily functions of an old man. Such ironic contrast between high literary reference and low burlesque is evident across much ECS output, and resonates with tensions between aspirations to cultural security and senses of reduced status, which constantly haunt the amateur cine movement itself. The whole film demonstrates a particular enjoyment in mocking figures of authority: the next scene shows a city gent, trying to impress a nanny with his natural affinity with babies, being covered in sick for his troubles. Then the "whining schoolboy" goes from being thrown out of the house, to falling into the arms of the law. When the police drop him off at school, the schoolboy is shown sticking his tongue out at the officers, in a far cry from the civic amateur filmmaking Grierson endorsed. While the early part of the film is economical and precisely rendered via more or less emulatory cinematic codes, later sequences take on a somewhat more surreal character. The courtroom scene is a case in point. Here the visuals once again undermine the deliberate portentousness of the narration. For example, when the judge enters and takes his position, it is announced; "In fair round belly with good capon lined..." and we see that the actor portraying the judge has made his character into a caricature by adding a rotund fake belly. (see Fig. 5-6) "With eyes severe and beard of formal cut" accompanies close-ups of the judge as he looks sternly over his glasses at the accused—the same man thrown out of the pub at the beginning of the film. "Full of wise saws and modern instances"—the judge addresses the chamber (although we do not hear what he says) and the whole courtroom suddenly erupts in laughter in an unexpected manner. A policeman even nudges the accused man to laugh, and then he too joins in. "And though he plays his part" intones the narration, as the camera zooms in on the book in front of the judge to reveal that he is actually reading a cartoon strip about teachers, which bears a striking resemblance to the *The Dandy*, a well-known Scottish comic, assimilated into a wider British culture. Plainly this is burlesque comedy in its more serious sense: making fun of institutions and those appointed to uphold their values.

---

[33] Shakespeare, *As You Like It*, Act II, Scene 7, 87.

Amateur Film Re-Located: Localism in Fact and Fiction 175

Fig. 5-5 frame enlargement from *Seven Ages* (1957)
Source: Scottish Screen Archive

Fig. 5-6 frame enlargement from *Seven Ages* (1957)
Source: Scottish Screen Archive

While the satire is frequently rendered with conviction, there seems to be less technical cohesion than is perhaps evident from the above description. The courtroom episode is bizarre for its unexplained laughter, but the soldier sequence that follows involves still more incongruous juxtapositions that seem to point towards problems in execution rather than any deliberate eccentricity. Quite simply, it seems as if the sequence is being improvised. The movement from a soldier being attacked by "natives" appearing from behind trees, then fighting in bushes where they find an annoyed golfer, before ending up with the soldier being shot by a cannon, is the most extreme example of the very loose associational logics involved. As Zimmermann comments, such an apparent loss of expressive coherence is symptomatic—the desire to make a technically accomplished film is frequently undermined by poor execution of certain scenes—of peculiarly amateur anxieties:

> Amateur films more often than not lack form, structure, style, and a coherence of normative visual tropes, precisely because they occupy psychic realms and psychic fantasies that are themselves unformed and forming. These various "lacks" and "insufficiencies," if you will, are exactly what make the amateur film such a complicated social document, where the larger political world collides with psychic terrains, where invisibility vies with visibility.[34]

Written with the example of home movies in mind, her remarks highlight a tendency also traced in many amateur fiction films. Variously describing the resulting aesthetic consequences as those of a "primitive cinema" or a body of "artistically inchoate works", this aesthetic of "lacks" is seen as especially troubling for fiction films made in the community mode, such as *Seven Ages*.[35] In practical terms, film scripts for such projects were often not fully worked out, leaving gaps to be improvised on the set itself. Minus the financial pressures that constrain professional productions, opportunities for improvisation amongst amateur actors routinely present themselves. At the same time, forward planning means that films made for the community mode were less likely to be "unformed and unforming" than home movies were. As a result, these more elaborate productions, which have some sense of the overall narrative, coupled with improvisation, can more accurately be described as having *semi-formed and unforming* production histories.

---

[34] Zimmermann, "Morphing History into Histories", 112.
[35] Ibid., 112-113.

While amateur fiction films such as *Seven Ages* feature many elements that betray geographical origins—such as the pubs and shops of Edinburgh, or the soldier with the Scottish flag—in general, amateur fiction films do not emphasise their locations in the same way as their amateur non-fiction counterparts. Although they remain available for acts of recognition by the audience, the locations in amateur fiction films seem largely irrelevant to the stories that are told. As in their professional equivalents, locations may be exploited for spectacle, but largely remain subservient to a fundamentally narrative economy. Rather than being the main focus of investigation, as the town of Wishaw was in *Fit O' the Toon*, Edinburgh instead merely becomes a background to the unfolding narrative of *Seven Ages*, whose very incongruity may add a further amusing dimension. Are these amateur films which therefore attempt to suppress their cultural origins, in order to appeal to audiences elsewhere? This possibility suggests clear overlaps with what Wayne describes as "disembedded" professional films, such as *Four Weddings and a Funeral* (1993) or *Bean: The Ultimate Disaster Movie* (1997):

> These are the films which have the budgets and the cultural potential to succeed...The cultural materials which they exploit in doing this are, as we have seen, the repertoire of national imagery that has already been achieved or may achieve wide circulation in the international market. It is in this sense that the films are disembedded from the national context.[36]

Notting Hill (1999) and *Love Actually* (2003) are more recent examples of disembedded British films designed to incorporate cultural material that would be easily exported to the American and international market. Wayne continues by noting that "...there is a real sense in which images designed for international consumption find it difficult to be attuned to the social specificities and diversities of national life."[37] While amateur films were not made for consumption to the same extent, similar processes of cultural masking are detectable at more local levels. Amateur fiction films that aspired to national or international circulation beyond their immediate surroundings often conformed to what might be termed a *disembedded localism*.

As with their professional others, amateur fiction films required more resources, both financial and in terms of personnel, to achieve access to audiences from other parts of the country, and the wider world. From a practical perspective, entering these fiction films into amateur film

---

[36] Wayne, *The Politics of Contemporary European Cinema*, 42.
[37] Ibid., 42.

festivals both nationally and abroad certainly might achieve this. In Britain, the winners of *Amateur Cine World's* Ten Best film contest, held every year from 1936 to 1984 in London, were packaged together and distributed as a feature for regional film theatres around both the U.K. and abroad. The winners of this contest often drew on recognised film genres in order to enhance the cultural mobility of their work. Amateur films that were *disembedded* had a much greater chance of being seen by a wider audience. This was the case then, and it remains the case now, in relation to potential access to amateur films through the both the archive and the Internet. However, regional archives have tended to focus their promotional activity on embedded non-fiction films, which have a cultural capital that tax payers and funding bodies understand, a value that currently eludes amateur fiction films.

Conclusions

Case studies of non-fiction and fiction amateur films support a strong argument that localism should no longer be seen as synonymous with the parochialism often invoked to devalue or marginalise non-professional modes. Amateur output across the genres represented by *Fit O' The Toon* and *Seven Ages*, displays rather a nuanced awareness of both the local sphere's articulation with the national and the international, and considerable ingenuity in negotiating self-definitions made simultaneously across these overlapping registers. The categories of *embedded localism* and *disembedded localism* have been introduced here to enable a more precise understanding of this often complex process, and the characteristic contradiction between desires for separation and participation marking so much amateur film practice. However, it should be noted that these "are not mutually exclusive categories; films can occupy more than one category".[38] It is certainly possible to imagine future studies that will complicate the framework that I have suggested here somewhat. The fact that these categories, developed for the study of commercial cinema, could with slight modifications be so easily transferred to the consideration of the amateur sector, demonstrates once again the relatively *relational* cultural geographies of the films produced by both lone workers and amateur cine clubs.

---

[38] Wayne, *The Politics of Contemporary European Cinema*, 40.

Works Cited

Anderson, Benedict. *Imagined Communities: Reflections on the Spread of Nationalism*. London: Verso, 1991.

Chalfen, Richard. "Cinema Naiveté: A Study of Home Moviemaking as Visual Communication." *Studies in the Anthropology of Visual Communication* 2, no.2 (1975): 87-103.

Foucault, Michel. *The Archaeology of Knowledge*. New York: Pantheon, 1972.

Fullerton, John, ed. *Film History* 17, no. 1 (2005). (special issue on local film)

Higson, Andrew. "The Concept of National Cinema." *Screen* 40, no. 4 (1989): 36-46.

Hill, John. "Scotland doesna mean much tae Glesca: Some notes on *The Gorbals Story*." In *Scotch Reels: Scotland in Cinema and Television*, edited by Colin McArthur, 100-111. London: British Film Institute, 1982.

Hogenkamp, Bert and Mieke Lauwers. "In Pursuit of Happiness? A Search for The Definition of Amateur Film." In *Jubilee Book: Essays on Amateur Film*, 107-116. Charleroi: Association Européenne Inédits, 1997.

Ishizuka, Karen. "Artifacts of Culture." *Journal of Film Preservation* 52 (1996): 15-20.

—. "The Home Movie: A Veil of Poetry." In *Jubilee Book: Essays on Amateur Film*, edited by Nancy Kapstein, 45-50. Charleroi: Association Européenne Inédits, 1997.

Jenkins, Keith. *Re-thinking History*. London: Routledge, 1991.

Malthouse, Gordon. "John Grierson Discusses the A.C.W. 'Commended' Films and Throws out a Challenge to Amateur Movie-Makers." *Amateur Cine World* 13, no. 2 (1949): 150-153.

McArthur, Colin. "Scotland and Cinema: The Iniquity of the Fathers." In *Scotch Reels: Scotland in Cinema and Television*, edited by Colin McArthur, 40-69. London: British Film Institute Publishing, 1982.

Norris Nicholson, Heather. "British Holiday Films and The Mediterranean: At Home and Abroad With Home Movies, 1925-1936." *Film History* 15, no. 2 (2003): 152-165.

Shakespeare, William. *As You Like It*. Harmondsworth: Penguin, 1973.

Shand, Ryan. *Amateur Cinema: History, Theory, and Genre (1930-80)*. PhD thesis submitted to the University of Glasgow, 2007.

—. "Theorising Amateur Cinema: Limitations and Possibilities." *The Moving Image: The Journal of the Association of Moving Image Archivists* 8, no. 2 (2008), forthcoming.
Sherington, Jo. *"To Speak Its Pride": The Work of The Films of Scotland Committee*. Glasgow: Scottish Film Council, 1996.
Southgate, Beverley. *History: What and Why: Ancient, Modern and Postmodern Perspectives*. London: Routledge, 1996.
Speirs, Norman. "Edinburgh Ciné & Video Society: A Brief History." *Cine Chat* 29 (1996): 6-8.
Stone, Melinda and Streible, Dan, eds. *Film History* 15, no. 2 (2003).
Toulmin, Vanessa and Martin Loiperdinger. "Is it You? Recognition, Representation and Response in Relation to the Local Film." *Film History* 17, no. 1 (2005): 7-18.
Wayne, Mike. *The Politics of Contemporary European Cinema: Histories, Borders, Diasporas*. Bristol: Intellect, 2002.
Zimmermann, Patricia R. *Reel Families: A Social History of Amateur Film*. Bloomington and Indianapolis: Indiana University Press, 1995.
—. "Morphing History into Histories: From Amateur Film to the Archive of the Future." *The Moving Image* 1, no. 1 (2001): 108-130.

Films Cited

Bean: The Ultimate Disaster Movie
(Polygram, Working Title, Tiger Aspect, 1997) 35mm., 90 mins.
Fit O' The Toon
(Enrico Cocozza, 1978) Super-8mm., 110 mins.
Four Weddings and a Funeral
(Channel Four, Polygram, Working Title, New World, 1993) 35mm., 117 mins.
The Gorbals Story
(New World Pictures, 1949) 35 mm., 74 mins.
Love Actually
(Universal, Studio Canal, Working Title, DNA Films, 2003) 35mm., 135 mins.
Notting Hill
(Polygram, Working Title, Bookshop Productions, Notting Hill Pictures, 1999) 35 mm., 124 mins.
Seawards the Great Ships
(Crown Office of Information, Clyde Shipbuilders Association, Schoenfeld Films, Templar Film Studios, 1960) 35 mm., 28 mins.

Seven Ages
(Ian Brock, 1957) 16mm., 15 mins.
A Study in Reds
(Miriam Bennett, 1927) 16mm., no running time available.

CHAPTER SIX

LOCATING THE FAMILY FILM: THE CRITICS, THE COMPETITION AND THE ARCHIVE

IAN GOODE

The holdings of the Scottish Screen Archive contain around 2700 items catalogued under the label "amateur". This represents roughly 26% of the collection: of this total, around 330 films have been assigned the more specific generic label of "home movie". The "family film" of concern here is a close derivative—or perhaps sub-set—of this more familiar category, and refers to those items that take the immediately available environment— usually but not exclusively the home, and the family within it—as their subjects. The grouping thus implies a work that privileges domestic themes, with, particularly in the British social context, accompanying connotations of ownership, propriety and belonging. However, not every home accommodates a family, and not every home movie need necessarily feature the family. A home movie also importantly suggests therefore a mode of production, a literal process of *making* in the home (i.e. shot, edited, projected and viewed) that separates it from its professional and commercial counterparts.

On the evidence of the archive, the narrower sub-set of the family film represents one of the most commonly chosen means of deploying the camera for the amateur filmmaker, although the enterprise involved has gained little serious critical recognition. The following survey of the family film therefore addresses a small sample of the substantial holdings of the Scottish Screen Archive, and considers a number of critical issues posed by this material. The enquiry is intended less as a populist reclaiming of the family film, than as an assertion of its critical potentials: it prefers to pose questions concerning the family film's positioning in and by the amateur film movement, about the paths followed as particular family films have found their way into the archive, and contemplates the issues that these findings raise for the study of this specific mode of amateur filmmaking.

At the centre of the essay is a concern for the amateur family film as a form of specific cinematic practice, hitherto a troubling emphasis. Patricia Zimmermann, for example, has argued that "amateur film deploys no systematic cinematic language" a supposedly implicit lack registering a problematic position in relation to the study of film *per se*, because it undermines assumptions about what a film is, and what the study of film can legitimately be concerned with.[1] Jane Simon underwrites such uncertainty, when she suggests that Zimmerman's account of amateur film, "leaves open the question of how to give critical attention to the field of amateur film when it is so difficult to physically—and sometimes conceptually—locate."[2] This is particularly true of the family film, because whilst archive holdings suggest that the home movie featuring the family is one of the most common and immediately available subjects for amateur filmmakers, its status even within the film culture of Scottish (and British) amateur cinema itself remains noticeably ambiguous. Amateur cinema critics write, often derisively, about the familiar "baby on the lawn" picture, because they want filmmakers to demonstrate more technical and creative ambition, but given that this subject is so commonplace in amateur filmmaking, it has to be accommodated in the critical discourse surrounding amateur cinema, as well as in the competitions and film festivals run by regional and national organisations and several key cine journals.

One productive consequence of such uncertain location of the family film within amateur cine culture, is that the significance of this sort of material can be appropriated for a variety of disciplinary ends. Film historian Rachael Low, for example, asserts of amateur films that:

> in their sheer inability to select and emphasise, to interpret and pre-digest the truth, the worst of these films from the artistic point of view have a strength for the historian as documents.[3]

From such a perspective, aesthetic insignificance does not necessarily equal historical insignificance, and it is this lack of status as *film*, attributed by Low and others, which ushers the study of amateur cinema firmly towards social history. Ironically perhaps, aesthetic status may be re-defined in such contexts: Richard Chalfen's anthropologically informed

---

[1] Zimmerman, *Reel Families: A Social History of Amateur Film*, 276.
[2] Simon, "Recycling Home Movies", 190.
[3] Low, quoted in Cookson, "Amateur Film and the Archives", 5.

accounts of what he clarifies as the "home mode of visual communication" do begin to acknowledge the typical *form* of such filmic material when he assigns the precept—"cinema naïveté" to the genre.[4] He also identifies a tension around the invaluable potential of the home mode to document, whilst remaining apparently free of the intentions and conventions of professional filmmaking:

> this mode of photographic representation is characterised by the non-professional use of communications technology for private "documentary" purposes rather than for public or "artistic" use.[5]

These different positions testify to the historical and anthropological value of the family film, whilst exposing the uncertain and problematic critical status of both this genre of non-professional filmmaking, and the peripheral and emerging status of amateur cinema within Film Studies. Ironically for the academy, it is the essentially non-filmic or non-cinematic characteristics of the material that recur throughout most writing on amateur cinema, characteristics arguably epitomised by the family film highlighted in this essay.

In this context, concerns with filmic quality necessarily sit side-by-side with an attention to social function, and the pursuit of more flexible definitions of amateur film such as those offered by Bert Hogenkamp and Mieke Lauwers, which seem helpful in granting important and different ranges of intent to the amateur filmmaker:

> it is possible to think of amateur film-makers as those who aim for technical perfection in their work and have clear artistic aspirations. They wear the label "amateur film-maker" as a sign of honour. They subscribe to specialist magazines, follow new developments in the field, and participate in competitions and festivals. Meanwhile, the term amateur film-maker also evokes an image of Dad capturing the highlights of family life on celluloid.[6]

The duality identified here by Hogenkamp and Lauwers suggests how easily the family film and the amateur filmmaker might fit these disciplinary assignations, whilst also departing from them, particularly when viewed through the critical discourse of amateur cinema. With this simultaneously parlous and culturally common presence of amateur

---

[4] Chalfen, "Cinéma Naïveté: A Study of Home Moviemaking as Visual Communication."
[5] Ibid., 87-88.
[6] Hogenkamp and Lauwers, "In Pursuit of Happiness", 110.

cinema and the family film in mind, what follows traces the position and the terms deployed to frame the discussion of the family film within amateur film criticism and culture in Scotland during the period between the early 1930s and around 1960.

The Family Film and the Amateur Critics

The journal *Amateur Cine World* was launched in 1934 and ran until 1967: its contents combined technical advice, organisational guidance and critical discussion on various issues pertinent to the amateur filmmaker, ranging from the acquisition of filmmaking equipment available to buy, to discussions of professional cinema releases. A survey of the journal through 1945-1960 reveals immediately how the family film stood at the centre of debates concerning amateur cine possibilities, and was critically positioned as potentially belonging to the category of both documentary and fictional filmmaking, thereby helping to cultivate skills in both modes.

It can be seen that the journal was keen to encourage amateur filmmakers not only to learn about filmmaking equipment and its use through the advice it offered, but to also recognise and appreciate the expressive and artistic possibilities of the medium made available through this equipment too. For example, the critic Jack Smith, writing a series of articles addressing the "committed" amateur in 1958, is keen to stress the perils of technophilia when he asserts that "the man who knows that a pair of eyes and a good imagination are more precious than half-a-dozen gadgets" increases his potential as a filmmaker.[7] There is clear evidence that *Amateur Cine World* was keen to offer a critical lead to more serious amateurs, and to aspire to a type of filmmaking that defied the stereotypical assumptions held about amateur cinema by, for example, the professional documentary and educational filmmaker Mary Field:

> It is several years since Mary Field told me she would like an amateur film to be made about unmarried mothers, and another about unwanted children. She complained then that our films are unbearably *trite*...[8]

If the amateur follows Field's request and ventures into a more public and topical forum, as the Claremont Cine Society of Bristol did in 1959, the results are commended in relation to the authentic criteria of documentary, rather than the manipulative mechanisms of fiction:

---

[7] Smith, "The Committed Amateur", 562.
[8] Davies, "A Movie Makers Diary", 925.

one of the ten best of 1959 has mentally retarded spastic children for its subject. The treatment is equally purposeful and sympathetic, yet never sentimental.[9]

Similarly, when the children of a family were used in the film *Big Fish* in 1948 to promote road safety, the clear social and public good of the film gains approbation as one of the "Ten Best"—the annual competition staged by *Amateur Cine World*.

The limits of merely recording the family on film are highlighted elsewhere by the filmmaker and critic H. A. Postlethwaite, who also raises the question of who the family film is essentially for, beyond the family featured in the film:

> there are few things more boring than sitting through two or three reels of somebody else's family record. It is all very well to say that such a film can be given a wider appeal by skilful editing, with touches of humour here and there and departures from the strictly family theme, but the fact remains that if it is a good family record, it will for that very reason be poor entertainment for the viewer outside the family.[10]

Postlethwaite regards the family film as belonging essentially to the field of non-fiction visual record-making, yet writing as a critic of film in a journal aimed at aspirational amateur filmmakers, also requires him to concede the limitations of this material. So whilst the content of this most prevalent genre of amateur cinema can be retrospectively claimed as "evidence" by historians and anthropologists, as I have noted, the critical discourse on the family as a potential stimulus to filmmaking projects beyond the impulse to record, steers the amateur towards the planned narrative scenarios of comedy/fiction.

In order to realise these enhanced scenarios, the writers of *Amateur Cine World* begin to identify what it is that amateur filmmakers should avoid, as Jack Smith pointedly suggests:

> it's true, of course, that the family film user will probably at some stage decide to try and make his holiday records and his scenes in the garden into something more coherent than just a random collection of odd shots. But (as I've tried to explain repeatedly) this is *not* film-making of the kind we're concerned with in these articles… [11]

---

[9] Smith, "The A.C.W. Ten Best Films of 1959 Competition Results", 1217.

[10] Postlethwaite, "'What's the date': Looking At The Family Film of Ten Years Ago", 42.

[11] Smith, "You Must Have an Audience", 1002.

Smith is referring here to that tendency of amateurs to use the film camera as if it were a modification of "still" apparatus, producing separate snapshot photographs of the family, without the necessity of any advance planning to link them together. As numerous commentators warn, one of the consequences of this habit when transferred to film-making is likely to be a pronounced lack of continuity between sequences. In order to avoid this random quality of pointing and shooting, the filmmaker must recognise the need to break free from, what the editor of *Amateur Cine World* Gordon Malthouse, described as "the stranglehold of photography":

> if the amateur is ever to make good films he must cease to look upon himself as a photographer. Let him by all means continue to make use of his affiliation to still photography, but let him also remember that still photography is one of several branches of endeavour to which he has an affinity.[12]

The branches of endeavour referred to here seemingly relate to location, story, plotting, editing and acting, and while these elements are seen as integral to the professional cine enterprise, they are apparently by no means common to the often random and unplanned recordings of the amateur family film.

The role of *Amateur Cine World* as creative advisor to its readership is demonstrated by the practitioner Kenneth Pople, who points out how consideration in advance of where the family were likely to be assembled can potentially function as a means of provoking ideas for plots:

> I know of one very successful amateur who finds it helps to develop the situation by choosing a specific location—a house, a garden, a wood over which he goes with a metaphorical toothcomb, noting every possible filmic location, and working out his plot from them... [13]

Advice can though sometimes take on the feel of critical stricture. In this example, quoted from an Eastman Kodak Handbook originating in the United States, advice also ushers in evaluative criteria concerning just what a *movie* should not be, if the quest for continuity is to be successful:

> continuity is the chief ingredient of the successful home movie. Between its first and last scenes every movie should tell a complete and interesting story. It should not record a succession of shots of different subjects, but

---

[12] Malthouse, "The Stranglehold of Photography", 272.
[13] Pople, "Looking for Plots", 1095.

rather a succession of sequences of different subjects... A movie should be as free as possible from posing...[14]

It is clear then how the advisory and instructive writing offered to filmmakers by *Amateur Cine World* encourages the amateur to improvise with resources that will lend family footage the appearance of a technically proficient *film* with certain formal competences, and avoid the pitfalls of random sequences:

> the best family films are usually those that contain brisk, purposeful action. But this is one of the hardest things to achieve under normal back-garden conditions. So a useful gambit is to introduce some incident-forming prop.[15]

In a similar vein, it is suggested that the self-consciousness typically exhibited in front of the camera—that reveals rather than conceals the familiarity between people in front and behind the camera—is undercut if the family are treated as a cast of *actors* with specified functions, as the critic Basil Harley states:

> we may segregate the type of "actors" that we are likely to encounter into three groups. First the members of the family whom we want to record on their holidays, or at their hobbies or even at their work. Secondly, the real amateur actor with whom we are producing a story film, and thirdly, the men on the farms, in the workshops or on the sea, around whose work we are making a documentary. How many times have we seen and suffered a screen full of embarrassed people, giggling at one another or mouthing meaningless nothings at the invisible cameraman, or mercifully perhaps, standing in dumb terror in front of the lens?[16]

Harley goes on to stress how the family must be *directed* by the filmmaker in order to avoid the pitfalls described.

In such ways, *Amateur Cine World* encourages its readership to break away from simply recording the events of family life, by using the location of the home as a suggestive setting, fabricating incident as a stimulus to action, and treating the family as potential cast members to construct "artificial" narratives:

---

[14] Double Run, "Success With The Family Film", 249.
[15] Sound Track, "Enliven Your Family Films With This Simple Prop", 1282.
[16] Harley, "The Art of Directing Amateur Actors", 24.

if you are looking for a theme for a family film this Christmas, why not centre your story round one of the presents the family is to receive? You might show how Junior makes some perfume for mother, or how father spends his time playing with his son's train, while the boy secretly tries out the pipe he gave his father.[17]

Not every critic however was entirely comfortable with the suggestion that the family film would remain a family film if it were cast, staged and performed using the conventions of narrative fiction. Harry Postlethwaite summarises wider anxieties succinctly:

a family film purports to be factual; if it is possible by rearranging scenes to construct sequences that seem to tell a story, well and good; but the story must have every appearance of truth... nor would I describe a family film in which a friend plays the part of father "as the genuine article..."[18]

Even a brief sketch of critical discourse on the family film confirms the uncertainties of locating such efforts within amateur cine culture, which are clearly inherited by subsequent academic criticism. If the family film ceases to be a visual record and the filmmaker seeks to develop the technical competences of continuity, editing and narrative, then the outcome could become defamiliarised, and take on the appearance of something other than a typical family film, as some of these views suggest.

A further problem rests upon what happens when a family film leaves its originating private and domestic context, and is circulated in a wider public sphere. *Amateur Cine World* clearly wants amateurs to exceed the familiar conventions of filming the family in the garden, but can a family film appeal to a wider audience? What is at stake for a filmmaker wanting to film the family whilst making technically competent films that follow the advice of the critics and the exemplary practitioners of *Amateur Cine World*? If a family film displays the typical conventions of informal familiarity between camera operator and subject(s), and is subsequently shown to an audience who do not know this family, then how are the stranger-spectators in this "secondary" audience positioned? As Roger Odin points out "in the home movie, those addressed by the film have lived the events depicted. Reading a home movie does not summon the documentarist mode of reading but the private one."[19]

---

[17] Double Run, "A Family Film for Christmas", 793.
[18] Postlethwaite, "'What's the date': Looking At the Family Film of Ten Years Ago", 43.
[19] Odin, "Reflections on The Home Movie as Document", 259.

So how can we account for the "public" spectator of the amateur family film, lacking any sense of ownership or "private" involvement? Few textual concessions aid the viewing activity of such a spectator, positioned as an uninformed witness to the record of the family, attending perhaps at an advertised time and place, scrutinising a re-located—perhaps even "orphaned"—film, now deprived of the shared provenance usually governing its intelligibility. Technical factors only seem to reinforce potential distanciation. Family films of this period were usually silent: and whilst some efforts such as the *Mavor Family Film* (1932) have inter-titles to ease transitions between scenes, most would lack even this degree of continuity. The absence of accompanying commentary only underlines the surrogate nature of looking at the unfamiliar family by the public audience. While points of recognition such as places, dress, and mannerisms may be caught within the image stream, these are not in themselves sufficient to hold the interest and attention of an audience unfamiliar with the family who have been placed before the public. The resulting uncertainty regarding who the family film is for and should be for—if it is made public—persists, for example, in accounts of the Scottish Amateur Film Festival (SAFF) through several decades.

The Family Film and the Scottish Amateur Film Festival

There is little evidence of either the presence or success of the family film in the early years of the Scottish Amateur Film Festival. However, the use of the family as a potential filmmaking resource in films that are not primarily films of record, is signalled most clearly through the endeavours of one of Scotland's most prolific amateur filmmakers—Frank M. Marshall. His film *Just One Thing After Another* (1936) was the novice prize-winner in 1937. The judging notes of Anthony Asquith confirm how members of the family can function effectively as part of the cast for dramatic scenarios: "whimsical film with children acting as grown-ups. The children are charming and the story quite well told. Colour photography very fair."[20] Asquith is clearly evaluating the film using professional criteria—and what seems clear is that such work was not valued by Asquith and the Festival as a family film in the non-fictional sense, but rather as a more expressive and imaginative project, incorporating a particular family as a supposedly more archetypal one, a strategy at which Marshall clearly excelled. The filmmaker's cine career is notable, as Ryan Shand confirms, for this ability to occupy positions

---

[20] Asquith, Scottish Screen Archive Ref. 2/3/13.

between fiction and non-fiction, addressing experiences assumed as common currency, while continuing to use his own immediate family to populate his films.[21] (see Fig. 6-1) The frequency of Marshall's output suggests that the camera became a common fixture of family life, allowing him to build the rapport that enabled him to treat and direct his children and relatives as performers, rather than as "posed" members of the family who would stare self-consciously at his camera, in the all too familiar manner of the more typical family film

Marshall's ability to construct humorous and concise narrative scenarios out of the situations and locations of family life is frequently awarded commendation and prizes by the judges of the festival. This produces a rather ambivalently located history that is not necessarily confined to non-fiction. The Marshall short *Tree for Two* (1957), and T. H. Thoms' drama *A Hit and a Miss* (1956), were awarded prizes in competition as the best family films, yet, they are understandably catalogued by the archive as amateur comedy, and amateur fiction, respectively.

Echoing his predecessors, competition judge Charles Frend clearly evaluates *A Hit and a Miss* (see Fig. 6-2) using criteria applicable to dramatic fiction:

> A splendid comedy. The story was good and extremely well put over. There was a considerable amount of character drawing. This was very successful, particularly in the case of the formidable old lady next door, who gave an excellent performance. The handling of the children was good. The husband creeping away was a shot he would remember for a long time. The editing was good, the film was well put together. Close-ups were cleverly used to get people from one place to another.[22]

There are examples of a family film being commended for its non-fictional qualities too. The *Amateur Cine World* annual "Ten Best" competition staged in London, and then touring nationally, included winners in the early 1950s including *Susan's Party* (1950) and *Portrait of Peter* (1952). In contrast to the comments of the SAFF judges, the evaluative criteria revealed by the critics of *Amateur Cine World* are clearly non-fictional *and* exceptional for the family films that are also functioning as films of record:

---

[21] Shand, "The Hobbyist Movement in Scottish Amateur Film: A Case Study of Frank Marshall", 2004.
[22] Frend, Scottish Screen Archive Ref. 2/3/43.

Fig. 6-1 frame enlargement from *Tree For Two* (1957)
Source: Scottish Screen Archive

This delightful film is a considerable achievement, for one really does get the impression that one is looking in on a real children's party rather than at a set piece carefully rigged up for the cameraman's benefit. *Susan's Party* has been planned and executed as a *film* rather than as a series of incidents.[23]

There is little of the familiar baby routine in this film. The symbolism which points the pre-natal sequences is perhaps scarcely very appropriate for what is essentially a family film. The film has been conceived as a lyrical essay on babyhood; a series of well arranged patterns, which evoke mood instead of merely stating fact.[24]

It is clear that such films are regarded as exceptional, not only because they are technically competent, but because they also manage to record the family with some degree of creativity without resorting to comic "set pieces" staged around the commonplaces of domestic life. Malthouse reveals how unusual this was in competition films:

---

[23] Malthouse, "Amateur Films worth Talking About". 444.
[24] Malthouse, "Family Affairs", 997.

> Family and holiday films which most of us favour are among the most difficult of all films to make, simply because it is so hard to inject any freshness into them. For this reason they seldom reach the prize-winning class in competitions which attract entries of a high level.[25]

A glance at amateur competition culture thus indicates that the family film is publicly accommodated in a critical discourse that traverses the boundary of fiction and non-fiction. It is immediately evident that the more typical non-fictional family film of record is less likely to appear in competition in this period, and that the critical challenges or "codes of expertise" such as dramatic continuity and character, set out by *Amateur Cine World*, were more likely to be taken up by the amateur filmmaker using the vehicle of comedy drama. It is on this basis that the films of Frank Marshall could occupy a joint public and private status, gaining frequent recognition at the festival as comedy fiction, whilst also serving as cherished films of record for the Marshall family.

Fig. 6-2 frame enlargement from *A Hit and A Miss* (1956)
Source: Scottish Screen Archive

The critical accounts of the SAFF appearing in Scottish newspapers, particularly those written by the film specialist Forsyth Hardy, also

---

[25] Malthouse, "Prizewinners and Why", 41.

confirm how difficult the family film was to accommodate for the critic, eventually necessitating the introduction of a specialised entry category, as this account from 1950 notes:

> In an effort to segregate some of the entries, a new class of "Personal Records" was created this year. Most of the films in this class were either holiday impressions or studies of baby in the back garden. Sometimes as in *Johnnie Looks Back* entered by John O'Russell of Balerno, they were both![26]

Hardy, as a practicing critic of professional cinema is required to give a cultural context to amateur cinema, as he does in the following extracts from 1951:

> The film is the most professional of all the arts in the sense that it's so expensive few amateurs can afford to practice it. Even of those who do, many are content with pictures of baby in the back garden, the annual summer holiday, or the occasional trip abroad. But potentially the amateur who is imaginative as well as affluent can use the film as excitingly as the professional, and he often does.[27]

It is apparent that for Hardy the criteria of value remain creative and artistic:

> films shown at the thirteenth Scottish Amateur Film Festival in Glasgow last weekend did not differ greatly from the films shown at the twelfth or the sixth or, except in number, the first. The film of baby in the back garden was there. So was the film about a visit to a farm. There was the film made during a motoring summer holiday. And there was domestic comedy in which the players are always all-but laughing at their own antics... of their kind these films were admirable. *A Busy Afternoon* again demonstrated that the two year old, preferably with curly hair, is the nearest rival to the Collie dog as the world's best natural actor. Unselfconscious seems too long a word to apply to the activities of this small child busily bathing her doll in the back garden. Here was the unaffected innocence of the small child, sensitively registered by a skilful camera.[28]

Hardy states that he expects and typically associates amateur cinema in the early 1950s with the family film or "baby in the back garden". Against this

---

[26] Hardy, "Amateur Has Lessons to Teach the Studios", 22.
[27] Hardy, "Scottish Amateur Film Festival", 24.
[28] Ibid.

pattern of familiarity, he is apparently searching for words of critical approbation relevant to the film he has isolated for comment, and seems to have doubts about its very inclusion in competition. Hardy does not know these family members, yet they have been viewed in a public context that requires his critical comment. It feels from his account here however that there is a deeper ambivalence pervading the peculiar publicness of the typical family film, particularly when it is not disguised as comedy fiction, an ambivalence that runs beyond problems of aesthetic or generic classification. This problem of public exhibition, that accompanies the passage of the family film out of the immediate family context and into the critical environments of *Amateur Cine World* and SAFF competition, is reiterated with variation in the case of the family films that go through subsequent processes of *donation* to the archive.

Entering the Archive

The non-competition family films that populate the Scottish Screen Archive tend to be given the title of the family name. Typical examples would be *Stein Family Life* (1932), and the *Mavor Family Film* (1932). Such family films, made in the 1930s but donated to the archive much more recently, are notable for the type of family captured on film—usually wealthy, and often owning and controlling a family business enterprise. Whilst such holdings certainly confirm that the technologies of amateur filmmaking were often restricted during this period to the affluent, there is something beyond questions of social class about the families of these films, raised by the very *presence* of such footage in the archive, namely *motivation*. What is it that prompts their owner to donate their family film collections to the archive, where the material will assume a public status and acquire a shared ownership, apparently at odds with the understanding that the typical family film is a predominantly private affair?

The journeys of family films produced in the 1930s *into* the archive are often initiated by subsequent generations of the families concerned, sometimes through interaction with the mediating cultural agencies of local museums or television programme-makers. Archive records show, for example, how the *Baxter Family Films* (1929-1950) were gifted by a member of the Baxter family, in collaboration with Shetland Islands Council and the Scottish Screen Archive. In this instance, the donor of the films wrote a letter to the archive in 1981, explaining how the watching of a BBC2 programme on the preservation of old footage prompted the consideration of their own family films, taken from the late 1920s onwards.[29] Given lack of access to projection equipment, the donor requests that the original reels be preserved in a more practical medium, requesting copies for Shetland's museum, and for sharing with the next generation of the family:

> My father died before I met my husband. It would mean a great deal to show him and my three children their Shetland great-grandparents and grandparents and me when young—on the move so to speak.[30]

The donor goes on to qualify their motives for donating the films:

> I am very interested in History myself but apart from that I consider it a duty to preserve such things, especially when change in Shetland is accelerating at such a pace.[31]

Shetland Islands Council then contribute to the process, by offering the funding to transfer the original 9.5mm films to 16mm, enabling subsequent copies to be made using videotape. The motivation for the Baxter family in this case seems to be a combination of family posterity and a citizen's commitment to community history.

The films of the Stein family go through a similar process, which involves the next generation of the family and the Smith Art Gallery and Museum in Stirling, during 1985.[32] Similarly, the extensive collection of Bowser family films (1927-1972) arrives at the archive via interaction with the Kilmadock Society—which exists "to promote interest in and appreciation of the history, heritage, environment and well being of Doune, Deanston and Landward."[33]

Certainly the passage of these examples into the archive reveals the importance of official agencies to ensuring that family films are preserved at a local and national level. However, what differentiates the Stein and Bowser families, from the Baxter family is the degree of public status already enjoyed by the families through their activities and influence as families of commerce. There are publications already in circulation that document the influence and status of Norman and Alastair Stein of Bonnybridge, and David Bowser of Argaty.[34] The donation of the films to the archive can be viewed in this context as a continuation of a historical

---

[29] Baxter, Scottish Screen Archive Ref. P/CN82c.
[30] Ibid.
[31] Ibid.
[32] Stein, Scottish Screen Archive Ref. P/CN122.
[33] Bowser, Scottish Screen Archive Ref. P/CN166.
[34] Sanderson, *Stein of Bonnybridge*.

process that maintains social status rather than, or as well as ensuring posterity, which is the case with the Baxter family. The content of the Stein and Bowser films donated to the archive also underlines this distinction.

In the Stein films catalogued as *Stein Family Life* (1932-1934) and *Castlecary Events* (1932-1937), the domestic life of the family is combined with the recording of the activities of the family brickworks in Bonnybridge, and local community events such as Gala day, the opening of Castlecary bowling green, and the Coronation Day celebrations in 1937. (see Fig. 6-3) This assurance in combining and extending the private and domestic into the locally public realms of industry and community leisure, differentiates these family films from those discussed within the critical discourse of *Amateur Cine World* and festival culture.

Fig. 6-3 frame enlargement from *Castlecary Events* (1932-1937)
Source: Scottish Screen Archive

Such emphases are maintained across a wide range of holdings. The Bowser family of Argaty by Doune, were a wealthy land-owning Perthshire family based at Argaty House, and boasting an estate of fourteen hundred acres, depicted frequently in the fifty or so films donated to the archive, traditionally worked through a system of tenant farming. The Bowser films were made by David Charles Bowser, who recorded family and estate life, as an enthusiastic cine enthusiast. Typical examples, fusing family record-keeping with broader documentary interests, include *Family at Nairn* (1933) *Argaty Scenes* (1932) *Jubilee Year* (1935) and *Bowser Fox Hunting and Sports Day* (1936). These films confirm the close relationship of the family to the estate and its working functions. *Family at Nairn* also includes footage of public events such as the Armistice Service at Whitehall, whilst *Agricultural and Highland Shows* (1928) indicates how invested the Bowser family were in the pageantry of the British state as land-owning gentry in rural Scotland. (see Fig. 6-4) Typically, the Bowsers screened the films to the estate workers and their families during the half-day holiday at Christmas, an occasion on which each worker received a gift from Bowser of a shirt and two collars, and their wives a half tea set or similar.[35]

Fig. 6-4 frame enlargement from *Agricultural and Highland Shows* (1928)
Source: Scottish Screen Archive

The Marshall *Family Films* (1931-1938) reveal a similar family status located in the urban context of Bridgeton, Glasgow. In the years following World War One, James Marshall in partnership with his brother, built up a successful family firm dedicated to the manufacture of wheat products such as semolina. The Marshall films such as *A Visit from Granny* (1931-

---

[35] Bowser, Scottish Screen Archive Ref. P/CN166.

1938) underline the wealth eventually commanded by the family, with a uniformed chauffeur delivering visitors to the Marshall family home. These films, in contrast with the more rural locations of the Steins and Bowsers, where the families clearly enjoy a significant relationship and influence in the local community, articulate a separation between the business of working life in the centre of the city of Glasgow, and the suburban home located in the emerging suburb of Bridge of Weir.

In these cases, the films and their families are united by their public status. The Steins, Bowsers and Marshalls were all successful commercial families, and key employers within their respective areas of Scotland. This social standing is affirmed in the films too which often show the family being extended into the community in a way that is noticeably patrician. Scottish families such as the Steins, the Bowsers, and the Marshalls enjoyed status, wealth and influence in the 1930s and beyond, and the films clearly confirm this, not least because the films and the apparatus needed to produce them, emerged in a period when, as Don MacPherson notes—the hobby of amateur filmmaking became a marker of social class.[36] The passage of their family films into the public realm of the archive effectively serves as a preservation and cultural confirmation of this standing. At the same time, with this exposure, the films potentially take on more critical status as evidential traces for social history that speaks powerfully to the unevenness of social development, and the related histories of class, family and gender. The domestic families shown in these films confirms the gendered division of the household with the man heading the family firm and the position behind the camera, and the women occupying the reproductive centre of the home, in front of the camera—an order of things confirmed by the etymological meaning of *family* as Leonore Davidoff et. al. point out:

> In its Latin root, *famulus* meant servant, which became *familia*, a household. For many centuries, the adult male head of that household was not considered part of it.[37]

It is also apparent in the way that these families exhibit themselves to themselves in their films, and in the extent to which the community around them underpins the ideological meaning of the family in British society, which Davidoff et. al. describe as nothing less than "a moral contract at the heart of a capitalist market society."[38]

---

[36] MacPherson, *Traditions of Independence. British Cinema in the Thirties*, 197.
[37] Davidoff et. al., *The Family Story: Blood, Contract and Intimacy, 1830-1960*, 8.
[38] Ibid., 101.

The family films isolated here perhaps reveal a degree of deportment and restraint contrasting with the comparatively spontaneous informality of the later and arguably more typical family film of the 1950s, where the relationship between the camera operator and subject is acknowledged rather than denied. The inclusion of local and state events within the referential range of events pertinent to the family film is indicative of the family's sense of status, and perhaps untypical proximity to the movement of "public" history. Nonetheless, this assurance with public exposure confirms the contention of Davidoff et. al. that "the moral and mythical meaning of family can be heavily drawn upon to exemplify the respective duties and responsibilities of state and citizen" reiterated in much more modest domestic film-making[39]

The proximity of Coronation Day in these films and the apparent ease of exhibition of the family members before the gaze of the camera, suggests people who are comfortable with and invested in this arrangement of appearance and display. The social status of these families lends credence to the suggestion that these family films represent a form of local pageantry that can be meaningfully related to the national pageants of the royal family. As John Stevenson notes of the period "the wealthiest families in the 1930s continued to maintain great house parties and function as important centres of social and political life."[40]

Exiting the Archive

Further issues arise from subsequent use of donated material. The localised meanings of family films are re-worked beyond the archive, when for example, agencies such as the BBC exploit the material—extracting footage for use alongside other historical sources in "attic archive" series such as *Scotland on Film* (BBC 2002-) and *Nation on Film* (BBC 2003-). Typically such programmes combine personal testimony with short clippings, and occasionally paper evidences. A good example of the resulting relationships is evident in an episode of *Scotland on Film* (tx. 16 February 2003) dedicated to the theme of food and drink. The section of the programme given over to alcohol consumption includes a recollection of an alcoholic father given by Caroline McLean-Smith (born 1934). Mclean-Smith is shot in colour and named and aged by subtitles as she describes how the wealth of the family—centred on "a beautiful house in Prestwick"—was lost as a consequence of her alcoholic father going

---

[39] Ibid., 10.
[40] Stevenson, *The Penguin Social History of Britain 1914-45,* 133.

Locating the Family Film: The Critics, the Competition and the Archive   201

bankrupt. As she addresses the camera directly, she states "my own father was an alcoholic. I don't ever remember seeing him drunk so it must have been kept away from the children. But I know he was." During this testimony there is a cut-away to a brief extract of a black-and-white family film, showing young children being ushered away from the front door of a sizeable house by a uniformed maid. There are no parents shown in the extract and the extract is not named or dated. The viewer is also shown another extract of a single toddler crying during McLean-Smith's recollection of her childhood. This sets up a relationship between the particularity of the oral testimony of memory disclosed by McLean-Smith and the illustrative generality of the archival film footage. The decision to not name and locate the films suggests that they are meant to provide illustration of the testimony rather than visual evidence for its occurrence.

Although the credit sequence at the end of the episode acknowledges the Scottish Film Archive as one of the sources used, the anonymity of the films in relation to the witness testimonies sets up a relationship between past and present that asks the viewer to trust the makers of *Scotland on Film* and the truth of the relationships assembled by the programme. The archive films most probably do not show Mclean-Smith herself as a child, but they do show a putatively representative child from the period that she is recollecting. The children in the extracts are clearly part of a wealthy family but there is nothing in the film extract shown to suggest that they are the children of an alcoholic parent.

The status of the archives credited by the programme also underpins the sometimes questionable micro-historiographic credentials of *Scotland on Film*. The interests of the people who appear in the extracts of the archived films are protected by the statement of principles agreed by the film archives in the UK and by the deposit agreement formed between the archive and the donors of the films. This requires subsequent use of the films deposited in the archive to be educational and concerned with the development and enlightenment of future generations.[41]

The recontextualisation of the archived family film by *Scotland on Film* not only confirms the recent popularity of personal and micro-histories as a genre of television but also reveals what the family film does not normally include in its range of subject matter. The ability of the viewer to see and to hear Caroline McLean-Smith briefly describe her experience as a child of her alcoholic father supplements the referential range of the family films deposited into the archive. Giving attention to this relay between the idealised families first captured and recorded by

---

[41] Scottish Screen Archive Licensing and Deposit Agreements. e-mail 22/4/08.

amateur filmmakers, and the broader social and historic contexts exhibited by public service television such as *Scotland on Film* underlines the secondary or fugitive nature of looking at these films and the invisible geography of their appearance on television. The spectator of these films, whether it is as a television viewer of *Scotland on Film* or a student of film in higher education, becomes implicated in a relay of looking at the lives of these *re-publiced* families that has still to be properly worked through, and which is accompanied by an ethics that emerges out of the formation of the relationship between past and present.

Conclusions

The influential work of Roland Barthes, Jo Spence and Annette Kuhn on images of the family captured in the form of the still photograph can be located at the disciplinary hinge of visual culture, between Film Studies and Cultural Studies. These accounts share the feature of being written from a personal and autobiographical perspective, a familiar way of revealing what was once private and unknown to the public.[42] The conventions of writing and narrating the self serve to offset the secondary and surrogate viewing that comes with watching and witnessing the exhibition of someone else's family film in public. However, as the visibility of archive holdings increases with the aid of the internet, and as the study of film begins to find ways of accommodating and including amateur cinema, then the need to identify appropriate frameworks for thinking about the family film that stretch beyond the personal and autobiographical impulse will also increase.

Heather Norris Nicholson has begun to assess the ethics of the increased public circulation of this kind of material: "who owns the right to put people and lifestyle on show?" she asks, in a social milieu within which:

> Cultural interpretation centres, museums and educational projects testify to new interests among many communities in expressing their own sense of history, belonging and identity through archival and modern visual form.[43]

The Scottish Screen Archive, as a founder member of the UK Film Archive Forum and International Federation of Film Archives, is governed

---

[42] Barthes, *Camera Lucida: Reflections on Photography*; Spence, *Putting Myself in the Picture: a Political, Personal and Photographic Autobiography*; Kuhn, *Family Secrets: Acts of Memory and Imagination*.
[43] Norris Nicholson, in Kapstein, *Essays on Amateur Film: A Jubilee Book*, 43-44.

by an agreed set of principles and code of ethics, tested especially clearly by the case of the family film.[44] Certainly the historical imperative which motivates much of the access to these films tends to occlude attention to the mechanisms of viewing and looking at this material, a situation in stark contrast to the thoroughly theorised spectatorship of cinema that is not amateur. Certainly, much amateur cinema and many family films refuse the mechanisms of identification and point of view that have defined the discipline of Film Studies, a refusal that is part of their fascination, and an invitation to the revision of some much-cherished theory. But it is the capacity initially identified by Low—to *resist* the "filmic" and yet also *pursue* the critical status of the "filmic"—that comes through most clearly in this study of the amateur family film

There is a bi-directional orientation here, which pulls the family film towards two areas of significance and meaning. The critical discourse of *Amateur Cine World* and festival culture from the 1930s to the end of the 1950s encourages the amateur to treat the family situation and environment as raw material for something that aspires to be more than a film of record, such as the comedy narratives of Frank Marshall's films. The contrast to this relatively defamiliarised family film is the deeply familiar and patrician family of the 1930s films, whose status is not only confirmed by the presence of the films in the archive, but also preserved for the potential benefit of wider public audiences in the future. The recirculation and recontextualisation of archived family film by "attic archive" programmes such as *Scotland on Film* demonstrates how the meaning of the family film can be historically amended through altered and *re-publiced* circumstances of exhibition.

It is this dialogic relation between the technical and creative competencies of the aspirant family filmmaker, the social and historical significance of the non-competition family films, and the implications of these particular kinds of visual attention that underline how the *cinema* of amateur cinema is much less fixed than professional cinema. The uncertain location of amateur film in general and the family film in particular demands that greater attention is given to the conditions of exhibition and critical reception surrounding the films. In this way the family film becomes the locus for the varying possibilities of the practice of amateur cinema and its subsequent study.

---

[44] http://www.fiafnet.org/uk/

Works Cited

Primary Sources

Adjudicator's Review of Entries, 1952. Scottish Screen Archive Ref. 2/3/35.
Asquith, Anthony. Notes by the Honourable Anthony Asquith, Adjudicator, 1937. Scottish Screen Archive Ref. 2/3/13.
Baxter, Rosemary. Family Film File, Scottish Screen Archive Ref. P/CN82c.
Bowser (family). Family Film File, Scottish Screen Archive Ref. P/CN166.
Frend, Charles. Adjudicators Comments for 1956 Scottish Amateur Film Festival. Scottish Screen Archive Ref. 2/3/43.
Stein (family). Family Film File, Scottish Screen Archive Ref. P/CN122.

Secondary Sources

Barthes, Roland. *Camera Lucida: Reflections On Photography.* London: Flamingo, 1984.
Davidoff, Leonore, Megan Doolittle, Janet Fink and Katherine Holden. *The Family Story: Blood, Contract and Intimacy, 1830-1960.* New York: Addison Wesley Longman, 1999.
Chalfen, Richard. "Cinéma Naïveté: A Study of Home Moviemaking as Visual Communication." *Studies in the Anthropology of Visual Communication* 2, no. 2 (1975): 87-103.
Cookson, Laraine. "Amateur Film and the Archives." In *Researchers Guide to British Film and Television Collections* 4th Revised Edition, edited by James Ballantyne, 5-14. London: British Film and Video Council, 1993.
Davies, Denys. "A Movie Makers Diary." *Amateur Cine World* 21, no. 9 (1958): 925.
"Double Run". "Success With The Family Film." *Amateur Cine World* 19, no. (1955): 249-251.
—. "A Family Film for Christmas." *Amateur Cine World* 21, no. 8 (1957): 793-794.
Hardy, Forsyth. "Scottish Amateur Film Festival." *The Scotsman* (April 1951): 24.
—. "Amateur Has Lessons to Teach the Studios." *The Scotsman* (April 1950): 22.

Harley, Basil. "The Art of Directing Amateur Actors." *Amateur Cine World* 10, no. 10 (1946): 24-26.
Hogenkamp, Bert and Mieke Lauwers. "In Pursuit Of Happiness? A Search For The Definition of Amateur Film." In *Essays on Amateur Film: A Jubilee Book*, edited by Nancy Kapstein, 107-116. Charleroi: Association Européene des Inédits, 1997.
Kuhn, Annette. *Family Secrets: Acts of Memory and Imagination*. London: Verso, 1995.
MacPherson, Don, ed. *Traditions of Independence: British Cinema In The Thirties*. London: British Film Institute, 1980.
McBain, Janet. "And the winner is...A Brief history of The Scottish Amateur Film Festival (1933-1986)." In *Essays on Amateur Film: A Jubilee Book*, edited by Nancy Kapstein, 97-105. Charleroi: Association Européene des Inédits, 1997.
Malthouse, Gordon. "Prizewinners and Why." *Amateur Cine World* 24, no. 1 (1960): 40-41, 88.
—. "Family Affairs." *Amateur Cine World* 15, no. 10 (1952): 995-998.
—. "Amateur Films Worth Talking About." *Amateur Cine World* 14, no. 5 (1950): 443-444.
—. "The Stranglehold of Photography." *Amateur Cine World* 12, no. 4 (1948): 271-272.
Norris Nicholson, Heather. "Moving Memories: Image and Identity In Home Movies." In *Essays on Amateur Film: A Jubilee Book*, edited by Nancy Kapstein, 97-105. Charleroi: Association Européene des Inédits, 1997.
Odin, Roger. "Reflections on the Home Movie as Document: A Semio-Pragmatic Approach." In *Mining The Home Movie: Excavations In Histories and Memories*, edited Karen Ishizuka and Patricia Zimmermann, 255-271. London: University of California Press, 2007.
Pople, Kenneth. "Looking for Plots." *Amateur Cine World* 12, no. 11(1958): 1095.
Postlethwaite, Harry, A. "'What's The Date': Looking at The Family Film of Ten Years Ago." *Amateur Cine World* 20, no. 1 (May 1956): 42-43.
Sanderson, Kenneth. *Stein of Bonnybridge*. Bonnybridge: K.W. Sanderson, 1986.
Shand, Ryan. "The Hobbyist Movement in Scottish Amateur Film: A Case Study of Frank Marshall", Session title: "Non-Fiction Filmmaking and Non-National Exhibition in Scotland", Postgraduate Symposium, Department of Theatre Film and Television Studies, University of Glasgow, 10th June 2004.

Simon, Jane. "Recycling Home Movies." *Continuum: Journal of Media and Culture Studies* 20, no. 2 (2006): 189-199.
Smith, Jack. "The Committed Amateur." *Amateur Cine World* 22, no. 6 (1958): 562-563.
—. "You Must Have An Audience." *Amateur Cine World* 23, no. 10 (1960): 1002-1003.
—. "The A.C.W. Ten Best Films of 1959 Competition Results." *Amateur Cine World* 23, no. 12 (1960): 1214-1217.
"Sound Track". "Enliven Your Family Films With This Simple Prop." *Amateur Cine World* 18, no. 12 (1955): 1282-1283.
Spence, Jo. *Putting Myself in The Picture: A Political, Personal and Photographic Autobiography*. London: Camden Press, 1986.
Stevenson, John. *British Society 1914-1945*. London: Penguin Books, 1990.
Zimmermann, Patricia. *Reel Families: A Social History of Amateur Film*. Bloomington: Indiana University Press, 1995.

Films Cited

Agricultural and Highland Shows
(David Charles Bowser, 1928) 16mm., 10 mins.
Argaty Scenes
(David Charles Bowser, 1932) 16mm., 4 mins. 47 secs.
Baxter Family Films
(Baxter family, 1929-1950) 16mm., 52 mins.
Big Fish
(Alan Simpson, 1948) 16mm., 10 mins.
Bowser Fox Hunting and Sports Day
(David Charles Bowser, 1936) 16mm., 4 mins. 59 secs.
A Busy Afternoon
(Iain Dunnachie, 1950) 16mm., 7 mins. 17 secs.
Castlecary Events
(Norman Stein, 1932-1937) 16mm., 17 mins. 29 secs.
Family at Nairn
(David Charles Bowser, 1933) 16mm., 5 mins. 9 secs.
Family Films
(James Marshall, 1931-1938) 16mm., 6 mins. 32 secs.
A Hit and a Miss
(T. H. Thoms, 1956) 16mm., 11 mins. 29 secs.
Johnnie Looks Back
(John O'Russell, 1950) 16mm., 8 mins. 20 secs.

Jubilee Year
 (David Charles Bowser, 1935) 16mm., 8 mins. 51 secs.
Just One Thing After Another
 (Frank Marshall, 1936) 16mm., 9 mins. 42 secs.
Mavor Family Film
 (Jack Mavor, 1932) 16mm., 7 mins. 58 secs.
Nation on Film
 (BBC, 2003-) TV series, 30 mins. per episode.
Portrait of Peter
 (A. E. Gillings, 1952) 16mm., 8 mins. 22 secs.
Scotland on Film
 (BBC 2002-) TV series, 30 mins. per episode.
Stein Family Life
 (Norman Stein, 1932-1934) 16mm., 27 mins.
Susan's Party
 (W. J. Shanks, 1950) 16mm., 12 mins. 7 secs.
Tree for Two
 (Frank Marshall, 1957) 16mm., 8 mins. 58 secs.
A Visit from Granny
 (James Marshall, 1931-1938) 16mm., 58 secs.

CHAPTER SEVEN

SCREENING CLASSICS:
FILM APPRECIATION CANONS
AND THE POST-WAR FILM SOCIETIES

RICHARD MACDONALD

It's the sixth time I've seen *Caligari*;
I've boarded *Potemkin* before;
Birth of a Nation's a long operation,
But must I be mid-wife once more?
Intolerance makes me intolerant,
Turksib is a tedious train—
I grant you that *Greed* is impressive, but need
I sit through the whole thing again?
I've seen quite enough of the savage
(*Tabu* and *Moana* and such),
And though Maxim Gorki's a theme for a talkie,
A trilogy is frankly too much.
To Pabst I address panegyrics
And Eisenstein's praises I sang—
But now I have *no* time for Erich von Stroheim,
And little for Lubitsch and Lang.
—From "Sunday Observance" by Anthony Brode

Originally published in *Punch* and later reprinted in *Film*, the magazine of the Federation of Film Societies, Anthony Brode's poem pokes knowing and affectionate fun at the "ranks of the devout" gathered at the film society on Sunday afternoon.[1] Unable to share their apparently limitless enthusiasm for reverential, repeated viewings of the canon of silent classics which characterises fellow club members, the poet confesses, "Even the tenth time they find it exciting/nobody's bored, the exception is me." In the decade that followed the Second World War, a period of

---

[1] Brode, "Sunday Observance", 27.

unprecedented growth in amateur film society exhibition, a number of film publications altogether more sympathetic to the movement, including *Sight and Sound, Documentary Newsletter* and *16mil Film User,* carried regular columns covering film society activity around the country, and helped circulate programme information nationally. Casting an eye over their reports, the recurrence of a relatively small number of silent films certainly evokes Brode's satirical sketch of film society programming, with all its perceived austerity and devotion. Could there have been a film society in the land that didn't show *The Italian Straw Hat* (1927) or *The Cabinet of Dr Caligari* (1919) or *Battleship Potemkin* (1925), sometime between 1945 and 1950?

The source of these films, and many of the other widely circulated titles, was usually the loan section of the National Film Library (NFL), later renamed the National Film and Television Archive (NFTA). Such titles also enjoyed widespread endorsement elsewhere. When the National Film Theatre (NFT) began regular screenings in its "Telekinema" after the 1951 Festival of Britain, these same films were programmed as part of a popular history of cinema series, subsequently screened on a yearly rotation throughout the 1950s. By the time the NFL films were shown in the context of this annual series at the NFT, we can assume that many of the titles would already have been seen by a sizeable proportion of the then 40,000-50,000 members of the film societies. This conjunction of the ubiquitous presence of films from the NFL collection within the amateur exhibition sector, and the conspicuous growth in film society membership in the first five years after the war, offers fertile ground for an examination of the shifting relationship between centralised, publicly-funded film bodies such as the British Film Institute (BFI), and the dispersed network of amateur-run film societies, at a time of change for both institutions.

The Film Institute Branches

A tracing of the figuration of the film societies might begin productively with the 1930s, and with moves made during the decade to create a national film institute. Establishment of such an organisation had been a central proposal of the Commission on Educational and Cultural Films, formed in 1929 following a conference convened by a broad coalition of educational and scientific organisations, to debate ways in which such bodies might best become involved with film in the national interest, in both the classroom and beyond. The Commission's terms of reference were firstly, to consider methods to improve the use of film in education, and secondly, to explore ways to raise standards of public appreciation of the medium.[2] Crucially, the Commission also found itself investigating the desirability of establishing a "permanent central organisation" to promote and co-ordinate nationally all educational initiative in relation to film.[3] The detailed arguments in favour of such an organisation, and proposals concerning its possible constitution and objects, were persuasively set out in their final report, entitled *The Film in National Life*. Co-ordination was clearly deemed urgent: by the time the document was published in 1932, a vigorous amateur exhibition movement was already well established; the London Film Society was completing its seventh season in the West End, whilst provincial societies had formed in at least a dozen other major centres. Perhaps of greater concern, a parallel development of workers' film societies, based in some of the larger industrial cities, was also becoming evident.

In basic terms, film societies acted as independent exhibitors of films unavailable through commercial cinema outlets. Most also aspired to be educators of a sort, encouraging the study of film, both by showing material variously described as unusual, artistic or cultural, and through the arrangement of lectures, discussions and exhibitions. Essentially, a film society was a private club, organising "closed" performances of films for a restricted membership. As such, film societies were vulnerable to attack as élitist bodies, and often regarded as places where cinema was "worshipped" by an intellectual clique. From very early in the movement's history therefore, warnings of the dangers of "highbrow" smugness and self-satisfaction were a persistent theme in writings about film societies, even from individuals broadly sympathetic to the movement—Paul Rotha for example, would question their tendency towards "effeminate dilletantism".[4] Such warnings were usually a prelude to discussion of a film society's public responsibilities. In response, the aspirations of a film society were rarely limited to the provision of private screenings; broader objectives were usually also to try to influence public opinion in support of good films. What justified the private film show then was nothing less than the impulse to reform the public commercial cinema beyond its highly circumscribed sphere.

The Film in National Life acknowledged the film societies as pioneers of the "constructive use of cinematography" at several points. Such altogether worthy and liberating engagement with the medium was significantly contrasted with the confining influence of the prevailing censorship apparatus. To look to the censor to bring about improvements

---

[2] Commission on Educational and Cultural Films, *The Film in National Life*, 1.
[3] Ibid., 1.
[4] Rotha, *Celluloid: The Film Today*, 68.

in the quality of film was to mistakenly expect "to make a restrictive force into a positive agent of improvement".[5] Equally negative in approach, according to the report's authors, were the moral guardians and educationalists fond of generalising about the harmful effects of the medium, but doing so without knowledge or discrimination. Against this background, the report set out a progressive vision of how to improve the entertainment film, a project which placed the education of the public at its core. The production of better films could be encouraged it was felt, by creating an audience that demanded them. Changing public taste would necessarily begin in the classroom, training the next generation of filmgoers to appreciate what was good. It would also involve other means of suggestion such as the publication of authoritative and informed criticism, and the development of educational initiatives such as lectures and meetings. Responsibility for these tasks would rest with a new, centralised organisation, a national film "institute", whose relationship with the already operating amateur exhibitors of the societies initially however remained unclear.

When it considered the movie audience, the report made key distinctions between the "general" public and the "educated film-goer", although the reformist rhetoric seemed reluctant to denigrate the tastes of the average ticket-buyer.[6] The "educated" audience segment was itself composed of two camps, the occasional patron of quality films at the local cinema, and the ardent student of the medium, specifically the men and women of the film societies. Collectively, the audience as a whole was likened to a pyramid; the general public made up nine-tenths of the base, on top of which was a thin layer of educated film-goers, and at the apex, the film society members. Within this model, the envisaged value of amateur exhibitors as collaborative partners of a professionalised film institute was explicit. As the report argued:

> What we need today is to enlist the interests of (the film societies)... They will provide the nucleus of effort in the provinces to promote cultural activity... Their enthusiasm should be used and their knowledge may be of great service.[7]

Above all, the film societies were valued then for retaining a vital connection between, on the one hand, a cinema of artistic expression and

---

[5] Commission on Educational and Cultural Films, *The Film in National Life*, 145.
[6] Ibid., 82.
[7] Ibid., 83.

cultural enrichment, and on the other, the commercial cinema as it existed for the majority audience.

Such initiatives answered widespread concern over the social and cultural effects of mass culture in the 1930s. The publication of *The Film in National Life,* for example, coincided with the appearance of *Scrutiny,* a literary journal associated with a group of Cambridge students and academics centred on F. R. and Q. D. Leavis. The verdict of the *Scrutiny* group on cinema was unambiguous, regarding the medium as one of the key forces levelling down taste, and sponsoring a trivialisation that was destroying valid cultural ideals. Reiterating the rejection of the "culture of the machine", so directly and comprehensively also condemned by the authors of *The Film in National Life,* positive values were seen to lay elsewhere, in more deeply-rooted traditions. The preservation of such cultures, threatened and undermined by industrial civilisation, and their restoration in the modern world, formed the *Scrutiny* group's single-minded ambition from the outset. Significantly, the journal's launch manifesto had argued that the "defenders of culture" were "scattered and unorganised", and practical organisation of this minority as an effective force soon emerged as a key objective.[8] Similarly, the central function of any future film institute would be to organise the disconnected strands of constructive critical opinion into a coherent rhetoric. But where *Scrutiny* envisaged the defenders of culture as professional literary critics stationed in the Universities, *The Film in National Life* reserved an important role for co-ordinated, but essentially amateur initiatives in the more public sphere of the film society.

Once established in 1933, the BFI encouraged the formation of local branches. These were independently run groups, composed of a dozen or more members, committed to pursuing the objects of the national organisation on more local grounds. A number of film societies including Merseyside, Manchester, Belfast and Leeds became fully-affiliated Film Institute branches, usually launched with a visit from national governors or officers. Other established societies such as Tyneside, Birmingham, Ipswich and Southampton guarded their independence however, and remained effectively unconnected to the Institute. Affiliation, it appears, became one way to emphasise the public service aspects of their activities, whilst lending a film society the air of legitimacy often derived from formal association with a public body. The advantages are apparent: these were difficult times for film societies; each was reliant on a local authority viewing their activities benignly, and allowances may have been made on

---

[8] Mulhern, *The Moment of Scrutiny,* 76.

the basis of a Film Institute affiliation. An editorial in *Cinema Quarterly* once quipped that the BFI had been brought into existence by a "mixed public of bishops, aldermen and schoolmasters"—perhaps a fair description of the philanthropic-progressive coalition organising local support for the organisation within the branches too.[9]

One of the most prominent advocates of affiliation was the Unitarian minister Heming Vaughan (father of Olwen Vaughan, later Secretary of the Institute) who organised the first Institute branch on Merseyside. Twelve months into the work, he wrote of the experience in *Sight and Sound*.[10] Over the course of the year, he recorded, the branch had organised lectures and discussions of "the classics", produced a monthly review of films screening at the local cinemas, and put on film shows for children and unemployed clubs; all thanks to voluntary labour. Reverend Vaughan added that local branches were imperative if the Institute was to function responsibly in the national interest. Intriguingly he noted, "It will necessitate generous grants from central funds", whilst reassuring the reader that "no money would be more legitimately or advantageously spent".[11] Generous grants however were not forthcoming. In fact it is difficult to see what, in practical terms, the BFI contributed to the branches that had sprung up in its name. The Institute did organise occasional lectures at the branch societies; the German pioneer of silhouette animation Lottie Reiniger and a young Henri Langlois of the newly formed Cinemathèque Française were, for example, among the visitors to the Manchester and District Institute Film Society.[12] However, the scale of such efforts was dwarfed by the independently-organised presence of documentary filmmakers, as speakers and lecturers throughout the film society movement.

The BFI's weak presence in the movement can perhaps be conveyed with reference to some of the key difficulties facing such organisations during the 1930s; the legal confusion concerning Sunday cinema shows, problems of film supply, and the inconsistent charging of entertainment tax. These were areas in which the Institute might have taken up the film society cause with greater conviction, but apparently chose not to do so. Again comparison might be made with the documentary sector, especially the Empire Marketing Board (EMB) and General Post Office (GPO) film units. Documentary producers actively cultivated links with the movement, for many of whom the film societies were considered a key

---

[9] Anon., "The Spectator", 4.
[10] Vaughan, "Organising a Branch", 114-115.
[11] Ibid., 114.
[12] Maddison, "Audio-Vision and the BFI".

part of the "new cinema public" that they intended to reach beyond mainstream cinemas.[13] The EMB and GPO Film Libraries were simultaneously a vital source of free films throughout the film society network. Close links between film societies and the documentary project can clearly be recognised in the journals *Cinema Quarterly* and *World Film News*. The former was started by film society activists at the Edinburgh Film Guild, and rapidly became an important forum for documentary writings. Likewise the latter, independently financed by filmmaker Basil Wright, was even adopted as the "official" journal of the pre-war Federation of Film Societies. Stimulated by these and other publications, arguments for a public service cinema, functioning as a tool of citizenship, preferably made by the documentarists, echoed through the film society movement, and found a receptive audience there.[14]

Constructing Authority—The National Film Library

The decisive moment in the BFI's gradual construction of authority over the art of film was undoubtedly the establishment of the NFL in 1935. Objectives were broad and ambitious, although the Film Library's means would remain meagre. Set up to preserve films of historical, scientific, artistic and educational value, it also aimed to facilitate the circulation of educational films to schools and other approved groups. Even commentators less than impressed with the Institute's record in other areas, regarded the library plan as an opportunity to "justify its existence"[15] whilst, more specifically, questions were raised concerning the practicability of the plans to be both a reference and circulating library.[16] Early on, Ernest Lindgren, appointed the first curator of the Film Library, formulated the principle that no print received for preservation should be subjected to the risk of wear and tear involved in projection; for films intended for preservation to be loaned, they would have to be reprinted.[17] The library's loan section was however conceived from the outset with educational and instructional films in mind; items primarily intended for classroom use, with titles like *Rice Cultivation* (1938), a film edited by the BFI educational committee, and *Winter Sports in Austria*

---

[13] Aitken, *Film and Reform: John Grierson and the Documentary Film Movement*, 102.

[14] Hardy, *John Grierson: A Documentary Biography*; Pleasance, *The Film Society Movement in Britain 1925-1939*.

[15] Anon., *Birmingham Post* (11 July 1935), BFI Special Collections.

[16] Ibid.

[17] Lindgren, "A National Film Library for Great Britain", 67.

(1930), donated by the Austrian State Travel Bureau, were amongst the early acquisitions.

In 1941 however, the National Film Library announced a major re-organisation of the loan section.[18] From now on, it would deal solely with reprints from the preservation collection, usually films chosen to illustrate the "core" history of cinema. Marking the occasion, the relevant catalogue was re-launched and advertised as a resource for film "appreciation", a concept that returns us momentarily to the "constructive engagement" envisaged by *The Film in National Life*. As a term, "film appreciation" drew together a bundle of educational ideas and practices, and was rooted in the notion that the commercial film could be improved by cultivating the taste of an increasingly demanding public. Encouraging such improvements in taste involved a range of initiatives, both informal and formal, from the presentation of films that were outstanding, unusual or artistic, to the study of film technique, in order to construct a sound basis for criticism and discrimination.

Within the discourse of film appreciation, the public taste in need of reform could be characterised in various ways; the philanthropically optimistic *Film in National Life*, remains striking for the way it tends to avoid judgement or condemnation of the general public, while a later film appreciation textbook such as Roger Manvell's *Film* (1944) becomes aggressively disparaging of the habits and preferences of the average movie-goer. The methods of reform and the ultimate goal were also the subject of much discussion. *The Film in National Life* had stressed the gradual nature of its project, and had conveyed a loose sense of the desirable standards to attain: one of its neater formulations is to praise films that are the best of their kind. A good film from such perspectives was neither obscurely highbrow, nor a morally improving "goody-goody film",[19] but one where no matter the particular genre:

> the acting was natural and true, the photography clear, ingenious and sometimes, literally and figuratively, brilliant; and [where, even] if the situations are fantastic the characters are likely to satisfy as three-dimensional men and women".[20]

More specifically, indigenous films should be an expression of British life and thought, "deriving character and inspiration from our national

---

[18] Anon., "New NFL Policy", *BFI 8th Annual Report*, 1941, 13.
[19] Commission on Educational and Cultural Films, *The Film in National Life*, 90.
[20] Ibid., 80.

inheritance" and on that basis, valued internationally.[21] Later inflections of the film appreciation discourse would be more explicitly bound up with promoting film as an art form.

The re-organisation of the NFL clearly responded to a growing demand for material that could be used to teach film appreciation, in a variety of both professional and amateur educational settings. Prioritisation of the Loan Section around reprints of selected titles, was therefore accompanied by the creation of study extracts to illustrate particular aspects of film technique. Composite films were assembled and soon added to the collection; a survey of the documentary entitled *Film and Reality* (1942) by Cavalcanti, and a history of animation called *Drawings That Walk and Talk* (1938) by Marie Seton, were early examples. Later, a series of shorts under the umbrella title of *The Critic and the Film* (1949), each featuring a talk by a prominent "authority" such as Dilys Powell of *The Sunday Times* or Jympson Harmon of *Kine Weekly*, were also commissioned. The new Loan catalogue itself was also re-organised chronologically into four sections, exploring the development of film technique in relation to changes deemed crucial to the history of the film industry and film culture generally. The first section, designated "The Primitives" included a small number of composite films, illustrating the beginnings of cinema. The second grouping, headed the "One Reel Period", emphasised innovation in cinematic storytelling prefiguring later developments in editing. The third category was headed "Silent Films" and contained the titles most closely identified with the film appreciation canon. Here the text described the modern feature film as reaching full maturity with *Quo Vadis* (1912) and *The Birth of a Nation* (1915). The flourishing of new artistic consciousness embodied in the national film traditions of Sweden, France, Germany and Soviet Russia was highlighted, as was their decline, due to competition from the United States of America. The constructivist school of Russian directors and their theories of film editing were also singled out. The final section included "Sound Films Since 1928". In contextualising this period, emphasis was increasingly given to the growth of minority film culture, and the development of a new spirit of film criticism, both of which were considered to have prepared the way for the documentary film in Britain and America.

The heart of the loan collection was undoubtedly the twenty or so films that made up the silent film section, and a dozen more sound films. Prominent among these were works that had made a major impact on the intellectual film culture of the 1920s and 1930s. In many cases, these had

---

[21] Ibid., 143.

received a British premiere at The Film Society, before becoming staples of provincial film society programmes. The list was dominated by films from Germany, *The Cabinet of Dr Caligari* (1919), *Warning Shadows* (1923), *Waxworks* (1924), *The Last Laugh* (1924), *Metropolis* (1926), and *Berlin* (1927). From Soviet Russia came *Battleship Potemkin* (1925), *Mother* (1926), *The End of St. Petersburg* (1927), *The General Line* (1929), *The Ghost that Never Returns* (1929), *New Babylon* (1929) and *Turksib* (1929). (See Fig. 7-1) Identifying these films as classics, and implying that they represented landmarks of film experiment, the narrative of film history developed by the loan catalogue was recognisably indebted to the lineage charted in Paul Rotha's *The Film Till Now* (1930) and its accompanying senses of aesthetic value. Traditions centring theatrical performance were rejected, and the true artistic potential of the cinema identified with more visually expressive aspects of the medium, epitomised above all by the editing techniques practiced by the Soviet filmmakers. The conception of film appreciation that the loan section supported was thus concerned with the structured, chronological study of a limited selection of films considered pivotal to aesthetic film history, a definition often elaborated via standardised programme notes. Over time however, the holdings of the loan collection slowly diversified. During World War Two, the NFL took over responsibility for the collection of The Film Society, and a small number of experimental films were reprinted and added to the loan section. In general though, additions to the loan catalogue were more of a trickle than a flood. Both the educational priorities and financial constraints of the NFL tended to reinforce an effective and austere process of canon-formation.

Classics at the Film Societies

From the point at which it was re-organised, there were year on year increases in demand for the films of the NFL loan section. The noticeable turn to historical programmes in the film society movement was however influenced by several other factors, including the unavailability of suitable contemporary features. Inevitably World War Two had an impact on the supply of contemporary films from the continent. The outbreak of hostilities disrupted activity considerably, with a number of prominent societies suspending meetings entirely. Those that continued operating faced a difficult time; dwindling stocks of suitable films tested booking and programming skills to the limit. Film shortages had in fact been a problem within the film society movement for several years, as traditional sources of material such as Germany, Russia, and to a lesser extent Italy dried up, indexing the wider political crisis of the 1930s. However with the fall of France, the importation of new films from the continent ceased altogether. Anticipating the effect of this on struggling film societies, Scottish activist Forsyth Hardy wrote a characteristically upbeat piece for *Sight and Sound*, that aimed to bolster morale whilst dispensing creative booking and programming advice. Addressing the film supply problem, Hardy drew attention to the growing loan section of the NFL as an important source of material. With resource and initiative, Hardy argued, "it should not prove difficult to maintain the tradition of the movement".[22]

Fig. 7-1 poster for film society favourite *Turksib* (1929)
Source: Author's collection

Lack of film availability also continued to be an issue for several years after the war, especially for the rapidly growing number of film societies operating with 16mm projectors, as the smaller gauge became standardised across the amateur exhibition sector. Certainly the technical profile of the film society movement altered dramatically between 1945 and 1950. Overall, the total number of film societies increased from about twenty in

---

[22] Hardy, "An Open Letter to Film Societies", 29.

1944 (not including societies in the armed services) to 213 in 1950.[23] In 1944, only seven of the twenty Film Societies were operating on 16mm projectors. Five years later, the number using only 16mm film shot up to 114, compared with 42 on 35mm, and 47 societies showing on both gauges. In 1948, the Head of Metro-Goldwyn-Mayer's 16mm Division wrote enthusiastically, and with considerable justification:

> Something like a revolution has quietly occurred in the film world since the end of the war. Although it has taken place without any fuss or publicity, it is almost as far-reaching as though the railways had suddenly put out extensions from their main lines to all villages in the country.[24]

The spread of 16mm technology, cheaper to own, and more easily operated by amateurs outside mainstream cinemas, meant that film societies could form where there were much smaller populations, in towns and rural areas often devoid of 35mm facilities. Certainly the average size of Film Societies was shrinking. By 1950 nearly two-thirds of the groups in England and Wales had less than 150 members.[25] By contrast, the big pre-war societies often had in excess of ten times that number; the Billingham Film Society on Teeside, for instance, regularly reported audiences approaching two thousand in the 1930s, likewise the Edinburgh Film Guild and Merseyside Institute Film Society. Unfortunately, the supply of 16mm titles had not kept pace with the diffusion of the new "substandard" gauge projectors. For several years, only a small proportion of continental films that became available to the 35mm societies (principally those imported by the specialist cinemas in London) were released in 16mm versions (the specialist renters who made such a big impact on film supply to the film societies in the 1950s such as Contemporary had not yet entered the market). By contrast, many of the classics of the NFL were only available, or could only be properly projected, on 16mm. Consequently a divergence is noticeable in the programmes of film societies in the immediate post-war period, with current films largely restricted to the 35mm societies, and 16mm societies giving much of their available feature programming to the classics from the library collection.

The presence of the library's classics on film society programmes and the rising numbers of people joining film societies to watch them, should also be seen in the context of broader social and cultural change in the

---

[23] *BFI 11th Annual Report*, 1944, 9; *BFI 17th Annual Report*, 1950, 12.
[24] Russell-Roberts, "The Progress of the 16mm Film", 358.
[25] Federation of Film Societies, *Annual Report of the Honorary Treasurer 1950*.

aftermath of war. Film "appreciation", the project of a reformist minority in the 1930s, acquired a more urgent social-democratic boost in the later 1940s. From an educational point of view, raising the standard of popular culture was now just as imperative as disseminating "high" culture to the people, a project now supposedly safely undertaken by the Arts Council, and funded securely by the State. Through the "age of austerity" moreover, film emerged as *the* democratic medium, and the *people's art*, enabling leading film society activists to argue with justification that greater numbers could potentially be brought into contact with "great" art through film than via any other artistic medium. From this perspective, the low standard of entertainment film was constructed as evidence of glaring cultural inequalities that could be addressed and resolved through teaching film appreciation.[26] Post-war conditions thus renewed concerns about standards within popular culture, at a time when cinema admissions were at an all time high. Evidence also suggests that the field of adult education was increasingly receptive to film appreciation, as a result of the searching debates taking place concerning progressive methods of popular education provoked by the educational initiatives of the armed forces.[27] Undoubtedly more film societies were partnering adult education bodies; 16mm societies needed buildings, premises in which to meet, and these were often provided by adult education organisations. Co-operation between educators such as the Workers Educational Association (WEA) and film societies on the organisation of film appreciation classes was also widespread.

In this cultural climate, film societies inevitably emphasised their educational responsibilities. In 1946, thanks to lobbying from the BFI and the newly created Federation of Film Societies (FFS), such groups were ruled exempt from payment of the Entertainment Tax, on the grounds that their activities were partly educational. For several years, invoking the entertainment tax remission became a favourite way for activists to prick the movement's conscience, and remind their colleagues of their educational vocation. Forsyth Hardy, to take one example from many, wrote in the magazine of the Scottish Federation of Film Societies that when film societies did little more than repeat the programmes of the specialised cinemas of the West End "their claim to remission of entertainment tax was decidedly meagre".[28] Within a film society too, a reference to the tax exemption, like the reminder about the society's

---

[26] Wilson, "Film Societies—The Next Phase"; Reeves, "The Film Societies and Adult Education".
[27] Anon., "Adult Education: Its Place in Post-war Society".
[28] Hardy, quoted in Anon., "Editorial", *Federation of Film Societies Bulletin*, 3.

constitution, would often accompany insistence that the film society's purpose was to educate rather than entertain, to cultivate a sense of film history, and even to challenge the direction of contemporary cinema. (see Fig. 7-2) Films deemed "classics" by no less an authority than the NFL were obviously well suited to a society's efforts to introduce seriousness of purpose and educational value into its programming. In fact, because they were "classics" and had been institutionalised as landmarks in film history, they could be regarded as serious without being overly highbrow, and deemed educational without committing the now highly anachronistic sin of self-satisfied élitism.

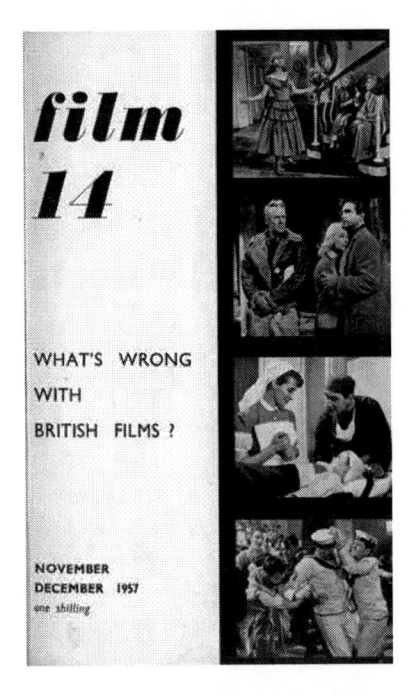

Fig. 7-2 Federation of Film Societies journal, *Film* (1957)
Source: Editor's collection

To some extent, the idea of the "classic" could be deployed to deflect the criticism of members. An example of this can be seen in the case of the South London Film Society (SLFS), a small 16mm group meeting in Camberwell. (see Fig. 7-3) In 1948, not long after the society's formation, an editorial on policy in the society's magazine stated their commitment to the film appreciation case succinctly:

The ideal aim of the present day societies can be summed up in three words "education in appreciation"...without some understanding of the artistic and technical background of any production an audience is not able to derive full benefit from seeing it. Members of a film society need guidance and education. We use the latter word, ugly and pretentious as it may seem without qualm.[29]

Fig. 7-3 South London Film Society Programme, 1951-1952
Source: Author's collection

In subsequent writings, society activists explained that in addition to organising lectures and discussions, it was vital for educational reasons that the programming was approached in a structured and systematic fashion. Accordingly, they proposed a season composed of three programming strands, the German classics, the Russian classics and Documentary. By the end of the season, the society's activists faced a minor revolt from the membership, which erupted on the letters pages of the magazine. Criticism of the programme took the form of a plea for films

---

[29] *South London Film Society Magazine*, 1948: 1, no. 1, 3.

that were less gloomy. A Mrs Hodges wrote: "We have had so much gloom and misery in the last ten years, please let us be cheered up when we go to the cinema".[30] A fellow member, Stanley Dinham concurred:

> I would like to see a film of a light nature occasionally as a curtain raiser... Now is the time to enrol members and extend a policy of "laugh while you learn". Later when the position of the society is secure, the laughter can be dropped if it is thought incompatible with the constitution.[31]

The response to these calls for brighter programmes artfully deflected the matter onto the textual properties of the classics of the NFL themselves. Such films were gloomy because this was the nature of the great film art of the 1920s and 1930s. Regrettably, they noted, the lighter French film classics of the period were as yet unavailable, adding archly, "Until the National Film Library deems it fit to extend its lists, film societies must study film as an art form and feel the more miserable for it".[32]

Film Society Exhibition

In a recent study of the Museum of Modern Art (MOMA) Film Library, Haidee Wasson has traced the efforts of the organisation to create an audience for the films it has long collected. Wasson describes a North American film society movement located predominantly within institutions of higher education, coming into existence in conjunction with the MOMA Film Library, and more or less exclusively fed by its programmes. She goes as far as to suggest that the MOMA film programmes and accompanying film notes created the conditions in which such a movement was even possible in the United States. For Wasson, the MOMA film programmes promulgated a shift from ideas and practices of film study that were locally specific and eclectic to:

> a nationally organised, highly co-ordinated system that could be run with regularity and reliability. Film Library programs offered the advantage of expert curation, steady film supply, and authoritative sanction: they were based on standard sets of films and also on regulated methods for analysis around which a curriculum could be established and maintained.[33]

---

[30] *South London Film Society Magazine*, 1948: 1, no. 5, 24.
[31] Ibid., 25.
[32] Ibid., 4.
[33] Wasson, *Museum Movies: The Museum of Modern Art and the Birth of Art Cinema*, 164.

In the British context, despite the extraordinary visibility of the NFL titles within the film society movement testifying to their enormous appeal, it would be difficult to argue that the Institute's impact was so generative or comprehensive.

Like MOMA, the NFL strongly recommended that its users book complete programmes, and schedule their film shows to exemplify sequences which respected the historical categories of the catalogue. Forewords in successive editions of the publication through the 1940s, introduced the films as a collection "illustrating the development and technique of the film as a medium of entertainment and expression", before advising that:

> If these films are shown singly or as items in a miscellaneous programme their value will in most cases not be fully realised and their purpose may even be misunderstood. It is therefore strongly recommended that they be shown in programmes or in sequences arranged to illustrate developments in film technique. To facilitate this, brief historical notes have been included in the catalogue and the films themselves are supplied with short introductory titles.[34]

Advice on how to programme and directions towards suitable reading could also be provided by the curator on request. The library catalogue's historical notes were certainly reproduced in film society programmes, along with excerpts from sources such as Paul Rotha's *The Film Till Now* (1930) and Lewis Jacobs' *The Rise of the American Film* (1939). Sometimes the sources would be stitched together in a review written by a film society member.

Was the recommendation to programme in chronological sequences taken up in the amateur exhibition sector? Certainly many of the new film appreciation courses offered jointly by film societies with adult educators such as the WEA, would have worked with the Film Library's categories and developmental sequence. There were also instances where a film society, often newly formed, reported showing a complete sequence of NFL films, from the beginnings of cinema to the sound films in the collection. But in terms of the broader tendencies of film society exhibition practice, it is unlikely that the Curator's recommendation to show the library's titles in strict historical sequences would have been widely followed. Encouragement to programme so as to illustrate the chronological development of film technique conflicted with at least two interrelated, yet quite distinct, priorities for the film society exhibitor,

---

[34]*National Film Library Catalogue of the Lending Section*, 1.

which informed the arrangement of individual programmes and the composition of entire seasons, namely variety and balance.

Film societies everywhere tended to plan their shows around the single feature programme. This gave scope to include two, sometimes three, shorter films with the main picture, confirming that the supporting programme was considered to be a very important part of an evening's entertainment. The supporting shorts might be any combination of animation (Disney films were always popular as were United Artists or Halas and Batchelor cartoons, and experimental pieces by Norman McLaren and Len Lye), public relations or sponsored film (anything from a Richard Massingham comic public information films to medical or scientific works—a short docudrama entitled *Penicillin* (1944) was a popular supporting film for several years), and of course related to that, current documentary fare, including films such as Humphrey Jennings's *Diary for Timothy* (1945), or Paul Rotha's *Land of Promise* (1946) and *The World is Rich* (1947).

One tendency in film society programming was to emphasise the diversity of potential uses of the medium, and the range of possible film experiences. The pioneer of this approach was the original Film Society, where presenting a variety of film technique demonstrating the breadth of possibilities for the medium, was itself framed as a pedagogical aim.[35] We know from a recent study and interview that a similar programming practice was also pursued at New York's "Cinema 16".[36] Organiser Amos Vogel self-consciously aimed for juxtapositions of film style and practice both within an evening's programme and across a season as a whole. This created presentations where in Scott McDonald's view:

> one form of film collided with another in such a way as to create maximum thought—and perhaps action—on the part of the audience, not simply about individual films but about film itself and about the social and political implications of its conventional (or unconventional) uses.[37]

The emphasis on breadth and contrast is brought to mind when looking at some of the imaginative and adroit programming undertaken from the mid- to late-1940s in established film societies like those of Manchester, Edinburgh, Norwich and Tyneside. In this context, it is interesting to note an article on programme-building which appeared in *Documentary*

---

[35] Sexton, "The Film Society and the Creation of an Alternative Film Culture in Britain in the 1920s."
[36] MacDonald, *Cinema 16: Documents Toward a History of the Film Society.*
[37] Ibid., 10.

Newsletter in 1940, probably written by Norman Wilson of the Edinburgh Film Guild.[38] The article describes the key to success as the presentation of fresh and unorthodox material. An astute film society committee should be fully informed about film material available, and become avid collectors of as wide a range of distribution catalogues as possible. Its author observes that many societies already possess such expertise, commenting that: "At the present juncture most established societies have been busily collecting data for years, can locate almost every film in the country, and can estimate the value of each one", before suggesting that:

> Once all sources of information have been properly tapped, the programme builder will find a wide choice of subjects. Films of sociological or psychological value, continental films of outstanding merit, fantasies, satires; surrealist, abstract, cartoon, puppet and silhouette film; documentaries; experimental films involving new applications in colour or sound technique; and certain outstanding scientific, biological, economic and diagrammatic films.[39]

The article then urged schedulers to consider constructing programmes that created suggestive juxtapositions, and provocative comparisons between films grouped together according to various logics, such as those of nation, director, social theme or technique. Strategies should be considered such as running Vigo's *L'Atalante* (1934) with a Marx Brothers film, to enhance such illuminating contrasts. We can see this approach to programme building at work in the Edinburgh Film Guild; their 1945 season, for example, is striking for the variety of films screened, and displays remarkable breadth in terms of genres and modes of film practice represented, illustrating well the diverse logics bringing films together on a programme. *New Earth* (1934) by Joris Ivens, appears alongside *La Kermesse Heroique* (1935) in an all Dutch programme; Jill Craigie's celebrated documentary on modern art, *Out Of Chaos* (1944) shares the bill with *The Forgotten Village* (1941), a Mexican-set film scripted by John Steinbeck; an evening of items from the National Film Board of Canada features material ranging from documentary to experimental animation; the Soviet feature *Baltic Deputy* (1937) is shown with a selection of Mack Sennett shorts. Thanks to such consistently creative and resourceful programming, the Guild was soon nurturing large audiences often recorded as over a thousand-strong.

---

[38] Anon., "Programme Building", 14.
[39] Ibid., 14.

What ought to be stressed here is that such established societies in particular represented reservoirs of accumulated expertise in film availability, and real skill in programming. It was expected of an experienced booking secretary that he or she would maintain files of film library catalogues, familiarising themselves with the lists of the numerous small local photographic dealers that hired out silent films on the cheap, as well as those of the countless film libraries operated by manufacturers, distributive organisations, travel bureaux, royal societies, foreign embassies and so on. No self-respecting booking secretary would have been satisfied working solely from the lists of the NFL. Clearly the Film Library's film appreciation canon often had to sit alongside a very broad range of non-feature filmmaking, including experimental, scientific and educational material. In particular the film society movement however retained a strong allegiance to the principles of a documentary cinema, which regarded itself as using film to engage the citizen in similar matters of public concern. Following a period of terrible international conflict, these links were renewed as they articulated desires for international peace and understanding.

The Edinburgh Film Festival was just one manifestation of the welding of internationalist sentiments with documentary principles. A survey of films shown during the Festival's second year produced for a film society readership, noted the difficulties of recommending films for inclusion on a programme given the variety of subject matter, and the possible interest they might stimulate in any particular society:

> *Hill Sheep Farm*, for example would not find much response in Bloomsbury, would perhaps be subject to technical criticism in Lewis but would be generally acclaimed in Hereford. As it happens it is also an extremely well made film; but others on Indian midwifery, Italian paintings, measurements in engineering, or the Dunfermerline plan, are difficult to assess in relation to the growing Film Society movement as a whole.[40]

Nonetheless, the programming practices of many post-war film societies often demonstrated a sophisticated understanding of the multiple use-values of film. Where these possibilities were juxtaposed intelligently in the programming, they raised pertinent questions about alternative film practices, stimulating debates about taste and value within a non-professional exhibition context. As research presented here suggests, the attitudes to film and education cultivated in the societies sector in the

---

[40] Mathews, "International Festival of Documentary Films: Edinburgh 1948", 5.

immediate post-war years were increasingly resistant to the highly selective, hierarchical thrust of art film canon-formation constructed through the NFL.

The second principle informing film society exhibition practice was the idea of balance, in terms of both the balanced programme and the balanced season. The virtues of balance are enshrined in the exhibitors' wisdom that you can't please all the people all of the time, but that by producing a balanced programme and season you can still please everyone some of the time.[41] Clearly the film society movement's self-image was still to some extent that of an educator, cultivating film taste and using film to enrich personal and national life. Society organisers do though seem to have developed new senses of themselves as exhibitors post-war, and in this capacity clearly had to be more entrepreneurial, selling a season to a potential membership they knew to be more wary of overly explicit appeals to artistic or educational values. If they failed in this task, their societies faced possible dissolution, without the cushion of public funds to sustain their activities during lean times. So although the movement of the 1940s retained a strongly puritan streak, manifested in a somewhat "we're not here to enjoy ourselves" rhetoric of education over entertainment, many of the movement's activists were more keenly aware that their educational fervour was not shared by all their members. Clearly people joined a film society and attended its screenings for a variety of reasons, as one editorial in a Federation of Film Societies publication reflected:

> We shall always attract the client who "likes to go on Sunday afternoons", the few remaining French film snobs (and incidentally the linguists who don't care a fig for montage); but in amongst them are the future directors, critics and heads of our University schools of cinematography.[42]

The handbook *Forming and Running a Film Society*, produced by the BFI and the Federation, carried advice for would-be exhibitors informed by an understanding of the now diverse expectations and interests audience-members brought to their viewing of film.[43] The booklet concludes with an essay offering practical advice and defining film society good sense, written by Gerald Cockshott, a veteran film society organiser. Cockshott now advised caution in relation to the use of the words "educational" and "artistic" in the advance publicity of a new society. For many people, he noted, the latter "conjures up a vision of flaming shirts, bizarre ties and

---

[41] Cockshott, "Part Two: An Informal Essay", 27.
[42] Anon., "Editorial", 4.
[43] Cockshott, "Part Two: An Informal Essay", 1948, revised 1950.

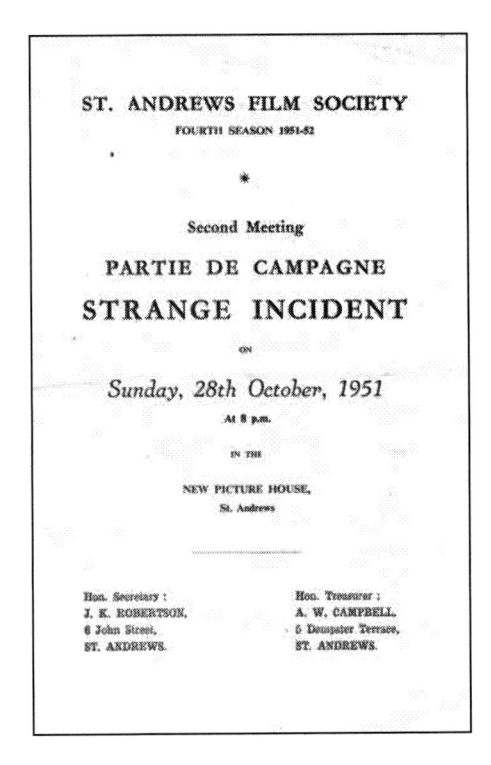

> ST. ANDREWS FILM SOCIETY
> FOURTH SEASON 1951-52
>
> *
>
> Second Meeting
>
> PARTIE DE CAMPAGNE
> **STRANGE INCIDENT**
>
> ON
>
> Sunday, 28th October, 1951
> At 8 p.m.
>
> IN THE
>
> NEW PICTURE HOUSE,
> St. Andrews
>
> ---
>
> Hon. Secretary :   Hon. Treasurer :
> J. K. ROBERTSON,   A. W. CAMPBELL,
> 6 John Street,   5 Dempster Terrace,
> ST. ANDREWS.   ST. ANDREWS.

Fig. 7-4 St Andrews Film Society Programme, 1951-1952
Source: Editor's collection

sandals".[44] Avoid a preliminary meeting, he suggested, as "the sight of a few beards and corduroy trousers may be enough to send a proportion of your potential audience away damning you once and for all as arty".[45] Also to be avoided was letting the society's ardent communist take charge of the programme. Pleasing everyone some of the time apparently involved striking a balance across the season: programmes should go for "drama with comedy, French sophistication with Russian naiveté".[46] If the feature is a sombre drama, the secretary is advised to book a funny supporting short. The values associated with the concepts of variety and balance, are explicit here: the former can be framed as educational imperative promoting the discovery of unusual films in provocative

---

[44] Ibid., 1950, 19.
[45] Ibid., 19.
[46] Ibid., 27.

arrangements. Balance, on the other hand, becomes an aspect of the programmer's art that conjures up not cinematic expression and its diversity, but rather the tastes and interests of the film society membership. (see Fig. 7-4) Achieving balance across the season meant anticipating both cultivated and popular tastes, and attempting to accommodate them within a mix of films, programming comedy and drama, anticipating laughter and reflection, offering instruction and emotional release.

Over time, such programming strategies seem to have produced diminishing returns. Further attention to the South London Film Society, and the revolt of its members against the glum classics that filled their programme, certainly suggests a certain loss of momentum. After attempting to "break the brittle ice of the rudiments of film appreciation" through the kind of sequenced programming of the canon favoured by the NFL,[47] the society quickly faced falling membership, and a financial loss of £7 on every screening. Revised aims in booking films for the new season were announced, and "brighter presentations" promised, though still accompanied by a fair proportion of the classic masterpieces.[48] Making the season more attractive in this way shouldn't cause serious complaint it was argued, "a mixed diet never did anyone any harm so long as there is plenty of it".[49] A less precise sense of educational purpose was now being mooted; study now involved accepting films "in the proper spirit and with the genuine intention of learning".[50] Such exchanges indicated how far the burden of demonstrating educational purpose had shifted from the film society struggling to make ends meet, to the disposition of its members.

Conclusions

The film societies assimilated or modified the NFL's film appreciation canon in complex ways that depended on factors such as their size, their accumulated experience in booking and programming, and the distinctive pedagogical traditions they could draw on as exhibitors. Standardizing tendencies of canon-formation met subtle resistance in the form of distinctive practices of programming and ideas of educational purpose, within the post-war film society movement. The library's impact on film study however went beyond the construction of a narrative of film history

---

[47] *South London Film Society Magazine* 1, no. 2, (1948): 2.
[48] *South London Film Society Magazine* 2, no. 1 (1949): 2.
[49] Ibid., 2.
[50] *South London Film Society Magazine* 2, no. 2 (1949): 15.

to support the circulation of a canon of classics to exhibition societies and teachers. In the longer term, the archive movement also transformed the conditions of film scholarship itself. A new generation of scholars emerged who self-consciously presented their approach to film analysis as the product of a careful re-examination of archived films. For this new school of film criticism, the archive and the possibilities of detailed re-examination of films it created enabled more rigorous and self-conscious forms of film analysis than were previously possible. Ernest Lindgren, curator of the Film Library, and for a time the BFI's Research Officer, wrote an article in *Sight and Sound* at the time of the Library's re-organisation that sought to draw a clear line distinguishing the old from the new styles of film analysis. For Lindgren, the pre-war film art movement, the film society, and the critical magazines *Close Up* and *Cinema Quarterly* represented "a sharply defined, unified epoch which had passed away".[51] Whilst he acknowledged that the old criticism was now quaintly outmoded, invoking only nostalgia, and that new approaches were emerging, the film appreciation project remained central, in his view. Whilst the old criticism was marred by extravagant enthusiasms, and partisanship, with the essence of film art identified with one or other properties of the medium, a new criticism would pick through the "pseudo-aesthetic rubbish" for the kernel of common sense it contained, and this would soon form the basis of a re-balanced film judgement.[52] Crucially in the present context, it would also replace largely amateur enthusiasms with more professionalised approaches.

A series of works soon emerged to realise the vision. Lindgren's own book *The Art of Film: An Introduction to Film Appreciation* was first published in 1948, one of a trio of popular film appreciation textbooks, which included Roger Manvell's *Film* (1944) and Hugo Wollenberg's *Anatomy of Film* (1947). Emerging from the experience of teaching film appreciation, they addressed the growing demand for authoritative introductions to film technique and criticism that could form the basis of a curriculum. Interestingly, neither Manvell nor Lindgren claimed any particular originality for their theorisation of film art, and both drew extensively on Rudolph Arnheim's *Film* (1933), and Pudovkin's *Film Technique* (1929). Lindgren indeed wrote in his preface that his ambition was simply to systematically introduce the reader to the fundamentals of film technique. Previously, he remarked, the cultivation of taste through appreciation of the finest works had been nurtured by the film societies, and was now spreading into organised education, and reaching a wider

---

[51] Lindgren, "Nostalgia", 49.
[52] Ibid., 50.

audience: "The need of the moment is that ideas so familiar to a small group of enthusiasts shall be given the widest possible currency".[53] For Lindgren then, the needs of the present demanded a shift from informal-amateur to formal-professional modes of film education, supported by standardised textbooks. Once identified as the nucleus of effort in film appreciation, the amateur film societies were apparently no longer considered suited to the task, instead professional teachers, lecturers and scholars would carry the project forward. At the very point of the film society movement's breathtaking ascent within the minority film culture, here was a portent of its future marginality. After all from which institutional sites in the film culture would the challenge to the film appreciation discourse be launched?

Works Cited

Primary Sources

Maddison, J. "Audio-Vision and the BFI." Unpublished article, BFI Special Collections: BFI Archive Box No. 11.

Secondary Sources

Aitken, Ian. *Film and Reform: John Grierson and the Documentary Film Movement.* London: Routledge, 1992.
Anon. "The Spectator." *Cinema Quarterly* 2, no. 1 (1933): 2-4.
—. *Birmingham Post* (11 July 1935). BFI Special Collections: BFI Archive Box 85; Cuttings File on the National Film Library from 1935-1940.
—. "Programme Building." *Documentary Newsletter* 1, no. 6 (1940): 14.
—. "New NFL Policy." *Sight and Sound* 10, no. 37 (1941): 13.
—. "Adult Education: Its Place in Post-war Society." *Adult Education: A Quarterly Journal of the British Institute of Adult Education* 16 (1943): 35-67.
—. "Editorial." *Federation of Film Societies Bulletin* (1949): 3-4.
Arnheim, Rudolph. *Film.* London: Faber, 1933.
British Film Institute. *8th Annual Report* (1941).
—. *11th Annual Report* (1944).
—. *17th Annual Report* (1950).
Brode, Anthony. "Sunday Observance." *Film* 7 (1956): 27.

---

[53] Lindgren, *The Art of Film: An Introduction to Film Appreciation*, vi.

Cockshott, Gerald. "Part Two: An Informal Essay." In *Forming and Running a Film Society*, edited by J. R. Cottrill, 18-31. Leicester: The Federation of Film Societies/British Film Institute, 1950.

The Commission on Educational and Cultural Films. *The Film in National Life*. London: George Allen and Unwin Ltd., 1932.

Federation of Film Societies. *Annual Report of the Honorary Treasurer 1950*. BFI Special Collections: British Federation of Film Societies Collection.

Hardy, Forsyth. "An Open Letter to Film Societies." *Sight and Sound* 10, no. 38 (1941): 29-30.

—. *John Grierson: A Documentary Biography*. London: Faber, 1979.

Jacobs, Lewis. *The Rise of the American Film*. New York: Harcourt Brace, 1939.

Lindgren, Ernest H. "A National Film Library for Great Britain." *Sight and Sound* 4, no. 14 (1935): 66-68.

—. "Nostalgia." *Sight and Sound* 9, no. 35 (1940): 49-50.

—. *The Art of Film: An Introduction to Film Appreciation*. London: George Allen and Unwin Ltd., 1948.

MacDonald, Scott. *Cinema 16: Documents Toward a History of the Film Society*. Philadelphia: Temple University Press, 2002.

Manvell, Roger. *Film*. Harmondsworth: Penguin Books, 1944.

Mathews, L. "International Festival of Documentary Films: Edinburgh 1948." *Federation of Film Societies Bulletin* (1949): 7-8.

Mulhern, Francis. *The Moment of Scrutiny*. London: New Left Books, 1979.

National Film Library Catalogue of the Lending Section. London: British Film Institute, 1948.

Pleasance, F. E. *The Film Society Movement in Britain 1925-1939*. MA Dissertation. School of English and American Studies, University of East Anglia, 1991.

Pudovkin, Vsevolod. I. *Film Technique*. London: Gollancz, 1929.

Reeves, M. "The Film Societies and Adult Education." *Adult Education: A Quarterly Journal of the British Institute of Adult Education* 21 (1949): 175-178.

Rotha, Paul. *The Film Till Now*. London: Cape, 1930.

—. *Celluloid: The Film Today*. London: Longmans, Green & Co., 1931.

Russell-Roberts, F. D. "The Progress of the 16mm Film." In *Winchester's Screen Encyclopedia*, edited by M. M. Miller, 358-359. Winchester: Winchester Publications Ltd., 1948.

Sexton, Jamie. "The Film Society and the Creation of an Alternative Film Culture in Britain in the 1920s." In *Young and Innocent? The Cinema*

in *Britain 1896-1930*, edited by Andrew Higson, 291-305. Exeter: University of Exeter Press, 2002.
South London Film Society Magazine 1, nos. 1, 2 & 5 (1948); 2, nos. 1 & 2 (1949).
Wasson, Haidee. *Museum Movies: The Museum of Modern Art and the Birth of Art Cinema.* Berkeley: University of California Press, 2005.
Wilson, Norman. "Film Societies—The Next Phase." *Sight and Sound* 14, no. 54 (1945): 37-38.
Wollenberg, Hugo. *The Anatomy of Film.* London: Marsland Publications Ltd., 1947.
Vaughan, F. H. "Organising a Branch." *Sight and Sound* 4, no. 15 (1935): 114-115.

Films Cited

L'Atalante
  (Gaumont-Franco/Film-Aubert, 1934) 35mm., 89 mins.
Baltic Deputy
  (Lenfilm, 1937) 35mm., 96 mins.
Battleship Potemkin
  (Goskino, 1925) 35mm., 75 mins.
Berlin
  (Deutsche-Verenis-Film, 1927) 35mm., 53 mins.
The Birth of a Nation
  (Griffith Corporation/Epoch Producing Corporation, 1915) 35mm., 187 mins.
The Cabinet of Dr Caligari
  (Decla-Bioscop, 1919) 35mm., 71 mins.
The Critic and The Film (series)
  (British Film Institute, 1949-1967) 35mm., 20-28 mins.
Diary for Timothy
  (Crown Film Unit, 1945) 35mm., 39 mins.
Drawings That Walk and Talk
  (British Film Institute, 1938) 35mm., 20 mins.
The End of St Petersburg
  (Mezhrabpom-Russ, 1927) 35mm., 80 mins.
The Forgotten Village
  (Pan-American Films, 1941) 35mm., 67 mins.
Film and Reality (extract compilation)
  (British Film Institute, 1942) 16mm., 121 mins.

The General Line
   (Sovkino, 1929) 35mm., 121 mins.
The Ghost That Never Returns
   (Sovkino, 1929) 35mm., 67 mins.
Greed
   (Metro-Goldwyn-Mayer, 1923) 35mm., 140 mins.
Hill Sheep Farm
   (Campbell Harper Films, 1948) 35mm., 20 mins.
Intolerance
   (Griffith, 1916) 35mm., 163 mins.
The Italian Straw Hat
   (Films Albatros, 1927) 35mm., 121 mins.
La Kermesse Heroique
   (Films Sonores Tobis, 1935) 35mm., 110 mins.
Land of Promise
   (Paul Rotha Productions, 1946) 35mm., 68 mins.
The Last Laugh
   (Ufa, 1924) 35mm., 77 mins.
Metropolis
   (Ufa, 1927) 35mm., 153 mins.
Moana
   (Famous Players Ltd., 1926) 35mm., 85 mins.
Mother
   (Mezhrabpom, 1926) 35mm., 90 mins.
The New Babylon
   (Sovkino, 1929) 35mm., 120 mins.
New Earth
   (Capi-Holland, 1934) 35mm., 36 mins.
Out of Chaos
   (Two Cities Films, 1944) 35mm., 28 mins.
Penicillin
   (Realist Film Unit, 1944) 35mm., 35 mins.
Quo Vadis
   (Cinès Productions, 1912) 35mm., 120 mins.
Rice Cultivation
   (amateur/BFI Education, 1938) 35 mm., 20 mins.
Tabu
   (Murnau-Flaherty Productions, 1931) 35mm., 90 mins.
Turksib
   (Vostok-kino, 1929) 35mm., 90 mins.

Warning Shadows
(Pan-Film der Dafu-Film Verleih, 1923) 35mm., 90 mins.
Waxworks
(Neptun-Film, 1924) 35mm., 65 mins.
The World is Rich
(Films of Fact/Central Office of Information, 1947) 35mm., 35 mins.
Winter Sports in Austria
(Austrian State Travel Bureau, 1930) 35 mm., 20 mins.

Part III

Creativities

CHAPTER EIGHT

ANIMATED EXPLORATIONS: THE GRASSHOPPER GROUP 1953-1983

SHEILA CHALKE

To animate: "to breathe life into, to enliven, to make lively."[1]

Unlike live-action film, which fragments and re-constitutes existing motion, film animation involves the creative visualisation of artistic ideas that are not necessarily indexed to any pro-filmic kinetic reality. The mode's acceptance as "cinema" is founded largely on its dependence upon a projection process, whilst a graphic specificity also encourages its recognition as an art form, equally relevant to gallery and museum locations. As Alexandre Alexeieff suggests, this grants animated film remarkable creative potentials:

> Contrary to live action cinema, animation draws the elements of its future works from a raw material made exclusively of human ideas, those ideas that different animators have about things, living beings and their forms, movements and meanings. They represent these ideas through images they make with their own hands. [2]

The "frame by frame" basics of this process were already established in the optical toys of the pre-cinematic era, the "persistence of vision" studies of Peter Mark Roget in 1824, and displays such as Emile Renaud's Théâtre Optique, held at the Grevin Museum in 1092. Many other pioneers experimented with apparatus and filmmaking techniques, as bonds with the proto-history of cinema were slowly forged. In 1895, Birt Acres filmed Tom Merry's drawings of Kaiser Wilhelm, whilst George Méliès animated letters of the alphabet for an advertising film in 1898, and integrated live actors with animated backgrounds soon after. Arthur Melbourne Cooper's

---

[1] Fowler, *Concise Oxford Dictionary*, 45.
[2] Alexeieff's 1973 comments, quoted in Bendazzi, *Cartoons*, xxii.

Matches: An Appeal (1899) used moving matchsticks to solicit the public donation of matches to soldiers fighting in the Boer War. Later productions by the filmmaker created three-dimensional animations, using toys; for example, *Noah's Ark* (1906), *Dreams of Toyland* (1908), *Wooden Athletes* (1912), and *Toymaker's Dream* (1913). Another pioneer, Emil Cohl, made his first film in 1908, and went on to produce a prodigious number of illogical trick films, using puppets and objects, before being employed on war propaganda films during the First World War.[3]

During the 1920s, an *avant-garde* film animation movement emerged, centred on the work of artists seeking to explore kinetics in painting and the moving image. Much of their experimental production attempted to represent musical notation, through graphic forms evolving into abstracted shapes. The work of Oscar Fischinger, Hans Richter, Viking Eggeling, Len Lye and others employed line, form, colour and objects (all elements in the field of fine art), in combination with the temporality and movement of cinema, to create and extend visual experience. When Walt Disney entered the arena in 1927 however, the term "animation" became synonymous with entertainment, and categorised as a "cartoon" medium. The trademark of "visual reality" it brought with it, came to dominate the world of commercial animation, setting a benchmark for the larger mainstream studios.[4]

Epitomising in this variant the wider force of commercial cinema, and even the mass culture of the inter-war years in general, animation offered amateur filmmakers therefore a significant professional "other" from the outset, as both a standard to be emulated, and a practice to be contested on its own ground. The intrinsic characteristics of animated film in fact seem to have lent the mode a particular attractiveness for the would-be amateur participant. This chapter explores such appeals in relation to the work of one remarkable collective, The Grasshopper Group, which gained unprecedented prominence within the British amateur film movement from the 1950s to the 1970s. Offering an outline account of the group's largely unresearched history, wider currents in the organised movement are traced, through the controversies which "the Grasshoppers" inspired, the evolution of their distinctive ideology of amateurism, and the preoccupations of their remarkably diverse output. In doing so, the essay seeks to locate amateur animation in relation to the wider live-action amateur community, and to initiate scholarship into an area of film practice often marginalised even *within* the already marginal spheres conventionally occupied by amateur cine.

---

[3] Ibid., 3-10.
[4] Wells, *Animation, Genre and Authorship*, 2.

Amateur Animation

Although sometimes peripheral within an amateur film culture with such strong roots in still photography and amateur dramatics, animated filmmaking has represented a persistent strand of non-professional cine activity in Britain, since the origins of the organised movement in the 1920s. Many early enthusiasts explored the mode, either as "lone workers" or within animation "units" operating inside cine clubs and various production groups. The Bognor Regis Film Society, for example, created "Moko The Monkey", who appeared regularly in their public shows in the 1930s.[5] By this time, animation had frequently been proposed as an eminently suitable occupation for the hobby filmmaker. As early as 1932, articles on animation appeared in the two main British cine journals—*Home Movies and Home Talkies* (1932-1940), and *Amateur Cine World* (1934-1967). Several suggestive items with titles such as "Animated Cartooning" and "Practical Animation for Amateurs", encouraged the production of animated films, stressing the possibility of worthwhile work in the field, even for those without the basic ability to draw.[6] Much interest was also shown in professional animation, in essays such as "Mickey Mouse Methods: How Disney Works", which scrutinised current commercial releases for instructional value.[7] Elsewhere, advertisements for Harbutt's Plasticine and other such materials, implied a more three-dimensional approach, alongside recurrent articles which explored model-based techniques.[8]

Encouragement to animate was in keeping with broader tendencies towards the cultivation of discrete modes of amateur practice. In an early essay headed "What Should I Film?", Adrian Brunel, a professional filmmaker much involved with the amateur movement in the thirties, advised "specialisation" rather than "generalisation" for the serious-minded hobby filmmaker. According to Brunel, the amateur's *forte* should lay in burlesque, cartoons, silhouette and puppet films, as these were seen as realisable projects for small units to tackle. There were many positive benefits, it was underlined, recommending such activity to amateur movie makers. The need for extensive studio space was eliminated; problems involving casting and subsequent reliability were removed; amateur actors could be dispensed with, as could costs incurred for the sets, costumes and

---

[5] Eyles, Gray, Readman, *Cinema West Sussex*, 43.
[6] Shaw, "Animated Cartooning", 52, and Salt, "Practical Animation for Amateurs", 289-290, respectively.
[7] Anon., "Mickey Mouse Methods", 97.
[8] Butcher, "Cartooning in Clay", 81-83.

make-up necessary in live-action production.[9] Unparalleled degrees of control were deemed possible in the field of animation, with production easily broken down into small-scale tasks, and the protracted investments involved—demanding meticulousness and systematic organisation—regarded as cultivating good amateur discipline, and as providing an opportunity to involve significant numbers of people in a single production—always important in the club sector in particular. At more basic levels, by working indoors, animators might avoid the vagaries of weather which could so easily disrupt even the best laid of live-action plans. A proliferation of articles with titles such as "Making a Silhouette Film" further suggest that animation promised particular satisfactions for the technically-minded, and offered a persistent incentive to the improvisers of devices, processes and visual effects of all kinds.[10]

This is not to imply that film animation was considered easy. Then as now, it remained an enormously time-consuming business, especially for those squeezing filmmaking into scarce segments of leisure time. Replacing the "real" with more graphic elements related to Art, such as form, line, colour and the representational conventions of two-dimensional space, animation undoubtedly generates new difficulties for the filmmaker. At the same time, it also suggests fresh possibilities, which perhaps involve a particular continuity with ideologies of amateurism rooted in notions of freedom from dominant orders and related institutional constraints. For many would-be participants, the diverse vocabulary of animated forms and processes significantly expanded such freedom, providing space for seemingly unrestricted demonstrations of aesthetic control. Whilst amateur cinematography itself is often defined by such freedom from established conventions, the "impossibilities" and metamorphoses of the animated world also significantly expand, for many commentators, the subversive attributes inherent in this singular practice. Paul Wells's description of animation in 2002 as:

> The most important creative form of the twenty-first century... The omnipresent pictorial form of the modern era .... a medium of universal expression embraced across The Globe.[11]

only echoes the imaginings of his 1920s and 1930s antecedents within the amateur cine movement. Ever since Disney established a visual aesthetics of "realism" to reinforce the "orthodox" currency of the animated film, all

---

[9] Brunel, "What Shall I Film?", 386-388.
[10] Anon., "Making A Silhouette Film", 277-282.
[11] Wells, *Animation, Genre and Authorship*, 1.

other models have tended to be categorised as "developmental" or "experimental" in relation to this standard reference point.[12] The work of small European studios in particular—and amateur/semi-professional cross-over units, such as the Grasshopper Group—have generally been positioned under the hegemony of the avant-garde, and allied with broader "progressive" movements and agencies of social transformation. Closer scrutiny of the Group however suggests a range of more contradictory affiliations and ambitions, and a network of traditions within which the work of the team might be productively located, a network activated by the particular historical conjuncture from which its membership emerged.

Formation of the Grasshopper Group

In the early 1950s, John Daborn (1929-1990), then working as a visualiser for an advertising agency, formulated the idea of a group, consisting of amateur and semi-professional filmmakers, which would work communally to support each other in the promotion and encouragement of cartoon and experimental filmmaking. Daborn, at that time living in Ashley Drive, Walton-on-Thames, gathered together a group of friends, who initially called themselves The Ashley Film Unit. Using a basic 9.5mm camera, they quickly began production of two animated films, eventually entitled *The Millstream* (1951) and *The History of Walton* (1952). After two years' work on the latter, it was realised that more help, both technical and financial, would be needed to complete the project, encouraging amalgamation with a nearby group, The Kingston and District Cine Club (KDCC). The move proved mutually beneficial, generating additional practical support, and securing the use of KDCC resources. Daborn could now rely on assistance with graphic design from Ken Clarke, and with the actual filming, from William Archer, (a Canadian scientist in Britain working for the war office). Tytpical amateur improvisation and resourcefulness were immediately in evidence. A hand-built rostrum camera was soon constructed from all manner of spare parts—including materials salvaged from an old fire engine—an apparatus that resided in a cupboard in Daborn's bedroom/studio for many years thereafter.

When completed, both films swept the board as prize-winners in several contests, and received much public acclaim. In January 1953, the KDCC presented three screenings of *The History of Walton* to full houses, at the local public library. Subsequent showings took place in March the

---

[12] Furniss, *Art in Motion*, quoted in Wells, *Animation, Genre and Authorship*, 34.

same year, at a nearby commercial cinema, where the film played for a week, was given an impressive front-of-house display, and was accompanied by a synchronised music soundtrack, recorded on tape.[13] By this time, the film had already won the IAC's "Ten Best" Competition—the "Oscars" of the amateur cine world—and had begun a successful tour of the competitive amateur cinema circuit, where it would garner a host of other prizes.[14] Production of the 300ft. animation had taken three years, with filming on Kodachrome "A" stock, using a camera "stripped of all its mechanism and driven by a gramophone motor geared to a frame release" —a somewhat "Heath Robinson" arrangement, which, nonetheless, seems to have worked well.[15] Above all, the film offered early testimony to Daborn's dedication. The original work-plan had envisaged several artists covering a sequence each, but, one by one, they had dropped out, leaving Daborn himself to paint all 270 backgrounds.

In its early sequences, *History of Walton* incorporates a visual resumé of the first decades of screen animation, from pre-cinema lantern shows to the avant-garde experimentalisms of the 1920s and 1930s. In a typical amateur turn, this inherited "master" narrative is re-figured in insistently "local" terms. Prehistoric "Walton man" is shown inhabiting a few thatched huts gathered along the banks of the River Thames. Here these early "neighbours" tend their fires and animals, in actions marked by stylised gestures, evoking the restricted movements of lanternslide technology—a raised arm, the flickering flame of a cooking fire, the breaking of flints to form an axe-head. When clouds darken the moon, Caesar's Roman legions cross the river to do battle with the primitive tribespeople. Visuals quickly dissolve into a riot of abstraction, spinning circles, zig-zag lines and repetitive patterns, suggesting the movement and violence of battle, in a style reminiscent of filmmakers such as Len Lye, and other avant-garde artists' films of the inter-war years. A review of the

---

[13] Anon., "Club Report", 1953, 936.

[14] The film proved extremely popular, and received an excellent reception when screened at the British Kinematograph Society, and won the Barnitt Cup at the Federation of Cinematograph Societies' Annual Competition; it took the BFI Cup for Best Documentary in the Scottish Amateur Film Festival for that year and, by June 2nd 1953 (Coronation Day) it had been chosen as one of four British entries for the prestigious International UNICA Congress to be held in Brussels from August 20th–28th. *The Millstream*, a much shorter, more conventional animation was also successful, also winning a BFI Prize at the Scottish Amateur Film Festival.

[15] Anon., "Ten Best Films of 1952", 29.

film, as overall winner in the "Ten Best" Competition, describes the process well:

> The moving camera is used as a means of animation no less than the cels on which the action is drawn in successive stages. It glides over decorative drawings in the modern manner, dwelling on this, withdrawing from that. Clever use is made of symbolism and colour change. The Roman Army is a stylised phalanx; at the moment of battle the scene explodes in a riot of colour. Repetitive pattern emphasises the odds, which the defenders have to meet.[16]

Although such exposure suggests a certain moment of self-realisation perhaps, it is not clear exactly *when* the Grasshopper Group became fully functional as an autonomous production unit. From the beginning it had possessed a loosely structured membership, which excluded neither affiliation with other societies, nor more independent filmmaking. In November 1953 however, *Amateur Cine World* announced the emergence of "a new unit devoted entirely to the production of experimental and cartoon film... formed by John (*History of Walton*) Daborn."[17] According to this early report, the group would be innovative in organisation as well as output: there were to be no subscriptions, but members of each unit would share in the cost of their own particular film. The piece also sketched something of a network structure, rather than the concentration of a conventional group. While there was to be a designated meeting location for live-action filming, cartoon work, it was envisaged would be done on a more "virtual" basis, by exchanging material through the post.

Publicity gained from the success of *History of Walton* proved instrumental in attracting other founder members like Dick Horne. Having attempted, as a lone animator, to grapple single-handedly with artistic, technical and financial problems, Horne wrote to *Amateur Cine World* in December 1953, offering assistance to fellow enthusiasts: "if any London club can make use of my services as an animation-designer I shall be pleased to hear from them."[18] His announcement brought immediate contact with Daborn and an injection of considerable professional experience to Grasshopper, with the newcomer having worked at the celebrated Halas and Batchelor animation studios since leaving college.[19] Horne may indeed have been something of a reluctant amateur:

---

[16] Ibid., 39.
[17] Daborn, "News From Societies", 1953, 679.
[18] Horne, "Letter to *Amateur Cine World*", 769.
[19] On Halas and Batchelor, see Stephenson, *Animation in The Cinema*, 80-82.

unfortunately, working conditions in the commercial studios of the time did not provide job stability for even talented practitioners. Animation workers were usually employed on short-term contracts only when required for major productions, and dismissed when assignments were completed. As a result, many would-be animators clearly preferred to work professionally in other areas of the graphics industry, while indulging their specifically filmic creativities within the more amenable environments of amateurism. John Daborn himself was said to prize "the freedom of the amateur" and to have "turned down commercial offers so that filmmaking can remain for him a hobby."[20] Another key Grasshopper presence, Stuart Wynn Jones, certainly subscribed to a similar view. In a letter to *Amateur Cine World* entitled simply "Pleasing Oneself", he states in almost manifesto-terms:

> The amateur is free to experiment in ways not open to the professional... and he should not give up this creative freedom in the hopes of catching the eye of the large-scale distributor.[21]

With Horne and Wynn Jones involved, it is safe to say that, by the end of 1953, the Grasshoppers were constituted as a coherent group. A committee had been formed with Daborn as Chairman, Jean and Ken Clarke as joint Secretaries, and a committee that included Dick Horne, Stuart Wynn Jones, Derek Hill, Bob Godfrey, Kevin Brownlow, Jim Nicholson, John Kirby and Bill Archer. Indicating the reputation and ambition of the group even at this early stage, Norman McLaren enthusiastically consented to become their first President; his charismatic influence was already evident in the first club production—a "pixilated" live-action film, *Two's Company* (1952) shot in six sessions on Wimbledon Common, and performed by Richard Cox, Gerry Potterton and Audrey Vayro (later to become Audrey Daborn). A technique previously exploited by McLaren in his own film *Neighbours* (1952), "pixilation" applied the principles of stop-motion animation to live subjects, an apparently still novel process that the Grasshoppers would explore over a lengthy series of movies.

Although *Neighbours* exposed a darker side of human nature, the aim of *Two's Company* was simply to seek "The irresponsible light-heartedness of the animated drawing which flaunts all physical laws."[22] The actors move like puppets, as each character is filmed a frame at a time, moving only slightly between each exposure. The result is highly

---

[20] Anon., "Grasshoppers Jump Ahead", 38.
[21] Wynn Jones, "Pleasing Oneself", 51.
[22] Daborn, "A Pixilated Comedy", 963.

stylised action, as normal movement speeds are slowed and/or accelerated. The narrative involves a simple love triangle, in which two suitors fight over a girl who sits, throughout the action, picking petals off a giant daisy—"He loves me, he loves me not...". Suggesting an early awareness of publicity value, an account of the Wimbledon Common "shoot" appeared in *Amateur Cine World* in January 1955, in which it was noted that the interaction of picnickers, passers-by, and some rude boys, gave amusing insights into the problems of amateur filmmaking in public locations.[23]

Battles, Birdies and Brides

The mid-1950s became a period of remarkable creativity for the Grasshopper Group, which indexed the vitality of the wider amateur cine movement as a whole, and saw a significant expansion of activities soon demanding greater resources. Early meetings had taken place in a café in Bloomsbury, but with a rapid increase in membership, a more permanent home was found at the Mary Ward Settlement, located close to London's Euston Station. With *Two's Company* in production, a second unit had already begun planning a more ambitious 16mm colour cartoon, provisionally entitled *The Battle of Wangapore* (see Fig. 8-1) This was undoubtedly a large-scale project in amateur terms, since although only ten minutes long, it was to involve synchronised sound—still in the 1950s a considerable challenge for the non-professional. Based on an original story by Rudyard Kipling, the film emerged, under John Daborn's leadership, and thanks to his remarkable powers of organisation, as an amazing achievement in teamwork and postal communication. Storyboards, drawings, sound and scenario ideas were all distributed around the country by mail, and returned after revision prior to shooting. Records suggest that, throughout the whole production, it was only necessary to have about half-a-dozen group meetings, held in London, at roughly three-monthly intervals.

Whilst preserving a quintessential amateur "spirit", professional practice was emulated meticulously at all stages. The script was broken down into scenes, and a detailed storyboard prepared. Character model-sheets were drawn, and each sequence subjected to precise timing. Commentary, sound and theme music were then optically-recorded onto 16mm film stock, upon which the animation would be constructed—unlike live-action film, an animation soundtrack must be constructed *first*

---

[23] Ibid., 964-966.

in order not to waste drawings. Work on *Wangapore*, begun in late 1952, was completed after three years of strenuous effort, an investment which had stretched resources to the limit. During the course of production, the Group had frequently advertised for artists, and additional helpers to undertake tracing, painting and other repetitious, time-consuming tasks. Persistence however reaped dividends: on its completion in 1955, the film toured the amateur competition circuits to much acclaim, winning no less than fifteen national and international awards.[24]

Fig. 8-1 Grasshopper production meeting for *The Battle of Wangapore* (1955) Source: author's collection (courtesy of Mrs A. Daborn)

---

[24] Prior to the five awards gained at the Cannes Amateur Film Festival, *The Battle of Wangapore* had already received trophies from the IAC, securing the "Mini-Cup" for technical proficiency in 1955. The IAC Cinematography Trophy was also awarded to the film in 1956, after it gained a third place in the scenario section at the UNICA International Festival in Zurich, where it scored the highest marks for any British entry. The film was subsequently selected for showing at the Edinburgh Festival, and gained further accolades abroad. Winning films from the 1956 Ten Best Competition toured Canada and the USA in 1959, where the Motion Picture Division of the Photographic Society of America rewarded the film with an award for best club production.

Recognition of *The Battle of Wangapore* extended well beyond the confines of the amateur cine movement; the film was exhibited at The National Film Theatre and, in July 1956, was screened by Richard Dimbleby on BBC Television's *Panorama* programme. It soon became one of only four films selected to represent Britain at UNICA's prestigious international festival, held that year in Brussels. (see Fig. 8-2) No less than five "glittering prizes" awaited the Group at the Cannes Amateur Film Festival of 1956, where *Wangapore* collected not only the Grand Prix d'honneur (awarded by the President of the French Republic), but also the cup for animation, a trophy awarded by the Cannes Ciné Club itself, a gold medal from the Festival sponsors, and the additional prize of a tour of France awarded by L'Industrie Cinematographique Substandard. Festival recognition further spread the film's reputation closer to home. Screened at a Group meeting in March 1956, an occasion at which representatives of the press, and members of the professional film industry were invited to be present, the audience was so large that over sixty applications for tickets had to be refused. After such resounding success, a documentary about the film's production was made. Entitled *Let Battle Commence* (1957), it charted the complex assembly process, explaining the involvement of large numbers of "helpers", and the dedicated work of the core team. This too eventually won an Oscar in the Ten Best competition of 1958.

Fig. 8-2 animation cell from *The Battle of Wangapore* (1955)
Source: author's collection (courtesy of Mrs A. Daborn)

By this point, a range of other projects had been developed. During the long production of *Wangapore*, a sponsored film, *Cutting for Style* (1954), had been prepared for the Guild of Hairdressers, Perfumers and Wigmakers, and by April 1955 the Group were able to report that they were:

To be expanded into a full-scale circle for lone workers and club members. Membership may not necessarily [they stressed...] entail active filming within the group [and that...] it is enough that every Grasshopper should have an interest in experimental and cartoon work.[25]

The slate of production which followed illustrates both widening participation and increasing recognition within the "mainstream". John Daborn's effort *Paintbox Holiday* (1955) was one of the entries chosen by Associated Rediffusion's Television Cine Holiday Competition, for transmission in a fortnightly series of programmes. Another "pixilated" comedy was produced—*Bride and Groom* (1955), which placed live actors in a colourful, but eccentric, cartoon setting. (see Fig. 8-3).

Fig. 8-3 frame enlargement from *Bride and Groom* (1955)
Source: author's collection (courtesy of Mrs A. Daborn)

Shot in a studio in Barnes loaned to the Group, with stylised sets and impressive trickery, the piece once more evoked Norman McLaren's inspirational experimental style, and again proved a prize-winner.[26] The film's hectic pace perhaps suggests something of the filmmakers' own accelerating work rate during this period. By September 1955, no less than

---

[25] Clark, "News From Societies", 1291.
[26] *Bride and Groom*, made with backing from the BFI Experimental Film Fund, eventually won the Avant Garde Cup at the Cannes Amateur Film Festival in 1958.

250   Chapter Eight

five experimental pieces, including further cartoons, were in production, and two "sponsored" films were also well underway.

Other members were busy developing their own projects. Bob Godfrey joined forces with Vera Linnicar and Keith Learner to make *Watch The Birdie* (1956). For this remarkable animation, the team used an obsolete hand-cranked Kodak-A camera, and returned to the cut-out techniques employed by early animators. (see Fig. 8-4) Almost a reconstruction of primitive methods, the result was a decorative mingling of line, colour, shape and movement narrated through humorous and witty titling. Not surprisingly, *Watch The Birdie* won prizes both in Britain, and at various competitions and festivals abroad.[27]

Fig. 8-4 frame enlargement from *Watch The Birdie* (1954)
Source: author's collection (courtesy of Mrs A. Daborn)

Meanwhile, Stuart Wynn Jones (the most avant garde of the Grasshoppers according to accounts from fellow members) worked on *Theorem of Pythagoras* (1955) and *Short Spell* (1956), in which:

---

[27] *Watch the Birdie* gained second place in both the animation and genre sections at UNICA, establishing still further the Grasshopper Group's position as one of the leading societies in the amateur film movement.

He [tried] to emulate Norman McLaren by drawing straight onto 35mm film with an ordinary pen and Indian ink, and at the same time devising his own soundtrack which, he says, sounds like a "hoarse electric organ". Only 100ft. in length... the idea behind it is to exploit amusing variations on the alphabet.[28]

Wynn Jones, a musician himself, was dedicated for many years to such *musique concrète*, which he composed and introduced as impressionistic soundtracks into a number of his films. Not to be confused with electronic music, this often complex assembly was constructed from natural sounds, sometimes mixed with musical chords and long notes, which were subsequently re-recorded to create rhythmic patterns.

Brief notes such as these can give only an impression of the sheer quantity of work being undertaken by the Grasshoppers during this period. In structure and function however, and despite the professional connections of some members, the Group followed the traditional pattern of most amateur collectives. Live-action filming took place mainly in the spring and summer months, while the winter season was given over to planning future productions, social events and public screenings. Talks and discussion sessions were also regular features of the Grasshopper calendar. Derek Hill, himself a film critic and writer, often devised the programmes, which were attended by large audiences, despite catering for more experimental and artistic tastes perhaps than the typical Film Society offerings discussed elsewhere in this volume.[29] Programmes usually consisted of recent "rushes" of members' and group productions, avant-garde films, such as Lindsay Anderson's *O Dreamland* (1953) and Lorenza Mazzetti's *Metamorposis* (1954)—the latter proving a little *too* avant garde, even for a "Grasshopper" audience. Such serious items were often balanced with comedies, such as Richard Massingham's *Tell Me If It Hurts* (1934), and early Magoo cartoons.[30] Sessions were usually

---

[28] Clark, "Newsreel", 579.

[29] See Richard MacDonald's chapter in this volume on the development of post-war exhibition culture amongst the Film Societies.

[30] Anon., "Controversy Corner", 171. Evidence of the Grasshopper's links *with*, and interest *in* the extremes of experimental, and artistic production is offered by Derek Hill's importation of seven films made by the Gryphon Film Group from New York. These were screened at Grasshopper shows, and then made available for other clubs to borrow through Adventure Films distribution. They included three by Stan Brakhage—*Interim* (1952), (his first film, made at the age of eighteen), *The Way to Shadow Gardens* (1954), and *Reflections on Black* (1955), a four-minute experimental film, *Visual Variations on Noguchi,* (maker unknown),

introduced by Grasshopper members, and talks often given by eminent directors. Screening events clearly functioned as important recruiting opportunities, and the diverse programming seems to have been designed to attract those whose "appreciative" interests might eventually be transformed into more direct participation.

By 1957, membership of the Group had grown to 143, leading to a decision to join the Federation of Cine Societies, a move confirming the Group as well established in the amateur movement, and as seeking broader recognition. Exposure via the hobby literature also seems to have become a strategic aim. Several members were now contributing regularly to *Amateur Cine World*; Kevin Brownlow (who had by then formed his own filmmaking unit) pursued his passion for silent film in a monthly feature; Desmond Roe submitted technical advice, whilst Derek Hill reviewed mainstream releases, with a particular eye to their instructional value for amateurs. Both Stuart Wynn Jones and his wife, Hazel Swift, also became regular contributors, while John Daborn himself penned occasional articles and letters.[31]

Grasshopper's overall profile also owed much to the Group's emulation of professional marketing strategies, which underlined their commitment to reaching audiences beyond the "social world" of the amateur. Paul Hudsmith undertook the distribution of Grasshopper films, along with other experimental work, through Adventure Film Productions, in a brave attempt to place amateur film before the public at reasonable cost, and to generate a little revenue for the Group itself. Such initiatives were not seen as contradictory to the basic ideological perspectives of the Group, which were firmly rooted in notions of liberal support for both individual and collective ideas and practices. In the face of the criticism which so professional a style sometimes attracted, the Grasshoppers were anxious to preserve amateur principles, which were defined as a balancing of creative expression with a degree of social responsibility in the exercising of freedom beyond the marketplace of mainstream cinema. Very much in this spirit, the Group decided, in 1957, to cease production

---

and a profoundly complex essay on theology, *Image in the Snow* produced by Willard Maas, sometime in the 1950s.

[31] Besides contributing articles such as "A Fight to the Last Frame", 1050-1074—on the making of *The History of Walton*, Daborn wrote frequent letters to *Amateur Cine World* on contentious subjects. Stuart Wynn Jones provided instructive pieces on cartooning such as "Cartooning With A Compass", 702-703—while Hazel Swift, who had taken over from Iris Fayde as the only female contributor to *Amateur Cine World*, provided a series dealing largely with ideas for filmmaking, such as "The Ones That Got Away", 48-149.

of collectively-produced sponsored film for commercial companies, although individual members were still free to work in these fields.

Imaginative solutions to the challenge of reconciling amateur principles with economic realities were developed continuously. Dick Horne's experimental cartoon *The Window* (1956) became the first group film to be sponsored through an internal share issue, pitched at the rate of £1 per share. Members were subsequently encouraged to buy shares in forthcoming productions as a means of funding new work. Revenue could then be recouped *if* and *when* films were distributed through Adventure Film Productions. However, there were difficulties inherent in this scheme and, at the Group's Annual General Meeting in 1956, various questions were raised: in the event of films making a profit, should the shareholder be paid in full, *pro rata*, or should they only get £1 back? Should the rest go into Group funds? How much should go towards Group equipment? Other reservations about the scheme were perhaps more significant—would this mean that the Group were in danger of losing their cherished amateur status?[32]

Always somewhat self-conscious about their "professionalised" approach to production, and aware of the disquiet felt—and often vociferously expressed—by other amateur filmmakers, over their conspicuous competitive success, the Grasshoppers were keen to defend their position in print. One 1956 report expressed both the anxiety and their response especially succinctly:

> The committee is very perturbed at current rumours that the Group is making, or is out to make, profit on its productions. This, they say, is an entirely false impression and has probably arisen because the Group has managed, in some cases, to regain a little of the money expended. Efforts are being made to find a definite answer to the old question: "When is an amateur not an amateur?"[33]

Perhaps the Grasshoppers would have appreciated later interventions by scholars such as Patricia Zimmermann, who has summarised the polarity of the amateur and professional, on the basis of a division that "hierarchically balances the contradiction between rationalised wage labour and more integrated creative labour."[34] One fundamental difference between amateur and professional practice according to this formulation is that, for amateurs, the process and activity of filmmaking itself absorbs, to

---

[32] Kerby, "Newsreel", 276-278.
[33] Clark, "Cross-Channel Hop", 852.
[34] Zimmermann, *Reel Families*, 4.

some degree, the filmic product. Rigid standardisation of procedure, exemplified by structures within professional studio systems, is dissipated to promote more fluid communal integration in the amateur field, allowing for participation in the filmic process as a whole. Thus tasks and skills are interchangeable and new competences can be learned—almost a definition of the Grasshopper Group at work.

Undoubtedly the CVs of various Grasshopper members raised eyebrows. Dick Horne, Ken Clark, John Daborn, and other members of the Group had received early training in commercial studios, although had felt at odds with the ethos and organisation of such environments, finding creativity limited and their contributions to the work in progress necessarily fragmented. Experience of the whole process of animation, involving control and freedom to experiment, they now felt, could only be found through working autonomously, or as part of an interactive group with shared ideologies of co-operative creative labour. "Cross-over" *into* the amateur sector might provide this opportunity, but only ironically if they were to operate on quasi-professional lines in order to avoid unacceptably "amateur*ish*" output.

Uncertainties concerning amateur status had been an on-going problem since the 1930s, haunting debate, particularly in the context of amateur competition culture. Fairly liberal rulings had been established by festival organisers, but persistent ambiguities in attitude remained.[35] Polemical argument on this issue pursued the Grasshoppers well into the 1960s when Paul Briggs, then Chairman of the Group, defended them in response to criticism that they were mostly "professional workers" and, consequently, should be barred from amateur contests.[36] Briggs pointed out that group membership consisted of people in many different professions, including a mathematician, computer programmer, solicitor, and a lecturer in horticulture, an engineering draughtsman and others. In a membership of seventy, at this time, there were apparently only two or three assistant film editors, and one genuine card-carrying ACTT newsreel cameraman. Briggs suggested that their critics should visit Group meetings to obtain

---

[35] 1934 IAC Competition Rules stated that the contest was open to amateurs and amateur clubs anywhere in the world, who were either members of, or affiliated to the IAC. The UNICA. ruling (of 1948) defined a film as "amateur" when the non-professional filmmaker had no financial and commercial object in making it. The term "professional" was limited to the profession of cameraman and director. Therefore, a film made by a professional art-director or editor *for his own pleasure* [my italics] would be regarded as an amateur film.

[36] Nurse, "UNICA—Aired Again", 35.

"the full flavour of our particular combination of amateurism (in the worst sense) and enthusiasm (in the best)."[37]

Television: A Blessing or a Curse?

To understand *why* the practice of amateur animation should have expanded in the early fifties one might look no further than the march of television, and in particular to the introduction of an "independent" service in 1955, under the auspices of the Independent Television Authority (ITA). Initially received only by a small audience in the London area, viewing figures were rising by 50,000 per week by 1957, and just as significantly, demand for advertising was far outstripping supply.[38] Ex-Grasshopper member Dick Horne, recalls those early days in terms of new opportunities for animators:

> Throughout '53 and '54 studios were setting-up, doing pilot films, waiting for ITV to start. In those days you had "one man and his dog" churning out a commercial, and down the road there would be twenty people in another studio doing the same kind of commercial... But that was the market. Jobs for people, settled employment, and it coincided with people in the States starting to challenge Disney. So there was another market opening there.[39]

On a practical level then, television provided unanticipated sources of employment for animators of all kinds, whilst also creating a remarkable new showcase for their talents, well beyond the existing spheres. Whilst winning films from the largest British amateur competition (the Ten Best) were screened annually at London's National Film Theatre, before going on tour around the regions, and other key gatherings (especially the IAC Competition and the Scottish Amateur Film Festival) also generated packages of circulating films—more general exposure was limited and coverage decidedly uneven. When the new medium of television courted amateur filmmakers to supply programme items, it is hardly surprising therefore that many should have sought to embrace the possibilities involved.

Back in 1953, BBC Television had, in collaboration with the British Association of Amateur Cinematographers' (BAAC's) Central Committee, planned to transmit amateur film in four one-hour programmes, at three-monthly intervals. Viewers would be allowed to vote for their favourite

---

[37] Briggs, "Unfair To Grasshoppers", 150.
[38] O'Sullivan, "Post-war Television in Britain", 33.
[39] Horne, interview, 2006.

film, which would then be awarded the Television Amateur Cinematographer's Trophy. Claiming that they wished to put viewers in touch with "the country's growing amateur film movement", the cine press naturally welcomed this move from the BBC as recognition of the amateur's achievements:

> Surely this is proof that the amateur film has now grown up, that it is now recognised that it deserves a public beyond the family and the small audience of fellow enthusiasts.[40]

Readers were further reminded that, in the United States, outlets for amateur work were being created on television. Italian television, too, apparently featured weekly programmes of amateur film. It was even suggested that in Britain, the BBC and the new ITV channel, might foster further post-war rejuvenation of hobby cinematography, as both organisations evolved. In this exciting new context, Grasshopper films were often singled out to provide screenings, and club members invited to participate in discussion of the possibilities involved.

John Daborn's *Paintbox Holiday* was presented on television in 1956. Other works featured on the small screen included Bob Godfrey's *Watch The Birdie* and *The Big Parade* (1952), which were both presented by the Goons on their early BBC programme, *Idiots Weekly* (1956). Another prize-winner in the Ten Best, *Driftwood and Seashell* (1956), made by Grasshopper members Dr. and Mrs Jobson, was televised on ITV. When Stuart Wynn Jones's film *Short Spell* was shown on BBC's *Tonight* programme, in 1954, the Corporation asked to see more of the Ten Best wining films "which similarly escape from the professional mould."[41] The trend continued through the 1950s, and by 1962 episodes of the BBC *Film Club* series would be dedicated to screened extracts from Top Eight Competition films.[42] A certain nervousness around all this interest from the "goggle-box", was soon indicated however when the medium was recommended as potential subject matter for amateur productions: a storyboard idea, featuring a burglar entering a house while the family were watching television, appeared in *Amateur Cine World* in 1963.[43]

Although this new outlet appeared to promise increased visibility for amateur film, there were clearly reservations about television's effect on the organised movement. Some feared that only prize-winning amateur

---

[40] Malthouse, "Amateur Films on TV", 1098.
[41] Wynn Jones, "Anyone Can A-n-i-m-a-t-e", 996-997.
[42] Rose, "Top 8 on TV", 47.
[43] Anon., "Goggle-Box Burglar", 795.

films would reach the public, leading to comparison with professional productions, and subsequent pressure on amateurs to reach those standards. Concerns were further expressed about the decimation of home cinema, while discourses arose around the relevant value, to amateurs, of new filmmaking styles and techniques introduced by television. Legal conflicts surrounding the broadcasting of amateur work on television, particularly its relationship to the British film quotas, the Cinematograph Film Act and protection of professional ACTT workers were other issues in dispute. Despite these polemics, the industry itself clearly felt safe in assuming that amateurs were not in any position to secure significant infiltration of mainstream cinema—assumptions confirmed by developments surrounding the subsequent fate of the Grasshoppers.

Endell Street and the 1960s

During 1958-1959 the Group moved to new premises. Membership had outgrown the Mary Ward Settlement, and space was now required to accommodate more frequent gatherings, to provide a studio-base for filming, and to act as a secure equipment store. John Daborn remained adept at finding ways, both practical and economical, by which the Group could survive, and premises in Endell Street (nothing more than a collection of decrepit, disused rooms once used for shelving film cans), were identified as a suitably central location for Grasshopper activities. Fortunately, the rent was low, and an obliging landlord even donated £100 towards renovation. The spring and summer of 1958 were therefore spent decorating and fitting out the new venue (materials from a projection booth, once used to show films to the Cabinet during the war, found a new lease of life as "partitioning") and by October of that year it could be reported that:

> The Grasshopper Group is making a special effort to complete the decorating of their new Endell Street clubroom before the start of the winter season. In addition to animation equipment, the Group hopes to install full sound editing equipment designed by Desmond Roe.[44]

By January 1959 members could congratulate themselves: "Although we say it ourselves... our new clubroom—now at last finished—looks pretty good."[45]

---

[44] Scott, "Cut-outs and Mozart", 598.
[45] Scott, "Ten Best Story", 952.

Situated near Wardour Street, above a film editing company, the Group were now located at the very centre of London's commercial film world, with accommodation housing a well-equipped studio for both live-action and animation productions, and a comfortable 60-seat cinema for public screenings. Marking this new phase of development, the Group also acquired a new President (Norman McLaren having returned to Canada accompanied by Gerry Potterton) in the form of actor Peter Sellers, a celebrity with a long interest in amateur filmmaking and a keen practitioner himself. Sellers soon offered the loan of a 16mm Arriflex camera, with which the Group filmed *Stone Idols* (1963), a study of London statues, and *Chiffoonerie* (1966), a short exercise designed to take advantage of the borrowed camera's variable speeds. The latter used lengths of coloured chiffon weaving and gyrating in the glare of a spotlight, against a dark background, and represented an experimental exploitation of colour, light, movement and sound very much in line with current avant-garde and design trends. Illustrating the range that still characterised Grasshopper output, another film, made on location in the South of France, entitled *A Gift of Laughter* (1975) presented an informal view of the shooting of a "Pink Panther" film, with Sellers in his celebrated role as Inspector Clouseau.[46]

Time spent renovating Endell Street seems not to have interrupted filmmaking. With *Let Battle Commence* reaching its final production stage, a short drama entitled *Quiet Water* (1957) and *Spring Is In The Air* (1959), a puppet animation by Dorothy Rogers, were almost complete. Unfortunately, *Quiet Water*, a moody, monochrome film based on a story by Guy de Maupassant, was not well received, and considered by some as the most resounding failure in the annals of the club.[47] However, *Englishman's Holiday* (1956) by John Daborn and John Kerby, and Terry Nunn's *The Case* (1958) were both still awarded prizes in the Ten Best Competition of 1958.

During the 1960s "Grasshopper" fame was also spreading overseas. The State Film Centre of Melbourne, Australia, acquired copies of *The Battle of Wangapore*, *Raving Waving* (1957), an abstract film by Stuart Wynn Jones, and *Bride and Groom*, which were presented at the Melbourne Festival. Meanwhile, in Canada, Tony Collins, an ex-Grasshopper member, and organiser of the Vancouver Amateur Film Festival, was arranging for Canadian distribution of *The Battle of*

---

[46] *A Gift of Laughter* contains a fascinating interview with director Blake Edwards, who discusses "comedy", whilst clowning recorded both on- and off-set, provides significant examples to illustrate his theories.
[47] Spendlove, "Resounding Squelch", 498.

Wangapore, *Let Battle Commence* and *Bride and Groom*. Previous visits to UNICA Festivals had long attracted membership from abroad—particularly from Europe—and contact with the Group was often a prelude to successful amateurism elsewhere. Herman Wuyts, for example, who eventually founded Filmgroep 58 in Belgium, became a prolific filmmaker with the Grasshoppers, with subsequent work such as *Jukebox* (1957) frequently entered in competitions, and its maker regularly winning prizes for his strikingly innovative work.[48]

Widening visibility abroad indexed amateur cinema's new cultural conspicuousness at home, which found concrete expression in the increasing number of part-time film production, and film appreciation courses available though colleges, private organisations and public institutions such as the BFI. Few courses had been available for enthusiasts in the 1930s, and it was not until the early 1960s that public interest in amateur filmmaking began to be addressed outside the informal training-grounds of clubs and societies. Regent Street Polytechnic, and the London School of Film Technique, now catered for those planning a career in the professional industry, whilst attention also turned to the would-be amateur cinematographers who wished to learn the technique of filmmaking as a leisure activity. Bodies such as London County Council, and other local authorities and educational centres throughout the country, slowly introduced production and appreciation evening classes into their adult education programmes.

The Central London Institute, for example, introduced a weekly evening class designed for city commuters, whilst the Industrial Welfare Society held a three-day course to cater for business people who wished to enhance their occupational presentations with film. Once again the Grasshoppers were involved, forming, in association with the Federation of Film Societies, a central London Film Appreciation Group "for serious students of film and those who like to discuss and argue about films in sociable surroundings."[49] In this new climate of technical education the Group took a bold step in mentoring inexperienced new members, leading practical exercises in live-action filming, both on location and in the studio: instruction in animation was inevitably also included. Such initiatives helped to maintain membership, and also to raise much-needed revenue for filmmaking and the up-keep of their premises. Ironically, the emergence of these new non-professional film cultures in the 1960s would

---

[48] *Solitude* (1957), *Jukebox* (1957), *Oh Suzanna* (1959), *Hollywood Speaking* (1959), and *Raga to a Red Rose* (1959) are just a few examples of his surreal imagination.

[49] Spendlove, "Newsreel", 382.

soon index amateur decline on a range of fronts, and perhaps even mark the beginning of the end for the Grasshoppers.

When Endell Street was once more needed for commercial purposes in 1966, a temporary home was actually found at the newly formed London School of Film Technique in Shelton Street. The venue proved ideal in many ways for, while having their own private meeting room and use of the cinema classrooms, the studio area was also available during college holidays. With the upsurge in alternative sources of instruction for hobby filmmakers represented by the School, there was however a less pressing need to join clubs and societies in order to learn basic cinematographic techniques. As membership began to fall, and with little revenue from annual subscriptions, it soon became apparent that it would be necessary to explore other financial options to enable the Group to survive. Predictably perhaps, the Grasshoppers were forced to abandon earlier idealisms, and make another sponsored film, this time appropriately enough, for Lettraset Ltd. This humorous combination of animation and live action, *All About Titling* (1970), starred Noel Myers, and evoked now iconic graphic styles of the period, while also providing clear step-by-step instructions on the uses of Lettraset.

In spite of dwindling numbers, and looming penury, the Group still managed to continue its filmmaking activities, and maintained their position as one of the most productive and award-winning amateur film clubs of the decade. Gordon Rowley was successful in winning two places in the Ten Best Competition of 1966 with *Cactus Polonaise* (1961) and *Pipeline To Paradise* (1961), along with other awards.[50] John Daborn's cartoon film *Leave No Litter* (1965) won a prize in the 1966 "Top Eight" competition, as the Group embraced the smaller gauge and introduced an 8mm. magnetic sound section to their film library. A typical film of this standard, made in the mid-sixties, was a comedy entitled *A Lass and A Lock* (1966). Set in Medieval England, and based on a spoof folksong concerning a chastity belt, it was filmed in only five weeks on location at Farnham Castle. In this case the soundtrack was recorded first, transferred to optical film, and then transferred back to a portable recorder, in loop form, so that the actors could mime to playback.

With the Film School expanding, the Grasshoppers moved for the last time, to Neal's Yard in the late 1960s, but with the rent proving too high for such an amateur organisation, they now of necessity crossed the line into professionalism by forming a limited company—Teamwork Films—

---

[50] His experimental film, *Black Leader* (1963), which was neither drawn on film, nor taken through a camera, was awarded the Grasshopper Trophy, while *April Showers* (1969) gained second place in the Group Competition.

to do commercial work, and provide a base for group meetings. John Daborn headed the new company, with partners Stuart Wynn Jones and Derek Phillips still providing the usual back-up. The "cross-over" seems to have proved only temporarily effective however. Decline, which had begun with falling membership and minimal finance whilst at the School of Film Technique, continued with the move to the new premises. Teamwork Films was soon taken over, and re-born as Neal's Yard Studios, a commercial venture run by Stein Falkenburg, in partnership with Joseph Spalter and their former landlord. The 1970s extend therefore as the "dark ages" in Grasshopper history. By now, many of the originators of the Group had moved on, several to pursue professional work, and those who remained were getting older. Both television viewing at home and the availability of adult education and college courses had also taken their toll. *Animator's Newsletter* was only left to record somewhat morosely in 1982 how: "Twenty nine years after the realisation of a youthful dream" the Grasshoppers met together for the last time on February 20th 1982 at the Waldorf Hotel, where "with a flourish and a buffet" they performed the "last rites."[51]

Aesthetics and Other Ambitions

What of the films themselves, now gradually emerging from archives and private collections? Certainly it is difficult to characterise a "house style", representative of Grasshopper Group work. Committed to originality and variety, and following experimental methods, that served to validate diverse modes of production, the survival of any single aesthetic would be surprising. As amateurs, a basic desire was to escape from inhibiting industrial processes, and to make films for the sheer pleasure of exploring cinematic possibilities, and as personal expression. Derek Phillips, while admitting that he was "never very good at drawing" began using animation as a means of communicating ideas and philosophies: "I just saw it as a convenient way of locking myself away and saying something. It seemed to me, at the time, to be more interesting than just writing."[52] He also found that to overcome technological problems gave added senses of value to the work.

The creative diversity exhibited by the Group did not readily lend itself to any firm structure of collective conventions. Humour, parody and satire characteristic of both commercial and amateur production in Britain are

---

[51] Clark, comments in *Animator's Newsletter*, 18.
[52] Phillips, in interview, 2007.

clearly evident, but Grasshopper films used many techniques, singly and in combination—cel animation, cut-outs, painting and scratching directly onto film, puppets, manipulation of objects and pixilated live-action. There were even attempts to assimilate live-action and animation long before *Who Framed Roger Rabbit?* (1988) was deemed to be "pioneering". The variety of style, message and meaning to be found in Grasshopper films clearly stemmed from the diverse interests of particular animators, whose individuality was in no way stifled by group cultures. Wider socio-political influences, and the shifts of the decades in which they were produced, are also evident in the content and approach. Their films ranged from the pure abstraction of animated forms, complete with conceptual soundtracks (*Raving Waving, Billowing Bellowing* (1959), *Chiffoonery*), through decorative and fanciful pieces (*Victoria's Rocking Horse* (1962), *Watch The Birdie*), to the socially and morally contentious (*Bigger is Better* (1974), *Way Out* (1974)), and the seriously avant-garde (*The Spark*, (1960) *Aether* (1960) and *Jukebox* (1957).

Norman McLaren's influence on the Group is perhaps an integrating factor during the early stages, having himself pioneered many experimental techniques, and featuring prominently within the programmes of club screenings. As in other areas of amateur production however, the impact of dominant forms is clearly detectable; commercial animation supplies a constant referent within Grasshopper production, particularly in examples of their cel animation, which complied with the conventions of two-dimensional graphic style, and presentation of movement etc. Undoubtedly a number of the original members had worked, if only briefly, for commercial studios and had absorbed industrial norms, although the linkage runs deeper than this, underlining the persistent awareness of professional comparators laced through much amateur activity. Those who eventually set up professionally continued to tread a fine line between producing short cartoon series for children's television, while pursuing more adult themes in their personal work.[53] Expressions of socio-cultural concerns are often filtered through the Grasshopper output. Derek Phillips submits strong arguments for countryside conservation versus the sprawling urban development of the post-war period in *Bigger*

---

[53] Bob Godfrey set up his own company and produced *Roobarb and Custard* (1974-75), and a large number of independent films, such as *Kama Sutra Rides Again* (1971) and *Dream Doll* (1979). Dick Horne was responsible for *The Perishers* (1970-1971) and *Fred Bassett* (1973-91) while Derek Williams made thirty-nine episodes of *Aubrey* (1980), twenty episodes of *Crazy Crow* (1990) and thirteen episodes of *Little Brmm and his Friends* (1987) for television transmission.

Is Better and *For Your Pleasure* (1971). Ted Rowley's exploration of suicide, *Way Out*, banned from television transmission, ventilates a profoundly taboo subject with objective humour. *A Short Vision* (1956) made by Peter and Joan Foldes, dealt controversially with the destruction of the world by a robot atom bomb—when shown on *The Ed Sullivan Show*, it caused a furore with American television audiences, equal only to that of Orson Welles "Invasion from Mars" broadcast of 1938.[54] On a lighter note, the animated abstract designs featured in the work of Stuart Wynn Jones—*Oodles of Doodles* (n.d.), and *Billowing Bellowing, Raving Waving*—both predicted and reflected those psychedelic graphics prevalent in contemporary design culture, the interaction of vision and sound in the emerging pop-music scene and the immediacy and playfulness of popular culture as a whole.

Conclusions

The Grasshopper Group evolved as a unique organisation within which amateur filmmakers, interested in experimental animation and unconventional live-action production, could find support for their work, by engaging in the mutual exchange of ideas and expertise. Programmes of public screenings and lectures organised by the Group, widened the audience for these marginalised amateur genres, and encouraged practical involvement in the innovative and artistic potential of animated and experimental film. The Group's close social structure generated both comradeship and creative energy, whose legacies are detectable across amateur cine culture and beyond.

In these various respects, The Grasshopper Group pre-dated, in function and ideology, the fellowship of subsequent film "co-operatives", which later sought to extend the parameters of non-professional film through mutual support mechanisms and understandings of collective purpose. In the days before colleges and art schools provided instructional courses, such groups were vital for the development of practical work, particularly for those amateur "auteurs" who straddled boundaries between art and film. From the beginning, their intentions were to provide the drive, discipline, incentive and opportunity to explore innovative ideas and techniques in animation filmmaking. The diversity and quality of work produced undoubtedly resulted from the creative space, and collaborative assistance, afforded by an open structure and ethos, which encouraged new directions in the genre. As a product *of* and response *to* a specific era of

---

[54] Clark, comments in *Animator's Newsletter*, 7.

social and cultural change, the formation of the Group mounted a challenge, on behalf of amateurs, to the regimented professional codes of large commercial studios, replacing such practices with a spirit of artistic autonomy that heralded the unconstrained attitudes prevalent in the 1960s. The medium of animation proved peculiarly appropriate to this task. As Paul Wells argues, taboos are broken and legitimised by:

> The very language of animation [which] seems to carry with it an inherent innocence which has served to disguise and dilute the potency of some of its more daring imagery.[55]

The Grasshopper Group can fairly be said to have applied just such an "innocence of the animated form" while contributing "serious models of social enquiry" in a significant number of their films.[56] In blurring the boundaries between technical proficiency and the creative freedom of the avant-garde, they stand as a unique experiment in the possibilities of collaboration combined with authorial imagination, energy and, above all, an undiminished playfulness that above all confirms the persistence and energy of the amateur filmmaker.

Works Cited

Primary Sources

Horne, Richard. Interview with author, 2006.
Phillips, Derek. Interview with author, 2007.

Secondary Sources

Alexeieff, Alexandre. "Preface." In *Cartoons: One Hundred years of Cinema Animation* by Giannalberto Bendazzi, xix-xxii. London: Indiana University Press, 1994.
Anon. "Mickey Mouse Methods: How Disney Works." *Home Movies & Home Talkies* 2, no. 3 (1933): 97.
—. "Making a Silhouette Film." *Amateur Cine World* 6, no. 6 (1939): 277-282.
—. "The Films You'll Be Talking About." *Amateur Cine World* 17, no. 1 (1953): 40.

---

[55] Wells, *Understanding Animation*, 19.
[56] Wells, *Animation, Genre and Authorship*, 59.

—. "Review of Ten Best Films of 1952." *Amateur Cine World* 17, no. 1 (1953): 29.

—. "Club Report." *Amateur Cine World* 16, no. 9 (1953): 936.

—. "Grasshoppers Jump Ahead." *Amateur Cine World* 20, no. 1 (1956): 38.

—. "Controversy Corner." *Amateur Cine World* 21, no. 2 (1957): 171.

—. "The Goggle-Box Burglar." *Amateur Cine World* 5, no. 21 (1963): 795.

Bendazzi, Giannalberto. *Cartoons: One Hundred years of Cinema Animation.* London: Indiana University Press, 1994.

Briggs, P. "Unfair to Grasshoppers." *Amateur Cine World* 12, no. 5 (1966): 150.

Brunel, Adrian. "What Shall I Film?" *Home Movies & Home Talkies* 2, no. 10 (1934): 386-388.

Butcher, Douglas. "Cartooning in Clay." *Amateur Movie Maker* 1, no. 5 (1958): 81-83.

Clark, J. "News from Societies." *Amateur Cine World* 18, no. 12 (1955): 1291.

—. "Newsreel." *Amateur Cine World* 20, no. 5 (1956): 579-580.

—. "Cross-Channel Hop." *Amateur Cine World* 20, no. 8 (1956): 852.

Clark, K. *Animator's Newsletter* 3 (1982): 7-18.

Daborn, John. "News from Societies." *Amateur Cine World* 17, no. 7 (1953): 679.

—. "A Pixilated Comedy." *Amateur Cine World* 18, no. 9 (1955): 963-966.

—. "A Fight to the Last Frame." *Amateur Cine World* 20, no. 10 (1957): 1050-1052, 1074.

Eyles, Allen, Frank Gray and Alan Readman. *Cinema West Sussex: The First Hundred Years.* Chichester: Phillimore & Co., 1996.

Fowler, Henry W. and Francis G. *Concise Oxford Dictionary* (4th edition). Oxford: Clarendon Press, 1951.

Furniss, Maureen. *Art In Motion: Animation Aesthetics.* London and Montrouge: John Libbey, 1998.

Horne, Richard. Letter to *Amateur Cine World* 17, no. 8. (1953): 769.

Kerby, J. "Newsreel." *Amateur Cine World* 20, no. 3 (1956): 276-278.

Malthouse, Gordon. "Amateur Films on TV." *Amateur Cine World* 16, no. 11 (1953): 1098.

Nurse, T. "UNICA—Aired Again." *Amateur Cine World* 12, no. 1 (1966): 35.

O'Sullivan, Tim. "Post-War Television in Britain: BBC and ITV." In *The Television History Book*, edited by Michele Hilmes, 30-35. London: British Film Institute Publishing, 2003.
Rose, Tony. "Top 8 on TV." *Amateur Cine World* 3, no. 1 (1962): 47.
Salt, B. G. A. "Practical Animation for Amateurs." *Home Movies & Home Talkies* 6, no. 7 (1937): 289-290.
Scott, P. "Cut-Outs and Mozart." *Amateur Cine World* 22, no. 6 (1958): 598.
—. "Ten Best Story." *Amateur Cine World* 22, no. 9 (1959): 952.
Shaw, E. "Animated Cartooning—How it is Done." *Home Movies & Home Talkies* 1, no. 2 (1932): 52-53.
Spendlove, E. "Newsreel." *Amateur Cine World* 24, no. 4, (1960): 382.
—. "Resounding Squelch." *Amateur Cine World* 22, no. 5, (1958): 498.
Stephenson, Ralph. *Animation in the Cinema*. London: Zwemmer, 1967.
Swift, Hazel. "The Ones That Got Away." *Amateur Cine World* 24, no. 2 (1960): 148-149.
Wells, Paul. *Understanding Animation*. London and New York: Routledge, 1998.
—. *Animation, Genre and Authorship*. London: Wallflower Press, 2002.
Wynn Jones, Stuart. "Pleasing Oneself." *Amateur Cine World* 20, no. 1 (1956): 51.
—. "Anyone Can A-n-i-m-a-t-e! This does mean you!" *Amateur Cine World* 21, no. 10 (1958): 996-997.
—. "Cartooning With a Compass." *Amateur Cine World* 25, no. 17 (1961): 702-703.
Zimmermann, Patricia R. *Reel Families: A Social History of Amateur Film*. Bloomington: Indiana University Press, 1995.

Films Cited

Aether
 (Herman Wuyts, 1960) 16mm., 8 mins.
All About Titling
 (Grasshopper Group, sponsored film for Lettraset Ltd., 1970) 16mm., 16 mins.
April Showers
 (Gordon Rowley, 1969) 16mm., 7 mins.
The Battle of Wangapore
 (Grasshopper Group, 1955) 16mm., 8 mins.
Bigger Is Better
 (Derek Phillips, 1974) 16mm., 7 mins.

The Big Parade
(Bob Godfrey, 1952) 16mm., running time unavailable.
Billowing Bellowing
(Stuart Wynn Jones, 1959) 16mm., 5 mins.
Black Leader
(Gordon Rowley, 1963) 16mm., 2 mins.
Bride and Groom
(Grasshopper Group, 1955) 16mm., 9 mins.
Cactus Polonaise
(Gordon Rowley, 1963) 16mm., 5 mins.
The Case
(Terry Nunn, 1958) 16mm., 7 mins.
Chiffoonerie
(Grasshopper Group, 1962) 16mm., 3 mins.
Cutting for Style
(Grasshopper Group, sponsored film for the Incorporated Guild of wigmakers and perfumers, 1954) 16mm., 25 mins.
Dreams of Toyland
(Arthur Melbourne Cooper, 1908) 35mm., running time unavailable.
Driftwood & Seashell
(Richard H. Jobson, 1956) 16mm., 9 mins.
Englishman's Holiday
(John Daborn, John Kerby, Desmond Roe, Colin Smith, 1956) 16mm., 9 mins. 30 secs.
For Your Pleasure
(Derek Phillips, 1971) 16mm., 3 mins.
A Gift of Laughter
(Teamwork Films, 1975) 16mm., 27 mins.
The History of Walton
(John Daborn assisted by Ken Clark and Kingston & District Cine Club, 1952) 16mm., 17 mins.
Hollywood Speaking
(Herman Wuyts and Kik Kuijpers, 1959) 16mm., 25 mins.
Image in the Snow
(Willard Maas, 1950) 16mm., 29 mins.
Interim
(Stan Brakhage, 1952) 16mm., 25 mins. 30 secs.
Jukebox
(Herman Wuyts, 1957) 16mm., 22 mins.
A Lass & A Lock
(Grasshopper Group, 1966) 16mm., 4 mins.

Leave No Litter
   (John Daborn, 1966) 8mm., 4 mins.
Let Battle Commence
   (Grasshopper Group, 1957) 16mm., 17 mins.
Matches: An Appeal
   (Arthur Melbourne Cooper, 1899) 35mm., running time unavailable.
Metamorphosis
   (Lorenza Mazzetti, 1954) 16mm., running time unavailable.
The Millstream
   (John Daborn assisted by the Ashley Film Unit, 1951) 16mm., 3 mins.
Neighbours
   (Norman McLaren, 1952) 35mm., 8 mins. 6 secs.
Noah's Ark
   (Arthur Melbourne Cooper, 1906) 35mm., running time unavailable.
O Dreamland!
   (Lindsay Anderson, 1953) 16mm., 12 mins. 27 secs.
Oh Suzanna
   (Herman Wuyts, 1959) 16mm., 12 mins.
Oodles of Doodles:
   (Stuart Wynn Jones: details unavailable)
Paintbox Holiday
   (John Daborn, 1955) 16mm., 8 mins.
Pipeline To Paradise
   (Gordon Rowley, 1961) 16mm., 7 mins.
Quiet Water
   (John Hall, 1957) 35mm., 20 mins.
Raga to a Red Rose
   (Herman Wuyts, 1959) 16mm., 12 mins.
Raving Waving
   (Stuart Wynn Jones, 1957) 16mm., 5 mins.
Reflections On Black
   (Stan Brakhage, 1955) 16mm., 12 mins.
Short Spell
   (Stuart Wynn Jones, 1956) hand-drawn onto 35mm. then reduced in printing to 16mm., 3 mins.
A Short Vision
   (Peter and Joan Foldes, 1956) 16mm., 10 mins.
Solitude
   (Herman Wuyts, 1957) 16mm., 14 mins.
The Spark
   (Grasshopper Group, 1960) 16mm., 3 mins.

Spring Is In The Air
   (Dorothy Rogers, 1959) 35mm., 7 mins.
Stone Idols
   (Grasshopper Group, 1963) 16mm., running time unavailable.
Tell Me If It Hurts
   (Richard Massingham, 1934) 16mm., 20 mins.
Theorem of Pythagoras
   (Stuart Wynn Jones, 1955) 16mm., 4 mins.
Toymaker's Dream
   (Arthur Melbourne Cooper, 1913) 35mm., running time unavailable.
Two's Company
   (Grasshopper Group, 1953) 16mm., 8 mins.
Victoria's Rocking Horse
   (Errol Le Cain, 1962) 16mm., 7 mins.
Visual Reflections on Noguchi
   (Filmmaker and date unavailable)
Watch The Birdie
   (Bob Godfrey, Vera Linicar, Keith Learner, Dick Taylor, 1954) 16mm., 6 mins.
Way Out
   (Ted Rockley, 1975) 16mm., 4 mins.
The Way to Shadow Gardens
   (Stan Brakhage, 1954) 16mm., 11 mins. 30 secs.
Who Framed Roger Rabbit?
   (Touchstone Pictures, 1988) 35mm., 99 mins.
The Window
   (Dick Horne, 1956) 16mm., 2 mins.
Wooden Athletes
   (Arthur Melbourne Cooper, 1912) 35mm., running time unavailable.

Chapter Nine

Enrico Cocozza as Amateur Auteur—Ideas Above His Station?

Mitchell Miller

A common Italian surname, a "Cocozza" is either a market gardener specialising in onions and pumpkins, or as with the Gaelic "Canmore" (Ceann Mor) kings, a "Big Head". In Wishaw, a small town in the heart of industrial Lanarkshire, the Cocozza name is equally synonymous with foodstuffs (ice cream) and that oft-favoured resort of the big-headed king-for-a-day, making movies.

The reputation of Enrico Cocozza (1921-1997) as an amateur filmmaker of unusual verve, style and imagination has been growing of late. In the present context, he can be seen to embody the most generous view of the amateur as "renaissance man", broadly engaged in a range of "cultivated" interests, each feeding the other—in this case, cinema, literature and linguistics. Between 1948 and 1960 Cocozza conceived, scripted and produced around 50-60 films whilst simultaneously pursuing scholarly interests in film history, literary aesthetics, and grammatics. In his film work, he employed non-professional talent, worked almost entirely independently, and remained unabashedly (but sometimes furtively) *avant-garde* in his approach. For almost twenty years, Cocozza produced work of such distinctiveness and power that he regularly scooped awards at the Scottish Amateur Film Festival (SAFF), and gained considerable acclaim further afield. Disillusioned, despite such success, he withdrew from filmmaking in the early 1960s, before returning in the late 1970s to produce a range of very different "local" works—more conventional in their form and aspiration, but retaining much of the earlier intensity and sensibility.

A decade after Cocozza's death, his films remain of interest, in part for their intrinsic qualities, but also as testaments to an amateur who aspired to self-realisation as a professional artist (whilst simultaneously recoiling from its implications) and as a filmmaker whose critical reception offers revealing insights into the general situation of the ambitious amateur in mid-twentieth century British cinema. Three aspects of Cocozza's case are of particular interest here. Firstly, the films in themselves represent fine examples of creative virtues achievable on a small scale with few resources; secondly, questions raised by his career perhaps challenge critical definitions of "amateur" filmmaking as a specific sub-culture, and thirdly, issues arising from Cocozza's reception as Scottish filmmaker problematise the relation of such work to conventional understandings of nationally-conscious film practice. Cocozza's own take on such matters seems to have shifted over time. During his first phase of activity he aspired to professional status, craved a wider canvas, and dreamed of "breaking out" into a more creative sphere increasingly identified with the European Art cinema; by the 1970s and 1980s, he seemed much more content with amateurism itself—as both an operational and philosophical viewpoint. His films from this period are much less polished, more reflective of his private preoccupations, and clearly intended for a "local" rather than an "international" audiences.

What follows mostly concentrates on the first (1947-1960) batch of films, made collaboratively with friends, like-minded cine enthusiasts, and unwitting "volunteers", now priceless relics of one man's decade-long attempt to break through the barriers raised between amateur and professional filmmaking.

Primal Scenes

Enrico was born in Glasgow on 6th November 1921, to Giuseppe and Assunta Cocozza, recent economic migrants from the Molise region of central Italy.[1] As with many of their compatriots, the Cocozzas had entered the local service industries, graduating from selling ice creams from a cart, to ownership of retail premises on Wishaw High Street, eventually to be christened the Belhaven Café. As the son of hard-working migrants, Enrico enjoyed the benefits of his parents' early labours and his dual identity. Conversant in two languages, largely excused from local sectarian tribalisms, and encouraged to excel at school, he quickly developed into a flamboyant and precocious child with the potential either to make his mark on the world or perform the role of the local eccentric. In

---

[1] The family background is recorded in *Assunta: the Story of Mrs Joe* (1987), a fictionalised biography charting his mother's teenage years in Italy, her marriage to Giuseppe Cocozza, and their subsequent migration to Scotland. Fascinating detail is also given concerning Enrico's childhood, his movement into filmmaking, and relations with the amateur cine movement.

the event, he arguably did both, reflecting perhaps the paradoxical emphases of his distinctly "transcultural" up-bringing. Whilst his parents established a firm work ethic, they were also more than prepared to indulge (Assunta in particular) their only son's various "artistic" fads and interests. Early proclivities towards theatre and opera, experienced though *libretti* and recorded *arias* soon gave way to an abiding fascination with cinema, fuelled and encouraged by father-and-son excursions to the local picture house. At the age of eleven, Rico announced his intention, we are told, to "relinquish the hazardous career of the theatre and turn instead to the more remunerative profession of the cinema." [2]

Perhaps sharing visions of lucrative "professional" development, Giuseppe agreed to set Enrico on this new career path, provided his son worked three hours every day behind The Belhaven's counter, over the summer of 1932. By 1933, Cocozza had earned his reward—a home cinematograph, and a few reels of second-hand film—the first, and not the last time the café would fund his cinematic ambitions. A camera seems to have been acquired around 1937—and was soon turned on the nearby streets which would provide playing spaces in so many subsequent productions.

If there were by-products of this first encounter with a camera they do not survive, although new discoveries of footage from the early- to mid-1940s (the period when Cocozza's filmmaking seems to have become a serious pursuit) are slowly surfacing within the Scottish Screen Archive.[3] For a while cinema might have appeared a passing fad: Cocozza's main profession would be language, the most stable and consistent outlet for his obvious intellect and cultural interests, which gained him entry to Glasgow University in October 1940. On graduation, his fluency in Italian soon saw him drafted as Staff Sergeant Interpreter for the Italian Labour Battalion in Gorton, Manchester, working with "co-operator" Italian prisoners of war from 1944-46. During this time, he also broadcast to Italy for the BBC, and edited the cultural review *Speranza*.[4] A snippet of one film, curiously titled *At W.H.S. Fete* (1945) records something of this time, including the

---

[2] Cocozza, *Assunta*, 191.
[3] The Scottish Screen Archive, 39-41 Montrose Avenue, Hillington Park, Glasgow, G52 4LA (www.nls.uk/ssa/index.html), retains the bulk of Cocozza's private papers and original film material. Holdings exist in varying states of preservation and stages of cataloguing.
[4] Very little is known about *Speranza*, save that it was produced by Cocozza during his time at the prisoner of war Camp in Manchester, for the consumption of its Italian occupants. Publication dates are likely to have spanned 1944-1946.

setting of a P.O.W. camp, and incorporating scenes depicting the prisoners of war whose welfare he so assiduously protected.

His father's premature death in 1943 meant that Cocozza returned from military service as the man of the house, and nominal master of The Belhaven. Demobilisation seems to have coincided with a difficult phase in Enrico's personal life: in *Assunta,* a biographical account of his mother, he alludes to a troubled romantic entanglement during his army years, that left him depressed, restless and in desperate need of distraction.[5] This was also the year Cocozza left his first identifiable celluloid footprint, in the shape of the somewhat Neo-Raphaelite *La Mort Et Le Poete* (1943) and the more naturalistic *Bryan Welcomes Raffles* (1943), two films which suggest at an early stage the extraordinary range of inspirations informing his subsequent output. The archive catalogue credits *Bryan* to Giuseppe, presumably before his death that year, though the onscreen credit is for "Henry Cocozza", the anglicised version of Enrico. Perhaps the filmmaker is exhibiting some form of authorial schizophrenia; the simple tale of an airman returning to his family maybe reflecting the English-speaking social-realist, *La Mort* answering the polyglot, with links to the continent and an early interest in *avant-garde* and neorealist films.

As the earliest artefacts of Cocozza's filmmaking career, *La Mort* and *Bryan Welcomes Raffles* are rough essays, indicative of the talent which excited so many in the Scottish film world. *Bryan* is arguably the better realised of the two pieces, and more successful as a film, being carefully lit, exact in its eye for detail, and touching in its simplicity. *La Mort* however offers a clearer premonition of themes Cocozza would routinely explore in the creative burst that spanned the 1950s, involving a grim allegory concerning a poet drowned in a burn by a robed killer. After lighter cinematic excursions,[6] the morbid subject matter, technical ingenuity and highly expressive style of *La Mort* would re-surface decisively in a string of remarkable short dramas. Following these first

---

[5] In the novel, Cocozza strongly hints that this was an unrequited love, but with whom is never made clear. Former colleague Joe Farrell maintains that Enrico was an in-the-closet gay: "One of the fundamental things about Rico was the fact that he was gay. Now, sometimes I wonder whether he knew that himself... this meant that he never had a proper relationship, and I do, in some ways, without wanting to go into psycho-babble, think that this did condition an awful lot of the way he actually was." See *Surreally Scozzese* television documentary, 2001.

[6] In 1947, for example, Cocozza produced *The Capella of Enchantment*, a melodrama set on the Italian coast, and an uncharacteristically gentle romantic foray. Trips to Italy often encouraged less introspective essays, and travelogues such as *Genova and Milano* (1947) and *Alassio* (1954), often well-received in "official" amateur circles.

efforts, and fuelled by his need to find a satisfying creative expression, Cocozza's filmmaking grew still more complex and ambitious, epitomising the dedication of the committed amateur increasingly intent on recognition and reward. By the later 1940s, he had clearly developed both a sense of direction and the pliable pool of non-professional talent that would contribute enthusiastically to a string of later projects.

From around the time of his father's death, Cocozza's attentions had gradually returned to the cinematograph under the bed—or more precisely, a Bell & Howell "70" camera, and its 50ft spools. Recent research has uncovered significant footage from this period of "reawakening", including fragments, and more finished "home movies", that give the impression of flexing unused muscle and recalling old tricks. Found on the same reel as the *La Mort Et Le Poete* and *Bryan Welcomes Raffles*, for example, are fleeting images of the filmmaker's personal life—some beautiful nature photography, coverage of a bus trip, and a dreamlike sojourn to the quadrangles of Glasgow University where, between two smiling girls, Cocozza's rotund form and chubby, effeminate features appear in affectionate close-up. With no absolute date for these fragments, it is uncertain whether they are contemporaneous with the shorts, or represent earlier or later experiments. At this stage, they remain an unaccounted-for piece of the Cocozza puzzle, whilst suggesting a moment of positivism and futurism that resonates elsewhere through the wider amateur cine culture as it emerged from wartime.

Little Hollywood

By 1947, Cocozza was dividing his time between teaching Italian at Glasgow University, and helping his mother with The Belhaven. Filmmaking remained however a key fascination, pursued with increasing determination and growing resourcefulness. This was the year the first of many "dips" were made into the café's till, and saw a basic production unit created. According to Cocozza, he simply:

> gathered together some cine enthusiasts and formed a film unit. [Thereafter...] Films were planned and quickly put into production. The actors and actresses were recruited from the café customers, some of whom were already playing an active part in local amateur dramatics. A film society was constituted. Enrolments were promising and soon there were more than 200 members.[7]

---

[7] Cocozza, *Assunta,* 254-255.

Judging by the ephemera surviving from this period, the group soon formalised as the Wishaw Film Society garnered considerable interest, was taken remarkably seriously by those involved, and became highly active in the area, with members regularly travelling from Motherwell, Hamilton, Newmains and the Shotts.[8] Relations between film-goers and film-makers require further research and it is unclear whether film production or "appreciation" came first, but tentative efforts certainly began to appear by late 1947. This initiated a period—book-ended by the sale of The Belhaven in 1960—proving one of the most fertile in the history of Scottish amateur filmmaking. As Cocozza himself put it (less than modestly, although with unmistakeable irony):

> Within a year, Rico made a name for himself as an outstanding and imaginative producer of fantasy films, winning many national awards. The phone never stopped ringing. It was like living in a little Hollywood.[9]

In reality, the small production unit worked out of the café's back rooms, before an adjoining garage and auction house were converted (probably around 1948) into a 100-seat cinema (flamboyantly named "The Connoisseur") for the use of film society members. Here Cocozza would screen everything from the shorts made in the next room, to the latest arthouse features by Jean Cocteau, Vittorio de Sica or Jean Renoir, to favourite gangster pictures or cartoons. Production and screening sessions would often culminate in repairing to The Belhaven, always more than a mere source of funds and facilities—epitomising rather the sense of community and life blood of the whole operation. As a place to drink coffee, buy sweets or cigarettes, pick up girls or get noticed by boys, the café stood at the centre of what was fast emerging as a vibrant local cine culture. Outside the shop-front was just as lively, the favoured stoop of the local "hairies" (referred to even then, as "neds"—localised versions of the "Teddy Boys" elsewhere defining British youth culture in the 1950s). Street life in Wishaw usually gravitated to The Belhaven at some point, a fact which Cocozza exploited to the full, turning work in the café into a

---

[8] *The Enrico Cocozza papers 1921-1998* (hereafter *Cocozza Papers*) held at the Scottish Screen Archive, include personal letters, publicity materials and various manuscripts. The collection also contains (audio) records, miscellaneous materials relating to the Wishaw Film Society, and press clippings retained by Cocozza himself. Unfortunately, few of these were dated precisely, and some are misattributed. Effort has been made here to identify the year in which these were published, through reference to originals of relevant local press publications (many now defunct). Clippings cited throughout are held in this collection.
[9] Cocozza, *Assunta*, 255.

recruiting operation, where faces fit for the screen could be found and, with a bit of persuasion, coaxed in front of the camera. One such like-minded Wishavian was James "Jimmy" Craig, who directed, scripted and acted in a number of films, most auspiciously, the heavily Cocteau-influenced *Nine O'Clock* (1951).

Membership of the production group always waxed and waned, in synch with Cocozza's own ambitions—in the late 1940s and early 1950s it was however extraordinarily active, with several of its films achieving limited theatrical distribution, and many others winning awards in both domestic and foreign competitions. In his reminiscences, Craig is quite clear that Cocozza was the dominant figure: "Compromise with EC was letting him have his way!" he comments, suggesting that the coterie was not so much a "collective" perhaps, as an entourage.[10] A variety of banana-republic companies were credited to the work produced—"Supramont Films", "Tongue in Cheek Productions", or the one that tended to stick, "Connoisseur"—perhaps because it best represented Cocozza's underlying dreams of artistic credibility.[11]

*Fantasmagori*a (1948), the first film produced by the group, strongly reflected Cocozza's own tastes, and is in effect, a remake of *La Mort Et Le Poete*. Premiering at the 1948 SAFF, the film was made for a cost of about £100, by no means a small amount in 1947, but still modest for a "story film" film of this kind. (see Fig. 9-1) The existence of any kind of budget is perhaps indicative of Cocozza's ambitions to make films suitable for widespread exhibition, with resources that would allow him to tackle more complex projects. As Craig recalled in an interview with Janet McBain much later, the Connoisseur group as a whole had very definite goals, which clearly lay beyond the horizons of the local cine community, seeing themselves as "avant-garde—surrealist—pushing the edges of film and enjoying the controversy that they created at SAFF".[12] As implied in published accounts of the non-professional scene appearing at this time,

---

[10] Quoted in interview with Janet McBain, curator of the Scottish Screen Archive, in July 2000. See *Cocozza Papers*.

[11] In his interview with Janet McBain, James Craig refers to the "Connoisseur Group" as if it formed a persistent identity for the production unit that assembled around the Wishaw Film Society. Certainly the name conveyed the aspirational dimension of the group's work well. "Connoisseur" was also the name of the 100-seater cinema built at the back of the Belhaven Café, which occasionally also provided studio space.

[12] McBain, Interview with James Craig, 2000.

Cocozza specifically identified success, or perhaps more accurately, cultural validity, with leaving amateurism behind.[13]

Fig. 9-1 frame enlargement from *Fantasmagoria* (1948)
Source: Scottish Screen Archive

Romantic fantasies such as those represented by *Fantasmagoria* stood at some remove from the preferred aesthetic standards and social values of contemporary amateur filmmaking, and undoubtedly Cocozza's proclivity for the metaphysical set the filmmaker apart from many of his peers, even at this early stage. The obvious intellectualism of the work may also have been an issue. *Fantasmagoria* indicates Cocozza's wide reading, and acquaintance with nineteenth century authors as diverse as Edgar Allen Poe, Georg Buchner, Robert Louis Stevenson and several others. Certainly this literary sensibility was noticed by at least one SAFF adjudicator, who remarked that "The film created a mood, just as some writers did."[14] Literary connections persist from here onwards: adapted from a poem by

---

[13] Hardy, "Amateur has lessons to teach the studios."
[14] From *Cocozza Papers,* as noted on a copy of the SAFF Adjudicator's feedback from the 1949 event. Outside of filmmaking, Cocozza wrote fiction and non-fiction prose throughout his life, most notably in *Assunta*, and in a series of unpublished short stories such as "Merle" (1988).

Wilfred Rowland Childe, *Before Time Came* (1958) has all the tragic starkness of a Scottish ballad, which, when cross-referenced to the elf-queen of *The White Lady* (1949), reveals an abiding interest in the fatalistic folk mythologies that underpinned the work of the filmmaker's favourite writers.

While not the best of Cocozza's films (cuts could be more decisive and the pacing seems laboured rather than leisurely) *Fantasmagoria* introduces most of the filmmaker's signature features. One of these is a barely subliminal misogyny, sometimes very pronounced in the later output, where women repeatedly figure as vampish antitheses to the matronly Assunta. The emphasis returns in subsequent work: in *The White Lady*, young men are lured to their doom; a girl drives Alex to suicide in *Nine O'Clock* (1951); in *Porphyria* (1960) the title character inveigles the artist into her own murder, whilst the female vampire of *Fantasmagoria* literally sucks the life out of the men she ensnares. This recurring motif often emerges alongside a fascination with water—usually the waves in a loch, river or pond, but also sinks, baths and buckets—that invokes ancient associations between femininity and the abyss. By contrast, young male protagonists are often objects of erotic fascination, idealised embodiments of truth and beauty often doubling unwittingly as lambs to the slaughter.

Whilst such efforts earned recognition within the amateur cine sector, Cocozza was clearly reluctant to keep to the path of the dedicated hobbyist, and early on sought "cross-over" routes into more esteemed cinematic circles. As formal training schemes spread slowly in Britain, Cocozza took advantage of his cultural connections and language skills, and in 1951 attended the summer school of The Centro Sperimentale Cinematografia in Rome, where he became immersed in realist technique and theory.[15] The experience, reinforcing his long-standing appreciation of the Neorealist project, nurtured during frequent Italian holidays, had a profound impact on his subsequent practice. His approach to shot design and composition, and sometimes his choice of theme and subject matter, can be usefully understood in relation to the movement. Claims that, along with fellow Centro-alumni Margaret Tait, Cocozza might be enshrined as one of Scotland's few *bona fide* neorealists may however somewhat force the issue, as over time his work would synthesise a far wider range of inspirations.[16] Early horror films and crime pictures seem as deep an

---

[15] See Sheila Chalke's essay in this volume, which offers further detail on the training opportunities for British amateurs in the later 1940s.

[16] Margaret Tait (1918-99) was an Orcadian General Practitioner and filmmaker, author of a series of film poems, abstract animations and experimental documentaries, and increasingly recognised as a pioneer of the British avant-garde.

influence on Cocozza as the canonical "classics" circulating through the Film Societies movement, examined elsewhere in this volume.[17]

Most conspicuously, Cocozza's work echoes Neorealism's particularly intense sense of place—a stress shared with amateur filmmaking more widely—exploiting opportunities presented by localised narratives and immediate environments. In Cocozza's hands, the emphasis takes on further dimensions however, with location pressed into the service of altogether more fantastic scenarios. A distinctive "double-vision" ensues: grotesque or supernatural encounters are curiously offset by the familiarity of Wishaw's closes, country estates and walkways, resulting in striking juxtapositions of the extraordinary and the mundane—generating a form of "magical realism" or "realist fantasy" indexing Cocozza's peculiar desire to turn surroundings into dreamscapes, as much as the amateur's ever-pressing need to "make do" with limited resources. Even the most surreal of sequences rarely banish "pro-filmic" awareness of commonplace buildings, old army barracks or the brackish links outside of town, reconstructed as "elemental" wastelands and limbo-worlds. In *The White Lady*, the Coltness country estate on the outskirts of Wishaw becomes Elfhame through nothing more than good photography, clever editing work and tight camera angles; in *Nine O'Clock*, a stairway to hell is obviously formed from a set of corporation-built concrete risers; the peculiar *largesse* of *Scherzo* (1955) references familiar Glasgow streetscapes and landmarks such as the university tower (see Fig. 9-2), while inviting the viewer to "read" Hollywood Boulevard or the Sunset Strip, thus inaugurating a suggestive play between recognition and misrecognition, between sheer silliness and highly suggestive *simulacra*.

Appropriately enough, several films deliberate upon the transformative powers and responsibilities of the artist-filmmaker: in *Bongo Erotico* (1959), Cocozza's own painted face looms into shot to initiate a disorienting sequence where a naked body, seemingly half-man, half-woman, writhes on a bed. In *Robot 3* (1951), the protagonist is again an agent of dangerous manipulation, a mad scientist whose human-like robots turn on him with predictably grim results. *Masquerade* (1953) likewise, borrows megalomaniac themes from Powell and Pressburger's *The Red Shoes* (1948) although in both its light-footed energy and its sympathy toward the female protagonist, is otherwise far removed from Cocozza's typical horror output. Comedic variants on the same themes include *Ad*

She seems to have attended the Centro at much the same time as Cocozza. See Sarah Neely's essay on Margaret Tait elsewhere in this volume and Miller, "Hold it Simple, Hold it Direct", 30-36.

[17] See Richard MacDonald's chapter elsewhere in this volume.

280   Chapter Nine

Infernum Buddy (1952), effectively the film society staple *Quo Vadis* (1912) re-made locally with the help of local school children in the wake of its professional re-make by M.G.M. (1951), and with Cocozza himself appearing as a classically *louche* Emperor.

Fig. 9-2 frame enlargement from *Scherzo* (1955)
Source: Scottish Screen Archive

Struggles for control are similarly tangible in the organisation of sound and image. The use of commentary to hold together and convey the narratives proves a particular bone of contention. Often an expedient amateur solution to routine difficulties of sound synchronisation and continuity, the device functions here as a further symptom of Cocozza's egocentric ambitions, regulating interpretation, and inscribing his presence between the audience and the fictional world unfolding onscreen. Responses were mixed: regular reviewer Harold Benson read it as a "get-out" clause for films which ultimately failed to satisfy their maker—in *The Mirror* (1957), a piece lambasted as unbearably pretentious, it is also used to lampoon Cocozza himself: "I wouldn't take too much notice of this shot; we just put it in to pad out the film a bit" insists the commentary—even as it asserts his organisational authority over the image stream.[18]

---

[18] Benson, "The Private World of Enrico Cocozza", 292.

Wishavian Realism

Cocozza's filmography records realist interests well prior to his spell at The Centro, although most projects are as clearly inspired by Anglo-American product exhibited in the local Odeon, as by continental developments encountered through the Film Society. Even films such as *Chick's Day* (1951), possibly his most conventional effort at social realism, show Cocozza as chimeric and idiosyncratic in his treatment of "the actual" as in articulating his more private fantasy worlds.

Work on this granite-edged, hard-boiled tale of juvenile delinquency began in 1949. It was inspired by the youths who loitered on his front doorstep (and occasionally attempted to steal The Belhaven's merchandise)—a very different demographic from the cinephile clientele of the Wishaw Film Society, meeting just behind the same building. Cocozza seems to have gone to great trouble to gain an authentic sense of how his subjects lived and behaved. Recollection of the project is suggestive of the approach adopted in developing such local fare, and of the sense of familiarity and intimacy of the finished film:

> I went out with a camera and whenever I found suitable types standing at a close mouth or a corner I just went up to them, asked if I could take their picture, then began chatting. The camera wasn't always loaded... but they were frank and friendly.[19]

Neorealist influences combine here with the anthropological perspectives of what would later emerge in Britain as Free Cinema, and the more didactic emphases of contemporary "riff-raff" pictures and even the American *film noir*.[20] By the time Cocozza reached The Centro in 1951, *Chick's Day* would in any case already be in the can, although the subsequent addition of a typically unsynchronised narration, voiced by its central character in a thick Lanarkshire accent, may reflect more specific neorealist interest in "native" or "mean" dialects.[21] Perspectives clearly

---

[19] From an article entitled "Butcher's Boy will be the star", appearing in the "Bill Knox Calling" column reprinted in several local newspapers. Knox (1928-1999) was a celebrated local journalist, broadcaster and author of mystery novels. He wrote for a number of publications including the *Glasgow Citizen* and *Evening Times*—this article is dated c.1958, and held within the *Cocozza Papers*.
[20] Murphy, "Riff-Raff: British Cinema and The Underworld", 286-305.
[21] Neorealism had an abiding interest in dialect as another technique that, "that suggested a 'direct take', an objective and unadulterated approach to the real", a trend also reflected in novels and poetry. Other neorealist practices involved a more synthetic, literary approach, that incorporated dialect and slang expressions

shifted as the exercise took shape, and the externalised "case study" account suggested by notes on pre-production, is quickly abandoned.[22] (see Fig. 9-3) As a finished film, *Chick's Day* has the character of a more private testimony, introducing an almost supernatural "from beyond the grave" or "in the dock" voice-over from Chick as he reflects on his own downfall, in a manner reprised in the more rambling, angry, and frequently obscure dreams of the young male protagonist of *The Living Ghost* (1960).

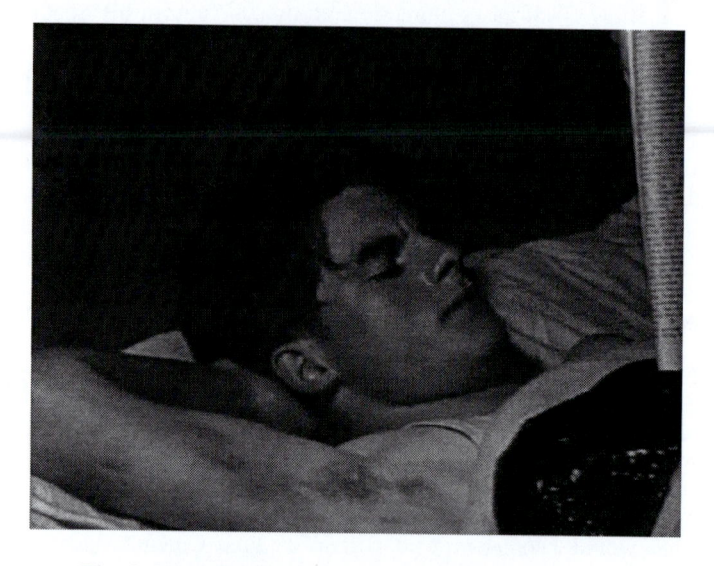

Fig. 9-3 frame enlargement from *Chick's Day* (1951)
Source: Scottish Screen Archive

Played with easy naturalism by John Graham, Chick is a youth who "never knew his faither" only his mother, a scurrilous, boozy and licentious anti-Assunta. With no job or prospects, Chick spends his time in search of a purpose; in well observed scenes, we gain insight into the less respectable pursuits of the day: pitch-and-toss games, gambling, drinking and petty crime. Chick is typically beset by female antagonists; his slattern mother, the shrewish wife of a friendly gamekeeper and ultimately, the unsuspecting female victim of the crime that leads to the film's climactic

---

while preserving clarity. For a useful discussion of neorealist aesthetics see Bondanella and Ciccarelli, *The Cambridge Companion to The Italian Novel*, 110-111.
[22] Cocozza, "How I Made 'The Film of the Year'", 50.

murder. A sense of environmentalism however is evident in the final accounting; the world is now to blame for Chick's fate (not simply neglectful parenting) and the film terminates with shots of brooding, unsympathetic skies—a Cocozza trademark—though there's a nagging sense that the narration may be unreliable as the film reaches a conclusion. This is after all, only Chick's account, narratively detached by its technical unsyncronisation: events might just *appear* to be as described.

In some respects, James Cagney in the Clyde valley, in others a glimpse of Scotland through the eyes of a de Sica or Rossellini, *Chick's Day* was disparaged by Harold Benson as a melodrama "masquerading as a slice of life" but has probably aged better than the critic could have imagined.[23] Chick is always far more than a putative young "ned"—much more sympathetic, socially aware and open-minded. According to Julie Davidson the strong language introduced (the F-word is deployed) made it highly controversial, although it was one of Cocozza's films that received distribution well beyond the amateur festival circuit.[24] One wonders however whether Cocozza would have taken the following programme note as compliment or condemnation:

> For those who tire of the over-sophistication of cinema, this film will ably demonstrate that movies of simple unrefined charm are not a lost cause.[25]

Almost ten years later, *Corky* (1958) illustrates the evolution of Cocozza's realist interests, and ongoing fascination with private adolescent worlds. Altogether lighter than *Chick's Day*, the story is told once again via a personal voice-over, incorporating local dialect, and authentic scenes of children at play, to create a remarkably whimsical realism. The small-scale drama of childhood infatuation and quixotic deception, is played out through the eyes of its eleven year-old hero as another very dreamlike experience. The effect seems in part to have been serendipitous: because variable weather conditions made retaining a sense of a believable temporal continuity near impossible, Cocozza rearranged his sequences into a more imaginative narrative framework, abandoning linear time for an episodic continuum that suggests a collection of disparate childhood memories, purposefully reassembled in respect of

---

[23] Benson, "The Private World of Enrico Cocozza", 291.
[24] Davidson, c. 1979, publication unknown—clipping from *Cocozza Papers*. The less distinguished *Crabbit Granny* (1953) also gained commercial distribution by the London-based company, Contemporary Films.
[25] *Contemporary Films Brochure*, c. 1954.—held within the *Cocozza Papers*.

sentiment, rather than any chronology—the mirror opposite of Chick's dark recollections.

Once more, Cocozza adopted an ethnographic approach, taking time to observe the youths frequenting his shop, and carefully selecting his leading actor (real name Norman) from among them:

> Hovering in the background, I could overhear the patter he exchanged with his friends, acquaintances and enemies—and he had an abundance of all three. A few days of eavesdropping complemented my mental picture of the character, and also brought me up to date with the local slang... I became friendly with Norman's family and paid frequent visits to his house. From my observation of the people I met there, I was able to sketch the other characters in my film story which was gradually taking shape.[26]

The result is a charming short film introducing beautifully unaffected scenes of childhood, and intermingling comic exchanges straight from the *Oor Wullie* strip cartoon, *The Beano* comic, or Richmal Crompton's gently satirical *Just William* stories, whose juvenile, but worldly-wise outsiders Corky so resembles.[27] (see Fig. 9-4) The hero here is however, a tougher nut that Wullie or William, and more complex than Dennis the Menace. The character inspired critic Tony Rose to compare him to the greatest child-hero in all literature, Huck Finn, albeit "with a harder streak of arrogance where Huck was romantic."[28] Narrated ostensibly by the protagonist in a droll, self-admiring commentary, the high-pitched voice is in fact Cocozza's own, recorded at 16 frames per second and played back somewhat faster at 24 frames per second. As usual, the official explanation for the effect is a practical, rather than a creative, one: the score (provided by local musician Bob McLeod) clashed with the "piping" voice of Corky. Interviews with the filmmaker indicate however that there may have been other, more censorious reasons for the device:

---

[26] Cocozza, "Life with Corky", 291-293.
[27] Drawn initially by Dudley Watkins (1907-1969) the *Oor Wullie* strip cartoons have been published by D. C. Thomson Ltd. in *The Sunday Post* since 1936, and in annuals of collected stories since 1939; *The Beano* first appeared from the same company in 1938. See Watkins, *The Broons and Oor Wullie*, and Various, *The Beano Book*. Richmal Crompton (1890-1969) published her first *Just William* story in *Home Magazine* in 1919, and the first collection of stories in book form in 1922. See Crompton, *Just William*. See Perry and Aldridge, *The Penguin Book of Comics*, for further details of these publications.
[28] Rose, "*Corky* is a Corker!", 76-77.

I asked Corky to look at the film and comment on it in his own words. He had far too much to say, and too many of the things he said would have shocked any audience. Nevertheless, I recorded his remarks on tape and used them as the basis of the final commentary.[29]

Fig. 9-4 frame enlargement from *Corky* (1958)
Source: Scottish Screen Archive

Cocozza always made much of realistic goals achieved with meager means, yet inevitably the gap between ambitions and resources sometimes wore down morale. In his account of the production of *Corky*, the filmmaker describes a tortuous filming process using borrowed—or stolen—time that would regularly extend beyond the week or weekend scheduled.[30] The week of the Easter holidays set aside soon lengthened into the whole summer, with filming constantly plagued by a curious gallery of onlookers (according to James Craig an irritation on all the Connoisseur shoots), and the difficulties of working with simple equipment, demanding characteristic amateur improvisation (eg. using a camera and a pillow to capture the ground level shots which give *Corky* its sense of sympathy with its characters). Cocozza's patience in general seems to have been wearing thinner, and local connection sensed increasingly as a burden rather than an opportunity. With the real promise

---

[29] Cocozza, "Life With Corky", 293.
[30] Ibid., 293.

of amateur "cross-over" seemingly still out of reach in far off London, Cocozza perhaps now sensed he had too many such local ties to try his hand in the metropolis.[31] All that remained for certain was the continuing struggle to make and show films closer to home. Despite the work's unreservedly optimistic tone, he closes his account of the making of *Corky* on a surprisingly negative note:

> Two years seem a very long time to spend on the production of a short film. Perhaps that is what has soured me, for I have to confess that the final result does not please me at all. In fact, I am astonished that anyone should like *Corky*.[32]

This last comment gives some flavour of the sense of hopelessness that seems to have been gradually creeping in, irrespective of the merits or demerits of any given project. Audiences did like *Corky*. Reporting on the twentieth SAFF, Tony Rose wrote that the film was "the toughest, earthiest, most scintillating and human amateur comedy that has come my way."[33] Insistence on the "amateur" qualification may by now have been the point for Cocozza perhaps; at this stage he may well have taken it as damnation with faint praise, provoking a perverse return to filmmaking less "accommodating" of preferred amateur standards.

Sourness seems to have suffused Cocozza's subsequent treatment of youth culture, *The Living Ghost*. The film seemingly began its life as a follow up to *Chick's Day*—another warts-and-all drama set among Wishaw's "Teddies". Press surrounding plans for the film shows Cocozza at the outset in decidedly judgmental mood:

> This is one film in which there will be no attempt to glorify these youngsters, or to put the blame for their existence on parents or environment. This film will say the Teddies only have themselves to blame.[34]

In the event, *The Living Ghost* would prove more decidedly experimental and even more unashamedly dreamlike than *Corky*.[35] The lead character is

---

[31] The BFI's Experimental Film Fund launched the careers of many former amateurs including Lindsay Anderson, Peter Watkins and Karel Reisz. See Ellis, *BFI Productions: 1951-1976*.
[32] Cocozza, "Life With Corky", 293.
[33] Rose, "*Corky* is a Corker!", 76.
[34] Knox, Bill, "Butcher's Boy will be the Star", c. 1958—*Cocozza Papers*.
[35] This may be the final form of *The Young Ned*, a putative film mentioned in *The Wishaw Press and Advertiser* c. 1959, and in undated clippings found in *Cocozza*

an angst-ridden drama queen as isolated from his peers as he is from established authority. Autobiographical, insular interpretations are as a result, almost inescapable, and seem to be invited.

In 1979, Cocozza told reporter Julie Davidson of his "18 years of disaffection with the limitations of amateur work", and perhaps that simple explanation must suffice for what followed. Following the making of *Smart Boy Wanted* (1960), Cocozza gave up filmmaking, channelling his efforts into his studies of Italian language and cinema, his private literary pursuits, and exhibiting his cat as a pet-food model. Craig recalls that around 1960 Enrico was also experiencing difficulties with his eyesight, that were leading to short-temperedness and frequent fits of pique and melancholy. In press clippings for *The Living Ghost*, his last SAFF victory, Cocozza hints at "taking a rest" from the competition.[36] Assunta's own illness soon led to the sale of The Belhaven, the centre of operations and catalyst for Connoisseur's various activities. The closure of the café, distancing Cocozza from the immediate community, and displacing the matriarch who always gave her tacit, unflinching support (not to mention an easily reached source of funds), and the decision to cease operations is surely no coincidence. A filmmaker so interested in fate and determinism might even take the event as an omen. Over time thereafter, the Connoisseur group slowly dispersed; James Craig's move from Wishaw to Glasgow, cutting Cocozza off from perhaps his most creative and critical collaborator, was perhaps in the end the decisive factor here.

Of the clutch of films surviving from this period, *Chick's Day, The White Lady, Porphyria* and *Before Time Came,* are those that work first and foremost as films in their own right, regardless of the occasional technical stumble or dramaturgical *faux pas*. Cocozza's virtuosity is often stunning: the simulated eyelid in *Fantasmagoria*; the netherworld of the moor in *Nine O'Clock,* or the heavens weighing down on Chick in the final moments of *Chick's Day,* transcend their homespun origins. The film regarded by the filmmaker as his most perfect work avoids both technical and dramaturgical problems entirely. Produced as a favour for two drama students, *Petrol* (1957) is just three minutes long, contains no dialogue, and follows what seems to be a cyclical plot. A man is driving in a car along a deserted road. He runs out of fuel. From over the horizon, another

---

Papers—set to star Duncan Beaton, the film does but not appear anywhere in the archive collection. If *The Young Ned* did indeed become *The Living Ghost*, then Cocozza clearly dispensed with the services of Beaton, a butcher's assistant who once foiled an attempt by "Teddy Boys" to steal goods from the Belhaven Café.

[36] "Premier award for Cocozza film", undated clipping from *The Wishaw Press and Advertiser*, c. 1960, in the *Cocozza Papers*.

figure appears on foot, and in total silence confronts and then murders the motorist. The body is tossed in the backseat, and the killer drives his victim's car away—returning us to the original sequence. Only questions remain. Will this man also run out of fuel? Will another faceless stranger crest the new horizon? Will there be an endless succession of murders? One could easily imagine the footage looped into an art installation; its laconic, economic style dispensing with further need for explanation or exposition, give it a genuine timelessness and universalism.

Subsequent events suggested less dramatic outcomes for Cocozza himself. In 1962, he accepted a post at the Scottish College of Commerce, and returned to academic life, eventually becoming chairman of Italian Studies at Strathclyde University in 1964, his cinematic interests now largely confined to research on the work of Jean Cocteau.[37] In the 1970s, literature would be the dominant pursuit, along with the genealogical enquiries leading to the eventual publication of *Assunta* in 1987. Neglect of film production would last for twenty years, finally ended by *Fit O' The Toon* (1978), an impressionistic return to former realist interests, detailing everyday life around the road junction outside the former Belhaven Café.

Explanations for Cocozza's resumption of filmmaking must remain tentative at this stage. In 1975, the Italian government had decorated him as Cavaliere Ufficiale dell "Ordine a Merito della Republica Italiana" for services to Italian culture, and he may have sensed responsibilities attaching to new found status, although Cocozza clearly wore the title with only semi-ironic pride, as the opening exchange of *Fit O' The Toon* between Cocozza and a would-be interviewer demonstrates:

Interviewer: Is the Cavaliera in?

Cocozza: I have a feeling the cavaliera is off looking for a horse at the moment, but come in...

By now, Cocozza's earlier celebrity had faded, requiring local journalists to remind their readers of earlier achievements:

Thirty years ago, Cocozza was an innovator among amateur film makers, one of an élite school of Scottish amateurs whose work, according to Ron McLusky, Director of the Scottish Film Council, was "Abstract, experimental and often superior to the work of professionals."[38]

---

[37] See Cocozza, *The Poetic Imagery and Existential Dilemma of Jean Cocteau*. See also McIntyre's obituary, 1988, and Davidson, "Filmmaker Returns With a Celebration of Street Life".

[38] Davidson, "Filmmaker Returns With a Celebration of Street Life".

With *Fit O' The Toon*, Cocozza returned to his camera for a very different type of project to those orchestrated by the counter-jumping impresario of the 1950s, and for the uninitiated the results would have given little clue to the character of the earlier works. Shot on Super-8, in approach, visual quality and execution, it much more closely resembles the domesticated amateur cinema he had previously so assiduously held himself apart from. Focused on the local people with whom Cocozza explicitly identifies, its emphasis is observational and preservative, introducing many moments of rough-hewn beauty, documenting a still vital community, and validating the numerous lives lived in such close proximity to his own.

Ryan Shand has analysed *Fit O' The Toon* and other of Cocozza's more locally engaged films, such as *Scenes from West Cross* (1979), citing the filmmaker's engagement with the local as a value that suggests a very different way of viewing cinema practice, in essence, one whose importance lies more with process than product.[39] Continuities with earlier work remain however; the wit and candour of the Cocozza who incited his neighbours to participate in *Fit O' The Toon* were the same qualities that fuelled Little Hollywood during the 1950s, where enthusiasm and goodwill had to act as substitutes for time and money.

Cocozza's remaining output consists mainly of "videograms", produced from the mid-1980s, with the help of protégé Iain Leslie. Very different from the first-phase films, which extended Cocozza's imaginative powers to draw in and include an entire community, these "end works" describe a certain process of withdrawal. Few escape the confines of his flat, though some gaze, squirrel-like, at Wishaw High Street from its window. In places barely edited, these introverted surveillance pieces can seem a disappointing coda. Some, such as the preamble to *Triptych* (1983) betray occasional flashes of Cocozza's previous flair and ingenuity, where Leslie uses his neck, arms and shoulders to form a striking simulacra of a face, before revealing himself, and initiating a capering dance in front of a drape. *Route 66* (1983) is an overlong, largely disinterested meditation from Cocozza's sitting room window, documenting a day in the life of an auto-supplies shop across the road from his flat. Almost akin to unfinished doodles, the tapes seem at best "pre-visualisations" awaiting fuller realisation, and perhaps at worst, as belated concessions to what Cocozza would once have seen as a decidedly "substandard" amateurism.

---

[39] Shand, "Amateurism and Localism", 21-25.

Reception and Reputation

From early on in the Connoisseur group's activities, Cocozza circulated the entirely false rumour that he had worked with Jean Cocteau and King Vidor. Perhaps such self-mythologisation underpins a persistent expectation in the press clippings that Cocozza might transcend his origins, and re-enter the ranks of a professional film élite. It may explain too, a certain disillusion at his failure to do so. During the 1950s, the Connoisseur group had hungrily courted and exploited publicity, securing the attentions of much-respected critics such as Forsyth Hardy, and local-interest commentators such as the *Glasgow Evening Citizen*'s Jack House—who paid a visit to the Connoisseur Cinema in 1948.[40] The local press in Wishaw remained a follower of Cocozza's activities over the years, even to the extent that a certain fatigue seems evident in some of the later cuttings—leader writers at the *Wishaw Press and Advertiser* refer to him simply by surname in the 1958 headline "Cocozza on Television", implying eyes rolled in only semi-convinced admiration at the newsdesk.[41] Senses of unrealised potentials resonate from much of this material. Since the first scandalous appearance of his work at SAFF, Cocozza had been earmarked as a man with potential. Forsyth Hardy, one of few professional critics regularly observing the Scottish amateur scene, had encouraged his ambitiousness, recognising a refreshing break from amateur conformisms:

> Enrico Cocozza... is clearly a man capable of thinking and feeling in cinema terms. He will make simpler and better films than *Fantasmagoria* and he should feel no resentment over the laughter which it occasionally provoked from the Cosmo audience. He should remember that it is a little startling to find a surrealist orchid among the film daisies and buttercups.[42]

Just a few paragraphs earlier, Hardy had chastised other entrants for their slavish imitation of Hollywood, while supporting work more readily shaped by official definitions of suitably amateur projects—films about idiosyncratic behaviours, the natural environment or local history. Within the world of an organised amateur movement, often caught between such polarised understandings of film practice, Cocozza cut a conspicuous

---

[40] House, "Super Cinema Built in the Backyard", *Glasgow Evening Citizen*, c. 1948—clipping held in the *Cocozza Papers*.
[41] *Wishaw Press and Advertiser*, c. 1958—clipping held in the *Cocozza Papers*.
[42] Hardy, "Critics Verdict on the Film Festival", 5.

figure, and SAFF judges continued (sometimes to the annoyance of other competitors) to reward Connoisseur for its willingness to experiment.[43]

Scanning surviving reports, there is a sense that critics divided the amateur world very much into the left and right of the shadow cast by the professional industry; some had the potential to "cut it" and should thus be elevated as "proven" practitioners; others existed along a different cinematic continuum with little interest in or ambition to "escape" amateurism, viewing their filmmaking as a recreational, or very limited instrumental practice. There is however a sense that some critics—Lindsay Anderson among them, and Hardy to an extent—opted for a more nuanced view of a less partitioned cinema, with the ethic and aesthetic of amateurism pointing the way towards "simpler and better films" that were more truthful and engaged than those conceived through slick professionalism—films that could help renew cinema as a whole.[44] Such sentiments often (still) find expression in the welcome reception of "substandard" technologies and less institutionalised practices as democratising and inspirational.[45] In its best moments, Cocozza's work fulfilled the promise that such critics saw in the amateur movement of a re-vitalised cinema, reminding us of pleas by SAFF judge Clive Donner in 1959; "Be bold, experiment with New Ideas. Avoid the Conventional. Don't Ape the Professionals."[46]

Translating such potentials into paid employment, whilst "avoiding the conventional" of course proved tricky. Cocozza remained imaginative in

---

[43] A number of references suggest Cocozza's ability to attract the admiration of SAFF judges irked fellow competitors and audiences alike. See comments on *Fantasmagoria*: "I do not pretend that I fully understood the film, and there many in the audience who remained unpersuaded...", in Hardy, "Critics Veridct on The Film Festival", 5. In *Surreally Scozzese*, McBain comments; "I think perhaps there is something in Enrico's work which these professionals (the adjudicators invited to judge each SAFF) recognised and awarded and rewarded with prizes, which I have to say, I think the rank and file of the amateur film societies wouldn't have agreed with."
[44] In the programme notes to *Free Cinema 3*, 1957, Anderson remarked "With a 16mm camera, and minimal resources, and no payment for your technicians, you cannot achieve very much in commercial terms. You cannot make a feature film, and your possibilities of experiment are severely restricted. But you can use your eyes and ears. You can give indications. You can make poetry."
[45] See Buckingham, Pini and Willet, "Take Back The Tube!", who provide a fascinating survey of discourses of "democratisation" circulating through amateur film and video publications from the 1920s to the present day.
[46] From proceedings of the 21st Scottish Amateur Film Festival, 1959. The Scottish Screen Archive. Reference no. 8469.

seeking patronage in a range of directions, to improve his employability,[47] but as accounts of other "cross-over" amateurs such as Lindsay Anderson or Kevin Brownlow demonstrate, structures of resistance and convention within the professional cinema often acted as antibodies to amateur ethics and aesthetics.[48] The stormy relationships between former amateur practitioners such as Peter Watkins and his patrons at the BBC, only crystallise the difficulties faced by many such filmmakers in their encounters with the professional film and television sectors.[49] So it was, to some extent, with Cocozza. Finding outlets for his most daring pieces beyond SAFF proved extremely difficult. More particularly, his brand of fantasy, romance and surrealism struggled to find financial support in a Scottish film culture centred around non-fiction. Despite eventually turning professional in 1956, he found little opportunity to make the sorts of films the Connoisseur group had enjoyed, and which SAFF adjudicators had regularly celebrated: his only professional output consists of factual shorts made for public service or commercial clients such as *Glasgow's Docklands* (1956) made for Educational Films of Scotland, or *Meet the Stars* (1960) funded by the Scottish Co-operative Wholesale Society.

Arguably Cocozza's finest professional work is contained in the monochrome *Docklands,* an information film about the life of the Clyde dockyards that dramatises via stark blacks and whites, and introduces deep

---

[47] Cocozza was not above using his own ethnicity to further the cause. Negotiations began with Luigi Pignatelli of the Italian consulate (12th July 1951) over the possibility of making a documentary on Scotland's Italian community, a project never realised despite a flurry of optimistic correspondence. Correspondence retained in the *Cocozza Papers*

[48] See Anderson, *Never Apologise*, 2004, for a sustained discussion of cinema and non-professional aesthetics; the programme notes for *Free Cinema 3,* 1957, and *The Diaries*, 2005, where Anderson remarks of his practice, "… very few, if any, are even aware of the felicity of style we are working to achieve. 'Perfection is not an aim', we announced among our Free Cinema principles all those years ago", 476. In *How It Happened Here*, 1968, Kevin Brownlow relates a much more contentious relationship between aspirations of sleek perfection and the virtues of amateurism. Amateurism has produced many of British cinema's most notable mavericks. Lindsay Anderson, while London-based, had drawn heavily on amateur ideals in developing Free Cinema. Peter Watkins also came to the BBC's attention through his outstanding amateur work. Festivals gave professionals an opportunity to scout emerging talent; Cocozza was just one of many amateurs who found their way into professional practice through his competition and festival appearances.

[49] See Peter Watkins' own monologue on the difficulties of working with BBC on *Culloden* (1964) and *The War Game* (1965), included on the "BFI Archive" DVD, 2003, and Cook, "The Last Battle: 2003.

compositions along the river banks, that reiterate the visual tendencies of his more highly subjective amateur explorations. The sequences shot with local children are particularly effective, recalling Free Cinema shorts such as *The Singing Street* (1952) and *One Potato, Two Potato* (1957),[50] and anticipating subsequent efforts on his "return" to amateurism, where he is still greeted with a kind of appreciative puzzlement:

> his is an intriguing as well as a prolific talent, and the films which he seems to turn out in an endless stream are just the things to stir up cine club controversy... Cocozza, make no mistake, is one of the most individual film makers the amateur movement knows.

In retrospect, Benson's article provides clues to the persistent problems attending assessment of Cocozza's amateur work. A sense of frustration at the filmmaker's mercurial approach, and resulting inconsistency in quality and vision is very apparent, leading to uncertainty as to whether Cocozza really is an artist, or a mere prankster. Benson quickly seems to lose patience with the experimental, avant-garde work that makes him fascinating to current scholarship. Having observed Cocozza closely throughout his career, Benson's exasperation with his capriciousness shines through: "I wouldn't believe it was possible for one man to be so lofty yet crawl around at rock-bottom level", he comments. Cocozza's best work apparently arises "when he's not really trying, and when he comes out of his private world into everyday surroundings" and operates in more standardised genres and modes, which make assessment of his individual achievements an altogether easier business.[51]

Sincerity seems to be the underlying issue. Cocozza was clearly not above spoof (several of his comedies were, after all, released under the title of "Tongue in Cheek" productions) although a sense of seriousness and ambition usually infiltrates these selfsame films. Benson comments on *The Mirror*, for example:

> It looks far too elaborate for a joke. My theory is that this was made as a genuine essay in the avant-garde, and that Cocozza felt that it either didn't come off or succumbed to friend's criticisms to such an extent that he decided to guy it.[52]

---

[50] See Lambert, "Free Cinema", 173-177, and the recent DVD collection *Free Cinema*, produced by the British Film Institute, 2006.
[51] Ibid., 292.
[52] Ibid., 292.

Fig. 9-5 frame enlargement from *The Mirror* (1951)
Source: Scottish Screen Archive

Jokes are certainly confined to commentary as described here, hinting at a lack of confidence in Cocozza over the validity of what he was doing—or perhaps, the validity of what he was doing in a town such as Wishaw, in a country such as Scotland. Being *avant-garde* was often something to sneer at north of the border, with *eminence gris* of the Scottish filmworld, John Grierson typically leading the way:

> The rebellion ... to the tradition of pure form in cinema is no great shakes as a rebellion. Dadaism, expressionism, surrealism are all in the same category. They present new beauties and new shapes. They fail to present new persuasions.[53]

Such critics, real or potential, seem to have been prominent in Cocozza's mind, and there are hints that suchl attention sometimes undermined and shook his confidence.[54] As a form of self-defence, Cocozza often sneered

---

[53] Hardy, *Grierson on Documentary*, 85.
[54] It is interesting to compare Cocozza's approach to the *avant-garde* with that of his fellow Centro alumnus, Margaret Tait. Working mostly in Edinburgh, and seemingly with little regard for prevailing taste, Tait's work comes across as much more committed and unequivocal. This may have been easier to accomplish in a

first, undermining his work at the very moment of its delivery. The example given by Benson of this "Cocozza-cringe" suggests a gnomic charm that could easily wear thin:

> Mr Watts said that one character, the old man, baffled him. He could not tell whether he was "Olivier playing Lear, or Santa Claus in a Glasgow Store"... Cocozza's reply to the press was wonderfully pretentious—the falseness of the beard, he claimed, was symbolic, representing the awakening consciousness of the young man to the "falseness" of Christianity.[55]

Wit rallies here to turn an apparent deficiency into an expression of comic genius, but it remains unconvincing. It was clearly hard to be Cocteau in the Clyde valley.

Conclusions

By the early 1990s, Cocozza was living alone above a chip shop which had replaced the Belhaven Café, his precious reels of film stuffed underneath his bed. Concerned at the proximity of hot fat and celluloid, he eventually contacted the Scottish Screen Archive to bequeath the collection to their care. The donation has preserved the material, and has quickly generated fresh interest in his activities. Four years after he died in 1997, a television documentary brought his work to public attention for the first real time in over four decades. Its title *Sureally Scozzese*, signals its essential take on Cocozza as peculiarly national fantasist and avant-gardist, a continental "intellectual manqué" stranded in the industrial heartland of 1950s Scotland.[56] Though attractive, such a framing of Cocozza's work loses much of the detail, ignoring both the particular conditions of his amateurism and the enduring implications of an identity always grasped in distinctly local, rather than national, terms.

Assessments must in any case remain provisional so long as new films continue to emerge from the archive. Some of the earliest efforts, that flesh out the initial period of proto-production are newly available, and will

---

city environment such as Edinburgh than the close quarters of a mining town. See Cook and Todd, *Subjects and Sequences: A Margaret Tait Reader*.

[55] Benson, "The Private World of Enrico Cocozza", 292.

[56] Following transmission of the documentary, entitled *Sureally Scozzese*, the programme and a trio of films were given a commercial VHS release by Scottish Screen—*Chick's Day, Petrol* and *Nine O' Clock*—a fairly representative sample of the best of the Cocozza output, innovative and unorthodox, blending Scottish avant-gardism with popular folklore and very modern expressions of angst.

undoubtedly help to cut through various mythologies. Many of the films referred to in the 1950s press have yet to re-emerge however, among them *Twilight* (1955), apparently one of his more visually stunning accomplishments, with "shots that would keep any cameraman, amateur or professional awake at night in incredulous envy."[57] According to Benson's assessment, it contains all of Cocozza's vices and virtues—virtuoso technique, imaginative power, serious pretension and a self-subversive humour. This is the film too that inspired Benson's comments about lofty intentions at "rock bottom" level, and may be the representative statement of who—amateur artist, would-be professional auteur, practical joker—Cocozza really was. Perhaps though dreams of such finalising definitions are in themselves fantasies, ironically akin to distinctly amateur idealisations of supposedly more integrated professional identities.

Material already available for viewing suggests that whilst meager resources could inspire bravura acts of technical and aesthetic virtuosity, such constraints also apparently combined with a lack of self-confidence and professional validation that crippled future ambitions. Caught between the movie-mogul egotism parodied in *Scherzo* and the victimhood of *Nine O'Clock*, Cocozza sometimes behaved as if he were an auteur, a strong-willed director orchestrating a professional apparatus, when in fact, he was working with local shopboys and café patrons—no mean feat, but an achievement perhaps only within the narrow confines of amateurism. Clearly Cocozza troubled amateurism's aesthetic standards: the notion of the moving image as the most eloquent expression of a film's intent enjoyed uneven support with a film culture often struggling to escape its still photographic roots, whilst at the same time, Cocozza's "failings" apparently seemed even more glaring from the theatrical/literary perspectives inherited from British film commentary of the time.[58]

Perhaps Cocozza's cosmopolitanism would have been more at home in the metropolis. If he had moved to London, and gained entry to the circle of pioneering filmmakers clustered around the BFI's Experimental Film Fund, who knows? Perhaps he would be a household name by now; perhaps he would also be much less interesting. For his case is one of cinematic devolution, of cinema de-centred, reaching into the forgotten corners of industrial Scotland. In this respect, Wishaw formed not so much a cage as a muse, focusing the creative tension between his boundless imagination and the subdued greys and pinks of the sandstone streets

---

[57] Benson, "The Private World of Enrico Cocozza", 292.
[58] Grierson provides many examples of this style in his early criticism. See for example, Hardy's edited collection, *Grierson at the Movies,* 1981, or Derek Hill's review of Michael Powell's *Peeping Tom*, entitled "Cheap Thrills", 1960.

supposedly so resistant to transformation as spaces for fantasy. The *Surreally Scozzese* television documentary depicted Cocozza as a millennial man out of time and place—his surviving film reels however complicate such comfortable separations of past and present, professional and amateur, still fresh and contemporary half a century later

Works Cited

Primary Sources

The Enrico Cocozza Papers 1921-1998, Scottish Screen Archive. (Scottish Archive Network no. GB2120/SSA 3/7) [referenced as *Cocozza Papers*]

McBain, Janet. Interview with James Craig, conducted in July 2000, transcript retained within the *Cocozza Papers*.

Secondary Sources

Anderson, Lindsay. *The Diaries*. London: Methuen, 2005.
—. *Free Cinema 3. Programme Notes*. London: National Film Theatre, 1957.
—. *Never Apologise: The Collected Writings*. London: Plexus Publishing, 2004.
Archive DVD. *Free Cinema*, British Film Institute, 2006
Archive DVD. *The War Game/Culloden*, British Film Institute, 2003.
Benson, Harold. "The Private World of Enrico Cocozza." *Amateur Movie Maker* 2, no. 6 (1959): 291-292.
Bondanella, Peter and Andrea Ciccarelli, eds. *The Cambridge Companion to the Italian Novel*. Cambridge: Cambridge University Press, 2003.
Brownlow, Kevin. *How It Happened Here*. London: Secker and Warburg, 1968.
Buckingham, David, Maria Pini and Rebekah Willett. "Take Back The Tube!: The Discursive Construction of Amateur Film and Video Making." *Journal of Media Practice* 8, no. 2 (2007): 183-201.
Cocozza, Enrico. "How I Made The 'Film of The Year': The Production of *Chick's Day*." *Amateur Cine World* 15, no. 1 (1951): 50-53.
—. "Life with Corky." *Amateur Movie Maker* 2, no. 6 (1959): 291-293.
—. *The Poetic Imagery and Existential Dilemma of Jean Cocteau*. PhD diss. University of Strathclyde, 1979.
—. *Assunta: The Story of Mrs. Joe*. New York: Vantage Press, 1987.

Cook, Benjamin and Peter Todd, eds. *Subjects and Sequences—A Margaret Tait Reader*. London: Lux, 2004.
Cook, John and Patrick Murphy. "The Last Battle: Peter Watkins on DVD." *Film International* 1, no. 1 (2003): 54-56.
Crompton, Richmal. *Just William*. London: George Newnes, 1922.
Davidson, Julie. "Filmmaker returns with a celebration of street life." c. 1979, publication unknown. Clipping from *Cocozza Papers*.
Ellis, John. *BFI Productions: 1951-1976*. London: British Film Institute, 1977.
Hardy, Forsyth, ed. *Grierson on Documentary*. London: Collins, 1946.
—. "Critics Verdict on the Film Festival." *The Scotsman* (24 March 1949): 5.
—. "Amateur has lessons to teach the studios." *The Scotsman* (24 April 1950): 5.
—. *Grierson on The Movies*. London: Faber & Faber, 1981.
Hill, Derek. "Cheap Thrills." *The Tribune* (29 April 1960): 5.
Lambert, Gavin. "Free Cinema." *Sight & Sound* 25, no. 4 (1956): 173-177.
McIntyre, J. Unidentified obituary, contained within the *Cocozza Papers*.
Miller, Mitchell. "Heavenly Mandates: Enrico Cocozza, Filmmaker." *The Drouth* 3 (2002): 9-15.
—. "'Hold it Simple, Hold it Direct' Margaret Tait's Reverberant Notes." *Filmwaves* 26 (2005): 30-36.
Murphy, Robert. "Riff-Raff: British Cinema and the Underworld." In *All Our Yesterdays: Ninety Years of British Cinema*, edited by Charles Barr, 286-305. London: British Film Institute, 1986.
Rose, Tony. "*Corky* is a Corker!" *Amateur Movie Maker* 2, no. 2 (1959): 76-77.
Shand, Ryan. "Amateurism and Localism—Notes towards a de-centred history of Scottish Cinema." *The Drouth* 21 (2006): 21-25.
Various. *The Beano Book*. London. D. C. Thomson, 1950-2003.
Watkins, Dudley. *The Broons and Oor Wullie: The Fabulous Fifties*. London: D. C. Thomson, 1998.
Wilkin, Andrew, ed. *Mosaico: A Miscellany of Writings Presented to Cav. Uff. Dr. Enrico Cocozza, on His Retirement from Teaching*. Glasgow: University of Strathclyde, 1985.

Films Cited

Ad Infernum, Buddy?
(James Craig, 1952) 16mm., 6 mins.

Alassio 1954
 (Enrico Cocozza, 1954) 16mm., 24 mins.
At W. H. S. Fete
 (Enrico Cocozza, 1945) 9.5mm., 3 mins. 23 secs.
Before Time Came
 (Enrico Cocozza, 1958) 16mm., 18 mins.
Bongo Erotico
 (Enrico Cocozza, 1959) 16mm., 9 mins.
Bryan Welcomes Raffles
 (Henry Cocozza/Enrico Cocozza, 1943) 9.5mm. 8 mins.
The Cappela of Enchantment
 (Enrico Cocozza, 1947) 16mm., 20 mins.
Chick's Day
 (Enrico Cocozza, 1950) 16mm., 31 mins. 55 secs.
Corky
 (Enrico Cocozza, 1958) 16mm., 20 mins.
Crabbit Granny
 (Enrico Cocozza, 1953) 16mm., 10 mins.
Culloden
 (Peter Watkins/BBC, 1964) 16mm, 73 mins. 30 secs.
Fantasmagoria
 (Enrico Cocozza, 1948) 16mm., 31 mins. 28 secs.
Fit O' The Toon
 (Enrico Cocozza, 1978) 8mm., 110 mins.
Glasgow's Docklands
 (Enrico Cocozza, 1956) 16mm., 11 mins.
La Mort Et Le Poete
 (Henry Cocozza/Enrico Cocozza, 1943) 9.5mm., 12 mins.
The Living Ghost
 (Enrico Cocozza, 1959) 16mm., 26 mins.
Masquerade
 (Enrico Cocozza, 1953) 16mm., 16 mins. 30 secs.
Meet The Stars
 (Enrico Cocozza, 1960) 16mm., 12 mins. 30 secs.
The Mirror
 (Enrico Cocozza, 1957) 16mm., 18 mins.
Nine O' Clock
 (Enrico Cocozza, 1951) 16mm., 20 mins.
Petrol
 (Enrico Cocozza, 1957) 16mm., 2 mins. 35 secs.

Porphyria
  (Jimmy Craig, 1960) 16mm., 8 mins.
Quo Vadis
  (Cinès Productions, 1912) 35mm., 80 mins.
Quo Vadis
  (Metro-Goldwyn-Mayer, 1951), 35mm., 171 mins.
The Red Shoes
  (Gaumont Film Distributors/The Archers, 1948) 35mm., 136 mins.
Ric has a bath
  (Enrico Cocozza, 1950) 16mm., 7 mins. 34 secs.
Robot Three
  (Enrico Cocozza, 1951) 16mm., 12 mins.
Route 66
  (Enrico Cocozza, 1983) VHS., 100 mins.
Sail to Inverary
  (Enrico Cocozza, 1956) 16mm., 10 mins.
Scenes at West Cross
  (Enrico Cocozza, 1949) 16mm., 16 mins. 9 secs.
Scenes at West Cross
  (Enrico Cocozza, 1979) 8mm., 19 mins. 26 secs.
Scherzo
  (Enrico Cocozza, 1956) 16mm., 5 mins.
Smart Boy Wanted
  (Enrico Cocozza, 1960) 16mm., 20 mins.
Sureally Scozzese
  (Caledonia, Sterne and Wyld, tx. 27 May 2001) TV, 26 mins.
Triptych
  (Enrico Cocozza, 1983) 16mm., no running time available.
Twilight
  (Enrico Cocozza, 1955) 16mm., 15 mins.
The War Game
  (Peter Watkins/BBC, 1965) 16mm., 50 mins.
The White Lady
  (Enrico Cocozza, 1948) 16mm., 13 mins. 12 secs.

CHAPTER TEN

"PLOUGHING A LONELY FURROW": MARGARET TAIT AND PROFESSIONAL FILMMAKING PRACTICES IN 1950S SCOTLAND

SARAH NEELY

Margaret Tait—poet, painter, and short story writer—has frequently also been cited as a truly independent filmmaker. Her first and only feature credit, *Blue Black Permanent* was released in 1992, but she is primarily remembered as a prolific creator of shorter films, ranging from vivid character studies, to cinematic poems and mobile graphic works often painted directly onto blank stock. When a selection of her films was screened at Calton studios in 1979, she was billed with justification as a "one woman film industry".[1] Hugh McDiarmid, himself the subject of one of Tait's film portraits, had much earlier described her as "ploughing a lonely furrow", and the majority of her work, although sometimes aided by family and friends, was produced largely on her own with very limited budgets.[2]

Although Tait's film *Colour Poems* was financed by the Scottish Arts Council's "filmmaker as artist" competition in 1974, the majority of her attempts at securing funding, including a number of approaches made to the Scottish Film Council, were thwarted. (see Fig. 10-1) To some extent, this was because her work, crossing a range of disciplines as it did, proved difficult to place within familiar traditions. Her own operational status also seemed uncertain—experimental methods were on more than one occasion misread as "unprofessional" by a variety of funding bodies, more focused on the strengths and definitional standards of Scotland's documentary revival.[3] Despite this lack of backing, Tait managed to

---

[1] Film programme Calton Studios, 6 May 1979, D97/25.
[2] McDiarmid, "Intimate Filmmaking in Scotland", 417.
[3] Neely, "Contemporary Scottish Cinema", 151-165.

achieve a degree of success, distributing her films internationally through diverse mechanisms. Yet it is hardly surprising that the oversight of her work on a funding level in Scotland, is reflected in the filmmaker's absence from emerging critical histories of Scottish cinema.

Tait's work could however also be read as part of a more general and problematic history of the critical reception of women avant-garde artists, a reality that has prompted a number of feminist initiatives to begin the recovery of this still fragmented film history. As various commentators have noted, the material most at risk of being lost is often driven by personal, intimate narratives dealing with issues perceived as having lesser value than those deemed to be of cultural, "collective" importance.[4] As with Tait, such filmmakers also often risk being overlooked because of difficulties in identifying their work with existing genres or filmmaking practices, and their often attendant designation as "substandard" with reference to aesthetic as well as technical measures. Robin Blaetz has countered such instincts, and criticised the narrow vision of previous film scholars for not realising that the play with focus, the haphazard framing, the disjunctive editing, and the often abbreviated length—found in the films of Gunvor Nelson, Chick Strand, and others working in the 1960s and beyond—were not signs of incompetence, but marks of a radically different vision, often exercising remarkable influence on surrounding filmmakers. Only in recent years has Marie Menken been credited with influencing Stan Brakhage and others, many of whom have been lionised for half a century for displaying Menken-like qualities, while she herself was forgotten, and her own films allowed to disappear.[5]

In company with the avant-garde filmmakers mentioned earlier, Tait's work focused on the particular and the personal. Like other non-narrative films exploring the materiality of the medium, their primary focus is not upon "collective" issues of national identity, resulting in neglect from standard critical perspectives on cinema in Scotland. Such oversight can be seen as part of a general tendency explaining the relative invisibility of avant-garde filmmakers within studies of national cinema, where such artists are relegated to more international frameworks, and marginalised for their apparent reluctance to contribute to debates around national development and destiny.[6] Exclusion may of course be rationalised on other grounds, and appeal to other evaluative parameters. Similar to the critics' misreading of Nelson and Strand's work as unprofessional and therefore incompetent, Tait's work has often been described as "amateur"

---

[4] Rabinovitz, "The Future of Feminism", 42.
[5] Blaetz, "Rescuing The Fragmentary Evidence", 154.
[6] Morgan, "Life on The Margins".

in the most negative sense of that term. When she sent her work to BBC Scotland in the 1960s, the response was that the "filming and editing were technically inadequate" and that it was "difficult to find a theme of interest". Somewhat perversely, from local perspectives, it was also suggested that she try furth of Scotland, or more specifically, London.[7]

Fig. 10-1 frame enlargement from *Colour Poems* (1974)
Source: Scottish Screen Archive

In many respects, Tait's methods of working encapsulated those of the "true" amateur. Essentially she was a one-woman show, although freelance assistance was very occasionally brought in. Production was often protracted, and assembly driven by opportunity rather than deadline. On average she produced one film a year, but like many amateurs, would usually have several projects in various developmental or production stages. For some films, it would take a number of years for her to collect the material necessary for their completion. At the same time, her activity emulated professional models in certain respects, and sought to exploit the output commercially, if only to fund further filmmaking. Whilst she sold prints to various organisations however, she rarely garnered profit from her activities, and her company, Ancona Films, continually worked at a deficit. Although her work was included in a number of international

---

[7] Letter to Alex Pirie from Finlay J. MacDonald, BBC Scotland, 20 June 1967, D97/2.

filmmaker tours, she also frequently organised exhibitions of her own, and always remained committed to screening her work locally. This essay traces Tait's earlier filmmaking practices, and the fusion of amateur and professional instincts which constituted her very personal formulation of an "independent" film practice. Although Tait did not align herself with organised amateur filmmaking in Scotland, the account considers her work in relation to the general critical debates around the nature of amateur versus professional filmmaking.

Continental Optimisms

Like many other amateur filmmakers, Tait's work seems to have gained impetus from wartime experience, and to have developed post-war on return from active service. Shortly after qualifying in medicine, she had joined the Royal Army Medical Corps, before serving in the Far East from 1943-1946. It was there that she became increasingly interested in photography, and time spent in the region would provide material for a number of scripts and stories, which would be developed later in a wide range of mediums. Upon her return to Scotland, she enrolled in a night class at Edinburgh College of Art, moving to London the following year, where she was engaged in a series of writing projects. The most conspicuous output of the stay was a novel, "The Lilywhite Boys", drawing upon her experience of being stationed in Jhansi, a city in northern India that served as a recuperation point for troops returning from Burma.[8] A manuscript was eventually sent to publishers who were largely unresponsive, citing the current glut of war novels as cause for rejection. After a while, Tait moved on to Perugia's school for foreigners, improving her Italian for a year, before enrolling in The Centro Sperimentale di Cinematographia, in Rome, where she studied from 1950 to 1952.

Tait's presence at the Centro must have attracted a certain attention, for upon her return to Britain, Gavin Lambert approached her to arrange a screening of student films produced in the school, for the London Film Society. The previous year, the critic had written a lengthy account of post-war Italian cinema for *Sight and Sound*, and perhaps because of this, also requested that Tait draft a short article on the works, that might contextualise the screenings, and possibly find publication elsewhere.[9] Although the article never appeared in *Sight and Sound*, it may well have

---

[8] "The Lilywhite Boys", unpublished manuscript, D97/33.
[9] Lambert, "Notes on A Renaissance", 399-409, and "Further Notes on a Renaissance", 61-65.

been used to accompany the Film Society screenings. The surviving account captures Tait's optimistic mood after returning to Britain:

> Rome is a *centre* of cinema, that is of cinema as an art even more than of cinema as a speculative enterprise. The people are enthusiastic about the cinema; they love films and the comments one overhears in bars and restaurants are critical and a good deal more adult that the "Who's in it?" type of discussion I seem to have heard so much of. Intelligent persons discuss cinema as elsewhere they discuss literature or painting. This status of being a "centre" is kept up, and subject matter for the discussions is provided by the liveliness of production here. There are always two or three important directors making important films as well as countless minor productions going on. And everybody *knows* about the films in production—indeed one meets the companies filming in the streets all the year round. There in the Piazza di Spagna was Emmer making his "Le Ragazze della Piazza di Spagna", while at the top of the stairs Fellini was shooting another film, and at the same time De Sica, taking a rest from directing, was acting in "Buongiorno Elefante" in a suburban street.[10]

Within this heady atmosphere, Tait forged friendships that would prove influential throughout her own career as filmmaker. For the production of her first projects, *One is One* (1951) and *The Lion and the Griffin* (1952), she collaborated with fellow Centro students Peter Hollander (later a celebrated documentary filmmaker for the United Nations), and Fernando Birri (now an established director and co-founder of film schools in Argentina and Cuba).

After leaving the Centro, Hollander and Tait established the production company, Ancona films, named after lodgings in the Via Ancona, Rome. Early letterheads for the company cite offices in the Italian capital, New York (where Hollander resided), and Edinburgh. Later promotional materials list only the offices from which Tait worked in Edinburgh's Rose Street from the 1950s, until relocating to her native Kirkwall in 1974—she would remain there, making films, until her death in 1999. Electing to work from Edinburgh, but especially from the Orkneys, was frequently a source of amazement for fellow practitioners, puzzled by both her desire and ability to produce films in locations remote from the centre of industry activity. In a letter written to Tait in 1982, Lindsay Anderson commented on the frustration she must have felt working outside of London, where all of the "wheeling and dealing" occurred.[11] Her Ancona films partner Peter Hollander encouraged her, at various points in time, to

---

[10] Tait, "Independence: Small Budget Production in Rome", 1.
[11] Letter from Lindsay Anderson, 22 February 1982, D97/25.

move to London. Although Tait resisted such suggestions, exploring working methods that allowed her a greater deal of freedom in this sense, the contacts made in film school would form an essential basis for the success she subsequently achieved in distributing her films internationally.

The 1950s proved a particularly active period in Tait's filmmaking career, and fuelled by the optimism generated by her time in Rome, she produced a variety of works that serve as early indicators of things to come. The desire to master basic skills is combined with excitement about exploring new possibilities. Whilst many of the results seem inconclusive, they represent in essence disciplinary exercises, as her developmental notebooks remind us. Here shot lists appear, later edited and revised, and commented on by herself—to herself. There are also notes on editing, which are later responded to—after a job has been done. In relation to the making of *Orquil Burn* (1955), *Happy Bees* (1955) and *The Drift Back* (1956)[12] for example—the films to be discussed in this essay—Tait expressed the importance of knowing the medium, confirming that she had "learnt a lot about camera movements in making these films even if the ones I have used are very conventional".[13] Overall the notebooks confirm the period as particularly crucial to the development of Tait's approach to filmmaking. Her interest in experimental possibilities, alongside ambitions to master standard technique, and a surprisingly open-minded approach to more commercial ventures, provides a fascinating case study of tensions between amateur and professional impulses evident in the work of many "non-professionals". Tait pursued commercial opportunity thereafter whilst resolutely guarding her independence, always mindful of the balance to be struck between the supposed "integrities" of amateurism, and the economic necessities of engagement with professional bodies. In a brief statement of intention, she reveals her belief, for example, in the virtues of smaller budgets, and describes a plan to follow Italian methods of production that would avoid hazards later encountered by the neorealists, "forsaking their post-war economic way of working."[14]

Balancing ambition and economic necessity often proved difficult. Although Tait did manage to accrue funding from various sources, Ancona films always operated at a significant loss. For the most part, her films were supported from her own earnings as a General (medical) Practitioner.

---

[12] Although the date given to this film is 1956 in several different sources, Tait completed this before *Happy Bees* and *Orquil Burn,* usually dated as 1955. According to the filmmaker's notes and details of their first screening dates, *The Drift Back* was completed before or at least around the same time.
[13] Tait notebooks, D97/3.
[14] Tait notebooks, D97/38.

Like many amateurs therefore, she practiced a kind of creative parsimony, and was particularly frugal with available stock, re-using old sequences as a basis for new projects. For *Calypso* (1955), one of Tait's hand-painted films, she recycled found, 35mm stock discovered in Rome, working with its existing optical musical soundtrack. Tight budgets led to the equally resourceful approaches that informed much of her other filmmaking. *Portrait of Ga* (1952), the first film produced by Tait as a truly "lone worker", was made for under £100. *Happy Bees* and *Orquil Burn* were both made for a total of £700.[15] Certainly no external funding seems to have been available for films such as these, although some recouped a portion of their costs through later sales and rental.

The Drift Back, one of Tait's few wholly sponsored short works, was produced for £87, supported by the Orkney Education Committee, and intended for distribution via the Rural Cinema Scheme. A local initiative, set up to offer cinema projections in parts of mainland Orkney and on several of the outer islands, the Scheme enjoyed some early success. Despite the practical difficulties involved, feature films were eventually shown regularly (either weekly or fortnightly) in twenty-seven different locations. Such was the confidence of the Scheme's sponsors, that by 1953 the committee had chosen to book films independently of the local Film Society—the Highlands and Islands Film Guild (HIFG)—not only to curb expenditures, but also to allow for an approach to programming that would be more considerate of the preferences of local audiences.[16] After a successful screening of an amateur film of the Queen's visit to Kirkwall, which nearly doubled audience figures, the Committee had agreed to consider the future programming of local interest films, and even proposed the production of a monthly cinemagazine, with camera-owning local enthusiasts provided with the necessary film stock for its production.

The first film completed under the Scheme eventually emerged as *The Drift Back*, which explores issues around migration and depopulation, following the movement of people from mainland Scotland, back to Orkney, or from the Orkney mainland, back to one or other of the smaller islands. (see Fig. 10-2) Unlike several later films, which employ a personally narrated commentary, *The Drift Back* makes some concession to its sponsors, and incorporates a conventional voice-over, delivered here by Harald R. Leslie, an Edinburgh barrister, originally from Orkney. Produced as a pilot for a local cinemagazine, it was hoped that by

---

[15] Minutes of the Orkney Education Committee, Kirkwall, 7 May 1957, 1340.
[16] The Highlands and Islands Film Guild was a mobile cinemas scheme operating throughout the region that would provide screenings—usually in village halls—of feature films, newsreels and educational films.

addressing themes of Orcadian interest, the film would appeal to local filmgoers, as such materials had in various other locales. Such magazines were staples of the amateur film movement elsewhere in the 1950s, often playing an important role within local information services. Although the expense of *The Drift Back* proved considerable for the council, it was suggested by Alex Doloughan, member of the committee and locations manager of the film, that prints could be sold to gain additional income. Despite the costs involved, it was also proposed that Tait should continue with the magazine, producing six films a year, with a budget of £1,500. Unfortunately, the sums envisaged proved too large for the council, and the project was swiftly abandoned. A camera was however eventually purchased for more limited use, and some short films were produced by employees of the Scheme. Doloughan and principal projectionist, Sandy Wylie's film of a royal visit in 1960, is just one example.

Fig. 10-2 frame enlargement from *The Drift Back* (1957)
Source: Scottish Screen Archive

The Rural Cinema Scheme was itself soon in difficulty. Shows were often cancelled because of bad weather, and projectors and equipment damaged by snowstorms and hurricanes. Attendances also declined, as television was reported to have "hit the islands with a vengeance."[17] Such was the impact that, just a few years after *The Drift Back* was made, it was proposed that all of the mainland screening centres be shut down, whilst several of the island locations were also considered for permanent closure. It was not until 1965, almost a decade after *The Drift Back*, that Tait could complete what might be considered the second installment of the Orkney cinemagazine, in the form of a short film of the Kirkwall sporting event—akin to rugby—*The Ba,* followed by footage of the Stromness ploughing match. Although prints of this footage were again sold for nominal sums, Tait's production costs were not covered in the same way as with *The Drift Back*. With the Rural Cinema Scheme facing financial hardships, and the committee now capable of filming its own local material to accompany screenings of commercial rental fare, it soon proved financially prohibitive to generate further films in this way.

Despite such setbacks, Tait remained imaginative in her exploration of support mechanisms. Around this time, she was in contact with the HIFG, and in 1964 approached the organisers to arrange a screening of her film *Rose Street* (1956), shot long ago around her studio in Edinburgh. Although the Guild was keen to exhibit the piece, issues again emerged around funding. Films for the organisation were generally booked as entire programmes from renters in London. In this context, the hire of additional titles was clearly deemed an extravagance, particularly difficult to justify when the material's subject matter did not relate to the local interests of the Highlands. In May of 1965, Tait nonetheless again wrote to the secretary of the HIFG, Hugh Ross, suggesting that they "might be of mutual help to each other".[18] Offering to shoot local events for exhibition on the circuit, with no imagined financial gain, she requested only occasional use of a 16mm projector in return. The Guild seems, on the basis of surviving records, to have been in even less of a position to assist her than had the Orkney Education Committee. Ross responded quickly to Tait's request, but felt unable to take the proposal forward. Television again seems to have been the key factor. The secretary writes simply:

> There was a day perhaps when such mutual help as you suggest might have been of some benefit, but in these days of almost complete coverage by

---

[17] Annual report from the Minutes of the Orkney County Council Education Committee, Kirkwall, 2 October 1962, January 1959-December 1961, C05/1/20.
[18] Letter to Hugh Ross, Secretary, Highlands and Islands Film Guild, Inverness, 22 May 1965, D97/37.

television, I doubt if such a scheme would be viable from the point of economics.[19]

Alternative support-structures seem to have remained unexplored for loosely ideological, or perhaps merely instinctive, reasons. The rapid expansion of the Film Societies movement, a distinctive feature of Scottish film culture through this period, might in other circumstances have provided the backing for Tait's local production that it offered filmmakers elsewhere.[20] Close to home, the Kirkwall Film Society (KFS) was certainly experiencing a period of revival, with *The Orkney Herald* optimistically reporting in 1957, for example, that the society "defies TV".[21] One of the few to be established during the Second World War, a time when many Scottish groups were disbanding, the Society was run by close contacts broadly sympathetic to Tait's situation. KFS Secretary Alex Doloughan had been Tait's partner on *The Drift Back,* and key to the development of the experimental cinemagazine. Despite such familiarity however with those involved, Tait herself had little direct involvement in the group, occasionally offering advice regarding programming, but remaining at a distance from its actual gatherings. Film Society culture and its emphasis on "appreciation", seems to have been a certain source of anxiety. Whilst on occasion Tait looked to the societies as a source of information, useful for locating skilled professionals, a deep-rooted cynicism about the movement's culture is apparent in her condemnation of the Edinburgh Film Festival, which she likens to a "film society movement rather than commercial cinema", an exercise akin to collecting antiques—"what Scots do when they want to be artistic."[22]

Localised Illustrations

Perhaps as a result of the filmmaker's apparent aloofness, Tait's films always drew a good deal of interest from "cultural" societies, with Scotland or, more specifically Orkney, as their focus. In April 1956, for example, a screening was held by The Dunedin Society for the Promotion of The Scottish Arts, of which Hugh MacDiarmid, was then president. Various Orkney- and Shetland-based associations also generated supportive audiences. In 1961, when Tait was still living in the capital, screenings were arranged as part of an "Orkney night" for the Edinburgh,

---

[19] Letter from Hugh Ross, Film Guild, 26 May 1965, D97/37.
[20] See essays by Melanie Selfe and Richard MacDonald elsewhere in this volume.
[21] Anon., "Kirkwall Film Society Defies TV", 4.
[22] Tait notebooks, D97/33.

Leith and District Orkney Association. In 1964, she accompanied her films north, for a screening at the Aberdeen branch of the Orkney and Shetland Association. The visit was to prove significant, as the event caught the attention of James Wilson, producer of the BBC's television magazine programme *The Talk of the North*, who subsequently approached the filmmaker to request viewing copies of *The Drift Back* and *Orquil Burn*. Tait, by now living in Sutherland, again offered to film local events for the programme, although the initiative seems not to have been realised. Wilson's fascination with Tait's activities would endure however, and his own study *Poet With A Camera*, a short television documentary on her work, would eventually be screened in 1979.

Involvement and interest in cinemagazine series in Orkney could simply be interpreted as testament to Tait's financial acumen, but the move also reveals deeper commitment to providing local images of the community. In a press book for *Orquil Burn*, she explains how the motivation for the film was two-fold:

> partly to provide entertainment (and attract bigger crowds to the rural cinemas and help to make the scheme pay) and partly to counteract the "call away" effect of the average exotic film by presenting an equally interesting "look what you've got here" sort of document.[23]

Such commitment would seem welcome, particularly through the 1950s and 1960s, as fruitful relations developed between the Scottish Film Council and the Scottish Association of Amateur Cinematography, and their interests came together in bodies such as the Scottish Educational Film Association.[24] Although like many amateurs involved with such organisations, Tait prized the filming of local events, she approached the subjects, as always, on her own terms. The potential incompatibility of her dual aims was sometimes quickly exposed. On the one hand, the small amounts of funding involved would provide her with basic raw materials, allow her to work independently, and to pursue her own artistic concerns. On the other hand, as with the experience of the Orkney Education Committee, required emphasis on historically representative material, and its potential educational use, pulled against the experimentation towards which Tait was habitually drawn. It is not surprising then that when Tait sent her films to the Scottish Film Council in the mid-1950s, the work was assessed in terms of its instrumental value, and fared badly on this basis. In general, the films were described as "too bitty", "too long", "too

---

[23] D97/12.
[24] McBain, "And The Winner Is…", 100-101.

repetitive", and as "lack[ing] in unity", making them generally too difficult to use for school room purposes.[25]

Although hope for the continuation of an Orkney cinemagazine dwindled with the evidence of slow financial returns, and despite largely inappropriate criticisms from official bodies, Tait continued to make films about Orcadian life. During the production of her next effort, *Orquil Burn*, she sketched a rough plan for an Orkney series or "omnibus", presumably once again with the intention of appealing to the local film market. In addition to *Orquil Burn*, the seventy-minute series would have included *Happy Bees*, a film about an Orkney farm, a film about wild animals, and another on the subject of Skara Brae. Most of these sections would never be realised however, and only fragments remain to the archive.

Orquil Burn was produced, on a minimal budget, and relied on unpaid assistance from the family and friends who appear in the film, and The Orkney Strathspey and Reel Society, which provided the music. Tait's "poetic" approach is well illustrated by the making of the film. (see Fig. 10-3) Such projects often began life in the pages of Tait's notebooks, where lists of places, images or scenes carve out the rough sculptural forms. The premise for *Orquil Burn*, following a burn from Scapa Flow, back to its source, is based on a documentary that Tait had seen about a film crew tracing the course of the River Nile. Comparisons could also be made with the work of contemporary filmmakers such as William Raban's *Thames Film* (1986) or Chris Welsby's *Stream Line* (1976), both films re-working predictable treatments of actual locations as triggers for meditation and reminiscence. Like these works, *Orquil Burn's* examination of a particular place provides its loose ideological structure, whilst always foregrounding a distinctly personal context. Departing from the conventional narration of *The Drift Back*, Tait's own voice now provides the voice-over. Speaking about the landscape in a familiar and personal register, her words draw attention to "the old dog spot" and note that "the local farmer is Uncle Peter". Like the filmmaker's later *Land Makar* (1981), a portrait-like film of Mary Graham Sinclair, a neighbouring crofter, where interactions between filmmaker and subject during an interview are suffused with an intimacy and familiarity, the *Orquil Burn* stresses Tait's highly personal involvement.

Surviving notebooks for the project attest to the maintenance of a professional approach, clearly underpinned by her formal training, alongside commitment to the personal and poetic. A variety of shooting scripts, listing over two hundred proposed shots, are intertwined with

---

[25] Scottish Film Council, D. M. Elliot, 23 January 1956; SFC, Elliot, 26 April 1956; SFC, Elliot, 28 May 1956, D97/37.

reflective prose pieces on the burn—some poetic, others more like personal reminders. In one instance, Tait recollects how "The water used to meander and get lost in the fields. Uncle Peter had the burn channeled straight for the proper drainage of his lands. The flowers came and grew beside it."[26] Later, poems merge into lists of desired shots. A string of subjects, reading like the seeds of a poem, "caldale cows, meadowsweet, a small water fall" becomes a catalogue of what she will shoot—"must do trickles out of peat, sphagnum moss and cotton".[27] Sometimes the words on the page are translated into filmic images, and on occasion they form the basis for Tait's poetic voice-overs. Shooting then becomes an extension of her writing practices, a creative necessity when faced with industry constraints. Amongst the notes for *Happy Bees,* also developed in this caméra-stylo-like way, sketches for what would become *Rose Street* appear as: "Wet Monday: Make it in Edin. Weary and wet. Grim faces, pavement, etc."[28]

Fig. 10-3 frame enlargement from *Orquil Burn* (1955)
Source: Scottish Screen Archive

---

[26] Tait notebooks, D97/3.
[27] Ibid.
[28] Ibid.

Jonas Mekas' use of personal narration and collage techniques (especially in terms of his diary filmmaking) suggest further points of comparison.[29] What is read in Mekas as collage, is very reminiscent of what Tait described as "condensation", implying a certain filtering of sensation and idea, to produce a direct and immediate effect, akin to poetry.[30] In the programme notes for her film *Where I am is Here* (1964), she explains how when she started filming again in 1963, she:

> made a conscious decision that there was no use working in this lone way and at this sort of budget level, unless I was doing it at the level of poetry, that is on the same level as what I had been lately writing, and translating, and painting (particularly in twenty-nine illustrations, in aniline colours, for Lorca's "Poet in New York").[31]

Such creation of virtue from necessity, and rationalisation of limited resources as aesthetic incentive, echoes very amateur stresses on "accommodation" to one's circumstances as a basis for distinctive creativity, as well as Mekas' celebrated designation of "substandard" cinema as a potential folk art on the basis of its freedom from commercialised norms.[32] Other points of connection might be stressed: Tait's use of "unsynchronised" sound in particular might be compared to that of Mekas, although while both filmmakers play with the debasement of sound and image as an element of collage-making, specific emphases occur in their respective work (eg. Tait's sound is usually natural rather than synthesised) marking their highly distinctive sensibilities.

As the Scottish Film Council's response to Tait's films reveals, such divergences from familiar aesthetic norms and agreed professional standards, may well be construed as failures of realisation. Such choices of subject matter and styles of commentary, palpably comfortable in their origins in the nearby and personal, are probably more likely to be read as traces of an amateur cinema at its most functional, akin to "aide-memoire" or the home movie of intrinsically personal significance, rather than artistry of any wider, cultural value. Certainly appreciative critical reception has found it necessary to contest such standard readings. Mike Leggett, for example, has usefully defended Tait's work, stressing its transcendence of the casualisms often recognised in writings around the home movie. Writing about *Portrait of Ga* (1952), Tait's study of her

---

[29] Ruoff, "Home Movies of the Avant-Garde", 294-312.
[30] Tait notebooks, D97/25.
[31] *Where I am is Here,* programme notes, D97/37.
[32] Mekas, "8mm. Cinema as Folk Art", 83.

mother, Leggett suggests that the film "demonstrates a certain intensity of observation (motivated by affection) which is possible in intimate domestic circumstance but is entirely unrelated to the 'home movie' tradition... "[33] His stance against assimilation of Tait's work to conventional domestic cinema comes as little surprise. As Karen L. Ishizuka comments, apart from "visionaries such as Jonas Mekas, most people don't take home movies seriously", and need to re-locate them to fresh registers if they are to attempt to do so.[34]

The home movie is often read too along divisions of gender, and Tait's womanhood is an important factor here, possibly reinforcing designation of the films as amateur, in terms that assume a pejorative status for that classification.[35] Patricia Zimmermann describes how "by the 1950s, amateur film was almost completely isolated within the confines of the nuclear family" and how through that decade "children were photographed more than anything or anyone else".[36] Tait's preoccupation with the domestic may have some resonance here, especially in relation to her own *Happy Bees,* a film about a child's experience of summer in Orkney, which featured young members of her own family. (see Fig. 10-4) However, extracts from Tait's production notes for *Happy Bees* reveal a conscious resistance to labelling in such terms. The important distinction here is that for her, the film was to be made "*for* children not too much *about* children (note; difference between this and the home movie tradition—not just filming family!)".[37]

Tait's films remain personal and poetic in the domestic sphere as elsewhere, adopting a candid mode of address, whilst moving beyond biographical ambitions at every turn, just as postcolonial critic bell hooks employs a self-referential approach to feminist theory, incorporating biography into her writing. As Moore-Gilbert et. al. describe the latter:

> what hooks does is to reorient the idea of the self, and she would not certainly apologise for the emphasis she places on personal experience, seeing this instead as liberating, and as a crucial cultural component of the bases of her radical female subjectivity. Indeed, it is the erasure of the body and of a history of the self in white academe that hooks is in part exposing. Teaching to transgress entails making the teacher more visible in the classroom.'[38]

---

[33] Leggett, "The Autonomous Filmmaker", 2.
[34] Ishizuka, "A Veil of Poetry", 45.
[35] Zimmermann, "Democracy and Cinema", 74.
[36] Ibid., 76-77.
[37] Tait notebooks, D97/3.
[38] Moore-Gilbert, Stanton and Maley, "Introduction", in *Postcolonial Criticism,* 44.

Fig. 10-4 frame enlargement from *The Happy Bees* (1954)
Source: Scottish Screen Archive

Although it would be misguided to argue that Tait was adopting such a radical ideological stance, her personal mode of filmmaking certainly challenges professional filmmaking practices in a similar manner, through tendencies to reveal rather than "erase" personal contexts, and stress her own presence in the work, as a condition of its making and reading.

Interestingly however, such revelation was insistently confined to the films themselves. The filmmaker herself, whose projects were developed from her own personal experiences, did not embrace the media's focus on the biographical details of her own life. Television programmes made about her, for BBC Scotland's *Spectrum* series in 1979, and a Channel Four profile in 1983 for *The Eleventh Hour*, both supposedly highlighting her artistic achievements, were not greeted enthusiastically: the finished material, Tait felt, seemed more interested in her than the films she had produced.[39] Having agreed to the programmes, in the hope of re-

---

[39] *Poet with a Camera* (for *Spectrum* series), BBC Scotland, 30 mins., tx. 5 January 1979, 10.15pm; *Margaret Tait: Filmmaker* (for *The Eleventh Hour* series), Channel Four and the Arts Council of Great Britain, 35 mins., tx. 25 April, 1983, 11.00pm. Although Channel Four followed the 1983 documentary with a broadcast of *Where I am is Here,* and on 6 March 1987 screened a 55 mins. compilation of Tait's films as part of *The Eleventh Hour* series, the earlier BBC Scotland documentary relied solely on extracts. Tait was resistant to the use of extracts in

generating interest in the back catalogue, and attracting funding for future filmmaking ventures, her palpable disappointment is understandable.

The fact that more money was probably assigned to make programmes about her than had ever been granted to the filmmaker herself, must have been a bitter contradiction to resolve. While forging biographical accounts of little-known women filmmakers remains a constructive activity, as Lauren Rabinovitz argues in relation to the future of feminist film studies, much more is certainly required:

> The radical politics of lost-and-found scholarship lies not in merely correcting a record that swept away women's contributions but in refashioning film theory and historiography. It develops a women's history that teaches the centrality of intimate, personal and sexual issues, as well as of the spheres of the everyday that embrace subjects with lesser cultural status.[40]

In this sense, a biographical account of Tait's life and working method gave the filmmaker a certain degree of exposure, but remained incapable of addressing the reasons for her oversight in the first place.

Strategic Amateurism

The construction of Margaret Tait as amateur filmmaker, raises a number of important issues, both critical and concrete. As Zimmermann and others have stressed, such definitions may have serious implications for both the accounting of the past, and the very possibility of its study in the future. To label a film as "amateur" she recognises, often means, "to banish it forever to the territory of the inconsequential and the meaningless." Once defined in this way, such material becomes unusually vulnerable to physical degradation and prone to eventual disappearance. According to Zimmermann, "It is also, in the world of film preservation, to erase it from the historical record."[41] Cash-strapped archives, she suggests, will often prioritise the big picture over the smaller one for restoration, with value defined in terms of national, aesthetic, or technological histories. Thankfully, Tait's films have been largely restored through the efforts of the Scottish Screen Archive, and LUX (formerly The London Filmmaker's

---

the profiles, and voiced concerns that people would assume that what they were seeing were the actual films, D97/1.

[40] Rabinovitz, "The Future of Feminism", 42.

[41] Zimmermann, "Democracy and Cinema", 73.

Co-operative).[42] The latter's role in the preservation and circulation of Tait's films, and creation of a reader edited by Peter Todd and Benjamin Cook,[43] as well as a DVD of a selection of her films, is pleasingly consistent with the way in which her work was historically sustained, by the support of fellow artists.

During her lifetime, the exhibition and distribution of these films was heavily reliant on Tait's own efforts. Like other avant-garde artists, she often exhibited her work through semi-formal or utterly informal screenings. Films would be shown in village halls or even in her own home, with projection into a gilded frame in the living room. Shortly after leaving The Centro Sperimentale, Tait set up a film studio on Rose Street in Edinburgh which soon doubled as an exhibition space. Following the busy production period detailed in this essay, she held the first Rose Street film festival there in August 1954. The informal event provided the opportunity to screen her own work, alongside the films of fellow classmates. Tait later recalled the event in the following way:

> In my workrooms in Rose Street, Edinburgh, I fitted out a small theatre. The biggest room has a reasonable length of throw for the projector and very nice acoustics for sound reproduction. A couple of small windows daringly made in an intervening wall turned a neighbouring small room into a projection booth. Ingenious if slightly confusing manipulation of switches and leads by a colleague gave me adequate control of theatre lights etc. from a central point. My New York partner, Peter Hollander, designed us an excellent poster, I had invitation cards printed, and advertised as well as I could the coming of the "Rose Street Film Festival."[44]

After the festival, a review in an Edinburgh paper noted the attendance of John Grierson, whose response was reported thus: "Fantastic, I haven't seen anything so beautiful for a long time."[45] Unfortunately, Grierson's appreciation of Tait's work at the Festival would never extend beyond that initial praise. When she approached him in 1963, to ask if he would include her portrait of Hugh McDiarmid in his television series *This*

---

[42] The range of classifications given for Tait's films, from amateur (*Orquil Burn*), to fiction and avant-garde experimental (*Happy Bees*), and genre/sponsored (*The Drift Back*) is testament to the slipperiness of taxonomies, particularly when considering the work of an innovative artist, working across a variety of disciplines as a non-professional.
[43] Todd and Cook, *Subjects and Sequences: a Margaret Tait Reader*.
[44] Tait, "On Throwing a Film Festival", D97/13.
[45] Heriot, "Rose Street Come to Life—For 20 Minutes", 10.

Wonderful Life (1957-1966), she received a response suggesting that the film was felt to be unsuitable for transmission.

Outside Scotland, Tait's films were exhibited in a number of locations including India, Malmo, Riga, Berlin, etc., and Ancona partner, Peter Hollander was instrumental in the screening of *Calypso* and *Rose Street* by WGBH-TV of Boston. The University of California also purchased a few prints for their archives. Sales such as these helped to supplement production costs. Tait seems to have been particularly proactive and inventive with regard to marketing at this time, writing to a number of parties regarding the potential purchase or hire of her work, including various embassies. A catalogue printed in 1955, lists copies of the films as selling for £20-£25 each, the year in which *Happy Bees* was sold to the Government of India for £25. Perhaps on the back of the deal, Tait wrote a couple of years later, to the Eastern Railway Co. in New Delhi, to suggest that they hire her films for exhibition on their trains. No record exists unfortunately of the outcome of this ingenious proposal.

Many of the avenues Tait explored for distribution now seem surprisingly commercial, and complicate our usual conceptions of the "avant-garde" artist, a term Tait herself was outspokenly uncomfortable with. In some respects, the pursuit of such outlets for her films seems indicative of ambitions to be perceived as a professional, even as she clung to distinctly non-professional practices in her own production methods. Writing on the subject, Zimmermann identifies the term "amateur" as originating from nineteenth century capitalism: "professionalism was linked to rationalised work […] while amateurism was located within leisure, the private sphere and hobbies."[46] From this perspective, Tait's case represents a fusion of a very traditional amateurism of privatised distraction, with more modern formulations of the artist as opportunist-entrepreneur.

Particular moments seem to encapsulate the resulting stance. When the Guinness Company, for example, wrote to Tait in her capacity as a General Practitioner about the health-benefits of their product, Tait wrote back immediately, suggesting the possibility that she produce a film, similar to *Orquil Burn*, about the organisation of the hops harvest. In 1957, she was in correspondence with J. Davis, director of the Scottish Associated News Theatres, following an encounter at the Edinburgh Film Festival, suggesting that she produce a number of short comedies for their cinemas. Gaining a positive response she drafted a number of proposals, including an idea for several ten-minute portraits of Edinburgh residents,

---

[46] Zimmermann, "Democracy and Cinema", 74-75.

based on her experience of filming *Rose Street*. It seems unlikely that anything ever came of this, but the effort is emblematic of Tait's way of thinking about her work in relation to very popular cinema.

Tait also devoted considerable effort to ensuring that *Happy Bees* garnered a wider audience. In addition to Walt Disney, *Happy Bees* was sent to the London-based Children's Film Foundation, for potential commercial distribution. In a detailed letter to the Foundation, she described the positive reception of her films by children in attendance at the Rose Street festival:

> During the Edinburgh Festival last year we put on a show of short films here at 91 Rose Street. All sorts of people came to see it, among them the children of Rose Street. Rose Street is rather a tough street and I know the children just came up in the first place because it was a free show. But some of them came several times and watched apparently with great interest the several shorts which we showed. The films were all products of Ancona Films or of Sperimentale Film co-op. r.l. of Palermo, and mostly of a documentary character. Only one film was actually devised for children.[47]

Such initiatives in distribution reflect deep-seated tensions between amateur and professional instincts, detected by others in their encounters with the filmmaker. Within a commercial context, her work was perceived to be *outside* the mainstream. Encounters with various funding bodies, by contrast, reveal a tendency to equate the practice of her filmmaking *with* the commercial. In 1957, a funding application submitted to the Carnegie Trust, was rejected on the grounds that the trustees did not support filmmaking conducted for profit. Tait's detailed response to the Trust questions their lack of support for filmmaking, highlighting their general statement of encouragement for the Arts, "in particular amateur music and drama activities", and stressing her own non-commercial status.[48] In addition to detailing the deficit Ancona operated under, she identifies the significance of the 16mm gauge as testament to the small scale distribution intended, deliberately playing upon general assumptions associating the gauge with amateur filmmaking, if this might prove to her own advantage.[49]

---

[47] Letter to Mary Field, Children's Film Foundation Ltd., 10 February 1955, D97/37.

[48] Letter to D. N. Lowe, Secretary Carnegie Trust, 14 May 1957, D97/30.

[49] In the programme notes written for Gavin Lambert, mentioned at the beginning of this essay, Tait described how 16mm did "offer a freedom and a close contact with the medium which is not always so easy to get in 35 mm. work." See Tait, "Independence: Small Budget Production in Rome", 5.

Although the term amateur is often employed to imply a sort of deficiency, Maya Deren's defence of amateur filmmaking in 1965 offers a more optimistic account, and relates well to Tait's own approach. Deren champions the poetic, rhythmic potential of an amateur filmmaking "never forced to sacrifice visual drama and beauty [...] to the relentless activity and explanations of a plot."[50] Whilst Tait undoubtedly found comparable liberations beyond the mainstream, it is important to note that her method of working was dictated as much by necessity, as any deliberate choice. Tait's ultimate belief was simply that:

> The real masterpieces of cinema have mostly been made within the Film *Industry*; in spite of all the pressures of working with others to a timetable to a large budget, and for a market, which one might expect or imagine to be restricting, out comes a work of art, surprisingly often.[51]

She may have cited the experience working with 16mm as "invaluable" but she was also clear about her intention "to work in 35 mm. as soon as possible". For Tait, 16mm was a platform for experimentation that would hopefully lead into filmmaking on a larger scale, or as she later expressed in one of her film notes: "The short films were done, keeping the concept of big-film making in mind".[52] Although filmmakers like Maya Deren, champion the mobility of the truly independent or amateur filmmaker, Tait's positive response to working with a team on *Blue Black Permanent* suggests she would have continued that way if possible. In a letter to Peter Hollander in 1995, she is doubtful of further opportunities for feature filmmaking and is considering new approaches. She writes:

> that sort of 16mm filming is hardly possible anymore. Having worked with a team, with a crew and a cast—if I "go back" to lonesomes working it might be better to try video and really DO something with that.[53]

Conclusions

Margaret Tait's work on *Blue Black Permanent* suggests immediate connections with other British filmmakers such as Derek Jarman, Peter Greenaway, or Sally Potter eventually achieving "cross-over" into the mainstream; yet unlike them, she was only able to produce one feature

---

[50] Deren, "Amateur Versus Professional", 45.
[51] Tait Notebooks, D97/37.
[52] Letter to Sharon Morris, Slade School of Fine Art, 1 October, 1992, D97/27.
[53] Letter to Peter (Hollander?), 15 May 1995, D97/3.

film in her lifetime. As has been suggested here, based in Edinburgh and Orkney, it may be that Tait was in the wrong place, but in many respects it may also have been the wrong time. In the programme notes for the NFT's third International Avant-Garde Film Festival, Malcolm Le Grice described Tait as "the only genuinely independent, experimental mind to precede the current movement which began here (Britain about 1966)".[54] In later years however, Tait achieved much greater degrees of recognition in Scotland, when a retrospective of her work appeared at the Edinburgh Film Festival in 1970. Without doubt, as Le Grice's comments attest, she was a pioneering British experimental filmmaker, but as this more historiographical account of Tait's work reveals, within 1950s and 1960s Scotland her work failed to register with a variety of influential funding bodies.

Thankfully, like many pioneers, Tait was able to remain independent, working towards a clear vision. As for her amateur or professional status, it is apparent where Tait's own preferred identity would rest. In her opinion, Ancona Films was one of the few companies in Scotland making films in a professional manner with "serious artistic intentions".[55] In a letter to *The Scotsman* in 1957, she questions the legitimacy of the Films of Scotland Committee, of which she argues "only one member (John Grierson) is a professional film-maker." All of the rest, she describes as perhaps distinguished in other fields, but "amateurs at production."[56]

Hugh MacDiarmid, writing in 1960, noted the gap between the opportunities for filmmakers in other countries and those available in Scotland, but predicted that the lonely furrow ploughed by Tait had "set a process in motion [that was] bound to develop".[57] Although MacDiarmid's prediction proved partially accurate, in that Tait was eventually given enough support to produce a feature film, the process set in motion, and the significant attempts made by Tait to establish funding and distribution opportunities for experimental film, sadly failed to gather much further significant momentum.

---

[54] See Le Grice's, *Film London: 3rd Avant-garde International Festival* (Programme notes).
[55] Letter to Malcolm Nixon, Glasgow Arts Centre, 14 February 1956, D97/37.
[56] Tait, "Making Films about Scotland", 7.
[57] McDiarmid, "Intimate Filmmaking in Scotland", 417.

Works Cited

Primary Sources

Minutes: minutes of the Orkney Education Committee. January 1957- December 1959, Orkney Archive, Kirkwall, C05/1/20.

Notebooks: material from the notebooks, correspondence and pressbooks also available from the Margaret Tait Papers, D97, Orkney Archive, Kirkwall.

Tait, Margaret. "Independence: Small Budget Production in Rome." Unpublished programme notes for Gavin Lambert, 1-5. Margaret Tait Papers, Orkney Archive, Kirkwall, D97/31.

—. "The Lilywhite Boys", unpublished manuscript, Margaret Tait Papers, Orkney Archive, Kirkwall, D97/33.

Secondary Sources

Anon. "Film Experiment in Orkney: *The Drift Back.*" *The Scotsman* (15 April 1957): 8.

—. "Kirkwall Film Society Defies TV." *The Orkney Herald* (2 June 1959): 4.

Blaetz, Robin. "Rescuing The Fragmentary Evidence of Women's Experimental Film." *Camera Obscura* 21, no. 3 (2006): 153-156.

Cook, Benjamin and Peter Todd, eds. *Subjects and Sequences: A Margaret Tait Reader.* London: Lux, 2004.

Deren, Maya. "Amateur Versus Professional." *Film Culture* 39 (1965): 45-46.

Heriot, Nan. "Rose Street Comes To Life—For 20 Minutes." *The Bulletin* (10 July 1957): 10.

Horak, Jan-Christopher. "The First American Film Avant-Garde, 1919-1945." In *Experimental Cinema, The Film Reader*, edited by Wheeler Dixon and Gwendolyn Foster, 19-43. London and New York: Routledge: 2002.

Ishizuka, Karen L. "The Home Movie: A Veil of Poetry." In *Jubilee Book: Essays on Amateur Film*, edited by Nancy Kapstein, 45-50. Charleroi: Association Européene Inédits, 1997.

Krikorian, Tamara. "*On The Mountain* and *Land Makar*: Landscape and Townscape in Margaret Tait's Work." In *The Undercut Reader: Critical Writings on Artists' Film and Video*, edited by Nina Danino and Michael Mazière, 103-105. London: Wallflower, 2003.

Lambert, Gavin. "Notes on a Renaissance: The Italian Cinema." *Sight and Sound* 19, no. 10 (1951): 399-409.
—. "Further Notes on a Renaissance." *Sight and Sound* 22, no. 2 (1952): 61-65.
Leggett, Mike. "The Autonomous Filmmaker: Margaret Tait: Films and Poems—a correspondence between Mike Leggett and Margaret Tait" [edited by Richard Kwietniowksi—unpublished]. British Artists' Film and Video Study Collection, Central Saint Martins College of Art and Design.
LeGrice, Malcolm. "Programme notes" in *Film London: 3rd Avant-garde International Festival.* London: National Film Theatre, 1979.
McBain, Janet. "And The Winner Is… A Brief History of the Scottish Amateur Film Festival, 1933-86." In *Jubilee Book: Essays on Amateur Film*, edited by Nancy Kapstein, 97-106. Charleroi: Association Européene Inédits, 1997.
MacDiarmid, Hugh. "Intimate Film Making in Scotland." *Scottish Field* (1960), reprinted in *Hugh MacDiarmid: The Raucle Tongue, Hitherto Uncollected Prose, Vol. III*, edited by Angus Calder, Glen Murray, and Alan Riach, 421-417. Manchester: Carcanet, 1998.
Mekas, Jonas. "8mm Cinema as Folk Art." *The Village Voice* (18 April 1963): 12, reprinted in *Movie Journal: The Rise of The New American Cinema,* 83. New York: Collier Books, 1972.
Moore-Gilbert, Bart, Gareth Stanton and Willy Maley. "Introduction." In *Postcolonial Criticism*, edited by Bart Moore-Gilbert, Gareth Stanton and Willy Maley, 1-72. London: Addison, Wesley and Longman, 1997.
Moran, James. *There's No Place Like Home Video.* Minneapolis: University of Minnesota Press, 2002.
Morgan, David. "Life on the Margins: The Scottish Avant-garde Film." *Filmwaves* 19 (2003). Available: http://www.futuremovies.co.uk/filmmaking.asp?ID=13
Neely, Sarah. "Contemporary Scottish Cinema." In *The Media in Scotland*, edited by Neil Blain and David Hutchison, 151-165. Edinburgh: Edinburgh University Press, 2008.
Rabinovitz, Lauren. "The Future of Feminism and Film History." *Camera Obscura* 21, no. 1 (2006): 39-44.
Ruoff, Jeffery K. "Home Movies of the Avant Garde." In *To Free the Cinema: Jonas Mekas and the New York Underground*, edited by David E. James, 294-312. Princeton, New Jersey: Princeton University Press, 1992.

Sobchack, Vivian. "Towards a Phenomenology of Nonfictional Film Experience." In *Collecting Visible Evidence*, edited by Jaine M. Gaines and Michael Renov, 241-254. Minneapolis: University of Minnesota Press, 1999.
Tait, Margaret. "Making Films about Scotland." *The Scotsman* ["Points of View" section] (2 February 1957): 7.
Zimmermann, Patricia. "Democracy and Cinema: A History of Amateur Film." In *Jubilee Book: Essays on Amateur Film*, edited by Nancy Kapstein, 73-80. Charleroi, Belgium: Association Européene Inédits, 1997.

Films Cited

The Ba
(Margaret Tait, 1965/75) 16mm., 62 mins. 42 secs.
Blue Black Permanent
(British Film Institute, Channel Four Television, Viz Permanent, 1992) 35mm., 84 mins.
Calypso
(Margaret Tait, 1955) 35mm., 4. mins. 29 secs.
Colour Poems
(Margaret Tait, 1974) 16mm., 11 mins. 20 secs.
The Drift Back
(Margaret Tait, 1957) 16mm., 10 mins. 56 secs.
Happy Bees
(Margaret Tait, 1954) 16mm., 16 mins. 07 secs.
Land Makar
(Margaret Tait, 1981) 16mm., 31 mins. 32 secs.
The Lion and the Griffin
(Margaret Tait, with Peter Hollander, 1951) 16mm., 13 mins. 33 secs.
Margaret Tait: Filmmaker (for *The Eleventh Hour* series)
(directed by Margaret Williams, producer Fizz Oliver, for Channel Four and the Arts Council of Great Britain, tx. 25 April 1983, 11.00pm) 35 mins.
One is One
(Margaret Tait, with Peter Hollander, 1951) 16mm., 33 mins. 03 secs.
Orquil Burn
(Margaret Tait, 1955) 16mm., 35 mins. 40 secs.
Poet with a Camera (for *Spectrum* series)
(directed by Keith Alexander, producer James Wilson, for BBC Scotland, tx. 5 January 1979, 10:15pm) 30 mins.

Portrait of Ga
(Margaret Tait, 1952) 16mm., 4 mins. 27 secs.
Rose Street
(Margaret Tait, assisted by Alex Pirie, 1956) 35mm., 14 mins. 44 secs.
Stream Line
(Chris Welsby, 1976) 16mm., 8 mins.
The Talk of the North
(BBC Television, 1962-1967) 86 x 30 min. episodes
Thames Film
(William Raban, 1986) 16mm., 66 mins.
This Wonderful Life
(producer John Grierson, for Scottish Television, tx. 1957-1966)
350 x 30 min. episodes
Where I am is Here
(Margaret Tait, producer Alex Pirie, 1964) 16mm., 32 mins. 48 secs.

Appendix A

Chronology

The chronology notes moments and events suggestive of the wider development of amateur cinema in Great Britain. Inclusions have been selected to mark symptomatic trends and ruptures, rather than to canonise particular instances or figures, and to indicate conjunctures and parallel narratives rather than to fix any definitive teleology. Organisational, technological and critical interventions provide the main focus here, although some reference is also made to the creation of particular films of tangible influence within the cine movement as a whole.

1888 *Amateur Photographer and Cinematographer* (1888-1945) first published;

1899 Birt Acres demonstrates "Birtac" 17.5mm film, closely followed by the 17.5mm Biokam, manufactured by Alfred Darling of Brighton;

1901 17.5mm film marketed;

1905 first 35mm home projector;

1910 "non-flam" acetate film manufactured in sub-standard (22mm) gauge;

1912 Edison's 22mm Home Projecting "Kinetoscope" released in the US; Pathéscope develops (non-inflammable) 28mm film for home use (adopted as safety standard with approval of SMPE);

1919 *Scottish Cinema* first published; Cinema Club of Glasgow established;

1920 Imperial War Museum Film Archive established; *American Cinematographer* first published;

1921 Pathé demonstrates 9.5mm stock;

1922 Cambridge University Kinema Club formed by Peter Le Neve Foster; Pathé introduce 9.5mm "Baby" projector; Kodak Panchromatic cine film introduced;

1923 Kodak introduces reversal-processed 16mm safety film; Kodak market first movie "outfit", including Cine-Kodak camera and Kodascope projector;

1924 Oxford University Film Society formed; Pathé 9.5mm "Baby" camera introduced in GB;

1925 The Film Society (London) established;

1926 Amateur Cinema League (ACL) founded in New York City, and publishes journal *Amateur Movie Makers* (1926-1954); *American Cinematographer* introduces regular amateur supplement (*Amateur Movies*); in GB, Amateur Film Players Club formed by Ben Carleton;

1927 *Close Up* (1927-1933) first published; *Cinema World International* first published; British Association of Amateur Cinematographers (BAAC) established; London Amateur Film Club founded; Newcastle ACA established;

1928 Devon Amateur Film Productions organises first "Amateur Kinematograph Convention" in Torquay; *Amateur Films* journal (1928-1930) first published by BAAC; Stockport Amateur Cine Players Club founded; 16mm Kodacolor film introduced;

1929 first national convention of Amateur Cinematographic Societies held in London, decides to form short-lived Amateur Film League of GB and Ireland, *Pathéscope Monthly* first published (1929-1955); "Talkiephone" sound-on-disc system demonstrated by Sheldon-Wilkinson; Jewish Amateur Film Society formed; Ace Movies (Streatham) formed; Thanet Amateur Cinematographers Association formed;

1930 first "amateur talkie" (*Shadows of Limehouse*) screened in London; first general meeting of London Workers' Film Society;

Edinburgh Film Guild established; short-lived British Association for Amateur Cinematography (BAAC) formed, with Sinclair Hill as President, drawing together around 120 active clubs; Pathé re-introduce 17.5mm "Rex" equipment; Crystal Productions (Bournemouth) formed; ACL begin annual "Ten Best" competition;

1931 Dundee Film Society founded; first international amateur film competition held in Brussels; "The Era" Challenge Cup Contest; abortive *Amateur Cinematography* journal published for two months; *The Screen: Magazine of the Amateur and Semi-Professional Cinema* first published (1931-33);

1932 *Home Movies and Home Talkies* (1932-1940) first published; Kodak introduce standard-8 equipment; Institute of Amateur Cinematographers (IAC) formed by Percy Harris, William Chadwick, George Sewell and Stanley Bowler; report by Commission on Educational and Cultural Films (*The Film In National Life*) published; *Sight and Sound* first published; Cine-Kodak Standard 8mm (double run) marketed; *Cinema Quarterly* (1932-1936) first published; demonstration of amateur cinematography at (London) Selfridge's department store; *IAC Bulletin* first published; IAC organise first "national" movie-making contest; Bradford Cine Circle established; in USA, *Movie Makers* (1932-1954) first published;

1933 first Scottish Amateur Film Festival (SAFF); British Film Institute (BFI) established (with amateur "panel"); *Cinema Quarterly* "Amateur" section changes to "Independent" section; Kodak introduce Standard-8 ("bootlace") film; G.B., DeVry and Paillard-Bolex all market domestic sound-on-disc systems; Meteor Film Producing Society (Glasgow) established; *Film Art* (1933-1937) first published; Independent Film Makers Association (IFA) established;

1934 *Amateur Cine World* (1934-1967) first published; Scottish Film Council (SFC) established (with Amateur Cinematography "panel"); Federation of East Midlands Amateur Film Societies established; 17.5mm home talkie system announced by Pathéscope; Federation of Scottish Filmmakers Society founded;

Planet Film Society (London) founded (first affiliated club to IAC); Stoke-on-Trent ACS founded;

1935   National Film and Television Archive established; estimated 200 amateur film clubs in GB; Kodachrome 16mm filmstock introduced; Stoke-on-Trent Cine Club established; Union Internationale du Cinéma d'Amateurs (UNICA) constituted in Barcelona; *British Journal of Photography* (1935-1970) first published (with "sub-standard" cine section);

1936   Kodak introduce 8mm Kodachrome film, and 16mm "magazine" camera; IAC incorporated into British Institute of Cinematography; *Journal of the British Institute of Cinematography* first published (1936-1938); ACW organises first "Ten Best" competition; Waverley (Edinburgh) Amateur Cine Club formed; Warrington Cine Society formed (with George Formby as President);

1937   formal establishment of UNICA at Paris World Fair; British Amateur Cinematographers Central Council (BACCC) established to represent GB at UNICA (with representation from BFI, IAC, SFC, RPS, *Movie Maker*, *Amateur Photographer*); Edinburgh Cine Society established; Federation of Cine Societies founded by Harry Walden and F. P. Barnitt; Pathé introduce 9.5mm sound stock; Kodak introduce Kodascope sound-on-film projector;

1938   British Empire Exhibition Film Festival, Glasgow; Films of Scotland Committee established; first Edinburgh and South-East Scotland Amateur Film Festival; *Miniature Camera World* first published (1938-);

1939   SFC establishes Scottish Central Film Library (distributes prize-winning amateur films); IAC activities suspended, and Emergency Committee created, with William Valon as chairman; *IAC Members' Newsletter* (1939-1941) circulated;

1940   *Home Movies and Home Talkies* ceases publication;

1943   Cinematograph Film (Control) Order, assigns film supply to discretion of Board of Trade;

1945	*IAC Bulletin* emerges from wartime as *IAC News*;
1946	Glasgow People's Film Society founded; J. Arthur Rank becomes President of the IAC; *The Mini-Cinema* (1946-1952) first published;
1947	Glasgow Cine Club re-established; first Cannes Amateur Film Festival; Crewe Photographic Society (with "cine section") established;
1948	ACW reports around 190 Film Societies in GB;
1949	Scottish Association of Amateur Cinematographers (SAAC) founded; abolition of wartime price-controls boosts trade in amateur cine equipment; Circle Nine-Five Cine Club (Walthamstow) established; Sheffield City Films established;
1950	ACW "Ten Best" re-designated as "National Amateur Film Awards"; Harrogate Cine Club formed;
1951	BBC transmits *Film Club* programme (scripted by Tony Rose); tenth UNICA Congress, hosted in London and Glasgow (organised by British Amateur Cinematographers Central Council);
1952	first magnetic sound-on-film systems introduced for substandard gauges; BFI establishes Experimental Film Fund;
1953	Grasshopper Group (London) formed; BBC "Television Amateur Cinematographer's Trophy" competition;
1954	Glasgow Dawn Cine Group established; *Film* first published (by Federation of Film Societies)
1955	ACL merges with Photographic Society of America; SFC records 41 Scottish Film Societies; *Pathéscope Monthly* renamed *Pathéscope Gazette* (-1959); Associated-Rediffusion television broadcast amateur cine series;
1956	*IAC News* renamed *Amateur Film Maker*; Vintage Film Circle established (publishes *Flickers*); first "Free Cinema" programme

Appendix A

at National Film Theatre; Associated-Rediffusion Television Film Contest (4 episodes of *Ciné Holiday* transmitted);

1957   *Amateur Movie Maker* (1957-1964) first published;

1958   Federation of Cine Societies disbanded; Weymouth Cine Club established;

1959   Britain resigns from UNICA; August Grundig demonstrates monochrome video camera at Berlin Radio Show aimed at the amateur market; UNICA accepted as member of UNESCO;

1960   BBC transmits *Personal Cinema* programme (with Michael Aspel as presenter); Pathéscope announce withdrawal from 9.5mm market; Association of Home Movie Producers (AHMP) formed to protect interests of importers of movies for domestic exhibition; *Cine Camera: The International 8mm Magazine* magazine (1960-1964) first published; North London Association of Cine Clubs formed as "regional" council of the IAC; Southern Sound and Cine Club (Bognor Regis) established;

1961   9.5 Group started by Paul Van Someren and Larry Pearce; Borehamwood Cine Club established; Westcliff Cine and 35mm Club (Rayleigh) established; *Amateur Cine World* goes weekly; *The Leader* (9.5mm newsletter) first published (1961-1963) by 9.5 Group;

1962   Group Five/Clansman (Aberdeen) formed by Ron Miller; North West Regional Council of IAC formed; *8mm Magazine* (1962-1969) first published;

1963   International Film Associates established; *Amateur Film Maker* re-named (again) as *IAC News*; British "Telcan" videotape recorder for home-taping of television programmes demonstrated on BBC; *The Leader* renamed as *The 9.5 Review* (1963-1972);

1964   *Amateur Movie Maker* re-named as *8mm Movie Maker and Cine Camera* (1964-1967);

1965	Super-8 introduced; Mary Stevenson first woman editor of *IAC News*; Sony launch (½ inch tape) "Videocorder 2000"; *Ninefive News* (newsletter) first produced by George Whitfield (1965-?);
1966	Southern Counties and East Midlands Regional Councils of IAC established;
1967	*Amateur Cine World* re-launched as *Movie Maker* (1967-1985), incorporating *8mm Movie Maker and Cine Camera*; Altrincham Cine Club established; BBC *Making Home Movies* series transmitted;
1969	Scottish Federation of Film Societies joins what becomes the British Federation of Film Societies; Britain re-joins UNICA;
1970	*Film Making* (1970-1980) first published; Philips gives first public demonstration of its Video Cassette Recorder (VCR) system; Sony introduces ½ inch portable VCR and editor units;
1971	Sony introduces first videocassette system;
1972	SAAC International Competition (Glasgow); Granada Television's *Clapperboard* programme (1972-1982) first transmitted; East Anglian Regional Council of IAC established; Sony introduces "U-matic" video system; *The 9.5 Review* renamed as *9.5* (1972-present day);
1973	Kodak introduces Super-8 sound cartridge; BBC "Scope" Film Competition; Akai/Magnavox introduce first low-cost colour video camera;
1974	Frome and District Cine Club established;
1975	first British International Amateur Film Festival staged in Brighton; Sony announces launch of Betamax home video system;
1976	Scottish Film Archive established by Scottish Film Council; East Anglian Film Archive established; JVC unveils its VHS (Video Home System) half-inch videocassette recorder;

Appendix A

1977   North-West Film Archive established;

1978   SFC withdraws support to Scottish Amateur Film Festival; first practical home colour video camera for VHS;

1979   *IAC News* again renamed as *Amateur Film Maker* (1979-1990); Magnavox introduce "Magnavision" home videodisc system;

1981   BBC "Young Filmmaker" Contest; Kodak manufactures last "home movie" camera;

1982   Northern Ireland Regional Council of IAC formed; major Japanese manufacturers agree standard for (8mm) home video and coin term "camcorder";

1984   Yorkshire Film Archive established; Eastman Kodak demonstrates first 8mm videotape system;

1985   Sony introduces "Mini-8" camcorder; *Movie Maker* renamed as *Making Better Movies* (1985-1989);

1986   final Scottish Amateur Film Festival;

1987   Film Archive Forum (FAF) established; Cornwallis Camcorder Club (Maidstone) established;

1988   Wessex Film and Sound Archive established; Scottish Association of Amateur Cinematographers (SAAC), re-named as Scottish Association of Moviemakers (SAM);

1989   Wales Film and Television Archive established (becomes National Screen and Sound Archive of Wales in 2001); Scarborough Videographic Society established; *Making Better Movies* renamed as *Amateur Film and Video Maker*;

1990   ECS re-named as Edinburgh Cine and Video Society; Association of Moving Image Archivists (AMIA) formally established; *Amateur Film Maker* re-launched as *Amateur Film and Video Maker* (1990-1996);

1992	South-East Film and Video Archive established; Mid-Cheshire Videographic Society established;
1993	TSW Film and Television Archive established (becomes South-West Film and Television Archive in 2001); Spalding Camcorder Club formed;
1996	*Amateur Film and Video Maker* re-titled as *Video Maker* (1996-);
1997	Kodak withdraws pre-striped Super-8; Kingston Camcorder Club established;
1998	Northern Region Film and Television Archive established; "Straight Eight" collective organise first event at the Metro Cinema, London;
2000	Media Archive for Central England established;
2001	Mac Movies (Greenock) formed.

APPENDIX B

SELECT BIBLIOGRAPHY

A bibliography is included for general reference, and is loosely organised around topics addressed in preceding chapters. It supplements details of works cited by individual authors, and draws together literatures offering practical advice and information, with more historical, theoretical and critical responses to the diverse phenomenon of amateur filmmaking. The listing is indicative only, and seeks to register the range of materials pertinent to the synthetic approaches represented in the volume. Excellent further bibliographies are noted below, containing information on the location of, in particular, invaluable non English-language materials.

1) Overviews

Buckingham, David, Maria Pini and Rebekah Willett. "Take Back The Tube!: The Discursive Construction of Amateur Film and Video Making." *Journal of Media Practice* 8, no. 2 (2007): 183-201.

Chalfen, Richard. *Snapshot Versions of Life*. Bowling Green, Ohio: Bowling Green State University Popular Press, 1987.

Erens, Patricia, ed. *Journal of Film and Video* 38, no. 3-4 (1986). [Special issue: "Home Movies and Amateur Filmmaking"]

Hoberman, Jan. *Home Made Movies: Twenty Years of American 8mm and Super 8 Films*. New York: Anthology Film Archives, 1981.

Hogenkamp, Bert and Mieke Lauwers. "In Pursuit of Happiness? A Search for The Definition of Amateur Film." *CBG Nieuws* 24 (1993): 19-28.

Horak, Jan-Christopher, ed. *Lovers of Cinema: The First American Film Avant-Garde, 1919-1945*. Madison: University of Wisconsin Press, 1995.

Kapstein, Nancy, ed. *Essays on Amateur Film: Jubilee Book*. Charleroi: Association Européenne Inédits, 1997.

Kattelle, Alan. *Home Movies: A History of the American Industry, 1897-1979*. Nashua, New Hampshire: Transition Publishing, 2000.

Kilchesty, Albert. *Big As Life: An American History of 8mm Films*. San Francisco: Foundation for Art in Cinema, 1998.

Lipton, Lenny. *The Super 8 Book*. San Francisco: Straight Arrow Press, 1975.
Lovell Burgess, Marjorie A. *A Popular Account of the Amateur Cine Movement in Great Britain*. London: Sampson Low, Marston & Co., 1932.
MacPherson, Don. "Part V: Amateur Films." In *British Cinema: Traditions of Independence,* edited by Don MacPherson, 191-207. London: British Film Institute, 1980.
McKee, Gerald. *Film Collecting*. London: Tantivy Press, 1978.
Malthouse, Gordon. "Milestones in the March of Amateur Movies." *Amateur Cine World* 20, no. 10 (1957): 1035-1037.
Randall, Valentine. *The Amateur Cinema*. [self-published for the Institute of Amateur Cinematographers], 1977.
Swanson, Dwight. "Inventing Amateur Film: Marion Norris Gleason, Eastman Kodak and the Rochester Scene." *Film History* 15, no. 2 (2003): 126-136.
Zimmermann, Patricia R. *Reel Families: A Social History of Amateur Film*. Bloomington and Indianapolis: Indiana University Press, 1995.
—. "Democracy and Cinema: A History of Amateur Film." In *Essays on Amateur Film: Jubilee Book,* edited by Nancy Kapstein, 73-80. Charleroi: Association Européenne Inédits, 1997.

2) Concepts and Definitions

Ashton, Elwyn T. *People and Leisure*. London: Ginn Press, 1971.
Barzun, Jacques. "The Indispensable Amateur." *Juilliard Review* 1 (1954): 19-25.
Buchanan, Thomas. "Commitment and Leisure Behaviour." *Leisure Sciences* 7, no. 4 (1985): 401-420.
Czurles, Stanley. "Art Creativity Versus Spectatoritis." *Journal of Creative Behaviour* 10, no. 2 (1976): 104-107.
Dubin, Robert. "Central Life Interests: Self-Integrity in a Complex World." *Pacific Sociological Review* 22, no. 4 (1979): 405-426.
Gelber, Steven M. "A Job You Can't Lose: Work and Hobbies in the Great Depression." *Journal of Social History* 24, no. 4 (1991): 741-766.
Glasser, Ralph. *Leisure: Penalty or Prize?* London: Macmillan, 1970.
Friedson, Eliot. *Professionalism: The Third Logic*. Chicago and Oxford: Chicago University Press/Polity Press, 2001.
Huizinga, Johan. *Homo Ludens: A Study of the Play Element in Culture*. Boston: Beacon Press, 1955.

Lewis, Roy and Angus Maude. *Professional People*. London: Phoenix House, 1952.
Parker, Stanley. *Leisure and Work*. London: George Allen & Unwin, 1983.
Perry, Bliss. *The Amateur Spirit*. Boston, Mass.: Houghton, Miflin and Co., 1904.
Shamir, Boas. "Unemployment and 'Free Time'—the Role of the Protestant Work Ethic and Work Involvement." *Leisure Studies* 4, no. 3 (1985): 333-345.
—. "Commitment and Leisure." *Sociological Perspectives* 31, no. 2 (1988): 238-258.
Stebbins, Robert. *Amateurs on the Margin Between Work and Leisure*. London: Sage, 1979.
—. *Amateurs, Professionals and Serious Leisure*. Montreal: McGill-Queen's University Press, 1992.
—. *Between Work and Leisure: The Common Ground of Two Separate Worlds*. New Brunswick and London: Transaction Publications, 2004.
—. "Project-Based Leisure: Theoretical Neglect of a Common Use of Free Time." *Leisure Studies* 24, no. 1 (2005): 1-11.
Truzzi, Marcello. "Toward a General Sociology of the Folk, Popular and Elite Arts." In *Research in Sociology of Knowledge, Sciences and Art: Vol. I*, edited by Robert A. Jones, 279-289. Greenwich, Conn.: JAI Press, 1978.
Yates, Peter. "Amateur Versus Professional." *Arts in Society* 3, no. 1 (1964-66): 19-24.

3) Social and Political Contexts

Addison, Paul. *Now the War is Over: A Social History of Britain, 1945-51*. London: Jonathan Cape, 1985.
Allen, Douglas. "Workers' Films: Scotland's Hidden Film Culture." In *Scotch Reels: Scotland in Film and Television*, edited by Colin McArthur, 93-99. London: British Film Institute, 1982.
—. "Dawn: A New Start for Scottish Workers' Films." *AMES Journal* (Autumn 1996): 3-5.
Allsop, Kenneth. *The Angry Decade*. London: Peter Owen, 1964.
Baird, Thomas. "Film and Civic Education." *Sight and Sound* 5, no. 17 (1936): 17-19.
Bartlett, C. J. *A History of Post-War Britain, 1945-1974*. London: Longman, 1977.
Berger, John: "Look at Britain." *Sight and Sound* 27, no. 1 (1957): 12-14.

Bogdanov, Vernon and Robert Skidelsky. *The Age of Affluence, 1951-1964*. London: Papermac, 1970.
Bowle, John. *The Imperial Achievement: The Rise and Transformation of the British Empire*. London: Penguin, 1974.
Calder, Angus. *The People's War*. London: Granada, 1971.
Childs, David. *Britain Since 1945*. London: Methuen, 1979.
Green, M. *Dreams of Adventure: Deeds of Empire*. London: Routledge & Kegan Paul, 1980.
Hewison, Robert. *Too Much: Art and Society in the Sixties*. London: Methuen, 1986.
—. *In Anger: Culture in The Cold War, 1945-1960*. London: Methuen, 1988.
Hoggart, Richard. *The Uses of Literacy*. London: Chatto & Windus, 1957.
Hogenkamp, Bert. *Film, Television and The Left in Britain, 1950-1970*. London: Lawrence and Wishart, 2000.
Hopkins, Harry: *The New Look: A Social History of Forties and Fifties Britain*. London: Secker & Warburg, 1963.
LeMahieu, D. L. *A Culture for Democracy: Mass Communication and the Cultivated Mind in Britain between the Wars*. Oxford: Oxford University Press, 1990.
Lewis, Peter. *The Fifties*. London: Book Club Associates, 1978.
Marwick, Arthur. *Britain in the Century of Total War: War, Peace and Social Change, 1900-1967*. Harmondsworth: Pelican, 1970.
—. *British Society Since 1945*. Harmondsworth: Penguin, 1984.
Masters, Brian. *The Swinging Sixties*. London: Constable, 1985.
Medlicott, W. N. *Contemporary England, 1914-1964*. London: Longman, 1967.
Morgan, Kenneth O. *Labour in Power, 1945-51*. Oxford: Oxford University Press, 1984.
Mowat, Charles Loch. *Britain Between The Wars, 1918-1940*. London: Methuen, 1978.
Napper, Lawrence. "British Cinema and the Middlebrow". In *British Cinema: Past and Present*, edited by Justine Ashby and Andrew Higson, 110-123. London: Routledge, 2000.
Pawling, C. ed. *Popular Fiction and Social Change*. London: Macmillan, 1984.
Sinfield, Alan. *Literature, Politics and Culture in Post-War Britain*. London: Continuum Impacts, 2004.
Sissons, Michael and Philip French, eds. *Age of Austerity*. Oxford: Oxford University Press, 1986.

Stevenson, John. *The Pelican Social History of Britain: British Society, 1914-1945*. Harmondsworth: Pelican Books, 1984.

4) Archival Issues

Baird, Thomas. "Film and Civic Education." *Sight and Sound* 5, no. 17 (1936): 17-19.

Benedict, Karen. *Ethics and The Archival Profession: Introduction and Case Studies*. Chicago: Society of American Archivists, 2003.

Carroll, Nathan. "Mitchell and Kenyon, Archival Contingency and the Cultural Production of Historical License." *The Moving Image* 6, no. 2 (2006): 52.

Cookson, Laraine. "Amateur Film and the Archives." In *The Researcher's Guide to British Film and Television Collections*, edited by James Ballantyne, 5-14. London: British Universities Film & Video Council, 1989.

Dupin, Christophe. "The Origins and Development of the National Film Library, 1929-1936." *Journal of Media Practice* 7, no. 3 (2006): 199-217.

Film Archive Forum. *Moving History: Towards A Policy for The UK Moving Image Archives*. London: British Universities Film and Video Council, 2000.

—. *Film in England: A Development Strategy for Film and The Moving Image in The English Regions*. London: British Universities Film and Video Council, 2000.

Francis, David. "Balancing the Accounts: Ernest Lindgren and the National Film Archive, 70 Years On." *Journal of Film Preservation* 71 (2006): 21-41.

Houston, Penelope. *Keepers of the Frame*. London: British Film Institute, 1994.

Jones, Janna. "Confronting the Past in the Archival Film and the Contemporary Documentary." *The Moving Image* 4, no. 2 (2004): 1-22.

McNamara, Peter. "Amateur Film as Historical Record—A Democratic History?" *Journal of Film Preservation* 53 (1996): 41-44.

Norris Nicholson, Heather. "Regionally Specific, Globally Significant: Who's Responsible for The Regional Record?" *The Moving Image* 1, no. 2 (2001): 152-163.

Read, Paul. "Film Archives on the Threshold of the Digital Era." *Journal of Film Preservation* 68 (2004): 32-45.

UK Audiovisual Archive Strategy Steering Group: *Hidden Treasures: The UK Audiovisual Archive Strategic Framework*. London: British Universities Film and Video Council, 2004.

Zimmermann, Patricia R. "Morphing History into Histories: From Amateur Film to the Archive of the Future." *The Moving Image* 1, no. 1 (2001): 108-131.

5) Technology

Aldred, John. "What Can We Expect From Kodak's New Gauge?" *8mm Movie Maker and Cine Camera* 8, no. 4 (1965): 168-169.

Coe, Brian. *The History of Movie Photography*. Westfield, N. J.: Eastview Editions, 1981.

Flory, John. "The Challenge of 8mm Sound Film." *Journal of the Society of Motion Picture and Television Engineers* 70, no. 8 (1961): 581-585. [special issue on 8mm]

Kattelle, Alan. "The Evolution of Amateur Motion Picture Equipment." *Journal of Film and Video* 38, no. 3-4 (1986): 47-57.

Gunter, Jonathon F. *Super 8: The Modest Medium*. Paris: UNESCO, 1976.

Macintosh, Douglas. *A Handbook of 9.5mm Cinematography*. Llandudno: Photoworld, 2000.

Malthouse, Gordon. "Milestones in the March of Amateur Movies." *Amateur Cine World* 20, no. 10 (1957): 1035-1037.

Matthews, Glenn E. and Raife G. Tarkington. "Early History of Amateur Motion-Picture Film." *Journal of the Society of Motion Picture and Television Engineers* 64, no. 3 (1955): 105-116.

Robinson, Jack Fay. *Bell & Howell Company: A 75 Year History*. New York: Bell & Howell Company, 1982.

White, Deane R. "8mm and Small-Format Film Systems." *Journal of the Society of Motion Picture and Television Engineers* 71, no. 8 (1962): 555-556.

Winston, Brian. *Technologies of Seeing*. London: British Film Institute, 1996.

Wratten, I. D. "The Progress of Sub-Standard." *Penguin Film Review* 1 (1946): 96-101.

Zavanda, Roland J. "The Standardization of the Super-8 System." *Journal of the Society of Motion Picture and Television Engineers* 79, no. 6 (1970): 536-541.

Zimmermann, Patricia R. "Trading Down: Amateur Film Technology in Fifties America." *Screen* 29, no. 2 (1988): 40-51.

6) Film Form and Aesthetics

Buchanan, Andrew. "Fictional or Non-Fictional Films?" *Amateur Cine World* 3, no. 8 (1936): 373-399.
Bulleid, H. A. V. *Special Effects in Cinematography: 16mm, 9.5mm, 8mm*. London: Fountain Press, 1954.
Burton, Alan. "Amateur Aesthetics and Practices of the British Co-Operative Movement in the 1930s." In *Essays on Amateur Film: Jubilee Book*, edited by Nancy Kapstein, 131-143. Charleroi: Association Européenne Inédits, 1997.
Herring, Robert. "Twelve Rules for the Amateur." *Close Up* 4, no. 5 (1929): 22-26.
Rose, Tony. *Let's Make Movies*. London: The New English Library, 1963.
Smith, Jack. "Good for a Laugh: The Surrealist Touch." *Amateur Movie Maker* 3, no. 8 (1960): 1003-1005.
Strasser, Alex. *Amateur Films: Planning, Directing and Cutting*. London: Link House Publications, 1937.
Zimmermann, Patricia R. "Hollywood, Home Movies and Common Sense: Amateur Film as Aesthetic Dissemination and Social Control." *Cinema Journal* 27, no. 4 (1988): 23-44.
—. "Professional Results with Amateur Ease: The Formation of Amateur Filmmaking Aesthetics 1923-1940." *Film History* 2, no. 3 (1989): 267-281.

7) Institutions, Organisations, Movements, Events

Bird, Lance. "Cinema Clubs and *The World of Tomorrow*." *Journal of Film and Video* 38, nos. 2-3 (1986): 39-45.
Bond, Ralph. "The Amateur Convention." *Close Up* 5, no. 6 (1929): 479-483.
Borneman, Ernest. "Films for International Understanding: The UNESCO Story." *Penguin Film Review* 7 (1948): 96-106.
Brown, Pat. *The First Fifty Years: A History of the Finchley Cine Society*. New Barnet: John Morin, 1980.
Butler, Ivan. *"To encourage the art of the film": The Story of the British Film Institute*. London: Robert Hale, 1971.
Coad, Mike and Jo Coad. *IAC: The Film and Video Institute: A History of The First Fifty Years, 1932-1982*. London: Institute of Amateur Cinematographers, 1982.
Cottrill, J. R., ed. *Forming and Running a Film Society*. Leicester: The Federation of Film Societies, 1950.

Duckworth, L. B. "The Future of the Amateur Film Movement." *Close Up* 8, no. 1 (1931): 52-54.
Kattelle, Alan. "The Amateur Cinema League and Its Films." *Film History* 15, no. 2 (2003): 238-251.
Lindgren, Ernest. "A National Film Library for Great Britain." *Sight and Sound* 4, no. 14 (1935): 66-68.
McBain, Janet. "And The Winner is ... A Brief History of The Scottish Amateur Film Festival (1933-1986)." In *Essays on Amateur Film: Jubilee Book*, edited by Nancy Kapstein, 97-106. Charleroi: Association Européenne Inedits, 1997.
Pierson, Michelle. "Amateurism and Experiment: The BFI's Experimental Film Fund, 1952-1966." *The Moving Image* 5, no. 1 (2005): 68-94.
Sewell, George. "The Ideal Cine Club: Parts 1-4." *Amateur Cine World* 2, nos. 2-6 (1935): 79-80, 163-164, 209, 255.
Sexton, Jamie. "The Film Society and the Creation of an Alternative Film Culture in Britain in the 1920s." In *Young and Innocent: The Cinema in Britain 1896-1930*, edited by Andrew Higson, 291-305. Exeter: University of Exeter Press, 2002.
Various. *Men With Bees in their Bonnets: The Story Behind Twenty-Five Years of the Scottish Amateur Film Festival*. Glasgow: Scottish Film Council, 1963.

8) Manuals

Abbott, Harold B. *The Complete 9.5 Cinematographer*. London: Iliffe & Sons, 1937.
Alder, R. H. *Family Movies Outdoors*. London: Fountain Press, 1950. Cinefacts, No. 3.
Arrowsmith, Frank. *Beginner's Guide to Super 8 Film Making*. London: Newnes Technical Books, 1981.
Baddeley, Walter. *How to Edit Amateur Films*. London: Focal Press, 1951.
Blakeston, Oswell. *How to Script Amateur Films*. London: Focal Press, 1949.
Broderick, Peter. *Amateur Film Making*. London: Arco Publications, 1964.
Brown, Bernard. *Amateur Talking Pictures and Recording*. London: Sir Isaac Pitman & Sons, 1933.
Brunel, Adrian. *Filmcraft: The Art of Picture Production*. London: George Newnes, 1933.
—. *Film Production*. London: George Newnes, 1936.
Burnford, Paul. *Filming for Amateurs*. London: Sir Isaac Pitman & Sons, 1940.

Callaghan, Barry. *The Thames and Hudson Manual of Filmmaking*. London: Thames and Hudson, 1973.

Davis, Denys. *Tricks With Movies*. [Cinefacts, No. 11]. London: Fountain Press, 1956.

Donaldson, Leonard. *Cinematography for Amateurs: A Handbook for Beginners in Motion-Photography*. London: Hazell, Watson & Viney, 1916.

Emerald, Jack. *Make-Up in Amateur Movies, Drama and Photography*. London: Fountain Press, 1966.

Ferguson, Robert. *Group Film-Making*. London: Studio Vista, 1969.

Gibson, Brian. *Lighting for Cine—Indoors and Out*. London: Fountain Press, 1962.

Golding, Richard L. *Sound and Cine for Beginners*. London: Miles Henslow Publications, 1962.

Grosset, Philip. *Planning and Scripting Amateur Movies*. London: Fountain Press, 1963.

—. *The Complete Book of Amateur Film Making*. London: Evans Bros., 1967.

Impey, Eric F. *The Handbook of 8mm Cinematography*. London: Edward Bagshawe, 1934.

Langlands, Thomas F. *Popular Cinematography: A Book of the Camera*. London: W. and G. Foyle Ltd., 1925.

Lescaboura, Austin C. *The Cinema Handbook*. New York: Munn and Co., 1921.

Lewis, Roland. *The Video Maker's Handbook*. London and Sydney: Pan Books, 1987.

McKay, Herbert C. *Amateur Movie Making*. New York: Falk Publishing Company, 1924.

Molloy, Edward, ed. *Practical Photography and Amateur Cinematography*. [Vol. III] London: George Newnes, 1935.

Natkin, Marcel. *How to Film Children*. London: Focal Press, 1955.

Neale, D. M. *How to Use 9.5*. London: Focal Press, 1951.

Ottley, Charles D. *Practical Set Construction for the Amateur Cinematographer*. London: Pitman, 1935.

Rawlings, F. *How to Choose Music for Amateur Films*. London, New York: Focal Press, 1955.

Reyner, J. H. *Cine-Photography for Amateurs*. London: Chapman and Hall, 1935.

Rose, Tony and Martin Benson. *How to Act for Amateur Films*. London: Focal Press, 1951.

Satariano, Cecil. *Canon-Fire! The Art of Making Award-Winning Amateur Movies.* London: Bachman and Turner, 1973.
Sewell, George. *Amateur Film-Making.* London: Blackie and Sons, 1938.
—. *Making and Showing Your Own Films.* London: George Newnes, 1954.
Sladen-Smith, F. *The Amateur Producer's Handbook.* London: University of London Press, 1933.
Smethurst, Philip. *Professional Quality on Amateur Reversal Film.* London: Link House Publications, 1938.
Strasser, Alex: *Ideas for Short Films: Simple Scripts for Amateurs.* London: Link House Publications, 1937.
Wain, George. *How to Film as An Amateur.* London: Focal Press, 1958.
Wallace, Carlton. *Cine Photography for Amateurs.* London: Evans Press, 1961.
Watson, Ivan. *How to Shoot a Motion Picture: 12 Golden Rules for Better Camerawork.* London: Macmillan, 1979.
Wheeler, Owen. *Amateur Cinematography.* London, New York: Sir Isaac Pitman & Sons, 1929.

9) Home Movies

Bateman, Robert. *Home Movies.* London: Corgi, 1970.
Camper, Fred. "Some Notes on the Home Movie." *Journal of Film and Video* 38, nos. 3-4 (1986): 9-14.
Chalfen, Richard. "Cinéma Naïveté: A Study of Home Movie-making as Visual Communication." *Studies in the Anthropology of Visual Communication* 2, no. 2 (1975): 87-103.
Citron, Michelle. *Home Movies and Other Necessary Fictions.* Minneapolis: University of Minnesota Press, 1998.
Fellows, Malcolm Stewart. *Home Movies.* New York: Drake Publishers, 1973.
Fry, Alec. *Film the Family: A Complete Practical Guide to Successful Home Movies.* London: Stanmore Press, 1965.
Ishizuka, Karen L. "The Home Movie: A Veil of Poetry." In *Essays on Amateur Film: Jubilee Book*, edited by Nancy Kapstein, 45-50. Charleroi: Association Européenne Inédits, 1997.
Ishizuka, Karen L. and Patricia R. Zimmermann, eds. *Mining the Home Movie: Excavations in Histories and Memories.* Berkeley: University of California Press, 2007.

Luckett, Moya. "Filming the Family: Home Movie Systems and the Domestication of Spectatorship." *The Velvet Light Trap* 36 (1995): 21-32.

Moran, James. *There's No Place Like Home Video*. Minneapolis: University of Minnesota Press, 2002.

Musello, Christopher. "Studying the Home Mode." *Studies in Visual Communication* 6, no. 1 (1980): 23-42.

Neumann, Mark. "Home Movies on Freud's Couch." *The Moving Image* 2, no. 1 (2002): 25-46.

Norris Nicholson, Heather. "In Amateur Hands: Framing Time and Space in Home Movies." *History Workshop Journal* 43 (1997): 199-212.

—. "Moving Memories: Image and Identity in Home Movies." In *Essays on Amateur Film: Jubilee Book*, edited by Nancy Kapstein, 35-44. Charleroi: Association Européenne Inédits, 1997.

—. "Seeing How It Was: Childhood Geographies and Memories: in Home Movies." *Area* 33, no. 2 (2001): 128-140.

Szczelkun, Stefan. "The Value of Home Movies." *Oral History* 28, no. 2 (2000): 94-98.

10) Amateur Story Film

Alder, R. H. *Making a Story Film*. [Cinefacts, No. 9]. London: Fountain Press, 1955.

Anon. "The Editor to His Readers: In Defence of the Film Play." *Amateur Cine World* 5, no. 5 (1938): 225-226.

Malthouse, Gordon. "The Amateur Story Film." *Amateur Cine World* 14, no. 2 (1950): 122-127.

—. "Can't Really Be Bothered." *Amateur Cine World* 14, no. 9 (1951): 868.

—. "The Easy Way to Successful Filming." *Amateur Cine World* 14, no. 12 (1951): 1175-1179.

Pople, Kenneth A. S. "The Plot's Not All That Important!" *Amateur Cine World* 15, no. 5 (1951): 429-432.

Salkin, Leo. *Make Your Own Movies: The Art of Story-telling Films for Amateurs*. London: Arco, 1959.

Sewell, George. *Film Play Production for Amateurs*. London: Sir Isaac Pitman, 1932.

Swift, Hazel. "Two-Minute Tales." *Amateur Movie Maker* 3, no. 2 (1960): 652-653.

11) Animation

Barton, C. H. *How to Animate Cut-outs for Amateur Films.* London, New York: Focal Press, 1955.
Daborn, John. *The Animated Cartoon.* London: Fountain Press, 1958. Cinefacts, no. 13.
Halas, John and Bob Privett. *How to Cartoon for Amateur Films.* London and New York, 1951.
Halas, John and Roger Manvell. *The Technique of Film Animation.* London and New York: The Focal Press, 1968.
Manvell, Roger. *The Animated Film.* London: Sylvan Press, 1954.
Stevenson, Ralph. *Animation in the Cinema.* London: Zwemmer, 1967.

12) Exhibition

Alder, R. H. *Home Movie Shows.* [Cinefacts, No. 8]. London: Fountain Press, 1951.
Barry, Anthony. *The Kinora: Motion Pictures for the Home, 1896-1914.* Hastings: Projection Box, 1996.
Bomback, R. H. *The Movie Projector.* London: Fountain Press, 1952. Cinefacts, No. 7.
Burgess, Alan. *16mm Projection from A to Z.* London: Cinema Press, 1951.
Edmonds, Gary. "Amateur Widescreen: or Some Forgotten Skirmishes in the Battle of the Gauges." *Film History* 19, no. 4 (2007): 401-413.
Gilmour, Edwyn. *Choosing and Using a Cine Projector.* London: Fountain Press, 1960.
Lawrie, James Pickett. *The Home Cinema.* London: Chapman & Hall, 1933.
McKee, Gerald. *The Home Cinema: Classic Home Movie Projectors, 1922-1940.* Bucks., UK: Gerald McKee, 1989.
Singer, Ben. "Early Home Cinema and the Edison Home Projecting Kinetoscope." *Film History* 2, no. 1 (1988): 37-69.

NOTES ON CONTRIBUTORS

Sheila Chalke trained in Fine Arts, and subsequently taught art and design as Lecturer in Art Education at Gipsy Hill College (now part of Kingston University) and part-time Lecturer in Design at the University of Calgary. After studying Theatre Design at The National Theatre School of Canada (1972-1975), she worked in theatre in Canada and the UK for many years. Awarded a Diploma in Media Studies (1999) and an MA in the History of Film and Visual Media (2002) from Birkbeck College, University of London, she is currently completing a PhD on the history of amateur filmmaking in Britain at Birkbeck College.

Ian Craven teaches Film and Television Studies at the University of Glasgow. His research interests include Australian cinema and television, film technology, and British amateur cinema. His edited publications include *Australian Popular Culture* (Cambridge University Press, 1994), and *Australian Cinema in The 1990s* (Frank Cass, 2001), and he has authored articles dealing with postcolonial screen culture, cinema and urban form, and the theory and practice of area studies, in a wide range of journals. From 1996-2002, he acted as editor of *Australian Studies*, the academic journal of the British Australian Studies Association. He is currently preparing a study of the South Australian Film Corporation, and a monograph entitled *Amateur Filmmaking in Britain 1920-1980*.

Ian Goode teaches Film and Television Studies at the University of Glasgow. His research interests include Scottish film and television, documentary and non-fiction, and film and television in rural contexts. His most recent critical articles have appeared in *Social Semiotics*, and *Portal: Journal of Multidisciplinary and International Studies*.

Richard MacDonald is completing a PhD thesis on Film Appreciation and the post-war Film Society Movement at Goldsmiths College, University of London. His research traces pedagogies of film in relation to the changing place of voluntary activism in British cinema culture. Related interests include the histories of ideas, and the institutions and movements of alternative cinemas; he has recently co-authored articles on the institutions of transnational cinephilia, and on competing modes of world cinema spectatorship. He currently teaches courses in film history and film and anthropology at Goldsmiths.

Mitchell Miller has been editor of the journal of cultural and critical studies, *The Drouth*, since 2001. His recent publications include: "Beyond the Vlogsphere" (*Artists Circles Collaborative Monograph*, 2006-07), "Tekkonkinkreet" (for *Varoom*, 2007), and "The Chic Goes on—Anita Loos" (*Product*, Winter 2008). Forthcoming essays include: "The Democracy of Lines—Strips, Plates, Doodles" (for *The Drouth*), and *Third Degree Burns* (edited with Johnny Rodger, due 2009). He has acted as researcher for: "The Ghost Show Project—Travelling Showpeople and the Birth of Cinema" (HLF funded, March-November 2008). Mitch acts as curator/programmer at the Glasgow Film Theatre, contributes to the MLitt in Film Journalism at The University of Glasgow, and teaches within the Centre for Visual and Cultural Studies, at Edinburgh College of Art. He is currently Director, Rushes Development, MIMAC-Rushes C.I.C. Ltd.

Sarah Neely is a member of the Stirling Media Research Institute, and Lecturer in the Department of Film, Media & Journalism at the University of Stirling. Her journal articles have appeared in *Screen* and *The Drouth*, and her reviews in *Scope* and *Textual Practice and English*. Her chapter in the present volume draws upon continuing research on Margaret Tait, and was supported by a small research grant from the Carnegie Trust for the Universities of Scotland, awarded in 2006.

Heather Norris Nicholson is a Research Fellow at the Manchester Centre for Regional History, Manchester Metropolitan University. She has written on socio-cultural and landscape-related change in relation to interpretations of visual evidence, and the politics of representation within British and international contexts. Her film-related publications include the monograph *Screening Culture: Constructing Image and Identity* (Rowman and Littlefield/Lexington Books, 2003), chapters in the collections *Landscape and Film* (Routledge, 2006), *Mining The Home Movie* (University of California Press, 2007) and *Moving Pictures/Stopping Places: Hotels and Motels on Film* (Wallflower, 2008), and articles in journals including *The Moving Image, History Workshop,* and *Tourist Studies*.

Melanie Selfe recently completed her PhD for the University of East Anglia, and is currently an RCUK academic fellow at the Centre for Cultural Policy Research, University of Glasgow. Her PhD explored the role of provincial film societies in the development of "serious" film culture in post-war Britain. Current research extends these concerns, and considers the relationship between regional interests and national policy in relation to subsidised cinema provision. She also continues to investigate the role of amateurs in arts provision more generally.

Ryan Shand gained his PhD at the University of Glasgow in 2007, and is currently a post-doctoral Research Fellow at the University of Liverpool. His thesis was entitled *Amateur Cinema: History, Theory, and Genre (1930-80)*, and was made possible with support from the Arts and Humanities Research Council. He also holds an MPhil in Screen Studies from the University of Glasgow, and a BA in Film and Television Studies from Brunel University. His essays on amateur cinema have appeared in *The Drouth*, *Northeast Historic Film: Moving Image Review*, *Scope: An On-Line Journal of Film Studies* and *The Moving Image: The Journal of the Association of Moving Image Archivists*.

Rush Washbrook is Education and Outreach Officer at the Scottish Screen Archive (SSA), of the National Library of Scotland. She holds a BA in Film, Television & Radio Studies from Staffordshire University, an MA in Gender, Society and Culture from Birkbeck College, and a PGCE (FE) qualification from the University of Greenwich. Articles dealing with her education and outreach work at the SSA have appeared in the Scottish film industry magazine *Roughcuts*, and in the National Library of Scotland magazine, *Discover*.

Clare Watson is a graduate of the MA programme in Film Archiving at the University of East Anglia, where she is also currently completing her PhD on the circulation and reception of Charles Chaplin's pre-1923 comedies in Britain, with a particular emphasis on non-theatrical distribution and exhibition. In addition to her work on amateur cinema, Clare is also researching the role of women in the British film industry during the silent era and is a member of the Women's Film History-UK & Ireland network.

INDEX

"home mode" production, 2
"kailyard" narratives, 1
16mil Film User, 209
A Hit and a Miss, 191
A Study in Reds, 159
Abbott, Harold B., 88
Acres, Birt, 71, 238, 327
Adorno, Theodor and Horkheimer, Max, 14
Alexeieff, Alexandre, 238
All About Titling, 260
All On A Summer's Day, 38
amateur
   "cross-over", 9, 20, 24, 42, 242, 254, 261, 278, 286, 292, 321
   competitions, 40, 43, 47, 98, 249, 256, 260, 301
   controversialism, 22
   employment status, 254, 257, 319
   ideology, 19
   inferiorism, 13, 16, 17, 321
   social world, 6
   subjectivity, 5–19
   superiorism, 18
   voluntarism, 6, 140
Amateur Cine World, 4, 5, 9–10, 37, 49, 112, 165, 185–97, 203, 240–46, 252, 256, 329–33, 341–47
Amateur Cinematography, 45, 61, 101, 311, 329, 344, 345
Amateur Movie Maker, 9
American Cinema League, 173
Ancona Films, 303
Anderson, Benedict, 169
Anderson, Lindsay, 305
Anderson, Violet, 41, 47, 60, 62, 63
Annand, Louise, 54, 55, 61, 62
Archer, William, 242

Arnheim, Rudolph, 231
Arts Council, 220
Asquith, Anthony, 43, 44, 59, 190, 204
avant-garde
   animation, 239
   festivals, 322
   influences, 251, 270, 273, 276
   politics, 242
   women artists, 302
Barker Scarr, John, 99, 100, 124, 125, 127
Battleship Potemkin, 209
Baxter Family Films, 195
BBC *Film Club*, 256
Bean: The Ultimate Disaster Movie, 177
Benson, Harold, 280, 293
Bernstein, Sidney, 84
Biggar, Helen, 41
Bigger Is Better, 263
Birrell, Harry, 54, 63
Birri, Fernando, 305
Blue Black Permanent, 301
Bride and Groom, 249
British Association of Amateur Cinematographers, 255
British Board of Film Censors, 83
British Film Institute, 25, 42, 45, 53, 137, 151–52, 209, 214, 209–30, 232, 243, 249, 259, 292
British Transport Films, 43
Brock, Ian, 173, 181
Brode, Anthony, 208
Brownlow, Kevin, 82, 91, 245, 252, 292
Brunel, Adrian, 240
Buchanan, Andrew, 41
Cairns, Elsie, 54

Cannes Amateur Film Festival, 248
Castlecary Events, 197
casual leisure, 7
Cavalcanti, Alberto, 47, 216
Chalfen, Richard, 2, 5, 117, 160, 183, 184
Chaplin, Charles, 78–89, 91, 92, 109, 350
Chick's Day, 281
children, 43–58
　cinema clubs, 85
　cinemagoing, 82
　viewing preferences, 86
Children's Film Society, 84
Chislett, Charles, 94, 109, 111, 113
cine club
　constituencies, 9
cine journals, 9–11, 214
　as discursive field, 19
　reviewing, 18
Cinema Quarterly, 213, 231
cinemagazines, 307, 312
cinematic influences, 278, 281, 302, 306, 312, 322
city symphony film, 145
Claremont Cine Society, 185
Clarke, Ken, 242
Close Up, 24, 231
Cockshott, Gerald, 228
Cocozza, Enrico, 27, 51, 166, 281–96, 297, 298, 297–300
Cocteau, Jean, 26, 275, 288
Cohl, Emil, 239
Colour Cocktail, 42
Commission on Educational and Cultural Films, 209
Connoisseur Group, 290
Corden, Roy, 143, 144, 150, 153
Corky, 283
Craig, James, 287
Craigie, Jill, 226
Daborn, John, 27, 242
Deren, Maya, 26, 321
Disney, Walt, 239
Dobson, William S., 53
Documentary Newsletter, 209, 226

Donner, Clive, 54, 55, 291
Dream Holiday, 1
Dunedin Society, 310
Dunnachie, Iain, 54, 62, 63, 64, 206
Early Birds, 1
Edinburgh Cine Society, 53, 172, 330
Edinburgh Film Festival, 227, 319
Edinburgh Film Guild, 219, 226
Eggeling, Viking, 239
Elliot, Donald, 49
Empire Exhibition, 45, 46, 47, 330
Empire Marketing Board, 213
entertainment tax, 220
experimental film, 28, 225, 226, 239, 242, 251, 286, 306
Experimental Film Fund, 296
Falkenburg, Stein, 261
Family at Nairn, 198
Fantasmagoria, 276
Federation of Cine Societies, 252
Federation of Film Societies, 131, 208, 220, 259
Festival of Britain, 130, 132–40, 147, 151, 152, 153, 209
Field, Mary, 185
film appreciation, 151, 215, 217, 220, 231, 275
film society
　civic involvement, 138
　membership, 152
　movement, 24, 130–31
　post-war expansion, 130, 209
　productions, 132
　programming, 217
Film Society (London), 132
Films of Scotland, 28, 161, 100, 292, 322, 330
Fischinger, Oscar, 239
Fit O' The Toon, 157, 288
For Your Pleasure, 263
Foucault, Michel, 160
Four Weddings and a Funeral, 177
Frankfurt School, 14, 29
Frend, Charles, 54, 191
Furie, Sidney J., 56

Gallipoli: a Pilgrimage Cruise, 99
General Post Office (GPO) film units, 213
genre
   animation, 240–42
   civic filmmaking, 131–35
   documentary, 165–71
   family film, 54, 182–203
   holiday films, 93
   posterity production, 170
   story film, 2, 17, 276
Glasgow School of Art Kinecraft Society, 41, 42
Go East, Young Man, 99, 108
Godfrey, Bob, 245
Grasshopper Group, 26, 239
   Adventure Film Productions, 252
   share scheme, 253
   Teamwork Films, 260
Grey Seals, 54
Grierson, John, 41, 42, 46, 165, 172, 179, 214, 294, 318, 322
Haffner family, 114
Hair, 38
Halas and Batchelor, 225, 244
Happy Bees, 306
Hardy, Forsyth, 42, 48, 51, 52, 161, 193, 218, 220, 290
Harley, Basil, 143, 144, 188, 205
Harmon, Jympson, 216
Harris, Hilary, 164
Hell Unltd, 44
highbrow culture, 210, 221
Highlands and Islands Film Guild, 307, 309
Hill Sheep Farm, 227
Hill, Derek, 245, 251
Hindley, John, 109
Hitchcock, Alfred, 46–49, 51, 56
Hollander, Peter, 305
home cinema
   equipment, 68
   marketing, 43–58
   print distribution, 73
   programming, 78

Home Movies and Home Talkies, 9, 10
Horne, Richard, 244
Institute of Amateur Cinematographers, 2, 37, 329, 337, 342
   "Ten Best" competition, 178, 186, 243
Ishizuka, Karen, 159
Jacobs, Lewis, 224
Jenkins, Keith, 160
Just One Thing After Another, 190
Kirkwall Film Society, 310
La Mort Et Le Poete, 273
Lambert, Gavin, 304
Land Makar, 312
Langlois, Henri, 213
Le Neve Foster, Peter, 22
Learner, Keith, 250
Leisure Studies, 6–8
Lindgren, Ernest, 214, 231
Linnicar, Vera, 250
literary influences, 277, 284, 301
localism, 23, 156–57, 170, 172
locationism, 177
London Film Society, 210, 304
Love Actually, 177
Low, Rachael, 183, 203
Lye, Len, 225, 239, 243
Malthouse, Gordon, 187, 192
Manvell, Roger, 215, 231
Marshall, Frank, 1–5, 45, 47, 48, 51, 54–56, 190, 191, 193, 203
Massingham, Richard, 225, 251
Mavor Family Film, 190
McAllister, Stewart, 41
McArthur, Colin, 164
McGavin, Nettie, 54, 62
McKee, Gerald, 65, 73, 91, 347
McLaren, Norman, 40, 58, 225, 245, 258, 262
McLean, William J., 41
Mekas, Jonas, 26, 314
Meliès, George, 238
Menken, Marie, 302

Merseyside Institute Film Society, 219
Meteor Film Producing Society, 5, 36, 44, 45
Mickey Mouse, 78, 79–80, 85–87, 240, 264
modernity, 11–18, 97
Montagu, Ivor, 132
Morey, Geoffrey, 102
Mower Madness, 47
Museum of Modern Art Film Library, 223
Nation on Film, 200
National Film and Television Archive, 209
National Film Library, 209, 214, 224
  canon, 25
National Film Theatre, 139, 209, 248, 255
Neighbours, 245
Nelson, Gunvor, 302
Nine O'Clock, 51
Notting Hill, 177
Nottingham & District Film Society, 130–53
Nottingham: Variations on a Theme, 134
Nunn, Terry, 258
O'Grady, James, 105
Oakley, Charles, 37, 48, 51
Odin, Roger, 189
Old Market Square, 23, 130, 139, 141–45, 152, 153, 154
Orquil Burn, 306
Pathé Company, 20
Pathéscope, 20, 69–82, 86, 87, 88, 89, 90, 91, 92
Pathéscope Monthly, 72, 73, 87
Payment Deferred, 1
Penicillin, 225
Perry, Bliss, 6
Petrol, 287
Phillips, Derek, 261
Pills for All Ills, 53
Piper, John, 174

Pople, Kenneth, 187, 205, 346
Porphyria, 287
Portrait of Ga, 307
Portrait of Peter, 191
Postlethwaite, H. A, 186, 189, 205
Powell, Dilys, 216
Powell, Michael, 49, 296
Preston brothers, 99, 100, 106, 107, 111
Rees, Lorimer, 84
Reiniger, Lottie, 213
Rice Cultivation, 214
Richter, Hans, 239
Riesel, Oscar, 55, 61
Robot Three, 51
Roe, Desmond, 252
Rogers, Dorothy, 258
Rollier, Augustus, 97
Rose, Tony, 16, 284
Rotha, Paul, 210, 217, 224, 225
Route 66, 289
Rowley, Gordon, 260
Rural Blacksmith, 133, 136
Rural Cinema Scheme, 307
Russell, Stanley L., 36
Saville, Victor, 38
Scherzo, 279
Scotland on Film, 200
Scottish Amateur Film Festival, 19, 36, 37, 42, 43–58, 190, 192–95, 270, 276, 277, 287, 291
Scottish Association of Amateur Cinematographers, 5, 49, 50, 51, 53, 56, 57, 59, 331, 333, 334
Scottish Educational Film Association, 311
Scottish Federation of Film Societies, 220
Scottish Film Council, 5, 28, 37, 42, 45, 48, 49, 51, 55–58, 60, 180, 288, 301, 311, 312, 314, 329, 330, 331, 333, 334, 343
Scottish Screen Archive, 57, 59, 182, 190, 191, 195, 196, 198, 201, 272, 275, 276, 291, 350
Scrutiny, 212

Seawards the Great Ships, 157
serious leisure, 7–9
Seton, Marie, 216
Seven Ages, 157
Smith, Jack, 85, 86, 91, 185, 186, 187, 206, 267, 342, 345
Sontag, Susan, 110
South London Film Society, 221, 230
Speirs, Norman, 57, 59
Stebbins, Robert, 6
Stein Family Life, 195, 197
Stevenson, John, 15
Strand, Chick, 302
Susan's Party, 191
Sykes family holiday in the Lake District, 112
Tait, Margaret, 28, 301–22
Taylor, H. W., 103, 104, 127, 269
technology, 21, 219, 341
  28mm gauge, 70
  9.5mm gauge, 66–68
  toy projectors, 69, 74, 79
television, 255–57, 311, 316, 319
The Amateur Photographer and Cinematographer, 98
The Battle of Wangapore, 246–48
The Crowded Years, 139, 142
The Dandy, 174
The Day Thou Gavest, 44
The Drift Back, 306
The Film in National Life, 210–12, 215
The Gorbals Story, 158
The History of Walton, 242
The Italian Straw Hat, 209
The Millstream, 242
The Silent Avenger, 81

The Singing Street, 293
The White Lady, 278
Theatre Optique, 238
Through the Balkan States, 94, 102, 122
Todd, Elizabeth, 14
Tour in the USSR, 99, 104, 127
Tree For Two, 192
Twilight, 296
Two's Company, 245
UNICA, 2, 5, 51, 243, 247, 248, 250, 254, 259, 265, 330, 331, 332, 333
Union Internationale du Cinéma d'Amateurs. *See UNICA*, *See UNICA*, *See*
Unruh, David, 6
Vaughan, Heming, 213
Very Fishy Tale, A, 1
Vogel, Amos, 225
Watson, Ivan, 26
Watt, Harry, 52
Waverley Steps, 145
Wayne, Mike, 171
Wilson, James, 311
Wilson, Norman, 226
Winter Sports in Austria, 215
Wishaw Film Society, 275
Wollenberg, Hugo, 231
Workers Educational Association, 220, 224
World Film News, 214
Wright, Basil, 214
Wuyts, Herman, 259
Wynn Jones, Stuart, 245, 250
Zimmermann, Patricia, 158, 161, 172, 176, 183